Spurgeon's Sermons on 2 Timothy

(Sermons on the Whole Bible)

Charles H. Spurgeon

Bibliographic Information

Charles H. Spurgeon (1834 – 1892), affectionately known by many as "the Prince of Preachers," addressed more than 10 million people during his ministry, baptized thousands of converts, and wrote so extensively and persuasively that his sermons have sold more than 50 million copies. Spurgeon's sermons were previously published in 1855 in a multi-volume series known as *The New Park Street Pulpit*.

an Ichthus Publications edition

Copyright © 2014 Ichthus Publications
ISBN 10: 1502771632
ISBN 13: 978-1502771636

www.ichthuspublications.com

CONTENTS

1

Our Gifts and How to Use Them

(Sermon No. 1080)

"Therefore I remind you to you stir up the gift of God which is in you by the laying on of my hands" (2 Timothy 1:6).

I SUPPOSE THAT TIMOTHY was a somewhat retiring youth and that from the gentleness of his nature he needed to be exhorted to the exercise of the bolder virtues. He is bid not to be ashamed of the testimony of our Lord and to endure hardness as a good soldier of Jesus Christ. He is called to the front, though his modesty would have kept him in the rear, and he is exhorted to command and teach, suffering no man to despise his youth. Perhaps, also, he was not a man of very vigorous action and needed, every now and then, a little touch of the spur to induce him to put forth all his dormant energy and keep himself and his Church thoroughly up to the mark in labor for Christ.

His was a choice spirit and therefore it was desirable to see it strong, brave and energetic. No one would wish to arouse a bad man, for like a viper he is all the worse for being awake. But in proportion to the excellence of the character is the desirability of its being full of force. The Apostle Paul tells Timothy, in his first Epistle, not to neglect the gift that is in him. And in the text before us he bids him stir up that gift—in each case he is sounding the trumpet in his ear and summoning him to intense action. He speaks of the gift that was conferred by the laying on of hands, and in the former Epistle he connects that with the hands of the presbytery.

Now it was no doubt the custom to lay on hands at the ordination of Christian ministers by the Apostles and there was an excellent reason for it—for gifts were thereby conveyed to the ordained. And when we can find anybody who can thereby confer some spiritual gift upon us, we shall be glad to have their hands laid on our heads. But we care not for empty hands. Rites cease when their meaning ceases. If practiced any longer they gender to superstition and are fit instruments of priest craft. The upholding of the hands of the eldership, when they give their vote to elect a man to the pastorate, is a sensible proceeding, and is, I suspect, all the Apostle means when he speaks of the presbytery. But empty hands, it seems to me, are fitly laid on empty heads—and to submit to an empty ceremony is the most idle of all idle waste of time!

If Paul were here and could confer a gift, we should rejoice to receive it. Yes, and if the meanest man in Christendom, or woman, for that matter, could confer the smallest drachma of Divine Grace by the putting on of their hands, we would bow our head in the most humble manner. Till then we shall beg to decline submitting to the imposition, or assisting in it. For this reason, and others, we cannot use the text exactly as it stands in addressing this congregation. But leaving out the reference to laying on of hands, we may honestly, without violation of the current of Inspiration, proceed to exhort each one of you to stir up the gift that is in you!

There are many kinds of gifts. All Christians have some gift. Some may have but one talent, but all have one at the least. The Great Householder has apportioned to every servant a talent. No single part of a vital body is without its office. True, there are some parts of the body whose office has not been discovered—even the physician and the anatomist have not been able to tell why certain organs are in the human frame, or what office they serve—but as even these are found to be necessary, we are quite sure that they fulfill some useful purpose. Truly, there are some Christians who might be put in that category—it might puzzle anybody to know what they are capable of—and yet it is certain they have some charge committed to them to keep, and, if true Believers, they are essential parts of the body of Christ.

As every beast, bird, fish and insect has its own place in Nature, so has every Christian a fit position in the economy of Grace. No tree, no plant, no weed could be dispensed with without injury to Nature's perfection. Neither can any sort of gift or Grace be lost to the Church without injury to her completeness. Every living saint has his charge to keep—his talent over which he is a steward. A measure of gift is in all of us, needing to be stirred up. Some have gifts outside of them rather than within them—gifts, for instance, of worldly position, estate and substance. These ought to be well used, and considering that in these times we have a starving world to deal with, and that one of the great impediments to the spread of the Gospel is, with some of us, the lack of means for the maintenance of those who should preach the Word, it does seem a strange thing that professors should store up God's money and use it as if it were their own.

When for our orphans, our students, our tract distributors and our missionaries we need funds, how can men love the Lord with all their hearts and yet keep their thousands cankering at their bankers, or their tens resting in their purses? They have not learned to provide for themselves bags that wax not old. They do not understand that to keep their money they must give it away—that truly to preserve it they must dedicate it to God—that which is kept by the miserly for themselves is not really preserved, but wasted. That which is expended in the Master's service is laid up in Heaven where neither moth nor rust can corrupt.

But I am not going to speak about that. I have not much reason to speak upon that subject to those who are immediately connected with me, for I have rather to praise you than to upbraid. Most of our dear friends here serve the Lord with the gifts that are outside of them—not all as we should, but many with more than ordinary liberality and some up to the full measure of their means, if not beyond them. There are, however, exceptions to all rules and there are a few who attend this place who need more than a gentle hint to excite anything like generosity in them. But we must go at once to the point in hand—"the gift that is in you," we have now to speak of. First, the gift that may be in each one of us. And then, secondly, how we are to stir this gift up. And in conclusion, we will give reasons for the stirring of it.

I. First, then, WHAT GIFT IS THERE IN US? In some here present there are gifts of mind which are accompanied with gifts of utterance. It is no mean thing to be able to read the Scriptures and to see their inner meaning—to be able to compare spiritual things with spiritual and to be so taught in other matters so that we are able to see the hand of God in history and can, upon all such subjects, speak to edification. It is not everyone who has a mind who has also the gift of utterance, but where God is pleased to give to any man mind and mouth, he possesses a gift which he ought abundantly to use.

Many a man is mighty in the Scriptures but not eloquent. When the two things meet, as in Apollos, and are combined with a fervent spirit, a man of God has power, indeed! May I suggest that every Christian man here who is possessed of the faculty of eloquent discourse is bound to use it for Jesus Christ? Some young men spend their evenings in Debating Societies and the like, and I have not a word to say against that, but I have this to say—whatever you may do with this talent in other directions, the Lord, who has bought you with His blood, if you are a Christian man—has the first claim upon you and you are bound to use your powers of utterance in His cause.

"But I am not a minister!" What do you mean by that? Do you find anything in Scripture about clergy and laity? If so, you have read it with different eyes from mine! There were men called especially to the oversight of the Church and the preaching of the Word, but everyone, according to his gift, also had a call—and there is no man in the Church of God who has ability to speak who has any license to be silent. Not only the golden-mouthed orators, but the silver-tongued speakers—men of the second as well as of the first order—should serve in the Gospel of the Son of God. I shall not ask any young man whether he ought to preach, but whether he can prove that he ought not.

Every man is bound to tell another who is in danger, to escape from that danger. Everyone who has recovered from a dreadful disease is bound to tell others what remedy was made effectual in his case. Nothing can excuse us from, in some way or other, spreading abroad the Gospel of Jesus Christ! And if we have the ability to speak, it will go hard at last with us if we have been silent with our fellow men. The stones in the street might surely cry out against some religious professors who make the Houses of Parliament, the Council Chamber, the Courts of Justice, the Athenaeum, or the Mechanics' Hall ring with their voices, and yet preach not Jesus—who can argue points of politics and the like, but not speak a word for Christ—eloquent for the world, but dumb for Jesus?

From this may God deliver us! If you have any gift, young man, come out and use it—or old man, also, if you have laid it by till late in the day. In these straitened times when the harvest is ripe and the laborers are few, let every man that has his sickle come forth into the field. Let no man say, "I pray you have me excused," but by the blood that bought you, if you have tasted of the Water of Life, cry aloud and spare not, and be this your message—"Whoever will, let him take the Water of Life freely."

There are numbers of Believers who have not the gift of utterance with the tongue, who nevertheless can speak very fluently and admirably with the pen. If, then, you have the gift of the pen, are you using it for Christ as you ought? I need to stir up the gift that is in you. Letters have often been blessed to conversion! Are you accustomed to write with that view? Perhaps you are a great contributor to the postal revenue. Let me ask you what sort of matter it is with which you burden her Majesty's mails? Do you write letters to your children and friends full of loving testimony to what the Grace of God has done for you? If you have not done so, dear Friends, try at once! Jesus wants consecrated pens and in His name I claim your service!

The writing of tracts and the dissemination of holy Truth by means of the press are most important—any person who has any gifts in that direction should be sure to use them. Why are writers upon religion often so dull, while the world commands talent and vivacity? Many thousands of pens are running every day upon the most idle nonsense and mailing booksellers' shelves groan with the literature of fiction! Are there none who, with splendor of diction or in humbler guise, could write interestingly of the Gospel and tell of its power among the sons of men? If there is, in the tribe of Zebulon, any that handle the pen of the ready writer, let them not keep back from the help of the Lord—the help of the Lord against the mighty!

Another form of gift that belongs to us is influence. We have all of us influence of some sort—some more, some less. What an influence the parent has! To a great extent you mold your children's lives. Some of us owe what we never can repay to our mothers. What they have done for us shall make us grateful to them even when they shall slumber in the dust. The nurse girl who has the care of little children should be very careful, for a remark she may make without intention may shape the character—yes, mar or bless the child's character throughout eternity! And you who associate daily with working men—is there enough among Christian masters of earnest zeal to use a holy and affectionate influence among the employed?

If classes are alienated, one from the other, as it is to be feared they are, is it not because we meet each other just as a matter of business and that there is little of anything like Christian affection and communion between the one and the other? Indeed some laugh off the idea as ridiculous and tell me I know very little of the world to dream of such a thing! I will leave that question to the day which shall reveal all things, and I think I know who will prove to be right. Let every one of us reckon up what influence he has, and having done so, let us ask God's Grace that we may use it aright. I shall not go into details here. You are all affecting those round about you for good or evil. As Christian men you are either leading others to Christ even unconsciously, or else you are deadening their consciences and leading them to think there is not much in religion after all—and surely you would not wish to do that! If you have the gift of influence, I would stir you up to use it.

Many of the elder members of the Church have another gift, namely, experience. Certainly, experience cannot be purchased nor taught. It is given us of the Lord who teaches us to profit. It is a peculiar treasure each man wins for himself as he is led through the wilderness. An experienced Christian is put in the Church on purpose that he may guide the inexperienced—that he may help those who are distressed with a word of comfort derived from his own experience of God's helping hand in time of trouble—that he may warn the heedless by the mischiefs he himself has suffered through carelessness. Now, when an experienced Christian merely uses his experience for his own comfort, or as a standard by which to judge his fellow Christians, or makes use of it for self-exaltation as though he were infinitely superior to the most zealous young men—such a man mars his talent, does mischief with it—and makes himself heavily responsible.

Dear Brothers and Sisters, I, who am so young in years compared with many of you, beseech you who have long walked in the ways of godliness to use your experience continually in your visitation of the sick, in your conversations with the poor, in your meetings with young beginners and in your dealings with backsliders! Let your paths drop fatness! Let the anointing God has given you fall upon those who are round about you! May you be of such a sort as a certain clergyman I heard of the other day. I asked a poor woman "What sort of man is he?" She said, "He is such a sort of man, Sir, that if he comes to see you, you know he has been there." I understood what she meant—he left behind him some godly saying, weighty advice, holy consolation, or devout reflection which she could remember after he had left her cottage door. May our venerable friends always have this said of them!

Another gift which many have is the gift of prayer—of prayer with power—in private for the Church and with sinners. There are some who have learned by long practice how to knock at Heaven's door so as to get a readier opening of the door than others. Numbers of these have coupled with this the gift of utterance in public prayer. Such dear friends ought not to be absent from the Prayer Meeting except when absolutely necessary. They should not only be content with coming to Prayer Meetings that are established, but they should stir up the gift that is in them and try to establish others in neglected places. There was never a period when the Church had too much prayer. "The Sacraments," as they are called, may have been unduly exalted but who has ever unduly exalted prayer? Bible-readings may degenerate into mere discussion, and even preaching into a show of oratory—but prayer has vital elements about it which survive many an injury.

Alas! Alas for Churches that have given up Prayer Meetings! You shall judge of the Presence of God by the Prayer Meeting as accurately as you shall judge the temperature of the air by the thermometer. It is one of the truest signs that God is with the people when they pray—and it is one of the darkest signs that He has departed when prayer is lacking. You who have sweet communion with God in private, look upon your prevalence on the knee not only as a blessing for yourselves, but as a gift that is bestowed upon you for the good of others. There is another gift which is a very admirable one. It is the gift of conversation, not a readiness for chit chat and gossip—(he who has that wretched propensity may bury it in the earth and never dig it up again)—but the gift of leading conversation, of being what George Herbert called the "master-gunner."

When we have that, we should most conscientiously use it for God. There lived, some 50 years or so ago, a set of great table-talkers who were asked out to dine because of their lively conversational powers. Now if this is in any of you, never waste it in mere pleasantries, but say something worth saying and aim at the highest results. Remember Jesus was a mighty table-talker, as the Evangelists take care to note. I wish I could, with discreet adroitness, break in upon a conversation in a railway carriage and turn it round to the Savior—turn it round to something worth speaking of. I often envy those of my Brethren who can go up to individuals and talk to them with freedom. I do not always find myself able to do so, though when I have been Divinely aided I have had a large reward.

When a Christian man can get hold of a man and talk to him, it is like one of the old men of war laying alongside a French ship and giving her a broadside, making every timber shiver and at last sending her to the bottom. How many a soul has been brought to Christ by the loving personal exhortations of Christian people who know how to do it? To be able, like Elijah, to stretch yourselves upon the dead child—to put your hands upon his hands, your feet upon his feet and breathe the life by God's help into the dead—oh, some of you can do this better, perhaps, than those who are called to speak to hundreds and thousands! Do use it if you have the ability, and try to get the ability if you have it not.

Perhaps you possess it and have not found it out. No unconverted person should come to this place without your speaking to him. And as to a person attending the Tabernacle three Sundays without being spoken to by some Christian, it ought to be an impossibility and would be if all were in a right warm-hearted state, earnestly desiring the salvation of others! May God teach us, if we can converse personally with individuals, to furbish up the gift, keep it in good condition and continually use it. My inventory of the gifts which are in us is not complete, nor is it intended to be. Each person may have a separate gift. Even the gift to be able to lie still and suffer is not a small one. The gift of being able to be poor and content is not to be despised. The gift of nursing the sick or of interesting children should be lovingly employed. Neither ought any talent to be wrapped in a napkin. But, whatever it is, the word is, "Stir up the gift which is in you."

II. And this brings us, secondly, to the consideration of HOW WE ARE TO STIR UP OUR GIFTS. First, we should do it by examination to see what gifts we really have. There should be an overhauling of all our stores to see what we have of capital entrusted to our stewardship. May I ask you for a minute to sit quietly and take stock of all God has given you? Remember you shall assess yourself, for I am sure your manhood, not to say your self-esteem, will not let you put yourself down as utterly without gifts.

If somebody were to speak of you depreciatingly, you would very soon defend yourself and argue for your own capacity in many departments. I would put you on your mettle and bring you to acknowledge your capabilities. Now think of all the abilities you have, dear Brother, dear Sister. What has God trusted you with? Add up each item and compute the total sum. What trading-money have you of your Lord's? To whom much is given, of him much will be required. What, then, has been given to you? Such an enquiry will help you to stir up the gift that is in you. The self-examination of every mental faculty, every spiritual attainment, every form of characteristic force or individual influence will be an excellent commencement for a more vigorous course of action.

Enquire what you can do, what more you could do, what more you might learn to do, what more you ought at least to attempt. Diminish nothing from the just amount of your possibilities and it will greatly tend to stir you up, if you then enquire, "How far have I done what I could do? How far have I used all that has been committed to me? How much of my life has been allowed to rust and how much has been made bright by wear and tear in the service of my Master?" It is not a pleasant duty to which I have invited you. You would be much more gratified if I asked you to consider some precious promise of the Covenant and certainly I should find it more consolatory to myself, but this is necessary. Sweet things are pleasant, but sharp things are often the more beneficial. Pillows for our heads are not our main desire—we wish, as soldiers of the Cross— to be found faithful, first of all and above all! We shall have to give an account before God. Oh, let us give an account before ourselves, now, in the forum of our own conscience and so stir up the gift that is in us!

The next mode of stirring up our gift is to consider to what use we could put the talents we possess. To what use could I put my talents in my family? Am I doing all I could for the children? Have I labored all I ought for my wife's conversion—my husband's conversion? Then about the neighborhood—is there nothing more that I could do for the salvation of my poor godless neighbors? Perhaps I see them drunk, profane, unchaste, irreligious, full of all manner of disobedience to God— can I not, by God's Grace, uplift them? They never come to a place of worship—have I done all I could to get them there? I was not placed in that neighborhood without an object. If it is a dark part of London, I am put there to be a lamp if I am a Christian. Am I shining, then?

Some people prefer to live where there is light and for themselves the choice is wise, but I think, for usefulness, loving hearts might prefer to live in bad districts that they might do good. Are you doing all you can for Jesus? Come, answer like an honest man! Having done so, I have more for your self-inspection. Will you examine yourself in every relation in which you stand? As a master, stir up your gift in reference to those you employ. As a servant, stir up the gift towards your fellow servants. As a trader, stir up your gift in reference to those with whom you come in contact. Are you a sailor? Have you stepped in here tonight? What an opportunity you have, my Friend, in landing on many shores and doing something for Christ here, and there and everywhere!

Are you a commercial traveler and do you go to many places? Surely you might travel for our Lord with Gospel wares to be distributed without money and without price and yet attend to your own calling, none the less. If our Churches were in a right state of spiritual health, men would not first say, "What can I do to make money?" but, "What can I do to serve Christ, for I will take up a trade subserviently to that." But if we cannot bring men to that point, we must at least say, (to all of you who profess to be Christians, at any rate), in whatever condition you are placed, high or low, rich or poor, you should live unto Christ! You should each enquire, "What can I do for the Lord in my present condition? What peculiar service does my position involve?" In this way, dear Friends, stir up the gift that is in you.

But, next, stir it up not merely by consideration and examination, but by actually using it. We talk much of working, but working is better than talking about working. To get really at it and to do something for soul-winning and spreading abroad the Glory of God is infinitely better than planning and holding committees. Away with windbags! Let us get to acts and deeds. None of us know what we can do till we try. The sportsman will tell you that there may be many birds in a field, but you know not how many till you walk through and then you discover them and see them on the wing. When the wheel turns you will be able to see the force of the current. You will see the speed of the horse when you put him to his best. Work, work and the tool that is blunt will get an edge by being used! Shine, and the light you have shall grow in the very act of shining!

He who has done one thing will find himself capable of doing two, and doing two will be able to accomplish four—and having achieved the four will soon go on to twelve and from twelve to fifty! And so, by growing multiples he will enlarge his power to serve God by using the ability he has. Does this tire you? Does my subject seem too much like salvation by works? Nothing is further from my thoughts! I am not, now, speaking upon salvation at all! Neither am I addressing those who are seeking after salvation. I am speaking to you who have been saved already by the Grace of God! You are saved, and on that point all is done. You are resting in the finished work of Christ. Should it ever seem hard to you to be stirred up to serve Him? Let the vision of His tearful face come up to you.

Behold His crown of thorns! Let Him turn His back to you, and count the gashes the Roman scourges made! Look at Him—a spectacle of blood and love! And is it possible that any service for Him can, by you, be considered difficult? To burn at a stake! If we could do it a thousand times, He well deserves that we should make the sacrifice! To give Him every pulse and every drop of blood and every breath we breathe—He well deserves it, glory be to His name! He merits all our love a thousand times over. I shall not fear to press upon you again and again and again that you use the gifts which are in you by actual service of so precious a Master.

And then, dear Friends, in addition to using our gift, every one of us should try to improve it. We have for years endeavored to stir up the young Christians of this congregation to educate themselves. By our evening classes it is intended that young men who preach in the street may get education in order to better preach the Gospel of Christ. And out of this congregation have gone hundreds whom God has owned as ministers of Christ and many such are being trained now. I would have every man put himself in training. I think every man ought to feel,

"I have been Christ's man with a talent; I will be Christ's man with ten if I can. If now I do not thoroughly understand the doctrines of His Gospel, I will try to understand them. I will read and search, and learn."

We need an intelligent race of Christians, not an affected race of boasters of culture—mental fops who pretend to know a great deal and know nothing—but we need hard students of the Word, adept in theology like the Puritans of old. Romanism will never do much with people who know the doctrines of the Word of God—it is a bat and hates sunlight. Every one of us ought to be students and learners, trying to get more ability for usefulness as well as to be built up ourselves in our most holy faith. To the younger members of our Churches, especially, we speak this. Give yourselves to reading, study and prayer. Grow mentally and spiritually. You teach in the class—you do well—but could not you do better if you knew more? And if you address children in the Sunday schools we are glad of it—but would you not do that better if you studied more perfectly the Truth of God?

Apollos was not ashamed to be taught, nor need the most successful laborer be ashamed to learn! Improve your gift, for that is one way of stirring it up. And then pray over your gifts—that is a blessed way of stirring them up—to go before God and spread out your responsibilities before Him. In my own case I have often to cry,

> "Lord, You have given me this Congregation, and O it is hard to be clear of the blood of them all, and to speak with affection and prudence, and courage to all so as not to leave one unwarned, unhelped, untaught. Help me, my Lord, that I may leave no one without his portion of meat in due season. Who is sufficient for these things? Only Your Grace is sufficient for me."

It stirs one up to preach with all his might when he has laid before God in prayer his weakness. And the ability which God has given him, too, and asked that the weakness may be consecrated to God's Glory and the ability accepted to the Lord's praise. Should we not do just the same, whatever our calling is—take it to the Lord and say,

> "Assist me, great God, to live to You. If Your Grace in me is only as a handful of meal and a little oil, make it hold out—make it hold out! It is not much I can do, my Master. Help me to do it well and to continue steadfast and unwearied in it"?

Pray over yourself, as it were.

Put your whole self upon the altar and then let the drink-offering be the pouring out of your tears before God in prayer that He would be pleased to accept you, to qualify you, to anoint you, to direct you and bless you in all that you do. This would be the most excellent manner of stirring up the gift that is in you. O Spirit of the living God, lead all Your people to downright, earnest and actual service of the Redeemer, and especially work in us to that end!

III. I will not linger longer there, but close with the third observation—WHY IS IT THAT WE SHOULD STIR UP THE GIFT THAT IS IN US? There are many replies to this. One or two will answer our purpose. We should stir up the gift that is in us because all we shall do, when we have stirred ourselves to the utmost and when the Spirit of God has strengthened us to the highest degree, will still fall far short of what our dear Lord and Master deserves at our hands! Ah, what must Jesus think of us when He remembers His own love? Was there ever such a contrast between His furnace seven times hotter and our iceberg spirits?

He spared not Himself but we are always sparing ourselves. He gives us everything to the last rag and hangs naked on the Cross. We keep almost all to ourselves and count self-sacrifice to be difficult. He labors, is weary and yet ceases not. We are a little weary and straightway we faint. He continued to preach on, notwithstanding all the ill return men made. We take offense and throw up our work because we are not appreciated as we should be. Oh, the little things which put some workers out of temper and out of heart! Oh, the looks or the not-looks! The words, or the silence that will make some spirits give up any place and any service and any work!

"Forbearing one another" seems to have gone out of fashion with many people. "Forgiving one another even as God for Christ's sake has forgiven you," is forgotten. Brothers and Sisters, if being doormats for Christ for all the Church to wipe their feet upon would honor Him, we ought to think it a great glory to be so used! Among genuine Christians the contention is for the lowest place—among sham Christians the controversy is for the higher positions. Some will ask the question now-a-days—"Which is the higher office—that of elder or deacon," and so on. Oh, what triviality!

When the Master was going up to Jerusalem to die, there was a contention among the disciples which of them should be the greatest— and so it is with us. At times when Grace is low, our opinion of ourselves is very high, and then our love to Christ is so little that we soon take affront and are quick to resent any little insults, as we think them to be, where perhaps nothing of the kind was meant. Beloved, may we be saved from all this littleness of soul! And remember what obligations we are under to our Master—how we should have been dead in trespasses and sins but for Him—how we should have been in Hell but for Him—how our expectations tonight would have been "a fearful looking for of judgment and of fiery indignation" but for Him. But we are washed and cleansed and on the way to Heaven—and we owe it all to Him. Therefore let us stir up the gift that is in us and serve Him with all our might.

Another reason is that these are stirring times. If we are not stirring, everybody else is. The Church of God, it seems to me, is traveling along the road to Heaven in a broad-wheel wagon and all the world is going its own way by express speed. If men become at all earnest in the cause of God, worldly critics shout out, "Fanaticism! Excitement!" Did you ever stand on the Paris Bourse—ever hear the raving, raging excitement of those stock-jobbers as they are trying to buy various forms of scrip! Nobody says, "Look at these men! See how fanatical they are!" No, they expect to see excitement on the Bourse. But if we were half as excited for God and His Gospel, there would be a hue and cry all over the country, "Here's a set of madmen! Here's a set of fanatics let loose."

Of good Mr. Rowland Hill they said, "The dear old gentleman's too earnest." "Why," said he, "When I was at Wotton-Under-Edge I saw a piece of a gravel pit fall in upon two or three men when I was walking by, so I went into Wotton as fast as my aged legs could carry me and I shouted with all my might, 'Help! Help! Help!' and nobody said, 'the dear old man's too earnest.'" Oh, no, you may be as earnest as you like about saving people's lives, but if their souls awaken your sympathy, some lukewarm professor or other is sure to be ready with a wet blanket to cool your ardor. And yet were there ever times in which the wheels of life revolved so swiftly as now? The world marches with giant strides! Everybody is up and awake, but the Church is asleep to a great extent.

For other things men labor, and tug, and toil and make sacrifices— for an idea they slaughter their fellow creatures! For the unity of a race they fatten fields with blood and make rivers run with gore. But to preach Christ and snatch sinners from the jaws of Hell they require of us to be chilled—and insist that we must not be too earnest—we must not go too fast. We must be prudent! We must be cool! From "prudence" and "coolness" good Lord, deliver us! From "decorum" and "propriety," (wherein they stand in the way of our winning souls), good Lord deliver us! And from every conventionality and every idol that has been set up among us which prevents our being thoroughly useful and grandly serviceable to the cause of God, good Lord deliver us! Because these are stirring times, we ought to stir up the gift that is in us.

And then, again, we must stir up our gift because it needs stirring. The gifts and graces of Christian men are like a coal fire which frequently requires stirring as well as feeding with fuel. You must not stir it up too much—the poker does not give heat, and stirring up a man of itself does not make him better—indeed, it is as injurious to a weak man to stir him up as it would be to an expiring fire in the grate. But yet there must be stirring and fires go out sometimes for the lack of it. There are times with us when we become dull and heavy, doing little or nothing—restless, indifferent—and then it is that we require rebuking. If there is a solid bottom of real Grace in us, we only need the poker that we be stirred up and straightway the fire begins to burn.

How I like to stir up some of you! I remember a dear Brother dropping in one Thursday night to hear the Word preached—an excellent Christian, but sluggish—but the Lord touched his heart with the spoken Word and he began to preach in the streets of the city where he resides! He has now one of the largest houses of prayer and God has given him hundreds of souls! He only needed stirring up! Is there no other Brother here, who, hearing this earnest word shall find it like a live coal from off the altar, touching his lips and moving him to go forth and preach the Word and serve his Master according to his ability? We must, then, dear Friends, stir ourselves up because if we do not, we may lose the faculty and rob ourselves of the power of usefulness! The knife which is not used loses its edge and the man who does not work for God loses much of his ability to do so in the future.

I shall give you another reason, and that is this. If we will but stir ourselves, Beloved, or rather, if God's Holy Spirit will but stir us, we, as a Church may expect very great things! I can hardly tell you how comforted I felt last Monday evening. I said on Sunday, "The Elders and Deacons will meet to pray, and those of you who love souls and are concerned about them will kindly come, too, at six o'clock." I was glad to see many of you who I know love the Lord fervently, and through that warm Prayer Meeting which we had before our more public gathering, we felt that we had laid hold upon our God. I know there is a blessing coming! I am sure of it! I hear "a sound of a going in the tops of the mulberry trees." The Lord is with us! He never made His people agonize in secret and join together publicly in deep soul earnestness without intending to bless them!

We might as well fear, when the months are warm, that there will be no ripening of the wheat as to say when Christian's hearts are warm towards God that there will be no conversions. It can't be! Enquiring saints always make enquiring sinners. If we enquire of God for sinners, sinners will soon enquire for themselves. Up, therefore! Up, therefore, Beloved! Stir yourselves, for God is stirring us! And remember, there will be a great stir by-and-bye. Business will all end, politics will be done with and all the matters in which you are concerned will be eternally closed. What a stir there will be in that day! Fallen we shall stand before the Judgment Seat of Christ to give an account of the deeds done in the body!

What a stir about ourselves! What a stir about others! Where will they be? Will they be on the right hand, or on the left? Shall I see my boys in Heaven, or will they be cast out? What a stir there will be about your husband or your wife! What a stir there will be about your neighbors! Think of it! Think of it, I say, and be stirred now! If they die as they are, they will be damned—they must be. They must sink into Hell! There is no hope of their escape if they die unsaved.

What a stir there will be throughout all the nations in that day! And, surely, if we look at it in the light of eternity—in the light of that tremendous day when Christ, with clouds, shall come—we shall feel that there is nothing worth living for but serving God! We shall surely feel that the very core and center of all life is to bring glory to God by bringing sinners to Jesus Christ! God grant you may live as if you expected to die! We ought always to preach as though we should go out of the pulpit into Heaven and we should always to pray in that way. And we should always spend every day as if we had not another day to spend. For this we need much of the Holy Spirit's power.

And He rests upon His people! May He come and rest upon us, now, for Jesus Christ's sake. Amen.

2

Salvation Altogether by Grace

(Sermon No. 703)

"Who has saved us, and called us with a holy calling, not according to our works, but according to His own purpose and grace which was given to us in Christ Jesus before the world began" (2 Timothy 1:9).

I F WE WOULD INFLUENCE thoughtful persons it must be by solid arguments. Shallow minds may be worked upon by mere warmth of emotion and force of excitement, but the more valuable part of the community must be dealt with in quite another manner. When the Apostle Paul was desirous to influence his son in the faith, Timothy, who was a diligent and earnest student and a man of gifts as well as of Divine Grace, he did not attempt to affect him by mere appeals to his feelings. Paul felt that the most effectual way to act upon him was to remind him of solid doctrinal Truth of God which he knew Timothy believed.

This is a lesson for the ministry at large. Certain earnest preachers are incessantly exciting the people, but seldom, if ever, instructing them. They carry much fire and very little light. God forbid that we should say a word against appealing to the feelings—this is most necessary in its place—but then there is a due proportion to be observed in it. A religion which is based upon, sustained, and maintained simply by excitement will necessarily be very flimsy and unsubstantial, and will yield very speedily to the crush of opposition or to the crumbling hand of time.

The preacher may touch the feelings by rousing appeals as the harpist touches the harp strings, and he will be very foolish if he should neglect so ready and admirable an instrument. But still, as he is dealing with reasonable creatures, he must not forget to enlighten the intellect and instruct the understanding. And how can he appeal to the understanding better than by presenting to it the Truth which the Holy Spirit teaches?

Scriptural doctrine furnishes us with powerful motives to urge upon the minds of Christians.

It seems to me that if we could, by some unreasoning impulse, move you to a certain course of action it might be well in its way. But it would be unsafe and untrustworthy, for you would be equally open to be moved in an opposite direction by other persons more skilled in such operations. But if God enables us, by His Spirit, to influence your minds by solid Truth and substantial argument, you will then move with a constancy of power which nothing can turn aside. The feather flies in the wind, but it has no inherent power to move—and consequently when the gale is over it falls to the ground—such is the religion of excitement. But the eagle has life within itself and its wings bear it aloft and onward whether the breeze favors it or not—such is religion when sustained by a conviction of the Truth of God! The well-taught man in Christ Jesus stands firm where the uninstructed infant would fall or be carried away. "Be not carried about with every wind of doctrine," says the Apostle, and those are least likely to be so carried who are well established in the Truth as it is in Jesus.

It is somewhat remarkable—at least it may seem so to persons who are not accustomed to think upon the subject—that the Apostle, in order to excite Timothy to boldness—to keep him constant in the faith—reminds him of the great doctrine that the Grace of God reigns in the salvation of men! He gives in this verse—this parenthetical verse as some call it, but which seems to me to be fully in the current of the passage—he gives in this verse a brief summary of the Gospel, showing the great prominence which it gives to the Grace of God, with the design of maintaining Timothy in the boldness of his testimony for Christ.

I do not doubt but that a far greater power for usefulness lies concealed within the Doctrines of Grace than some men have ever dreamed of. It has been usual to look upon doctrinal Truth as being nothing more than unpractical theory, and many have spoken of the precepts of God's Word as being more practical and more useful. The day may yet come when, in clearer light, we shall perceive that sound doctrine is the very root and vital energy of practical holiness, and that to teach the people the Truth which God has revealed is the readiest and surest way of leading them to obedience and persevering holiness.

May the Holy Spirit assist us while we shall, first, consider the doctrine taught by the Apostle in this text. And secondly, the uses of that doctrine.

I. Very carefully let us CONSIDER THE DOCTRINE TAUGHT BY THE APOSTLE IN THIS TEXT. Friends will remember that it is not our object to preach the doctrine which is most popular or most palatable. Nor do we desire to set forth the views of any one person in the assembly. Our one aim is to give what we judge to be the meaning of the text. We shall probably deliver doctrine which many of you will not like, and if you should not like it we shall not be at all surprised! Or even if you should be vexed and angry we shall not be at all alarmed because we never understood that we were commissioned to preach what would please our hearers, nor were expected by sensible, not to say gracious men, to shape our views to suit the notions of our audience.

We count ourselves amenable to God and to the text. And if we give the meaning of the text, we believe we shall give the mind of God and we shall be likely to have His favor which will be sufficient for us, contradict us who may. However, let every candid mind be willing to receive the Truth of God if it is clearly in the inspired Word.

1. The Apostle, in stating his doctrine in the following words, "Who has saved us, and called us with a holy calling, not according to our works, but according to His own purpose and grace, which was given to us in Christ Jesus before the world began," declares God to be the Author of salvation—"Who has saved us and called us." The whole tenor of the verse is towards a strong affirmation of Jonah's doctrine, "that salvation is of the Lord."

It would require very great twisting—involving more than ingenuity, it would need dishonesty—to make out salvation by man out of this text! But to find salvation altogether of God in it is to perceive the Truth of God which lies upon the very surface. No need for profound enquiry. The wayfaring man, though a fool, shall not err here—the text says as

25

plainly as words can say, "God has saved us, and called us with a holy calling."

The Apostle, then, in order to bring forth the Truth that salvation is of Grace, declares that it is of God—that it springs directly and entirely from Him and from Him alone. Is not this according to the teaching of the Holy Spirit in other places where He affirms over and over again that the alpha and omega of our salvation must be found, not in ourselves, but in our God? Our Apostle, in saying that God has saved us, refers to all the Persons of the Divine Unity. The Father has saved us. "God has given to us eternal life" (1 John 5:11). "The Father Himself loves you." It was He whose gracious mind first conceived the thought of redeeming His chosen from the ruin of the Fall.

It was His mind which first planned the way of salvation by Substitution. It was from His generous heart that the thought first sprang that Christ should suffer as the Covenant Head of His people, as said the Apostle,

"Blessed be the God and Father of our Lord Jesus Christ, who has blessed us with all spiritual blessings in heavenly places in Christ. According as He has chosen us in Him before the foundation of the world, that we should be holy and without blame before Him in love: having predestinated us unto the adoption of children by Jesus Christ to Himself, according to the good pleasure of His will, to the praise of the glory of His grace, wherein He has made us accepted in the Beloved" (Eph. 1:3-6).

From the heart of Divine compassion came the gift of the only begotten Son: "For God so loved the world that He gave His only begotten Son, that whoever believes in Him should not perish, but have everlasting life." The Father selected the persons who should receive an interest in the redemption of His Son, for these are described as, "called according to His purpose" (Rom. 8:28). The plan of salvation in all its details sprang from the Father's wisdom and grace. The Apostle did not, however, overlook the work of the Son. It is most certainly through the Son of God that we are saved, for is not His name Jesus, the Savior? Incarnate in the flesh, His holy life is the righteousness in which saints are arrayed, while His ignominious and painful death has filled the sacred bath of blood in which the sinner must be washed that he may be made clean.

It is through the Redemption, which is in Christ Jesus, that the people of God become accepted in the Beloved. With one voice before the Eternal Throne they sing, "Unto Him that loved us and washed us from our sins in His blood, unto Him be glory." And they chant that hymn because He deserves the glory which they ascribe to Him. It is the Son of God who is the Savior of men, and men are not the saviors of themselves. Nor did the Apostle, I am persuaded, forget that Third Person in the blessed Unity—the Holy Spirit.

Who but the Holy Spirit first gives us power to understand the Gospel? "The carnal mind understands not the things that are of God." Does not the Holy Spirit influence our will, turning us from the obstinacy of our former rebellion to the obedience of the Truth of God? Does not the Holy Spirit renew us, creating us in Christ Jesus unto good works? Is it not by the Holy Spirit's breath that we live in the spiritual life? Is He not to us Instructor, Comforter, Quickener? Is He not everything, in fact, through His active operations upon our mind?

The Father, then, in planning. The Son in redeeming. The Spirit, in applying the redemption, must be spoken of as the one God "who has saved us." Brothers and Sisters, to say that we save ourselves is to utter a manifest absurdity! We are called in Scripture "a temple"—a holy temple in the Lord. But shall anyone assert that the stones of the edifice were their own architect? Shall it be said that the stones of the building in which we are now assembled cut themselves into their present shape and then spontaneously came together and piled this spacious edifice? Should anyone assert such a foolish thing we should be disposed to doubt his sanity! Much more may we suspect the spiritual sanity of any man who should venture to affirm that the great temple of the Church of God designed and erected itself!

No! We believe that God the Father was the Architect, sketched the plan, supplies the materials, and will complete the work. Shall it also be said that those who are redeemed redeemed themselves? That slaves of Satan break their own fetters? Then why was a Redeemer needed at all?

How should there be any need for Jesus to descend into the world to redeem those who could redeem themselves? Do you believe that the sheep of God, whom He has taken from between the jaws of the lion, could have rescued themselves? It were a strange thing if such were the case.

Our Lord Jesus came not to do a work of supererogation, but if He came to save persons who might have saved themselves, He certainly came without a necessity for so doing. We cannot believe that Christ came to do what the sinners might have done themselves! No, "He has trod the winepress alone, and of the people there was none with Him," and the redemption of His people shall give glory unto Himself only!

Shall it be asserted that those who were once dead have spiritually quickened themselves? Can the dead make themselves alive? Who shall assert that Lazarus, rotting in the grave, came forth to life of himself? If it is so said and so believed, then, no, not even then, will we believe that the dead in sin have ever quickened themselves! Those who are saved by God the Holy Spirit are created anew according to Scripture—but whoever dreamed of creation creating itself? God spoke the world out of nothing, but nothing did not aid in the creation of the universe! Divine energy can do everything, but what can nothing do?

Now if we have a new creation, there must have been a creator, and it is clear that not being, then, spiritually created, we could not have assisted in our own new creation, unless, indeed, death can assist life, and non-existence aid in creation. The carnal mind does not assist the Spirit of God in new creating a man, but altogether regeneration is the work of God the Holy Spirit, and the work of renewal is from His unassisted power. Father, Son and Spirit, we, then, adore, and putting these thoughts together, we would humbly prostrate ourselves at the foot of the Throne of the august Majesty and acknowledge that if saved, He alone has saved us, and unto Him be the glory!

2. We next remark that grace is in this verse rendered conspicuous when we see that God pursues a singular method, "Who has saved us and called us." The peculiarity of the manner lies in three things—first, in the completeness of it. The Apostle uses the perfect tense and says, "who has

saved us." Believers in Christ Jesus are saved. They are not looked upon as persons who are in a hopeful state and may ultimately be saved, but they are already saved.

This is not according to the common talk of professors nowadays, for many of them speak of being saved when they come to die. But it is according to the usage of Scripture to speak of us who are saved. Be it known this morning that every man and woman here is either saved at this present moment, or lost—and that salvation is not a blessing to be enjoyed upon the dying bed and to be sung of in a future state—but a matter to be obtained, received, promised and enjoyed NOW! God has saved His saints, mark, not partly saved them, but perfectly saved them. The Christian is perfectly saved in God's purpose. God has ordained him unto salvation, and that purpose is complete.

He is saved, also, as to the price which has been paid for him, for this is done not in part but in whole. The substitutionary work which Christ has offered is not a certain proportion of the work to be done, but, "it is finished," was the cry of the Savior before He died. The Believer is also perfectly saved in his Covenant Head, for as we were utterly lost as soon as ever Adam fell, before we had committed any actual sin, so every man in Christ was saved in the second

Adam when He finished His work. The Savior completed His work and in the sense in which Paul uses that expression, "He has saved us."

This completeness is one peculiarity—we must mark another. I want you to notice the order as well as the completeness—"who has saved us and called us." What? Saved us before He called us? Yes, so the text says. But is a man saved before he is called by Divine Grace? Not in his own experience. Not as far as the work of the Holy Spirit goes. But he is saved in God's purpose, in Christ's redemption, and in his relationship to his covenant Head. And he is saved, moreover, in this respect—that the work of his salvation is done, and he has only to receive it as a finished work. In the olden times of imprisonment for debt it would have been quite correct for you to step into the cell of a debtor and say to him, "I have freed you," if you had paid his debts and obtained an order for his discharge.

Well, but he is still in prison! Yes, but you really liberated him as soon as you paid his debts. It is true he was still in prison, but he was not legally there, and no sooner did he know that the debt was paid and that receipt was pleaded before proper authorities, than the man obtained his liberty. So the Lord Jesus Christ paid the debts of His people before they knew anything about it. Did He not pay them on the Cross more than eighteen hundred years ago to the utmost penny? And is not this the reason why, as soon as He meets with us in a way of Grace, He cries, "I have saved you. Lay hold on eternal life"? We are, then, virtually, though not actually, saved before we are called. "He has saved us and called us."

There is yet a third peculiarity, and that is in connection with the calling. God has called us with a holy calling. Those whom the Savior saved upon the tree are, in due time, effectually called by the power of God the Holy Spirit unto holiness. They leave their sins, they endeavor to be like Christ, they choose holiness—not out of any compulsion—but from the stress of a new nature which leads them to rejoice in holiness, just as naturally as before they delighted in sin. Whereas their old nature loved everything that was evil, their new nature cannot sin because it is born of God, and it loves everything that is good.

Does not the Apostle mention this result of our calling in order to meet those who say that God calls His people because He foresees their holiness? Not so! He calls them to that holiness—that holiness is not a cause but an effect—it is not the motive of His purpose, but the result of His purpose. He neither chose them nor called them because they were holy, but He called them that they might be holy, and holiness is the beauty produced by His workmanship in them. The excellences which we see in a Believer are as much the work of God as the Atonement itself!

This second point brings out very sweetly the fullness of the Grace of God. First—salvation must be of Grace, because the Lord is the Author of it, and what motive but Grace could move Him to save the guilty? In the next place, salvation must be of Grace because the Lord works in such a manner that our righteousness is forever excluded. Salvation is completed by God, and therefore not of man, neither by man.

Salvation is worked by God in an order which puts our holiness as a consequence and not as a cause, and therefore merit is forever disowned.

3. When a speaker desires to strengthen his point and to make himself clear, he generally puts in a negative as to the other side. So the Apostle adds a negative—"Not according to our works." The world's great preaching is, "Do as well as you can. Live a moral life and God will save you." The Gospel preaching is this—

"You are a lost sinner, and you can deserve nothing of God but His displeasure. If you are to be saved, it must be by an act of Sovereign Grace. God must freely extend the silver scepter of His love to you, for you are a guilty wretch who deserves to be sent to the lowest Hell. Your best works are so full of sin that they can in no degree save you—to the free mercy of God you must owe all things."

"Oh," says one, "are good works of no use?" Good works are of use when a man is saved—they are the evidences of his being saved. But good works do not save a man, good works do not influence the mind of God to save a man, for if so, salvation would be a matter of debt and not of Grace. The Lord has declared over and over in His Word, "Not of works, lest any man should boast." "By the works of the Law there shall no flesh living be justified." The Apostle in the Epistle to the Galatians is very strong, indeed, upon this point. Indeed, he thunders it out again, and again, and again! He denies that salvation is even so much as in part due to our works, for if it is by works, then he declares it is not of Grace, otherwise Grace is no more Grace. And if it is of Grace, it is not of works, otherwise work is no more work.

Paul assures us that the two principles of Grace and merit can no more mix together than fire and water—that if man is to be saved by the mercy of God—it must be by the mercy of God and not by works. But if man is to be saved by works, it must be by works entirely and not by mercy mixed with it, for mercy and work will not go together. Jesus saves, but He does all the work or none. He is Author and Finisher, and works must not rob Him of His due. Sinner, you must either receive salvation freely from the hand of Divine Bounty, or else you must earn it by your own unassisted merits, which is utterly impossible! Oh that you would yield to the first!

My Brethren, this is the Truth of God which still needs to be preached. This is the Truth of God which shook all Europe from end to end when Luther first proclaimed it. Is not this the old thunderbolt which the great Reformer hurled at Rome—"Justified freely by His grace, through the redemption which is in Christ Jesus"? But why did God make salvation to be by faith? Scripture tells us—"Therefore it is of faith, that it might be by grace." If it had been by works it must have been by debt—but since it is by faith we can clearly see that there can be no merit in faith. It must be therefore by Divine Grace.

4. My text is even more explicit, yet, for the eternal purpose is mentioned. The next thing the Apostle says is this: "Who has saved us, and called us with a holy calling, not according to our works but according to His own purpose." Mark that word—"according to His own purpose." Oh how some people wriggle over that word, as if they were worms on a fisherman's hook! But there it stands, and cannot be gotten rid of. God saves His people "according to His purpose." No, "according to His *own* purpose."

My Brothers and Sisters, do you not see how all the merit and the power of the creature are shut out here, when you are saved, not according to your purpose or merit, but "according to His own purpose"? I shall not dwell on this. It is not exactly the object of this morning's discourse to bring out in full the great mystery of electing love, but I will not, for a moment, keep back the Truth of God. If any man is saved, it is not because he purposed to be saved, but because God purposed to save him.

Have you never read the Holy Spirit's testimony: "It is not of him that wills, nor of him that runs, but of God that shows mercy"? The Savior said to His Apostles what He, in effect, says also to us, "You have not chosen Me, but I have chosen you, and ordained you, that you might bring forth fruit." Some hold one and some another view concerning the freedom of the will, but our Savior's doctrine is, "You will not come unto Me that you might have life." You will not come! Your wills will never bring you! If you do come, it is because Divine Grace inclined you! "No man can come unto Me, except the Father which has sent Me draw Him." "Whoever comes to Me I will in no wise cast out," is a great and precious general text, but it is quite consistent with the rest of the same verse—"All that the Father gives Me shall come to Me."

Our text tells us that our salvation is "according to His own purpose." It is a strange thing that men should be so angry against the purpose of God. We ourselves have a purpose—we permit our fellow creatures to have some will of their own, and especially in giving away their own goods. But is my God to be bound and fettered by men, and not permitted to do as He wills with His own? But be this known unto you, O men that reply against God, that He gives no account of His actions, but asks of you, "Can I not do as I will with My own?" He rules in Heaven, and in the armies of this lower world, and none can stay His hand or say unto Him, "What are you doing?"

5. But then the text, lest we should make any mistake, adds, "according to His own purpose and grace." The purpose is not founded on foreseen merit, but upon Divine Grace alone. It is Grace, all Grace, nothing but Grace from first to last! Man stands shivering outside, a condemned criminal, and God, sitting upon His Throne, sends the herald to tell him that He is willing to receive sinners and to pardon them. The sinner replies,

"Well, I am willing to be pardoned if I am permitted to do something in order to earn pardon. If I can stand before the King and claim that I have done something to win His favor, I am quite willing to come."

But the herald replies,

"No, if you are pardoned, you must understand it is entirely and wholly as an act of Grace on God's part. He sees nothing good in you. He knows that there is nothing good in you. He is willing to take you just as you are, filthy, and bad, and wicked, and undeserving. He is willing to give you graciously what He would not sell to you, and what He knows you cannot earn of Him. Will you take it?"

And naturally every man says, "No, I will not be saved in that style."

Well, then, Soul, remember that you will never be saved at all, for God's way is salvation by Grace! You will have to confess, if ever you are saved, my dear Hearer, that you never deserved one single blessing from the God of Grace. You will have to give all the glory to His holy name if ever you get to Heaven. And mark you, even in the matter of the acceptance of this offered mercy, you will never accept it unless He makes you willing! He does freely present it to every one of you, and He honestly bids you come to Christ and live. But come you never will, I know, except the effectual Grace which first provided mercy shall make you willing to accept that mercy. So the text tells us it is His own purpose and Grace.

6. Again, in order to shut out everything like boasting, the whole is spoken of as a gift. Notice—lest, (for we are such straying sheep in this matter), lest we should still slip out of the field—it is added, "purpose and grace which He gave us." Not, "which He sold us," "offered us," but "which He *gave* us." He must have a word here which shall be a death-blow to all merit—"which he gave us"—it was *given*. And what can be freer than a gift, and what more evidently of Divine Grace?

7. But the gift is bestowed through a medium, which glorifies Christ. It is written, "which was given us in Christ Jesus." We ask to have mercy from the wellhead of Divine Grace, and we ask not even to make the bucket in which it is to be brought to us! Christ is to be the sacred vessel in which the Grace of God is to be presented to our thirsty lips. Now where is boasting? Why surely there it sits at the foot of the Cross and sings, "God forbid that I should glory save in the Cross of our Lord Jesus Christ." Is it not Grace and Grace alone?

8. Yet further, a period is mentioned and added—"before the world began." Those last words seem to me forever to lay prostrate all idea of anything of our own merits in saving ourselves, because it is here witnessed that God gave us Divine Grace "before the world began." Where were you then? What hand had you in it "before the world began"? Why, fly back, if you can, in imagination, to the ancient years when those venerable mountains, that elder birth of nature, were not yet formed! Fly back when world, and sun, and moon, and stars, were all in embryo in

God's great mind—when the unnavigated sea of space had never been disturbed by wing of seraph, and the awful silence of eternity had never been startled by the song of cherubim—when God dwelt alone.

If you can conceive that time before all time, that vast eternity—it was then He gave us Grace in Christ Jesus. What, O Soul, had you to do with that? Where were your merits then? Where were you yourself? O you small dust of the balance, you insect of a day, where were you? See how Jehovah reigned, dispensing mercy as He would, and ordaining unto eternal life without taking counsel of man or angel, for neither man or angel then had an existence! That it might be all of Grace He gave us Grace before the world began!

I have honestly read out the doctrine of the text, and nothing more. If such is not the meaning of the text I do not know the meaning of it, and I cannot, therefore, tell you what it is. But I believe that I have given the natural and grammatical teaching of the text. If you do not like the doctrine, I cannot help it. I did not make the text, and if I have to expound it I must expound it honestly as it is in my Master's Word. And I pray you receive what He says, whatever you may do with what I say.

II. I shall want your patience while I try to SHOW THE USES OF THIS DOCTRINE. The Doctrine of Grace has been put by in the lumber chamber. It is acknowledged to be true, for it is confessed in most creeds. It is in the Church of England articles. It is in the confessions of all sorts of Protestant Christians, except those who are avowedly Arminian, but how little is it ever preached! It is put among the relics of the past. It is considered to be a respectable sort of retired officer who is not expected to see any more active service.

Now I believe that it is not a superannuated officer in the Master's army, but that it is as full of force and vigor as ever. But what is the use of it? Why, first, it is clear from the connection that it has a tendency to embolden the man who receives it. Paul tells Timothy not to be ashamed, and he gives this as a motive—how can a man be ashamed when he believes that God has given him Grace in Christ Jesus before the world was? Suppose the man to be very poor. "Oh," he says, "what does it matter? Though I have but a little oil in the cruse, and a little meal in the barrel, yet I have a lot and a portion in everlasting things! My name is not in Doomsday Book nor in Burke's Peerage—but it is in the book of God's election, and was there before the world began!"

Such a man dares look the proudest of his fellows in the face. This was the doctrine on which the brave old Ironsides fed—the men who, when they rode to battle with the war cry of, "The Lord of Hosts!" made the cavaliers fly before them like chaff before the wind. No doctrine like it for putting a backbone into a man, and making him feel that he is made for something better than to be trod down like straw for the dunghill beneath a despot's heel. Sneer who will, the elect of God derive a nobility from the Divine choice which no royal patent can outshine! I would that Free Grace were more preached, because it gives men something to believe with confidence.

The great mass of professing Christians know nothing of doctrine. Their religion consists in going a certain number of times to a place of worship, but they have no care for the Truth of God one way or another. I speak without any prejudice in this matter—but I have talked with a large number of persons in the course of my very extensive pastorate who have been for years members of other churches. And when I have asked them a few questions upon doctrinal matters it did not seem to me that they thought they were in error—they were perfectly willing to believe almost anything that any earnest man might teach them. But they did not know anything—they had no minds of their own—and no definite opinions.

Our children, who have learned "The Westminster Assembly's Confession of Faith," know more about the Doctrines of Grace and the doctrine of the Bible than hundreds of grownups who attend a ministry which very eloquently teaches nothing. It was observed by a very excellent critic not long ago that if you were to hear thirteen lectures on astronomy or geology you might get a pretty good idea of what the science was, and the theory of the person who gave the lectures—but that if you were to hear thirteen hundred sermons from some ministers, you would not know at all what they were preaching about or what their doctrinal sentiments were. It ought not to be so.

Is not this the reason why Puseyism spreads so, and all sorts of errors have such a foothold, because our people, as a whole, do not know what they believe? The doctrine of Election, if well received, gives to a man something which he knows and which he holds and which will become dear to him. Something for which he would be prepared to die if the fires of persecution were again kindled! Better still is it that this doctrine not only gives the man something to hold but it holds the man! Let a man once have burnt into him that salvation is of God and not of man, and that God's Grace is to be glorified and not human merit, and you will never get that belief out of him!

It is the rarest thing in all the world to hear of such a man ever apostatizing from his faith. Other doctrine is slippery ground, like the slope of a mountain composed of loose earth and rolling stones down which the traveler may slide long before he can even get a transient foothold. But this is like a granite step upon the eternal pyramid of Truth—get your feet on this—and there is no fear of slipping so far as doctrinal standing is concerned. If we would have our churches in England well instructed and holding fast the Truth of God, we must bring out the grand old verity of the eternal purpose of God in Christ Jesus before the world began!

Oh may the Holy Spirit write it on our hearts! Moreover, my Brethren, this doctrine overwhelms, as with an avalanche, all the claims of priest-craft. Let it be told to men that they are saved by God, and they say at once, "Then what is the good of the priest?" If they are told it is God's Grace, then they ask, "Then you do not want our money to buy masses and absolutions?" And down goes the priest at once! Beloved, this is the battering ram that God uses with which to shake the gates of Hell! How much more forcible than the pretty essays of many so-called Divines which have no more power than bulrushes, no more light than smoking flax!

What do you suppose people used to meet in the woods for in persecuting times? They met by thousands outside the town of Antwerp, and such-like places on the Continent, in jeopardy of their lives! Do you suppose they would ever have come together to hear that poor milk-and-water theology of this age, or to receive the lukewarm milk and water of our modern anti-Calvinists? Not they, my Brethren! They needed stronger meat, and a more savory diet to attract them. Do you imagine that when it was death to listen to the preacher, that men under the shadows of night, and amid the wings of tempest would then listen to philosophical essays, or to mere moral precepts, or to diluted, adulterated, soulless, theological suppositions?

No! There is no energy in that kind of thing to draw men together under fear of their lives. So what did bring them together in the dead of night amidst the glare of lightning, and the roll of thunder? What brought them together? Why, the doctrine of the Grace of God! The doctrine of Jesus and of His servants Paul, and Augustine, and Luther, and Calvin! For there is something in that doctrine which touches the heart of the Christian and gives him food such as his soul loves, savory meat, suitable to his Heaven-born appetite!

To hear this, men braved death and defied the sword! And it we are to see once again the scarlet hat plucked from the wearer's head, and the shaven crowns with all the gaudy trumpery of Rome sent back to the place from where they came—and Heaven grant that they may take our Puseyite Established Church with them—it must be by declaring all the doctrines of the Grace of God! When these are declared and vindicated in every place, we shall yet again make these enemies of God and man to know that they cannot stand their ground for a moment where men of God wield the sword of the Lord and of Gideon by preaching the doctrines of the Grace of God.

Brothers and Sisters, let the man receive these Truths! Let them be written in his heart by the Holy Spirit, and they will make him look up. He will say, "God has saved me!" and he will walk with a constant eye to God. He will not forget to see the hand of God in Nature and in Providence. He will, on the contrary, discern the Lord working in all places, and will humbly adore Him. He will not give to laws of Nature or schemes of State the glory due to the Most High, but will have respect unto the unseen Ruler.

"What the Lord says to me, that will I do," is the Believer's language. "What is His will that will I follow. What is His Word, that will I believe. What is His promise, on that I will live." It is a blessed habit to teach a man to look up, look up to God in all things! At the same time, this doctrine of Election makes a man look down upon himself. "Ah," he says, "I am nothing! There is nothing in me to merit esteem. I have no goodness of my own. If saved, I cannot praise myself. I cannot in anyway ascribe to myself honor. God has done it, God has done it." Nothing makes the man so humble, but nothing makes him so glad! Nothing lays him so low at the Mercy Seat, but nothing makes him so brave to look his fellow man in the face. It is a grand Truth of God! Would to God you all knew its mighty power!

Lastly, this precious Truth is full of comfort to the sinner, and that is why I love it. As it has been preached by some it has been exaggerated and made into a bugbear. Why, there are some who preach the doctrine of Election as though it were a line of sharp spikes to keep a sinner from coming to Christ! As though it were a sharp, glittering sword to be pushed into the breast of a coming sinner to keep him from mercy!

Now it is not so. Sinner, whoever you may be, wherever you may be, your greatest comfort should be to know that salvation is by Divine Grace. Why Man, if it were by merit, what would become of you? Suppose that God saved men on account of their merits? Where would you drunkards be? Where would you swearers be? You who have been unclean and unchaste, and you whose hearts have cursed God, and who even now do not love Him—where would you be?

But when it is all of Grace, why, then, all your past life, however black and filthy it may be, need not keep you from coming to Jesus. Christ receives sinners! God has elected sinners! He has elected some of the filthiest of sinners—why not you? He receives everyone that comes to Him. He will not cast you out. There have been some who have hated Him, insulted Him to His face—that have burned His servants alive, and have persecuted Him in His members—but as soon as they have cried, "God be merciful to me a sinner," He has given them mercy at once!

And He will give it to you if you are led to seek it. If I had to tell you that you were to work out your own salvation apart from His Grace it were a sad day for you. But when it comes to you yourself—filthy—there is washing for you! Dead—there is life for you! Naked—there is raiment for you! All undone and ruined—here is a complete salvation for you! O Soul, may you have Grace to lay hold of it, and then you and I together will sing to the praise of the glory of Divine Grace.

3

Faith Illustrated

(Sermon No. 271)

"For the which cause I also suffer these things: nevertheless I am not ashamed: for I know whom I have believed, and am persuaded that he is able to keep that which I have committed unto him against that day" (2 Timothy 1:12).

AN ASSURANCE OF OUR SAFETY in Christ will be found useful to us in all states of experience. When Jesus sent forth his seventy chosen disciples, endowed with miraculous powers, they performed great wonders, and naturally enough they were somewhat elated when they returned to tell him of their deeds. Jesus marked their tendency to pride; he saw that in the utterance—"Behold even devils were subject to us," there was mingled much of self-congratulation and boasting. What cure, think you, did he administer; or what was the sacred lesson that he taught them which might prevent their being exalted above measure? "Nevertheless," said he, "rejoice not in this, but rather rejoice because your names are written in heaven." The assurance of our eternal interest in Christ may help to keep us humble in the day of our prosperity; for when God multiplies our wealth, when he blesses our endeavors, when he speeds the plough; when he wafts the good ship swiftly onward, this may act as a sacred ballast to us, that we have something better than these things, and therefore we must not set our affections upon the things of earth, but upon things above; and let our heart be where our greatest treasure is. I say, better than any lancet to spill the superfluous blood of our boasting, better than any bitter medicine to chase the burning fever of our pride; better than any mixture of the most pungent ingredients is this most precious and hallowed wine of the covenant—a remembrance of our safety in Christ. This, this alone, opened up to us by the Spirit, will suffice to keep us in that happy lowliness which is the true position of the full-grown man in Christ Jesus. But note this, when at any time we are

41

cast down with multiplied afflictions, and oppressed with sorrow, the very same fact which kept us humble in prosperity may preserve us from despair in adversity. For mark you here, the apostle was surrounded by a great fight of affliction; he was compassed about with troubles, he suffered within and without; and yet he says, "Nevertheless I am not ashamed." But what is that which preserves him from sinking? It is the same truth which kept the ancient disciples from overweening pride. It is the sweet persuasion of his interest in Christ. "For I know whom I have believed, and am persuaded that he is able to keep that which I have committed unto him against that day." Get then, Christian brethren and friends, get assurance; be not content with hope, get confidence; rest not in faith, labor after the full assurance of faith; and never be content, my hearer, till thou canst say thou knowest thy election, thou art sure of thy redemption, and thou art certain of thy preservation unto *that day*.

I propose this morning in preaching upon this text to labor both for the edification of the saint and the conversion of the sinner. I shall divide the text very amply thus: First, we have in it *the grandest action of the Christian's life,* namely, the committing of our eternal interests into the hand of Christ. Secondly, we have *the justification of this grand act of trust*—"I know in whom I have trusted." I have not trusted one whose character is unknown to me, I am not foolish, I have sure grounds for what I have done. And then we have, thirdly, *the most blessed effect of this confidence*—"I am persuaded that he is able to keep that which I have committed unto him."

I. First, then I am to describe THE GRANDEST ACTION OF THE CHRISTIAN'S LIFE.

With all our preaching, I am afraid that we too much omit the simple explanation of the essential act in salvation. I have feared that the anxious enquirer might visit many of our churches and chapels, month after month, and yet he would not get a clear idea of what he must do to be saved. He would come away with an indistinct notion that he was to believe, but what he was to believe he would not know. He would, perhaps, obtain some glimmering of the fact that he must be saved through the merits of Christ, but how those merits can become available to him, he would still be left to guess. I know at least that this was my case—that when sincere and anxious to do or be anything which might save my soul, I was utterly in the dark as to the way in which my salvation might be rendered thoroughly secure. Now, this morning. I hope I shall be able to put it into such a light that he who runs may read, and that the wayfaring man, though a fool, may not err therein.

The apostle says, he committed himself into the hands of Christ. His soul with all its eternal interests; his soul with all its sins, with all its hopes, and all its fears, he had put into the hands of Christ, as the grandest and most precious deposit which man could ever make. He had taken himself just as he was and had surrendered himself to Christ, saying—

"Lord save me, for I cannot save myself; I give myself up to thee, freely relying upon thy power, and believing in thy love. I give my soul up to thee to be washed, cleansed, saved, and preserved, and at last brought home to heaven."

This act of committing himself to Christ was the first act which ever brought real comfort to his spirit; it was the act which he must continue to perform whenever he would escape from a painful sense of sin; the act with which he must enter heaven itself, if he would die in peace and see God's face with acceptance. He must still continue to commit himself into the keeping of Christ. I take it that when the apostle committed himself to Christ, he meant these three things. He meant first, that from that good hour *he renounced all dependence upon his own efforts to save himself.* The apostle had done very much, after a fashion, towards his own salvation. He commenced with all the advantages of ancestry. He was a Hebrew of the Hebrews, of the tribe of Benjamin, as touching the law a Pharisee. He was one of the very straightest of the straightest sect of his religion. So anxious was he to obtain salvation by his own efforts, that he left no stone unturned. Whatever Pharisee might be a hypocrite, Paul was none. Though he tithed his anise, and his mint, and his cummin, he did not neglect the weightier matters of the law. He might have united with truth, in the affirmation of the young man, "All these things have I kept from my youth up." Hear ye his own testimony: "Though I might also have confidence in the flesh. If any other man thinketh that he hath whereof he might trust in the flesh, I more." Being exceedingly desirous to serve God, he sought to put down what he thought was the pestilent heresy of Christ. Being exceeding hot in his endeavors against every thing that he thought to be wrong, he persecuted the professors of the new religion, hunted them in every city, brought them into the synagogue, and compelled them to blaspheme; when he had emptied his own country, he must needs take a journey to another, that he might there show his zeal in the cause of his God, by bringing out those whom he thought to be the deluded followers of an impostor. But suddenly Paul's mind is changed. Almighty grace leads him to see that he is working in a wrong direction, that his toil is lost, that as well might Sisyphus seek to roll his stone up hill, as for him to find a road to heaven up the steps of Sinai; that as well might the daughters of Danaus hope to fill the bottomless cauldron with a bucket full of holes, as Paul indulge the idea that he could fill up the measure of the laws' demands. Consequently he feels that all he has done is nothing worth, and coming to Christ he cries,

"But what things were gain to me, those I counted loss for Christ. Yea doubtless, and I count all things but loss for the excellency of the knowledge of Christ Jesus my Lord: for whom I have suffered the loss of all things, and do count them but dung, that I may win Christ, and be found in him, not having mine own righteousness, which is of the law, but that which is through the faith of Christ, the righteousness which is of God by faith."

And now, my dear friends, if you would be saved, this is what you must do. I hope many of you have already performed the solemn act, you have said to Jesus in the privacy of your closet, "O Lord, I have tried to save myself, but I renounce all my endeavors. Once I said, 'I am no worse than my neighbors; my goodness shall preserve me.' Once I said, 'I have been baptized, I have taken the sacrament, in these things will I trust,' and now, Lord, I cast all this false confidence to the winds.

'No more, my God, I beset no more,
Of all the duties I have done;

44

> I quit the hopes I held before,
>> To trust the merits of thy Son.
>
> The best obedience of my hands,
>> Dares not appear before thy throne:
> But faith can answer thy demands,
>> By pleading what my Lord has done.'"

You cannot be saved if you have one hand on self and the other hand on Christ. Let go, cannier, renounce all dependence in anything thou canst do. Cease to be thine own keeper, give up the futile attempt to be thy own Saviour, and then thou wilt have taken the first step to heaven. There are but two, the first is—out of self, the next is—into Christ. When Christ is thy all, then art thou safe.

But again, when the apostle says he committed his soul to the keeping of Christ, he means that he had *implicit confidence that Christ would save him* now that he had relinquished all trust in self. Some men have gone far enough to feel that the best performance of their hands cannot be accepted before the bar of God. They have learned that their most holy acts are full of sin, that their most faithful service falls short of the demands of the law; they have relinquished self, but they are not able yet to see that Christ can and will save them. They are waiting for some great revelation; they think, perhaps, that by some marvellous electric shock, or some miraculous feeling within them, they will be led to place their confidence in Christ. They want to see an angel or a vision, or to hear a voice. Their cry is, "How could I think that Jesus would save such an one as I am. I am too vile, or else I am too hardened; I am the odd man; it is not likely that Christ would ever save me." Now, I doubt not that the apostle had felt all this, but he overcame all this attacking of sin, and he came to at last Christ and said,

> "Jesus, I feel that thou art worthy of my confidence. Behold, I the chief of sinners am, I have nothing in myself that can assist thee in taking me to heaven; I shall kick and struggle against thee rather than assist thee. But behold, I feel that such is thy power, and such thy love, that I

commit myself to thee. Take me as I am, and make me what thou wouldst have me be. I am vile, but thou art worthy; I am lost, but thou art the Saviour; I am dead, but thou art the quickener; take me; I beseech thee; I put my trust in thee, and though I perish, I will perish relying on thy blood. If I must die, I will die with my arms about thy cross, for thou art worthy of confidence, and on thee do I rely."

And now, my friends, if you will be safe, you must, in the strength of the Holy Ghost, do this also. You say you have given up all trust in self—well and good; now place your trust in Christ, repose your all on him; drop into his arms; cast yourself into his power; lay hold on him. You know how Joab, when he fled from the sword of Solomon, laid hold on the horns of the altar, thinking that surely when he had laid hold on the altar he was safe. His was vain confidence, for he was dragged from the horns of the altar and slain. But if thou canst lay hold on the horns of the altar of God, even Christ, thou art most surely safe, and no sword of vengeance can ever reach thee.

I saw the other day a remarkable picture, which I shall use as an illustration of the way of salvation by faith in Jesus. An offender had committed a crime for which he must die, but it was in the olden time when churches were considered to be sanctuaries in which criminals might hide themselves and so escape. See the transgressor—he rushes towards the church, the guards pursue him with their drawn swords, all athirst for his blood, they pursue him even to the church door. He rushes up the steps, and just as they are about to overtake him and hew him in pieces on the threshhold of the church, out comes the Bishop, and holding up the crucifix he cries, "Back, back! stain not the precincts of God's house with blood! stand back!" and the guards at once respect the emblem and stand back, while the poor fugitive hides himself behind the robes of the priest. It is even so with Christ. The guilty sinner flies to the cross—flies straight away to Jesus, and though Justice pursues him, Christ lifts up his wounded hands and cries to Justice, "Stand back! stand back! I shelter this sinner; in the secret place of my tabernacle do I hide him; I will not suffer him to perish, for he puts his trust in me." Sinner, fly to Christ! But thou sayest, "I am too vile." The viler thou art, the more wilt thou honor him by believing that he is able to make thee clean. "But I am too great a sinner." Then the more honor shall be given to him that thou art able to confide in him, great sinner though thou art. If you have a little sickness, and you tell your physician—"Sir! I am quite confident in your skill to heal," there is no great compliment, but if you are sore sick with a complication of diseases, and you say—"Sir! I seek no better skill, I will ask no more excellent advice, I trust alone in you," what an honor have you conferred on him, that you could trust your life in his hands when it was in extreme danger. Do the like with Christ; put your soul in his care, dare it, venture it; cast thyself simply on him; let nothing but faith be in thy soul; believe him, and thou shalt never be mistaken in thy trust.

But I think I have not completely stated all the apostle meant, when he said that he committed himself to Christ. He certainly meant those two things—self-renunciation, and implicit belief in Christ's power and willingness to save, but in the third place, the apostle meant that he did make *a full and free surrender of himself to Christ,* to be Christ's property, and Christ's servant for ever. If you would be saved you must not be your own. Salvation is through being bought with a price; and if you be bought with a price, and thus saved, remember, from that day forward you will not be your own. To-day, as an ungodly sinner, you are your own master, free to follow the lusts of the flesh; or, rather Satan is your great tyrant, and you are under bondage to him. If you would be saved you must by the aid of the Holy Spirit now renounce the bondage of Satan and come to Christ, saying,

> "Lord I am willing to give up all sin, it is not in my power to be perfect but I wish it were, make me perfect. There is not a sin I wish to keep; take all away; I present myself before thee. Wash me, make me clean. Do what thou wilt in me. I make no reserve, I make a full surrender of all to thee."

And then you must give up to Christ all you are, and all you have by solemn indenture, signed and sealed by your own heart. You must say in the words of the sweet Moravian hymn—

> "Take thou my soul and all my powers;
>   O take my memory, mind, and will,
> Take all my goods, and all my hours,
>   Take all I know and all I feel;
> Take all I think and speak, and do;
>   O take my heart, but make it new."

Accept the sacrifice,—I am worthless, but receive me through thy owe merits. Take and keep me, I am, I hope I ever shall be thine.

I have now explained that act which is after all the only one which marks the day of salvation to the soul. I will give one or two figures however to set it in a clearer light. When a man hath gold and silver in his house, he fears lest some thief may break through and steal, and therefore if he be a wise man he seeks out a bank in which to store his money. He makes a deposit of his gold and his silver; he says in effect, "Take that, sir, keep it for me. To-night I shall sleep securely; I shall have no thought of thieves; my treasure is in your hands. Take care of that for me, when I need it, at your hands shall I require it." Now in faith we do just the same with our blessed Redeemer. We bring our soul just as it is and give it up to him.

> "Lord, I cannot keep it; sin and Satan will be sure to ruin it—take it and keep it for me, and in that day when God shall require the treasure, stand my sponsor, and on my behalf return my soul to my Maker kept and preserved to the end."

Or take another figure. When your adventurous spirit hath sought to climb some lofty mountain, delighted with the prospect you scale many and many a steep; onward you climb up the rocky crags until at last you arrive at the verge of the snow and ice. There in the midst of precipices that scarcely know a bottom and of summits that seem inaccessible, you are suddenly surrounded with a fog. Perhaps it becomes worse and worse until a snow-storm completes your bewilderment. You cannot see a step before you: your track is lost. A guide appears: "I know this mountain," says he.

"In my early days have I climbed it with my father. O'er each of these crags have I leaped in pursuit of the chamois;[1] I know every chasm and cavern. If you will follow me even through the darkness I will find the path and bring you down; but mark, before I undertake to guide you in safety, I demand of you implicit trust. You must not plant your feet where *you* think it safest, but where I shall bid you. Wherever I bid you climb or descend you must implicitly obey, and I undertake on my part to bring you safely down to your house again."

You do so—you have many temptations to prefer your own judgment to his but you resist them—and you are safe. Even so must you do with Christ. Lost to-day and utterly bewildered Christ appears. "Let me guide you, let me be an eye to thee through the thick darkness; let me be thy foot, lean on me in the slippery place, let me be thy very life; let me wrap thee in my crimson vest to keep thee from the tempest and the storm." Will you now trust him; rely entirely, simply, and implicitly upon him? If so, the grand act of your life is done and you are a saved man, and on the *terra firma* of heaven you shall one day plant your delighted feet and praise the name of him who saved you from your sins.

I must add, however, that this act of faith must not be performed once only, but it must be continued as long as you live. As long as you you must have no other confidence but "Jesus only." You must take him now to-day, to have and to hold through life and in death, in tempest and in sunshine, in poverty and in wealth, never to part or sunder from him. You must take him to be your only prop, your only pillar from this day forth and for ever. What sayest thou sinner? Does God the Holy Ghost lead thee to say "Ay?" Does thy heart now confide in Jesus? If so, let the angels sing, for a soul is born to God, and a brand is plucked from the eternal fire. I have thus described faith in Christ—the committing of the soul to him.

II. This brings us to our second point—THE JUSTIFICATION OF THIS GRAND ACT OF TRUST.

---

[1] The chamois is a goat-antelope species found in the mountainous regions of Europe and Western Asia.

Confidence is sometimes folly; trusting in man is always so. When I exhort you, then, to put your entire confidence in Christ, am I justified in so doing? and when the apostle could say that he trusted alone in Jesus, and had committed himself to him, was he a wise man or a fool? What saith the apostle? "I am no fool," said he,

"for I *know* whom I have believed. I have not trusted to an unknown and untried pretender. I have not relied upon one whose character I could suspect. I have confidence in one whose power, whose willingness, whose love, whose truthfulness I know. I know whom I have believed."

When silly women put their trust in yet more silly and wicked priests, they may say possibly that they know whom they have believed. But we may tell them that their knowledge must be ignorance indeed—that they are greatly deluded in imagining that any man, be he who he may, or what he may, can have any power in the salvation of his fellow's soul. You come sneaking up to me and ask me to repose my soul in you; and who are you? "I am an ordained priest of the Church of Rome." And who ordained you? "I was ordained by such a one." And who ordained him? "It cometh after all," saith he, "from the Pope." And who is he, and what is he more than any other man, or any other imposter? What ordination can he confer? "He obtained it directly from Peter." Did he? Let the link be proved; and if he did, what was Peter, and where has God given Peter power to forgive sin—a power which he should transmit to all generations? Be gone! The thick pollutions of thine abominable church forbid the idea of descent from any apostle but the traitor Judas. Upon the Papal throne men worse than devils have had their seat, and even a woman big with her adulteries once reigned as head of thine accursed church. Go purge the filthiness of thy priesthood, the debauchery of thy nunneries and the stygian filth of thy mother city, the old harlot Rome. Talk not of pardoning others, while fornication is licensed in Rome itself, and her ministers are steeped to the throat in iniquity. But to return. I rest no more on Peter than Peter could rest in himself, Peter must rest on Christ as a poor guilty sinner himself, an imperfect man who denied his

Master with oaths and curses. He must rest where I must rest, and we must stand together on the same great rock on which Christ doth build his church, even his blood and his ever-lasting merits. I marvel that any should be found to have such confidence in men, that they should put their souls in their hands. If however any of you wish to trust in a priest, let me advise you if you do trust him, to do it wholly and fully. Trust him with your cash-box, trust him with your gold and silver. Perhaps you object to that. You don't feel at all inclined to go that length. But, my friend, if you cannot trust the man with your gold and silver, pray don't trust him with your soul. I only suggested this because I thought you might smile and at once detect your error. If you could not trust such a fox with your business; if you would as soon commit your flocks to the custody of a wolf, why will you be fool enough to lay your soul at the feet of some base priest who, likely enough, is ten thousand times more wicked than your self.

Was Paul then justified in his confidence in Christ? He says he was because he *knew* Christ. And what did he know? Paul knew, first of all, Christ's Godhead. Jesus Christ is the Son of God, co-equal and co-eternal with the Father. If my soul be in his hand,

**"Where is the power can reach it there,
Or what can pluck it thence?"**

If the wings of Omnipotence do cover it, if the eye of Omnipotence is fixed upon it, and if the heart of eternal love doth cherish it, how can it be destroyed? Trust not thy soul my fellow-man anywhere but with thy God. But Jesus is thy God rely thou fully in him, and think not that thou canst place a confidence too great in him who made the heavens, and bears the world upon his shoulders. Paul knew too that Christ was the Redeemer. Paul had seen in vision Christ in the garden. He had beheld him sweat as it were great drops of blood. By faith Paul had seen Jesus hanging on the cross. He had marked his agonies on the tree of doom. He had listened to his death shriek, of "It is finished," and he felt that the atonement which Jesus offered, was more than enough to recompense for

51

the sin of man. Paul might have said, "I am not foolish in confiding my soul in the pierced and blood-stained hand of him whose sacrifice hath satisfied the Father and opened the gates of heaven to all believers." Further, Paul knew that Christ was risen from the dead. By faith he saw Christ at the right hand of God, pleading with his Father for all those who commit themselves to his hand. Paul knew Christ to be the all-prevailing intercessor. He said to himself "I am not wrong in believing him, for I know whom I have trusted, that when he pleads, the Father will not deny him, and when he asks, sooner might he even die than he become deaf to Jesus' prayer." This was again, another reason why Paul dared to trust in Christ. He knew his Godhead, he knew his redemption, he knew his resurrection, he knew his ascension, and intercession, and I may add, Paul knew the love of Christ, that love which passeth kindness; higher than thought, and deeper than conception. He knew Christ's power, that he was Omnipotent, the lying of kings. He knew Christ's faithfulness; that he was the God, and could not lie. He knew his immutability, that he was "Jesus Christ, the same yesterday today and for ever," and having known Christ in every glorious office, in every divine attribute, and in all the beauty of his complex character, Paul said, "I can with confidence repose in him, for I know him, I have trusted, and am persuaded that he is able to keep that which I have committed to him."

But Paul not only knew these things by faith, but he knew much of them by experience. Our knowledge of Christ is somewhat like climbing one of our Welsh mountains. When you are at the base you see but little, the mountain itself appears to be but one half as high as it really is. Confined in a little valley you discover scarcely anything but the rippling brooks as they descend into the stream at the base of the mountain. Climb the first rising knoll, and the valley lengthens and widens beneath your feet. Go up higher, and higher still, till you stand upon the summit of one of the great roots that start out as spurs from the sides of the mountain you see the country for some four or five miles round, and you are delighted with the widening prospect. But go onward, and onward, and onward, and how the scene enlarges, till at last, when you are on the summit, and look east, west, north, and south, you see almost all England lying before you. Yonder is a forest in some distant country, perhaps two hundred miles away, and yonder the sea, and there a shining river and the smoking chimneys of a manufacturing town, or there the masts of the ships in some well known port. All these things please and delight you, and you say, "I could not have imagined that so much could be seen at this elevation." Now, the Christian life is of the same order. When we first believe in Christ we see but little of him. The higher we climb the more we discover of his excellencies and his beauties. But who has ever gained the summit? Who has ever known all the fullness of the heights, and depths, and lengths, and breadths of the love of Christ which passeth knowledge. Paul now grown old, sitting, grey hair'd, shivering in a dungeon in Rome—he could say, with greater power than we can, "I *know* whom I have believed?"—for each experience had been like the climbing of a hill, each trial had been like the ascending to another summit, and his death seemed like the gaining of the very top of the mountain from which he could see the whole of the faithfulness and the love of him to whom he had committed his soul.

III. And now, I close by noticing THE APOSTLE'S CONFIDENCE. The apostle said, "I am persuaded that *he* is able to keep that which I have committed to him." See this man. He is sure he shall be saved. But why? Paul! art thou sure that thou canst keep thyself? "No," says he, "I have nothing to do with that:" and yet thou art sure of thy salvation! "Yes," saith he, "I am!" How is it, then? "Why, I am persuaded that he is able to keep me. Christ, to whom I commit myself, I know hath power enough to hold me to the end." Martin Luther was bold enough to exclaim "Let him that died for my soul, see to the salvation of it." Let us catechise the apostle for a few minutes, and see if we cannot shake his confidence. Paul! Thou hast had many trials, and thou wilt have many more. What if thou shouldst be subject to the pangs of hunger, combined with those of thirst. If not a mouthful of bread should pass thy mouth to nourish thy body, or a drop of water should comfort thee, will not thy faith fail thee then? If provisions be offered thee, on condition of the denial of thy faith, dost thou not imagine that thou wilt be vane, quashed, and that the pangs of nature will overpower thee? "No," says Paul, "famine shall not quench my faith; for the keeping of my faith is in the hands of Christ." But what if, combined with this, the whole world should rise against thee, and scoff thee? What if hunger within should echo to the shout of scorn without? wouldst thou not then deny thy faith? If, like Demas, every other Christian should turn to the silver of this world, and deny the Master, wouldst not thou go with them? "No," saith the apostle, "my soul is not in my keeping, else might it soon apostatize; it is in the hand of Christ. though all men should leave me, yet will he keep me." But what, O apostle, if thou shouldst be chained to the stake, and the flames should kindle, and thy flesh should begin to burn; when thy beard is singed, and thy cheeks are black, wilt thou then hold him fast! "Yea," saith the apostle, "he will then hold me fast;" and I think I hear him, as he stops us in the midst of our catechising, and replies,

> "Nay, in all these things we are more than conquerors, through him that loved us. For I am persuaded that neither death, nor life, nor angels, nor principalities, nor powers, nor things present, nor things to come, nor height, nor depth, nor any other creature shall be able to separate us from the love of God, which is in Christ Jesus our Lord."

Paul, Paul, suppose the world should tempt you in another way. If a kingdom were offered you—if the pomps and pleasures of this world should be laid at your feet, provided you would deny your Master, would your faith maintain its hold then? "Yea," saith the apostle,

> "Jesus would even then uphold my faith for my soul is not in my keeping, but in his, and empires upon empires could not tempt him to renounce that soul of which he has become the guardian and the keeper. Temptation might soon overcome me, but it could not overcome him. The world's blandishments might soon move *me* to renounce my own soul; but they could not for one moment move *Jesus* to give me up."

And so the apostle continues his confidence. But Paul, when thou shalt come to die, will thou not then fear and tremble? "Nay," saith he, "he will be with me there, for my soul shall not die, that will be still in the hand of him who is immortality and life." But what will become of thee when thy soul is separated from thy body? Canst thou trust him in a separate state, in the unknown world which visions cannot paint? In the time of God's mighty thunder, when earth shall shake and heaven shall reel. Canst thou trust him then? "Yea," saith the apostle, "until *that day* when all these tempests shall die away into eternal calm, and when the moving earth shall settle into a stable land in which there shall be no more sea, even then can I trust him."

"I know that safe with him remains,
Protected by his power,
What I've committed to his hands
Till the decisive hour."

O poor sinner! come and put thy soul into the hands of Jesus. Attempt not to take care of it thyself; and then thy life shall be hidden in heaven, and kept there by the Almighty power of God, where none can destroy it and none can rob thee of it. "Whosoever believeth on the Lord Jesus Christ shall be saved."

4

Assured Security In Christ

(Sermon No. 908)

"I know whom I have believed, and am persuaded that He is able to keep that which I have committed unto Him against that day" (2 Timothy 1:12).

IN THE STYLE OF THESE APOSTOLIC words there is a positiveness most refreshing in this age of doubt. In certain circles of society it is rare nowadays to meet with anybody who believes anything. It is the philosophical, the right, the fashionable thing, nowadays, to doubt everything which is generally received. Indeed, those who have any creed whatever are by the liberal school set down as old-fashioned dogmatists, persons of shallow minds, deficient in intellect, and far behind their age. The great men, the men of thought, the men of high culture and refined taste consider it wisdom to cast suspicion upon Revelation, and sneer at all definiteness of belief.

"Ifs" and "buts," and "perhaps" are the supreme delight of this period. What wonder if men find everything uncertain—when they refuse to bow their intellects to the declarations of the God of Truth? Note then, with admiration, the refreshing and even startling positiveness of the Apostle—"I know," says he. And that is not enough—"I am persuaded." He speaks like one who cannot tolerate a doubt. There is no question about whether he has believed or not. "I know Whom I have believed." There is no question as to whether he was right in so believing. "I am persuaded that He is able to keep that which I have committed to Him." There is no suspicion as to the future. He is as positive for years to come as he is for this present moment. "He is able to keep that which I have committed to Him against that day."

Now there is a positiveness which is very disgusting—when it is nothing but the fruit of ignorance and is unattended with anything like thoughtfulness. But in the Apostle's case, his confidence is founded not on ignorance, but on knowledge. "I know," says he. There are certain things which he has clearly ascertained, which he knows to be fact. And his confidence is grounded on these ascertained Truths of God. His confidence, moreover, was not the fruit of thoughtlessness, for he adds, "I am persuaded." As though he had reasoned the matter out and had been persuaded into it—had meditated long upon it, and turned it over—and the force of Truth had quite convinced him, so that he stood persuaded.

Where positiveness is the result of knowledge and of meditation, it becomes sublime, as it was in the Apostle's case. And being sublime it becomes influential. In this case it certainly must have been influential over the heart of Timothy, and over the minds of the tens of thousands who have, during these nineteen centuries, perused this Epistle. It encourages the timid when they see others preserved. It confirms the wavering when they see others steadfast. The great Apostle's words, ringing out with trumpet tone this morning, "I know, and I am persuaded," cannot but help to cheer many of us in our difficulties and anxieties. May the Holy Spirit cause us not only to admire the faith of Paul, but to imitate it, and to attain to the same confidence!

Some speak confidently because they are not confident. How often have we observed that brag and bluster are only the outward manifestations of inward trembling? They are but concealments adopted to cover cowardice! As the schoolboy, passing through the Churchyard, whistles to keep his courage up, so some people talk very positively because they are not positive. They make a pompous parade of faith because they desire to sustain the presumption which, as being their only comfort, is exceedingly dear to them.

Now in the Apostle's case, every syllable he speaks has beneath it a most real weight of confidence which the strongest expressions could not exaggerate. Sitting there in the dungeon, a prisoner for Christ, abhorred by his countrymen, despised by the learned, and ridiculed by the rude, Paul confronted the whole world with a holy boldness which knew no quailing. A boldness resulting from the deep conviction of his spirit. You may take these words and put what emphasis you can upon each one of them, for they are the truthful utterance of a thoroughly earnest and brave spirit. May we enjoy such a confidence ourselves, and then we need not hesitate to declare it—for our testimony will glorify God and bring consolation to others.

This morning for our instruction, as the Holy Spirit may help us, we shall first consider the matter in question, that which Paul had committed to Christ. Secondly, the fact beyond all question, namely, that Christ was able to keep him. Thirdly, the assurance of that fact, or how the Apostle was able to say, "I know and am persuaded." And fourthly, the influence of that assurance when it rules in the heart.

I. First, then, dear Friends, let us speak for a few minutes upon THE MATTER IN QUESTION.

1. That matter was, first of all, the Apostle's deposit of all his interests and concerns into the hands of God in Christ. Some have said that what Paul here speaks of was his ministry. But there are many reasons for concluding that this is a mistake. A great array of expositors, at the head of whom we would mention Calvin, think that the sole treasure which Paul deposited in the hands of God was his eternal salvation. We do not doubt that this was the grandest portion of the priceless deposit— but we also think that as the connection does not limit the sense, it cannot be restricted or confined to any one thing. It seems to us that all the Apostle's temporal and eternal interests were, by an act of faith, committed into the hands of God in Christ Jesus.

To the Lord's gracious keeping the Apostle committed his body. He had suffered much in that frail tabernacle—shipwrecks, perils, hunger, cold, nakedness, imprisonments, beatings with rods and stoning had all spent their fury upon him. He expected before long that his mortal frame would become the prey of Nero's cruelty. None could tell what would then happen to him—whether he should be burned alive to light up Nero's gardens, be torn to pieces by wild beasts to make a Roman holiday—or become the victim of the headsman's sword. But in whatever way he might be called to offer up himself a sacrifice to God, he committed his body to the keeping of Him who is the Resurrection and the Life.

He was persuaded that in the day of the Lord's appearing he would rise again, his body having suffered no loss through torture or dismemberment. He looked for a joyful resurrection and asked no better embalming for his corpse than the power of Christ would ensure it.

He gave over to Christ at that hour his character and reputation. A Christian minister must expect to lose his reputation among men. He must be willing to suffer every reproach for Christ's sake. But he may rest assured that he will never lose his real honor if it is risked for the Truth's sake and placed in the Redeemer's hands. The day shall declare the excellence of the upright, for it will reveal all that was hidden and bring to light that which was concealed. There will be a resurrection of characters as well as persons. Every reputation that has been obscured by clouds of reproach for Christ's sake shall be rendered glorious when the righteous shall shine forth as the sun in the kingdom of their Father. Let the wicked say what they will of me, said the Apostle, I commit my character to the Judge of the quick and the dead.

So also his whole lifework he delivered into the hands of God. Men said, no doubt, that Paul had made a great mistake. In the eyes of the worldly wise he must have seemed altogether mad. What eminence awaited him had he become a rabbi! He might have lived respected and honored among his countrymen as a Pharisee. Or if he had preferred to follow the Grecian philosophies, a man with such strength of mind might have rivaled Socrates or Plato! But instead, he chose to unite himself with a band of men commonly reputed to be ignorant fanatics who turned the world upside down. Ah, well, says Paul, I leave the reward and fruit of my life entirely with my Lord, for He will at last justify my choice of service beneath the banner of His Son. And then the assembled universe shall know that I was no mistaken zealot for a senseless cause.

So did the Apostle resign to the hands of God in Christ his soul, whatever its jeopardy from surrounding temptations. However great the corruptions that were within it, and the dangers that were without, he felt safe in the great Surety's hands. He made over to the Divine Trustee all his mental powers, faculties, passions, instincts, desires and ambitions. He gave his whole nature up to the Christ of God to preserve it in holiness through the whole of life. And right well did his life-course justify his faith.

He gave that soul up to be kept in the hour of death, then to be strengthened, sustained, consoled, upheld, and guided through the tracks unknown—up through the mysterious and unseen—to the Throne of God, even the Father. He resigned his spirit to Christ, that it might be presented without spot or wrinkle or any such thing in the Last Great Day. He did, in fact, make a full deposit of all that he was, and all that he had, and all that concerned him, into the keeping of God in Christ, to find in his God a faithful Guardian, a sure Defender and a safe Keeper. This was the matter, then, about which the Apostle was concerned.

2. But next to this, the matter in question concerned the Lord's ability to make good this guardianship. The Apostle did not doubt that Christ had accepted the office of Keeper of that which he had committed to Him. The question was never about Christ's faithfulness to that trust. The Apostle does not even say that he was confident that Jesus would be faithful. He felt that assertion to be superfluous. There was no question about Christ's willingness to keep the soul committed to Him—such a statement Paul felt it unnecessary to make. But the question with many was concerning the power of the once crucified Redeemer to keep that which was committed to Him.

Oh, said the Apostle, I know and am persuaded that He is able to do that. Mark, my dear Friends, that the question is not about the Apostle's power to keep himself. That question he does not raise. Many of you have been troubled as to whether you are able to endure temptation. You need not debate the subject. It is clear that apart from Christ you are quite unable to persevere to the end. Answer that question with a decided negative at once, and never raise it again. The enquiry was not whether the Apostle would be found meritorious in his own righteousness in the Day of Judgment, for he had long ago cast that righteousness aside.

He does not raise that point. The grand question is this, "Is Jesus able to keep me?" Stand to that, my Brethren, and your doubts and fears will soon come to an end. Concerning your own power or merit, write, "despair," straightway upon its forehead. Let the creature be regarded as utterly dead and corrupt, and then lean on that arm, the sinews of which shall never shrink. And cast your full weight upon that Omnipotence which bears up the pillars of the universe. There is the point—keep to it, and you will not lose your joy. You have committed yourself to Christ. The great question now is not about what you can do, but about what Jesus is able to do. And rest assured that He is able to keep that which you have committed to Him.

3. The Apostle further carries our thoughts on to a certain set period—the keeping of the soul unto what he calls "that day." I suppose he calls it, "that day," because it was the day most ardently expected and commonly spoken of by Christians. It was so usual a topic of conversation to speak of Christ's coming and of the results of it, that the Apostle does not say, "the advent," he simply says, "that day." That day with which Believers are more familiar than with any other day beside. That day, the day of death if you will, when the soul appears before its God. The Day of Judgment, if you please—that day when the books shall be opened and the record shall be read.

That day, the winding up of all, the sealing of destiny, the manifestation of the eternal fate of each one of us. That day for which all other days were made. Christ Jesus is able to keep us against that day. That is to say, He is able to place us, then, at the right hand of God, to set our feet upon the Rock when others sink into the pit that is bottomless. To crown us when others shall be accursed. To bring us to eternal joy when sinners shall be cast into Hell.

Here was the matter of consideration—can the Great Shepherd of souls preserve His flock? Ah, Brethren, if you have never searched into that question, I should not wonder but what you will! When you are very low and weak, and heart and flesh are failing. When sickness brings you to the borders of the grave and you gaze into eternity, the enquiry will come to any thoughtful man—Is this confidence of mine in the Christ of God warranted? Will He be able in this last article, when my spirit shivers in its unclothing, will He be able to help me now?

And in the more dreadful hour, when the trumpet peal shall awake the dead, shall I, indeed, find the Great Sin Bearer able to stand for me? Having no merit of my own, will His merit suffice? From ten thousand sins will His blood, alone, cleanse me? Nothing can ever equal this matter in importance. It is one of most pressing urgency of consideration.

II. It is a happy circumstance that we can turn from it to our second point, to dwell for a while upon THE FACT BEYOND ALL QUESTION, namely, that God in Christ is able to keep that which we have committed to Him.

The Apostle's confidence was that Christ was an able Guardian. So he meant, first, that Jesus is able to keep the soul from falling into damning sin. I suppose this is one of the greatest fears that has ever troubled the true Believer. Have you ever prayed that you might rather die than turn aside from Christ? I know I have, and I have sung bitterly in my soul that verse—

> **"Ah, Lord! With such a heart as mine,**
> **Unless You hold me fast,**
> **I feel I must, I shall decline,**
> **And turn from You at last."**

Now, troubled Christian, remember that your Lord is able to keep you under every possible form of temptation. "Ah," you say, "the Apostle Paul had not the trials I have." I think he had. But if he had not, Jesus had. And Christ has ability to keep you under them. Do I hear one say, "I am the only one of my household that has been called by Grace, and they all oppose me. I am a lonely one in my father's house"? Now, Paul was precisely in your condition. He was a Hebrew of the Hebrews, and he was regarded by his people with the most extreme hate because he had come out from among them to follow the Crucified One.

Yet Paul felt that God was able to keep him, and you may depend upon it—though father and mother forsake, and brothers and sisters scoff—He whom you trust will keep you also firm in the faith. "Ah," says another, "but you do not know what it is to strive with the prejudices of

62

an education hostile to the faith of Jesus. When I seek to grow in Grace, the things I learned in my childhood force themselves upon me and hinder me." And was not the Apostle in this case? As touching the Law he had been a Pharisee, educated in the strictest sect, brought up in traditions that were opposed to the faith of Christ. And yet the Lord kept him faithful even to the end.

None of his old prejudices were able so much as to make him obscure the simplicity of the Gospel of Christ. God is able to keep you, also, despite your previous prejudices. "Ah," says one, "but I am the subject of many skeptical thoughts. I often suffer from doubts of the most subtle order." Do you think that the Apostle never knew this trial? He was no stranger to the Greek philosophy, which consisted of a bundle of questions and skepticisms. He must have experienced those temptations which are common to thoughtful minds. And yet he said, "I know that He is able to keep me." Believe me, then, the Lord Jesus is equally able to keep you.

"Yes," says another,

"but I have so many temptations in the world. If I were not a Christian, I should prosper much better. I have openings now before me by which I might soon obtain a competence, and perhaps wealth, if I were not checked by conscience."

Do you forget that the Apostle was in like case? What might he not have had? A man of his condition in life—his birth and parentage being altogether advantageous—a man of his powers of mind and of his great energy! He might have seized upon any attractive position. But those things which were gain for him, he counted loss for Christ's sake. And he was willing to be less than nothing, because the power of Divine Grace kept him true to his profession.

But you tell me you are very poor, and that poverty is a severe trial. Brothers and Sisters, you are not so poor as Paul. I suppose a few needles for his tent-making, an old cloak, and a few parchments made up all his wealth. A man without a home, a man without a single foot of land to call his own, was this Apostle. But poverty and want could not subdue him—

Christ was able to keep him even then. "Ah," you say, "but he had not my strong passions and corruptions." Most surely he had them all, for we hear him cry,

"I find, then, a Law, that when I would do good, evil is present with me. For I delight in the Law of God after the inward man: but I see another Law in my members, warring against the Law of my mind, and bringing me into captivity to the Law of sin which is in my members. O wretched man that I am! Who shall deliver me from the body of this death?"

He was tempted as you are, yet he knew that Christ was able to keep him. O trembling Christian, never doubt this soul-cheering fact—that your loving Savior is able to keep you. But the Apostle did not merely trust Christ thus to keep him from sin—he relied upon the same arm to preserve him from despair. He was always battling with the world. There were times when he had no helper. The Brethren often proved false, and those that were true were frequently timid. He was left in the world like a solitary sheep surrounded with wolves. But Paul was not faint-hearted. He had his fears, for he was mortal—he rose superior to them, for he was Divinely sustained. What a front he always maintains! Nero may rise before him—a horrible monster for a man even to dream of—but Paul's courage does not give way.

A Jewish mob may surround him, they may drag him out of the city—but Paul's mind is calm and composed. He may be laid in the stocks after having been scourged, but his heart finds congenial utterance in a song rather than a groan. He is always brave, always unconquerable, confident of victory. He believed that God would keep him, and he was kept. And you, my Brothers and Sisters, though your life may be a very severe conflict and you sometimes think you will give it up in despair—you never shall relinquish the sacred conflict. He that has borne you onward to this day will bear you through, and will make you more than conqueror, for He is able to keep you from fainting and despair.

Doubtless, the Apostle meant, too, that Christ was able to keep him from the power of death. Beloved, this is great comfort to us who so soon shall die. To the Apostle, death was a very present thing. "I die daily," said he. Yet was he well assured that death would be gain rather than loss to him, for he was certain that Christ would so order all things that death should be but like an angel to admit him into everlasting life. Be certain of this, too, for He who is the Resurrection and the Life will not desert you. Do not, my Brothers and Sisters, fall under bondage through fear of death, for the living Savior is able to keep you, and He will.

Do not, I pray, look too much at the pains, groans, and dying strife. Look rather to that kind Friend, who, having endured the agonies of death before you, can sympathize with your sufferings, and who, as He ever lives, can render you available assistance. Cast this care on Him, and fear no more to die than you fear to go to your bed when night comes.

The Apostle is also certain that Christ is able to preserve his soul in another world. Little is revealed in Scripture by way of detailed description of that other world. Imagination may be indulged, but little can be proved. The spirit returns to God who gave it, this we know. And in the instant after death the righteous soul is in Paradise with Christ. This, too, is clear. Yet whether we know the details or not, we are assured that the soul is safe with Christ. Whatever danger from evil spirits may await us on our journey from this planet up to the dwelling place of God. Whatever there may be of conflict in the last moment, Jesus is able to keep that which we have committed to Him.

If I had to keep myself, I might, indeed, tremble with alarm at the prospect of the unknown region. But He that is the Lord of death and of Hell, and has the keys of Heaven, can surely keep my soul on that dread voyage across a trackless sea. It is all well. It must be well with the righteous—even in the land of death—for our Lord's dominion reaches even there—and being in His dominions we are safe. Paul believed, lastly, that Christ was able to preserve his body. Remember my statement that Paul committed all that he had, and was, to God in Christ?

We must not despise this body. It is the germ of the body in which we are to dwell forever. It shall be raised from corruption into incorruption, but it is the same body. Developed from weakness into power, from dishonor into glory, it never loses its identity. The marvel of the resurrection will not fail of accomplishment. It may seem an impossibility that the body which has rotted in the tomb, and, perhaps been scattered in dust over the face of the soil—which has been absorbed by vegetables, which has been digested by animals, which has passed through countless circles of change—should be raised again. Yet impossible as it seems, the Lord Jesus Christ will perform it.

It must be as easy to construct a second time as to create out of nothing at the first. Look at creation and see that nothing is impossible with God. Think of the Word, without whom was not anything made that was made, and straightway you will talk no longer of difficulties. With man it may be impossible, but with God all things are possible. In your entirety, my Brethren, in the integrity of your manhood, spirit, soul, and body—all that is essential to your nature, to its happiness, to its perfection. Every part of you and every power of you—you having placed all in the hands of Christ—shall be kept until that day, when in His image you shall stand, and prove in your own persons the power which in your faith you do, this day, devoutly trust.

III. We shall, in the third place, pass on to notice THE ASSURANCE OF THAT FACT, or how the Apostle Paul attained to it.

"I cannot talk like that," says one. "I cannot say, 'I know, and I am persuaded,' I am very thankful that I can say, I hope, I trust, I think." Dear Friends, in order to help you to advance, we will notice how the Apostle Paul attained to such assurance. One main help to him was the habit, as seen in this text, of always making faith the most prominent point of consideration. Faith is twice mentioned in the few lines before us. "I know whom I have believed, and am persuaded that He is able to keep that which I have committed to Him." Paul knew what faith was, namely, a committal of his precious things into the custody of Christ.

He does not say, "I have served Christ." No. He does not say, "I am growing like Christ, therefore I am persuaded I shall be kept." No. He makes most prominent in his thought the fact that he believed, and so had committed himself to Christ. I would to God, dear Friends, that you who are subject to doubts and fears, instead of raking about in your hearts to find evidences and marks of growth in Grace and likeness to Christ, and so on, would first make an investigation concerning a point which is far more vital—namely this—have you believed?

Dear anxious Heart, begin your search on this point. Do you commit yourself to Christ? If you do, what though marks should be few and evidences for awhile should be obscure, he that believes on Him has everlasting life. He that believes and is baptized shall be saved. The evidences will come, the marks will be cleared in due time. But all the marks and evidences between here and Heaven are not worth a single farthing to a soul when it comes to actual conflict with death and Hell.

Then it must be simple faith that wins the day. Those other things are good enough in brighter times. But if it is a question whether you are safe or not, you must come to this, "I have rested with all my heart on Him that came into the world to save sinners, and though I am the very chief of sinners, I believe He is able to save me." You will get to assurance if you keep clear about your faith.

The next help to assurance, as I gather from the text, is this. The Apostle maintained most clearly his view of a personal Christ. Observe how three times he mentioned his Lord. "I know whom I have believed, and am persuaded that He is able to keep that which I have committed to Him." He does not say, "I know the doctrines I believe." Surely he did, but this was not the main point. He does not say, "I am certain about the form of sound Words which I hold." He was certain enough about that, but it was not his foundation. No mere doctrines can ever be the stay of the soul. What can a dogma do? What can a creed do?

Brethren, these are like medicines—you need a hand to give them to you. You want the physician to administer them to you—otherwise you may die with all these precious medicines close at hand. We want a person to trust. There is no Christianity to my mind so vital, so influential, so true, so real, as the Christianity which deals with the Person of the living Redeemer. I know Him, I know He is God, I know that He is mine. I trust not merely in His teaching, but in Him. Not on His laws, rules, or teachings am I depending so much as on Himself, as a Person. Dear Brothers and Sisters, is that what you are doing now?

Have you put your soul into the keeping of that blessed Man who is also God? He who sits at the right hand of the Father? Can you come in faith to His feet and kiss the prints of the nails? Can you look up into His dear face and say,

> **"Ah, Son of God, I rely upon the power of Your arms, on the preciousness of Your blood, on the love of Your heart, on the prevalence of Your plea, on the certainty of Your promises, on the immutability of Your Character. I rest on You, and on You alone"?**

You will get assurance readily enough, now. But if you begin to fritter away your realization of the Person of Christ and live merely on dogmas and doctrines, you will be far removed from real assurance.

Brothers and Sisters, the Apostle attained this full assurance through growing knowledge. He did not say, "I am persuaded that Christ will save me, apart from anything I know about Him." But he begins by saying, "I know." Let no Christian among us neglect the means provided for obtaining a fuller knowledge of the Gospel of Christ. I would that this age produced more thoughtful and studious Christians. I am afraid that apart from what many of you gather from the sermon, or from the reading of the Scriptures in public, you do not learn much from the Word of God, or from those innumerable instructive books which godly men have bequeathed to us.

Men are studious in various schools and colleges in order to obtain knowledge of the classics and mathematics. But should we not be even more diligent that we may know Christ? That we may study Him, and all about Him—and no longer be children, but in knowledge may be men? Many of the fears of Christians would be driven away if they knew more. Ignorance is not bliss in Christianity, but misery. Knowledge sanctified and attended by the Presence of the Holy Spirit is as wings by which we may rise out of the mists and darkness into the light of fall assurance. The knowledge of Christ is the most excellent of sciences. Seek to be masters of it, and you are on the road to full assurance.

Once, again, the Apostle, it appears from the text, gained his assurance from close consideration as well as from knowledge. "I know and am persuaded." As I have already said, persuasion is the result of argument. The Apostle had turned this matter over in his mind. He had meditated on the pros and cons. He had carefully weighed each difficulty, and he felt the preponderating force of Truth swept every difficulty out of the way. O Christian, if you made your mind more familiar with Divine Truth, you would, under the guidance of the Holy Spirit, have much more assurance! I believe it is the doctrine which we have least studied in the Word which gives us the most trouble in our minds. Search it out and look.

The divisions among Christians, nowadays, are not so much the result of real differences of opinion as of want of accurate thought. I believe we are getting closer and closer in our theology, and that on the whole, at least among the Nonconforming Churches of England, very much the same theology is preached by all evangelical ministers. But some are not careful of their terms and words, and use them incorrectly. And so they seem to preach wrong doctrines when in their hearts they mean rightly enough. May we come to be more thoughtful, each of us, for a thousand benefits would flow from there.

Thinking of the Deity of Christ, considering of the veracity of the Divine promises, meditating upon the foundations of the Everlasting Covenant, revolving in our minds what Christ has done for us—we should come at last, by the Spirit's teaching—to be fully persuaded of the power of Christ to keep the sacred charge which we have given to Him. Doubts and fears would vanish like clouds before the wind. How many Christians are like the miser who never feels sure about the safety of his money, even though he has locked up the iron safe and secured the room in which he keeps it—and locked up the house—and bolted and barred every door?

In the dead of night he thinks he hears a footstep, and tremblingly he goes down to inspect his strong-room. Having searched the room and tested all the iron bars in the windows, and discovered no thief, he fears that the robber may have come and gone, and stolen his precious charge. So he opens the door of his iron safe. He looks and pries, he finds his bag of gold all safe, and those deeds, those bonds—they are safe, too. He puts them away, shuts the door, locks it, bolts and bars the room in which is the safe and all its contents. But even as he goes to bed he fancies that a thief has just now broken in! So he scarcely ever enjoys sound, refreshing sleep.

The safety of the Christian's treasure is of quite another sort. His soul is not under bolt and bar, or under lock and key of his own securing. He has transferred his all to the King eternal, immortal, invisible—the only wise God, our Savior—and such is his security that he enjoys the sleep of the Beloved, calmly resting, for all is well. If Jesus could fail us, we might wear sackcloth forever! But while He is Immutable in His love and Omnipotent in his power, we may put on the garments of praise. Believing as we do that eternal love neither can, nor will desert a soul that reposes in its might, we triumph in heart and find glory begun below.

IV. Now to close. What is THE INFLUENCE OF THIS ASSURANCE when it penetrates the mind? As time fails me, I shall but say that, as in the Apostle's case, it enables us to bear all the disgrace which we may incur in serving the Lord. They said Paul was a fool. "Well," replied the Apostle, "I am not ashamed, for I know whom I have believed. I am willing to be thought a fool." The ungodly may laugh at us now, but their laughs will soon be over, and he will laugh that wins forever.

Feel perfectly confident that all is safe and you can let the world grin at you till its face aches. What does it matter what mortals think? What difference does it make what the whole universe thinks if our souls are beloved of God? You will, my dear Friends, as you live in full assurance of God's love, grow quite indifferent to the opinions of the carnal. You will go about your heavenly service with an eye only to your Master's will—and the judgment of such as cavil and carp will seem to you to be too inconsiderable to be worth a thought.

If you doubt and fear, you will be hard put to it. But if you are serenely confident that He is able to keep you, you will dare the thickest of the fray—fearless because your armor is of God. Assurance will give you a serenity within which will qualify you for doing much service. A man who is always worrying about his own soul's salvation can have little energy with which to serve his Lord. But when the soul knows the meaning of Christ's words, "It is finished," it turns all its strength into the channels of service out of love to such a blessed Savior.

O you that doubt, and therefore fret and care, and ask the question, "Do I love the Lord or not? Am I His or am I not?"—how I wish this suspense were over with you! O you who fear daily, lest, after all, you will be castaways—you lose your strength for serving your God! When you are sure that He is able to keep what you have committed to Him, then your whole manhood, excited by gratitude, spends itself and is spent in your Master's cause. God make you men to the fullness of vigor by giving you a fullness of assurance.

Those who are unsaved in this place may well envy those who are. That which attracted me to Christ—I have not heard of others brought in this way, but this brought me to Christ mainly—was the doctrine of the safety of the saints. I fell in love with the Gospel through that Truth. What, I thought, are those who trust in Jesus safe? Shall they never perish and shall none pluck them out of Christ's hands? Everybody esteems safety. One would not insure his life where he thought there was a doubt as to the safety of the insurance. Feeling that there was perfect safety if I gave myself up to the Redeemer, I did so. And I entertain no regrets to this day that I committed my soul to Him.

Young people, you cannot do better than early in life entrust your future with the Lord Jesus. Many children at home appear to be very excellent. Many lads, before they leave their father's house, are amiable and commendable in character. But this is a rough world—and it soon spoils the Graces that have been nurtured in the conservatory of the home. Good boys very often turn out very bad men. And girls who were so lovely and pure at home have been known to become very wicked women.

O children, your characters will be safe if you trust them with Jesus! I do not say you will be rich if you trust Christ, nor that you will prosper after the manner of men. But I do say that you shall be happy in the best sense of that word, and that your holiness shall be preserved through trusting yourself with Jesus. I pray that you may be led to desire this, especially any of you who are leaving your father's house, or are setting up in business on your own account. Commit yourselves to God!

This first Sunday of a new year. What time more suitable for beginning aright? O may the Holy Spirit softly whisper in your ears reasons that shall persuade you to give yourselves to Christ! I say again, my testimony is that you cannot do a wiser or a better thing. Oh, the happiness my soul has known in resting on my Lord! I wish you knew it. I would not cease to be a Christian if I might be made a king or an angel. No character can be to me so suitable or so happy as that of a humble dependent upon the faithful love of my redeeming Lord.

O come and trust Him, dear young Friends! You older ones—do you need that I should speak to you, when you are getting so near your grave? You are now out of Christ—how soon may you be in Hell? You younger ones, I say, embrace this flying hour and let this be the day of which you shall sing in after years—

"It is done! The great transaction's done!
I am my Lord's, and He is mine—
He drew me, and by His Grace I followed on,
Charmed to confess the voice Divine.

"High Heaven, that heard the solemn vow,
That vow renewed shall daily hear—
Till in life's latest hour I bow,
And bless in death a bond so dear."

5

Knowing and Believing

(Sermon No. 3331)

"I know whom I have believed." (2 Timothy 1:12).

THE TEXT IS WHOLLY TAKEN up with three things—with knowing, with believing and with the Person who is known and believed. And upon both the knowing and the believing, Paul is very decided. He puts in no, "if," no word of change. He does not say, "I hope so," or, "I trust so," but, "I know I have believed and I know whom I have believed." It is all assurance and not a shadow of doubt! Let us imitate the Apostle, or ask for Grace to be able to imitate him, that we may shake off the dubious phraseology which is so common among Christians, nowadays, and may be able to speak with Apostolic confidence upon a matter upon which we ought to be confident if anywhere at all, namely—our own salvation!

As the text is thus taken up with knowing and believing, these two matters will be the subject of our meditation at this time. My first remark drawn from the text shall be—

I. THE ONLY RELIGIOUS KNOWING AND BELIEVING WHICH ARE OF A SAVING CHARACTER CONCERN THE PERSON OF THE LORD JESUS CHRIST. "I know," says the Apostle—not, "what"—but, "whom I have believed." He does not say, "I know the Catechism which I have believed," nor, "I know the Institutes of Calvin," nor, "I know the body and system of theology," but, "I know whom I have believed." Both the knowing and the believing center around the wondrous Person who for our sakes left His starry Throne and became a Man. Knowing whom is a saving knowledge and trusting whom is a saving trust—of which all other knowing and believing fall short!

Observe, then, that all other knowledge may be useful enough in itself, but if it does not concern Christ, it cannot be called saving

73

knowledge. Some persons know a great deal about Doctrine. Perhaps they have taken up with the Calvinistic theology, or even with the hyper-Calvinistic and they really understand the system thoroughly well—and they certainly hold it with quite enough tenacity, if not too much. We know some who we believe would very cheerfully go to the stake in defense of some points of Doctrine so convinced are they of the orthodoxy of what they have received! Others take up another theory and go upon the Arminian principle—and they, too, know their set of doctrines and know them well. But, dear Friends, I may know all the Doctrines in the Bible, but unless I know Christ, there is not one of them that can save me! I may know Election, but if I cannot see myself as chosen in Christ Jesus, election will do me no good. I may know the Doctrine of the Final Perseverance of the Saints, but if I am not in Christ, I would only persevere in my sins—and such a final perseverance will be dreadful, indeed! It is one thing to know the Doctrine of Justification by Faith, but it is quite another thing to be justified by faith and to have peace with God! You may stand up for Imputed Righteousness and fight for it, and yet the righteousness of Christ may never be imputed to you! It is not knowing the creed, though that is well, that can save the soul—the knowledge that is needed is to know Him whom Paul believed!

And, again, a man may know something more than Doctrine. He may know a great deal about experience. There is a class of persons who sneer at Doctrine. They call the doctrinal preacher a mere "letterman." As for themselves, they talk about deep experience. They have a consciousness of having a corrupt heart. They have discovered that they have evil tempers (by the way, other people, too, have discovered it)! They have discovered that they have defiled natures and everybody can see that they are not perfectly free from sin. But, strange delusion, because they know the disease, they fancy they have been healed! Because they have perception enough to see they are spiritually bankrupt, they, therefore, imagine that their debts are paid! Because they feel themselves to be in the Slough of Despond, they dream they are on the Rock!

But there is a vast difference between the two things. A man may think he has an experience of his own emptiness—no, he may truly possess it—but if it does not drive him to Christ, if he does not come and rest on the Lord Jesus, all his experiences are of no saving value! The foundation of the soul's salvation is not experience of any or every kind, but the finished work, the meritorious blood and righteousness of our Lord and Savior!

There are some, too, who not only know experience and Doctrine, but who also know how to talk of them. They have mingled with Christian people until they can get up their phraseology and, as some Christians have cant expressions, these people can "can't" in any quantity and to any extent. They can talk about their "poor souls" and about, "the dear Lord," and use all those other precious phrases of hypocrisy which lard some religious publications and which are to be found in the conversation of some people who ought to know better. They use these expressions and then, when they get in among the people of God, they are received with open arms! And they fancy that because they can talk as Christians talk, it is all well with them! But, oh, remember that if a parrot could call you, "father," it would not, for all that, have become a child of yours! A foreigner may learn the language of an Englishman but never be an Englishman, but still remain a foreigner. So, too, you may take up the language of a Christian, but may never have within you the Spirit of God and, therefore, be none of His. You must know Him. "Know yourself," said the heathen philosopher. That is well, but that knowledge may only lead a man to Hell. "Know Christ," says the Christian philosopher, "know Him and then you shall know yourself"—and this shall certainly lead you to Heaven, for the knowledge of Christ Jesus is saving knowledge— "whom to know is life eternal."

In addition to these valuable pieces of information, there are some who know a great deal *about* Christ, but here I must remind you that the text does not say, "I know about Christ," but, "I know Him." Ah, dear Hearer, you may have heard the Gospel from your youth up, so that the whole history of Christ is at your fingertips! But you may not know Him, for there is a deal of difference between knowing about Him, and knowing Him. You may know about a medicine, but still die of the disease which the medicine might have cured. The prisoner may know about liberty and yet lie and pine in his dungeon until, as John Bunyan put it, "the moss grows on his eyelids." The traveler may know about the home which he hopes to reach and yet may be left out at nightfall in the midst of the forest. Many a man of business knows about wealth, or even concerning the millions of the Bank of England, and yet is a bankrupt or on the verge of poverty. Many a sailor knows about the port, but his ship drifts upon the rocks and all hands go down. It is not enough to know about Christ, it is knowing Christ, Himself, that alone saves the soul!

And, over and above, and in addition to all this, you may know the Scriptures from youth up. I suppose I have some—perhaps many— before me who are well acquainted with almost every Chapter in the. Bible. You could not be questioned upon any part of it so as to be really nonplussed. You have read the Book and you continue to read it—and I approve of your wise choice in so doing—and beg you to always continue in so excellent a practice! But remember, if you have not the Word of God in your heart it is of small use to have it merely in your head. Oh, to know Christ is our supreme and tragic need! Not to merely know texts and Scripture, for—"the letter kills, it is only the Spirit that quickens"—and unless you know Christ you do not know the vital Spirit of the Word of God! The only saving knowledge, then, is knowing Christ.

Well, now, so is it with the exercise of faith. You may know a great deal about faith, but the only saving faith is belief concerning Christ. "I know whom I have believed." To believe Doctrine will not save a man. You may hold all the creed and be orthodox—and then be no better than the devil, for I suppose that the devil is a very sound theologian. He surely knows the Truth. He believes and trembles! But you may know it and not tremble—and so you may fall short of one virtue which even the devil possesses! A firm belief in what is preached to you is well enough in its way, but to believe a Doctrine as such cannot save you. Some have a belief in their minister—and I suppose that is so flattering to us that you will hardly expect us to speak against it—but of all vices, it is one most surely to be dreaded because it is so very dangerous! We charge you in the sight of God, always weigh what we have to say to you—and if it is not according to Scripture, cast it away as you cast away refuse! Take nothing merely because we say it! Let nothing that we preach be received upon our *ipse dixit*,[2] but let it be tried and tested by the Word of God, for otherwise you may be led by the blind. And "if the blind lead the blind, they shall both fall into the ditch." Ah, what multitudes of persons there are in England who are beginning to get their fellow man to perform their religion for them! They are too lazy to think! They are too idle to use whatever brains they have and so they get some mere simpleton who thinks that God is pleased with his putting on a white gown or a blue dress, or a black gown or green dress, a scarlet gown or mauve dress, is pleased with burning candles in the daylight and pleased with making a pungent odor in the church—they get such a creature as this to do their religion for them and then they lie down at night to rest, feeling perfectly satisfied that God is satisfied and they are all right! Oh, I charge you, believe not this delusion! It is not believing in a priest that will save you! Believing in the priest may be your ruin, but believing in Christ is the really vital point—the one thing that truly matters. He that believes in Christ is saved! But he that believes even the Pope of Rome shall find that he believes to his own eternal ruin!

Then again, it is not believing in ourselves. Many persons believe thoroughly in themselves. The doctrine of self-reliance is preached in many quarters now-a-days. I suppose that what is meant by the term is a good mercantile possession, a business virtue, but it is a Christian vice as towards spiritual things and emphatically towards the soul's salvation! Self-reliance in this matter always ruins those who practice it. Rely on self? Let night rely on her darkness to find a light! Let emptiness rely on its insufficiency to find its fullness! Let death rely on the worms to give it immortality! Let Hell rely upon its fire to make it into Heaven—such trusts as these would be equally strong with those of the sinner who relies upon himself for salvation! Your belief must not be that you can force your way to Heaven, but you must believe Him, for anything else is an unsaving faith.

You see, then, that the knowledge which saves, and the belief which saves, both hang upon the Cross. They both look to the wounds of that

---

[2] Latin for, "He himself said it." Also means, "an assertion made but not proved."

dear Man, that blessed God who was there the Propitiation for our sins and who suffered in our place. My Hearer, are you trusting Christ? Are you hanging upon Him as the vessel hangs upon the nail? Do you know Him as a man knows his friend? Do you seek to know more of Him? Is He all your salvation and all your desire? If not, take home this solemn warning—whatever else you know, you are still ignorant, and whatever else you believe, you are still an unbeliever—unless you know and believe in Him who is the Savior of men!

I pass on now to a second point, which is this—

II. THAT KNOWLEDGE WITHOUT FAITH IS VAIN.

This is to try to balance with but one scale—to run a chariot on one wheel. You have the double matter here. "I know whom I have believed." It is good to know, but knowledge must be crowned with faith! It has been remarked that Paul does not say, "I know of whom I have heard." He does not say, "I know of whom I have read." He does not say, "I know of whom I have preached," but, "I know whom I have believed." Here he hits the nail on the head. Knowledge is useful in the bud. Mere reading, preaching, too, are well as an exercise—but believing is the fruit which must grow upon the Tree of Knowledge or else the knowledge will be of little use to us!

Now, my dear Friends, I know that I am addressing many of your class, many who know Christ in a certain sense. Know much about Him. You know of His Nature, you believe Him to be true Deity. You know Him to be Human like yourselves and for man's sake made Man. You know His life. You have often read it. You often like to dwell upon the incidents of it. It is a genuine and great pleasure to sing of Bethlehem and its manger, of Cana and its marriage. You have turned over the pages of that Life of lives and felt enraptured with this matchless masterpiece of biography. You are well acquainted, too, with His death—it has often drawn tears to your eyes when you have thought of the shame and the spitting and the crown of thorns. You know something concerning His expiring cries. Your imagination has often pictured to you the wounded body of that dread Sufferer. You have thought that if you had been there, you would have wet His feet with your tears, you did so sympathize with

Him. You know of His burial and of His Resurrection, too, and you have sweetly joined with us when we have been singing—

"Angels, roll the rock away, Jesus Christ is risen today" and you have not been lacking when we have been singing of His Ascension! Your eyes have flushed with fire when you have heard the words—

> **"They brought His chariot from on high,**
> **To bear Him to His Throne,**
> **Clapped their triumphant wings and cried,**
> **'The glorious work is done.'"**

You know that He reigns in Heaven! You know that He has prepared mansions for His people. You know that He intercedes for sinners. You expect that He will come. You believe in His Second Advent and when the *Te Deum*[3] has been sung in your hearing—"We believe that You shall come to be our Judge," you have said, "Yes! I do—I do—I believe it." Now, if you know all this, you know that which it is very important to be known, but if you stop short here, where are you? Why, I have no doubt there have been hundreds who knew this, but who have given their bodies and souls to the devil and have lived in open sin, day by day! If you could go to the condemned cell tonight, I would not wonder if the wretch confined there knows all this. If you were to go into the flaunting gin palaces which are scattered to our shame and curse all over London—where men and women are drinking liquid fire at this very moment—you would find that half of them know all this, but they do not drink any the less for it! If you were to go into the lairs of vice, you would find that the most abandoned know all this, but it does them no good! And I will add also this—that the lost spirits in Hell went there knowing all this! And the devil, himself, knows it all, but he still remains a devil! Ah, my Hearer, I charge you before God, do not sit down and say, "I know, I know, I know." Do you believe? Do you *believe*?

---

[3] An early Christian hymn of praise. The title is taken from the opening phrase in Latin meaning, "Thee, O God, we praise."

The common answer given very frequently to the city missionary is just this—men say to them, "There is no need for you to come here and tell me anything. I know all about it." Ah, but do you believe in Jesus? What is the good of your knowing unless you believe? I do not think that the most of you who go to places of worship need so much instruction in Divine Truth as you need an earnest appeal to your hearts not to stop short at instruction! You do know, and that, indeed, shall be, indeed, part of your damnation—that you had the light but you would not see! That Jesus came into your street and came near to you, but you would not have Him! The medicine was there, but you died because you would not take it! The food was on the table, but you would sooner perish with hunger than receive it as the free gift of Heaven! Ah, my Hearer, your knowing will not benefit you, but will be a plague to you! The poor savage in his kraal in Central Africa who never heard the name of Jesus shall die with at least this mitigating circumstance—that he never rejected the Savior's love! The million a month who die in China, for a million do die every month in China—the million who die every month in China die with this one solace, at any rate, that they never sinned against the light of Christianity, nor rejected the Truth as it is in Jesus! This is more than you can say! This will never help to make a dainty couch for you, when you make your bed in Hell! The responsibility of having known shall add remorse to the whips of accusing conscience and make Hell still more terrible! Oh, may God grant that we may not stop short with knowledge, alone, but may know Christ as Him whom we have believed! But still we have in the next place—

III. FAITH WITHOUT KNOWLEDGE IS BUT A BIRD WITH ONE WING. The old faith of the fuller is coming back in some places today. You remember what the fuller said, "Yes, he believed" He believed—what did he believe? He believed, "What the Church believed." And what did the Church believe? "Well, the Church believed—well, what he believed." And, pray tell, what did he and the Church, together, believe? "Why, they both believed the same thing." Ah, how many there are of that sort today! They say,

"We think he ought to be sincere, you know, and if he is sincere, it does not matter much whether it is absolutely true. He need not trouble greatly to enquire whether what he believes is Scriptural or not, or whether it is according to God's Revelation—that will take up too much of his time and thought—and look too much like being obedient to God's will. Just be sincere, you know, and then, hit or miss, whatever your mother or father happened to be in religious character, go at it with all your might and it will be all right."

Now, unfortunately, that does not happen to be the Truth of God—and we do not find people in this world getting on in proportion to their sincerity. I suppose our friends who bought Overend and Gurney's shares were sincere enough in their belief that they were buying a good thing, but I should fancy that their opinions have undergone a change of late! No doubt there have been persons who have taken prussic acid,[4] sincerely believing that it would benefit them, but I suppose it has killed them, notwithstanding their sincerity. If a man should travel due south in order to get to the Orkney Islands, however sincere he might be, he would probably discover himself in the Bay of Biscay before long. The fact is, it is not sincerity, alone—it is the studious endeavor to find out what the right is and what the Truth is—that is the only safe way for us! We do not, therefore, ask you to believe without knowing what you are to believe. It is impossible. Do not think a man can hold in his hands four or five doctrines and say to you, "Do you believe them?" "Well, but what are they?" "Never mind! You are a true Believer and you must believe then without knowing them." A man who has no power of belief at all says, "Oh, yes, I believe. I will kiss your feet if necessary, or do anything you like to tell me." But the thoughtful man, the man who is likely to be saved, says at once, "I find it impossible to believe until I first know what I am to believe."

I have sometimes thought when I have heard addresses from some revival Brothers who had kept on saying time after time, "Believe, believe, believe," that I would like to have known for myself what it was we were to believe in order to our salvation. There is, I fear, a great deal of

---

[4] A colorless, extremely poisonous liquid.

vagueness and crudeness about this matter. I have heard it often asserted that if you believe that Jesus Christ died for you, you will be saved. My dear Hearer, do not be deluded by such an idea! You may believe that Jesus Christ died for you and may believe what is not true! You may believe that which will bring you no sort of good whatever. That is not saving faith! The man who has saving faith attains to the conviction that Christ died for him afterwards, but it is not of the essence of saving faith. Do not get that into your head or it will ruin you! Do not say, "I believe that Jesus Christ died for me," and because of that feel that you are saved! I pray you to remember that the genuine faith that saves the soul has for its main element—trust—absolute rest of the whole soul—on the Lord Jesus Christ to save me, whether He died in particular or in special to save me or not and, relying as I am, wholly and alone on Him, I am saved! Afterwards I come to perceive that I have a special interest in the Savior's blood, but if I think I have perceived that before I have believed in Christ, then I have inverted the Scriptural order of things and I have taken as a fruit of my faith that which is only to be obtained by rights—by the man who absolutely trusts in Christ, and Christ alone, to save!

The matter, then, which saves is this—a man trusts Christ, but he trusts Christ because he knows Him. See! He knows Christ and, therefore, he trusts Him. How does he come to know Him? Well, he has heard of Him, he has read of Him, he seeks Him in prayer and when he has learned His Character, he trusts Him. Occasionally young converts will say to us, "Sir, I cannot trust Christ." I never try to argue with them about it, but say, "Then you do not know Him, because to truly know Christ is sure to bring trust." I believe there are some men in the world whom you have only to know to trust because they are so transparently honest, so clearly truthful that you must trust them! The Savior is such a Person as that. Let me tell you, Sinner, God was made flesh and dwelt among us—do you believe that? "Yes." He lived a holy life. He died a painful death. The merit of His life and death is set to the account of everyone who trusts in Him and He declares that if you trust in Him, He will save you. Now surely you can trust Him! You say, "No, I cannot." Why not? Is He not able? He is Divine—therefore you cannot raise the question. Is He not willing?

He died—that argues willingness surely to do a lesser thing, since He has done the greater! Surely you cannot doubt that! The life of the Lord Jesus Christ is an answer to every form of doubt. Do you know, I feel with regard to Christ, myself, that instead of its being any difficulty to trust Him, I find it very difficult not to trust Him if I cannot find any reason why I should distrust Him. I was turning over the other day some odds and ends of my own brain to see if I could find any reason why Christ should not receive my soul. Well, I could not find half a one, but I could think of 20,000 reasons why I should believe in Him to save me, even if I had a million souls! I feel as if His way of saving is so magnificent and the working of it out so Divinely generous, that His offerings were so great, His Person is so glorious, that I could not only cast my one soul on Him, but 50,000 souls if I had them! Why, I cannot find any reasonable ground for doubting Him! Soul, I would to God that you would think of Him in the same light!—

"He is able, He is willing—Doubt no more!"

You know something of Him. Oh, may God give the Grace to add to your knowledge, trust, and then shall you have true saving faith!

Let it be remarked here that in proportion as our genuine knowledge of Christ increases, so we shall find that our trust in Him will increase, too. The more we know Christ, the more we shall trust Him because every new piece of knowledge will give new arguments for immovable confidence in Him! Oh, if you have not seen Christ, I can understand your doubting Him, but if you have leaned your head upon His bosom, if He has ever kissed you with the kisses of His lips, if He has ever taken you into His banqueting house and waved His banner of love over you, I know you will feel,

"Doubt You, Jesus, doubt You? Why, how can I? I know the power of Your arm. I know the love of Your heart. I know the efficacy of Your blood. I know the Glory of Your Person. I know the faithfulness of Your Word. I know the Immutability of Your oath and I can trust You and, either sink or swim, my soul casts herself upon You, You blessed Savior!"

But now there may be some present who are saying, "I cannot say I know whom I have believed."

IV. "HOW CAN I KNOW THAT I MAY BELIEVE IN HIM?" The answer is, search the Word of God with a desire to find Him. Seek out the most Christ-exalting ministry in your neighborhood, in whatever denomination you can find it, and listen to it with all your ears and with all your heart. Get to your chamber and there seek the Lord to illuminate you in the matter of the Lord Jesus Christ! Ask Him to reveal His Son in you. I tell you this—faith comes by hearing and by hearing the Word of God—and when to these is added earnest seeking, you shall not be long without finding Him! They who seek Christ are already being sought of Him. You who desire Him shall have Him! You who want Him shall not be long without Him. It is to have Christ to some degree, to hunger and to thirst after Him—and when you feel that you cannot be content without Him, He will not let you be, but will soon come to you! I believe there are some who will get peace with Christ tonight! Do you understand it, dear Friend? You have nothing to do. You have nothing to be. You have not even anything to learn, except that Jesus Christ came into the world to save sinners and that He is able to save unto the uttermost them that come unto God by Him! You know that. Now, trust Him, and if you do, it is all done and you are saved! If you have trusted in Him whom God has revealed as your Savior, it is not a matter of twenty minutes nor much less a matter of months, but you are saved at once!—

"The moment a sinner believes,
And trusts in his crucified God,
His pardon at once he receives,
Salvation in full through Christ's blood."

When a man once gets into the lifeboat, if it were certain that the lifeboat would never sink, he is saved as soon as he gets in. Now, the act of faith does, as it were, put us into the lifeboat of Christ Jesus and we are saved immediately! You may have many a tossing, but you will get safely to land at last. If you want faith you must get it, as I have told you, by knowing Him, studying the Word of God, listening to it and seeking His face. But make use of what you know, or else what you know will be like the stale manna and will be of no use to you. Believe it as you know it. Use it up as you get it. And if you already know Christ to be a sinner's Savior, and know that you are a sinner, then come tonight and put your trust in Him! And be of good cheer because He will never, never, never cast you away! And now, lastly, I should like to ask a question, and it is this—

V. HOW MANY ARE THERE WHO DO KNOW CHRIST?

We all know something of which we are a little proud, but, "I know, I know, I know," is a very poor thing to say when you do not know Christ! "I know," says my young friend over there who has been to Oxford or Cambridge University, "I know So-and-So." "I know," says another, "such-and-such a special line of distinguished thinking." But do you know Christ, my dear Friend? "Ah, thank God," says one upstairs, and another good soul below, "we can hardly read, Sir, but we do know Him." I would change places with you, Friends, much sooner than I would with the most learned of men who do not know Christ, because when they come to the gates of death, you know, he who keeps the gate will not say, "Do you know the classics? Have you read Horace? Have you studied Homer? Do you know mathematics? Do you understand logarithms or conic sections?" No, but he will say, "Do you know Christ?" And if you scarcely even know your own native tongue, yet if you know Christ, the gates of Heaven shall fly open to let you in!

Now, do you know Christ? Do let the question go round to each one, "Do I know Christ?" Well, then, do you believe Christ? Do you trust Christ? "Yes, thank God!" says one, "with all my imperfections I can sing the hymn—

**"On Christ the solid Rock I stand,
All other ground is sinking sand."**

Oh, then, Brothers and Sisters, let us be of good cheer, for, trusting Him, He will never fail us! Believing Him, He will never leave us! We shall see

His face in Glory. Oh, that the day were come! But when it does, to His name shall be all the praise! Amen.

EXPOSITION OF 2 TIMOTHY 4:1-11

Verses 1, 2. *I charge you, therefore, before God and the Lord Jesus Christ, who shall judge the quick and the dead at His appearing and His Kingdom, preach the Word of God.* We are not to use such strong language as this unless there is some sufficient reason for it. We must not be too hot upon cold matters, but even this is better than to be cold upon matters that require heat. When John Calvin wished to leave Geneva to complete his studies elsewhere, that man of God, Farrell, knowing how necessary it was for the Church that Calvin should remain at Geneva, charged him before God that he dared not go—and hoped that a curse might light upon all his studies, if for the sake of them he should forsake what he held to be his duty. So sometimes, like the Apostle, we may before the Judge of the quick and dead, charge men not to forsake their work and calling.

2. *Be instant in season and out of season.* The Greek word means, "Stand up to it," as when a man is determined to finish his work, he stands right up to it. Stand over your work, putting your whole strength into it— standing up over it. "In season and out of season," because the Gospel is a fruit which is in season all the year round! Sometimes these "out of season" sermons, preached at night or at some unusual time, have been of more service than the regular ordinances of God's House. Mr. Grimshaw used to ride on horseback from village to village throughout the more desolate parts of Yorkshire and wherever he met with ten or a dozen people, he would preach on horseback to them, preaching sometimes as many as 24 sermons in a week! That was being instant "out of season" as well as "in season." So should God's Timothy be and, indeed, all of us!

2. *Reprove, rebuke, exhort with all long-suffering and doctrine.* That is, do not exhort with mere declamation, but put some argument into your exhortation! Some men think it quite enough to appear to be in earnest,

though they have nothing to say. Let such exhorters remember that they are to exhort with *doctrine*—with solid teaching!

3. *For the time will come when they will not endure sound doctrine; but after their own lusts shall they heap to themselves teachers, having itching ears.* When men have not good preachers, they are sure to have a great many of them! Those nations which have the worst priests always have them in swarms. So let us be thankful if God sends us a glowing and zealous minister, for even those who count it an affliction to have a minister, would be more afflicted if they had not a good one! But how evil it is when men get itching ears, when they need someone to be perpetually tickling them, giving them some pretty things, some fine pretentious intellectualism! In all congregations there is good to be done, except in a congregation having itching ears. From this may God deliver us!

4. *And they shall turn away their ears from the Truth, and shall be turned unto fables.* When a man will not believe the Truth of God, he is sure, before long, to be a greedy believer of lies! No persons are so credulous as skeptics. There is no absurdity so gross but what an unbeliever will very soon be brought to receive it, though he rejects the Truth of God!

5, 6. *But watch you in all things, endure affliction, do the work of an evangelist, make full proof of your ministry. For I am now ready to be offered, and the time of my departure is at hand.* How complacently he talks about it! It is only a departure, though Caesar's sword might smite his head from his body! And truly death to the Believer is no frightful thing. "Go up," said God to Moses, and the Prophet went up, and God took away his soul to Him—and Moses was blessed! And so, "Come up," says God to the Christian, and the Christian goes up, first to his chamber and then from his chamber to Paradise!

7, 8. *I have fought a good fight, I have finished my course, I have kept the faith: henceforth there is laid up for me a crown of righteousness, which the Lord, the righteous Judge, shall give Me at that day: and not to me only, but unto all them also that love His appearing.* This seems, then, to be a distinguishing mark of a true child of God—he loves the appearing of Christ! Now there are some professors who never think of the Second Advent at all. It never gives them the slightest joy to believe that—

"Jesus the King will come,
To take His people up,
To their eternal home."

Truly they are mistaken and are surely wrong, for was not this the very comfort that Christ gave to His disciples? "If I go away, I will come again and receive you unto Myself, that where I am there you may be also." I trust, dear Friends, we are among those "who love His appearing," and if we are, it is a sure prophecy that we shall have a crown of righteousness!

9, 10. *Do your diligence to come shortly unto me: for Demas has forsaken me, having loved this present world, and is departed unto Thessalonica.* Demas was once almost a martyr! He was upon the very edge of suffering, but now you see he goes back to the world—he is not content to lie in the dungeon and rot with Paul, but will rather seek his own ease. Alas, Demas, how have you dishonored yourself forever, for every man who reads this passage, as he passes by flings another stone at the heap which is the memorial of one cowardly spirit who fled from Paul in danger!

10. *Crescens to Galatia, Titus unto Dalmatia.* It is likely that Paul had sent Crescens and Titus away upon a mission, but now, from certain intimations, the Apostle is sure that his time of death is coming on and so, indeed, it was, for his head was struck off by Nero's orders a few weeks after the writing of this Epistle—and now he somewhat laments that he had sent them away. And would not you and I want the consolation of kind faces round about us, and the sweet music of loving voices in our ears if we were about to be offered up?

11. *Only Luke is with me.* Take Mark, and bring him with you for he is profitable to me for the ministry. That is one of the prettiest verses in the Bible! You remember that the Apostle Paul quarreled with Barnabas about this very Mark, because John Mark would not go into Bithynia to preach the Word, but left Paul and Barnabas. Therefore Paul would not have Mark with him anymore because he had turned in the day of trouble. But now Paul is about to die and he wishes to be perfectly at peace with everyone. He has quite forgiven poor John Mark for his former weakness.

He sees Divine Grace in him and so he is afraid lest John Mark should be under some apprehensions of the Apostle's anger. And so he puts in this very kind passage, without seeming to have any reference at all to the past, but he gives him this great praise—"for he is profitable to me for the ministry."

6

Confidence and Concern

(Sermon No. 1913)

"For this reason I also suffer these things; nevertheless I am not ashamed, for I know whom I have believed and am persuaded that He is able to keep that which I have committed unto Him against that day. Hold fast the form of sound words, which you have heard of me, in faith and love which is in Christ Jesus. That good thing which was committed unto you keep by the Holy Spirit which dwells in us" (2 Timothy 1:12-14).

O
UR APOSTLE WAS IN PRISON. If he was confined in the Mammertine, those of us who have shivered in that dark underground dungeon may well pity him. And if he was confined in the prison of the Praetorian Guards, he fared no better, for the near company of such rough and cruel soldiers would involve much suffering. The Apostle was not only a prisoner, chained by his right hand to a soldier both day and night, but he was, to his intense sorrow, forsaken by his friends. The encouragements of Christian communion are exceedingly great and the loss of them is very bitter. Those who ought to have gloried in the Apostle for his fervor, his self-sacrifice, his courage and his zeal, had turned against him. He writes to Timothy, "This you know, that all they which are in Asia have turned away from me; of whom are Phygellus and Hermogenes." It would seem that these two notable persons were ashamed of Paul's chain and, to their endless disgrace, turned against him.

Deserted in his utmost need, deprived of his liberty and treated as a breaker of the laws, we could not have marveled if the Apostle had been somewhat dispirited. Active spirits are apt to fret in confinement and tender hearts bleed under desertion. Beside that, the man of God was in daily danger of execution by the tyrant's sword. He was not likely to be spared by the monster who occupied the Roman throne and already he had the sentence of death in himself. Any morning he might be awakened by a rough summons to come forth and die. See him, then—such a one as Paul the Aged! Wearing his chain, he sits in his cell, expecting soon to die a cruel death—but instead of being personally discouraged—he has encouragement to spare for others! He is thinking of young Timothy and not of himself! As for himself, he says, "Nevertheless, I am not ashamed." And then he charges his young Brother not to be disheartened nor shaken in faith, but bravely to carry on the great work committed to his charge. It is grand to see how calmly this man bore himself! In his case it was, indeed, true, that "stone walls do not a prison make, nor iron bars a cage." Paul ranged the world with his free missionary spirit and he reigned more royally in his prison than Caesar in his palace! No one envies Nero, but many have felt that Paul's sufferings might readily be embraced for the sake of his exalted life.

What was the cause of the cool courage of the Apostle? On what foundation was his peace built? How was his confidence sustained? He tells us in our text how his fears were removed—and he also informs us as to a matter which pressed upon his mind. Our discourse this morning will be an attempt to show at once Paul's confidence and his concern. I pray God to bring our minds into a parallel line with that of the Apostle so that we may enjoy the most serene peace, as Paul did, and may, at the same moment, feel a noble concern for higher interests than those which begin and end with ourselves! The honored Apostle had committed all his own matters into the hands of God and so was at perfect peace about them. But he experienced deep anxiety for another treasure which was committed to him—which he handed over to Timothy with an earnest entreaty that he would guard it by the Holy Spirit. The blending of deep peace and holy zeal will give us a condition of heart of a most desirable kind!

Our subject opens up to us under four divisions. First, we shall notice what Paul had done. Then, secondly, what Paul knew. Thirdly, what Paul was persuaded of. And lastly, what he was concerned about.

I. First, observe carefully WHAT PAUL HAD DONE. I will speak but briefly here.

He had trusted a Person—"I know whom I have believed." He had trusted that Person with full, clear knowledge of Him—so trusted that he did not alter his trust as years rolled by but, as he grew in the knowledge of that Person, he was also confirmed in his confidence in Him—"I know whom I have believed."

He does not say, "I know what I have believed," though that would have been true. He does not say, "I know when I believed," though that would have been correct. Nor does he say, "I know how much I have believed," although he had well weighed his faith. He does not even say, "I know in whom I have believed," but he goes still closer! He says expressly, "I know whom I have believed," as much as to say, "I know the Person into whose hand I have committed my present condition and my eternal destiny. I know who He is and I, therefore, without any hesitation, leave myself in His hands." Brothers and Sisters, it is the beginning of spiritual life to believe Jesus Christ! Is not this the one word that we preach to you continually? "Believe on the Lord Jesus Christ and you shall be saved." "He that believes on the Son has everlasting life." "He that believes on Him is not condemned." Many are the Scriptural assurances to the same effect. Paul had not ventured upon a fancy, but he had trusted in a well-known Friend! He had not done this in ignorance, nor in fanaticism, nor in desperation, but with cool, clear, deliberate judgement—knowing whom he had trusted. Ignorance is a wretched foundation, but sure knowledge is like a rock!

Paul had gone further and had practically carried out his confidence, for he had deposited everything with this Person. He had unreservedly committed his body, soul, spirit, character, life and immortality to the guardian care of that Person whom he knew and loved so well! I may believe in a person and yet I may never have committed anything to his charge—he might not wish that I would do so, nor be willing to accept any trust at my hands. But we must go that length with the Lord Jesus. While we are bound to believe in the Lord Jesus as faithful and true and able to save, this belief is not enough, in itself, to work salvation—we must, in consequence of this belief—actually and definitely convey out of our own keeping all our eternal interests and put them into His keeping.

We must make the Lord Jesus Christ the depository of all our anxieties and hopes. He must be to us the banker who has the custody of all our valuables, bonds and title-deeds—yes we must also leave ourselves with Him—all that we are, all that we have, all that we expect to have, we must confide with Jesus.

A poor idiot, who had been instructed by an earnest Christian, somewhat alarmed him by a strange remark, for he feared that all his teaching had been in vain. He said to this poor creature, "You know that you have a soul, John?" "No," said he, "I have no soul." "No soul!" thought the teacher, "this is dreadful ignorance." All his fears were rolled away when his half-witted pupil added, "I had a soul, once, and I lost it, but Jesus found it. And so I have let Him keep it." How could he better have expressed his faith? Is not that exactly what the Apostle meant—he passed his soul out of his own keeping into the care of Jesus, his Lord? As a man leaves his estate with a trustee, or as the patient entrusts his life to his physician, even so had the Apostle Paul committed himself into the hands of that glorious Person whom having not seen, he loved!

I pause here to ask whether we have all done the same. This is a vital question. If you, my Friend, are keeping your own soul, you have a poor keeper! You will lose your soul as surely as you attempt to be your own savior! Have you once and for all transferred salvation work from yourself to Jesus? Are you looking out of yourself and looking to Jesus, only? Are you leaning upon the Beloved? Are you living in Him? If so, your safety is secure. In the hands of Jesus, a soul must be safe. In the keeping of Jesus, nothing shall hurt you either night or day. In Him you dwell in a fortress and high tower—and no enemy shall molest you. Through time and eternity you are secure! Death shall leave you sleeping on His bosom! Resurrection shall awaken you in His likeness and endless ages shall display your security in Him forever and ever!

What Paul did is summed up in these words, "I know whom I have believed," "I have committed everything to Him."

II. The next thing is, WHAT DID PAUL KNOW? He tells us plainly, "I know whom I have believed." We are to understand by this that Paul looked steadily at the Object of his confidence and knew that he relied upon God in Christ Jesus. He did not rest in a vague hope that he would be saved, nor in an indefinite reliance upon the Christian religion, nor in a sanguine expectation that all things would, somehow, turn out right at the end. He did not hold the theory of our modern divines, that our Lord Jesus Christ did something or other, which, in one way or another, is more or less remotely connected with the forgiveness of sin. No, Paul knew the Lord Jesus Christ as a Person and he deliberately placed himself in His keeping, knowing Him to be the Savior!

His countrymen did not know Jesus, or they would not have crucified the Lord of Glory, but Paul knew Him. Those around the Apostle were strangers to the Lord Jesus and could not sympathize with Paul, yet he knew Him. Some of them curiously asked, "Who is this Christos of whom you sing?" Others asked, "Who is this Crucified One, of whom you make so much fuss?" Paul answers by avowing his own faith—"I know whom I have believed." He had no phantom Savior, no mythical Savior, no unknown Savior, no Savior sharing salvation with two or three others. Paul knew no company of saints and virgins, nor even a church to which he trusted his soul—he says, "I know whom I have believed." Jesus was a distinct Person to the Apostle, so real as to be known to him as a man knows a friend. Paul knew nobody else so well as he knew his Lord!

By faith he knew Jesus as He was born at Bethlehem, partaker of our humanity, bone of our bone, flesh of our flesh—a Brother born for adversity. He knew Him as He died on Calvary, bearing our sins in His own body on the tree. He knew Him as dead and buried in the tomb of Joseph—and as risen from the dead for our justification! He knew Him as gone up into Glory and sitting at the right hand of God, clothed with honor and majesty. Because of all this, the Apostle trusted his Lord. On what better ground could he have gone? What could be more reasonable than that he should entrust his all with One so fitted to preserve him till he day of His appearing?

Dear Friends, do you really know Christ Jesus as a real Person? Do you trust in Him as now living? I beseech you, do not trust the weight of your salvation upon a doctrine! A statement, an abstraction, cannot save you—you need the active interference of a Person. Do not trust in a form of faith, nor in a code of rules. What are they? Trust in the living Person of Him who, though He was dead, rose again and always lives to make intercession for us at the right hand of God, even the Father! I trust that you have no hesitation as to faith in Him, but that you can sing with me—

> "Jesus, my God, I know His name,
> His name is all my trust!
> Nor will He put my soul to shame,
> Nor let my hope be lost."

Paul also knew the Character of Jesus whom he trusted. His perfect Character abundantly justified the Apostle's implicit trust. Paul could have said,

> "I know that I trust in One who is no mere man, but very God of very God. I have not put my soul into the keeping of a priest, like unto the sons of Aaron, who must die, but I have rested myself in One whose Priesthood is according to the Law of an endless life—a Priest forever after the order of Melchizedek. He upon whom I confide is He without whom was not anything made that was made, who sustains all things by the Word of His power and who, at His coming, shall shake both the heavens and the earth, for all fullness of Divine energy dwells in Him."

Paul knew that his Christ was God as well as Man and so he felt safe in relying upon Him.

He knew also that this blessed Person was pre-eminently satisfactory to the heart of the eternal God. What manner of perfection must concentrate itself in Him in whom the Father, Himself, delights? Think of Him as the great Sacrifice for sin who has made a complete, absolute and everlasting Atonement, to which nothing can be added, from which nothing shall ever be taken away! Think of Him in whom the Justice of God is vindicated and the Love of God is displayed! When my own eyes dart a glance to Calvary and I picture the Lord of Glory dying there for my sake, I cannot allow a doubt to live—I feel compelled to trust—I cannot but rest in perfect peace when I see that great Sacrifice which has forever put away all the sins of Believers!

Beloved, Paul knew whom he had believed as being Divine in His Person and complete in His Sacrifice, but more than that. Paul knew that the Lord Jesus Christ, to whom he trusted his soul, was now adorned with all the Glory of Heaven and clothed with all the Omnipotence of the mighty God. He knew that, if he was bound, Jesus was not bound and that, if he must die, yet Jesus could not die. He knew that the Lord shall reign forever and ever and his expectant ears caught the hallelujahs of eternity when the Crucified shall be acknowledged Lord of All! "All power is given unto Me in Heaven and in earth," said Jesus, "Go you therefore, and teach all nations, baptizing them." Paul felt that such power was worthy of boundless confidence and, therefore, he said—"I know whom I have believed." Jesus was to Paul's faith no longer the despised and rejected Nazarene; no longer the condemned and crucified Man of Sorrows, but He was the acknowledged King of Kings and Lord of Lords! He knew Him in His risen Glory. Happy, happy, happy heart which has such knowledge of Jesus and such confidence in Him!

Now, Brothers and Sisters, I think I have shown you why Paul had much faith in Jesus. How could he do otherwise than trust in One of whom he knew such wonderful things? But how did Paul come to know Christ? I suppose he knew Him in great part by the Word of God. Every page of Scripture, as the Apostle perused it, revealed Jesus to him. These Scriptures are the swathing-bands of the Holy Child Jesus. Unroll them and there He is! This Book is a royal pavilion within which the Prince of Peace is to be met with by Believers who look for Him. In this celestial mirror, Jesus is reflected! This is a sure testimony—more to be trusted than the sight of the eyes, or the hearing of the ears. Do you know Christ by seeing Him in His Word?

Paul also knew Jesus in another way than this. He had personal acquaintance with Him. He knew Him as "the Lord Jesus, who appeared unto him in the way." When he was going to Damascus to persecute the saints of God, this same Jesus spoke out of the excellent Glory and said to him, "Saul, Saul, why do you persecute Me?" Brethren, have we any personal acquaintance with Christ? If not, our witness will not run parallel with Paul's utterance in our text, "I know whom I have believed." Did Jesus ever call you to Himself, and have you answered His call? Has He so spoken as to change the whole current of your life? Does He still speak to you? Do you remember a sacred place, a consecrated spot where Jesus has met you? Have you a chamber where He meets you and manifests Himself to you as He does not to the world? If so, you can well trust Him whose love is shed abroad in your heart by the Holy Spirit. You can well trust Him, for He is no stranger, but your near kinsman who is mindful of you and visits you. Cannot you join with our poet and softly sing—

> **"Yes, though I have not seen and still**
> **Must rest in faith alone,**
> **I love You, dearest Lord, and will,**
> **Unseen, but not unknown."**

There are other gates of the soul beside eyes and ears, other touches than those of the hands and other feelings than those of the flesh. Our inner spirit, when it would commune with the spiritual world, disdains to use the gross and inefficient instruments of this poor body—she cannot, with these, have fellowship with the Father and with His Son, Jesus Christ. By its own inner hands, our spirit has touched Him. With her own inner mouth she has kissed the Well-Beloved. With other than a material eyes she has beheld her unseen Spouse. Our eyes do not see—we see through our eyes even these temporal things—but we see eternal things without the need of eyes. Our spirit needs no intervening medium, but she sees in her pure spirit the pure spirit of Jesus, face to face! More than the senses could convey to the soul, she perceives without them! This is a Divine and blessed knowledge and the Apostle could, with all his heart, declare that it was his own. Though he had once known Christ after the flesh, he declared that after the flesh he knew Him no more, but he knew Him so well and so truly after the spirit that he said, without reserve, "I know whom I have believed."

He knew the Lord, also, by practical experience and trial of Him. Paul had tested Jesus amidst furious mobs, when stones fell about him, and in prison when the dampness of death chilled him to the bone! He had known Christ far out at sea, when Euroclydon drove him up and down in the Adriatic. And he had known Christ when the rough blasts of un-brotherly suspicion had beaten upon him on the land. All that he knew increased his confidence! He knew the Lord Jesus because He had delivered him out of the mouth of the lion. "I know," he said—he was past the age of speculation and theory. Look at his hoary locks and his scarred face—he is no fair-weather sailor—he has sailed with his Lord upon the great deeps and has suffered many things for His sake. And now, after all his experience, he does not say that he hopes, supposes, or thinks, but he writes, "I know."

Glorious dogmatist, we are not ashamed to follow in your track! Where is there any comfort or stimulus except in the Truth of God assuredly believed? To doubt is to be downcast and feeble. Only in solemn assurance is there courage and strength. Come on, you who quibble and criticize—Paul meets you with, "I know!" You demand that he shall maintain his thesis with logic? He answers, "I know!" What he knew of his Lord was as sure to him as his own consciousness. He had no reserve in his mind for future alterations of creed, for he had reached certainty. "I know whom I have believed." He could not doubt Him, nor distrust Him, nor stir an inch from the absolutely unlimited confidence which he reposed in Him. Beloved, I trust we know as much of Jesus as leads us to a living faith in our living Lord. Some people do not know much else, but they are well educated if they know this! Others are skillful in classics, mathematics and applied sciences, but if they do not know Jesus, in whom the saints believe, they are in the worst of ignorance! I pray God to send such untaught persons to His infant school, for it is written, "Except you are converted and become as little children, you shall not enter into the Kingdom of Heaven." May we be taught of God to know Jesus by that practical acquaintance which engenders trust in Him!

III. Thirdly, let us enquire—WHAT WAS THE APOSTLE PERSUADED OF? If one should say to a Christian man, "Pray, Sir, what are your opinions?" he might answer, "I have no opinions, but I know whom I have believed." If the enquirer then said, "But what is your persuasion?" he might answer, "I am persuaded that He is able to keep that which I have committed to Him." This method of treating matters is far better than forming mere opinions for ourselves, or borrowing persuasions from others.

Implicitly Paul declares his faith in our Lord's willingness and faithfulness. He does not mention these in words, but sometimes there is great instruction in omissions—things not said may, perhaps, be more conspicuous by their absence than things which are spoken. Silence is often more emphatic than speech. Paul does not raise the question whether the Savior was willing or faithful to keep what he had committed to Him—he takes that for granted. He will not even assert his knowledge of the Truth and Grace of his Redeemer—he leaves these among the things which could not be questioned for a moment! Dear Heart, if you have given yourself to Christ, Christ has given Himself to you—do not doubt His readiness to receive you! If you are leaning upon the Beloved, He is willing to be leaned upon and He will never fail you. If, in very truth His Word is your trust, the Lord will never run back from His promise. Has He not said it and will He not do it? Take this for granted! Receive it as an acknowledged principle which none may question.

But the point which the Apostle expressly mentions is the power of Christ—"I am persuaded that He is able." He had a solemn conviction of the ability of the Lord Jesus, who is able to save unto the uttermost. Let us hope that no Believer here has any doubt about the power of Christ. If he has, the doubt is most absurd! He that goes to the sea for salt water cannot rationally fear that he will be forced to come back with an empty bucket. He that lifts up his face to the sun can have no doubt but that his features will be bright with the light. So he that turns to Christ may be persuaded that there is no lack of sufficiency or ability in Him.

"Oh," one says, "I do not doubt the ability of Christ to save me!" May I ask you, then, what you do doubt? "Oh, I doubt my own merit, my own ability and so forth." What have any of these things to do with the matter in hand, which is the power of Jesus? These things are altogether out of the circle! All the salvation of a man depends upon the Lord Jesus Christ—and if He is able to save you, why are you full of fears? If you have committed your money to the banker and you say, "I am afraid it is not safe," the only justifiable reason for such suspicion must be because the bank is not solvent. Would you say, "I doubt about my money because I have a headache?" Would that be rational? Would you say, "I am afraid my money is unsafe because my eyesight is failing me?" Does that influence the safety of your deposit at the bank? Nothing can affect that matter but lack of stability in the bank, itself.

If you have committed yourself to the care of the Lord Jesus Christ, I cannot listen to those miserable, "ifs," and "buts"—they are unreasonable and irrelevant. I blow them away as so much chaff. If Jesus is able to save and you are trusting Him, there is no room for distrust. Can you doubt the Lord's ability? Have we not believed in His Godhead and in the almighty power with which the Father has girt Him as the God-Man, the Mediator, now that He has gone up into His everlasting reward? If these are facts, how can it be difficult to trust such a One? Trust my soul with Christ? Why, if I had all your souls within my body, I could trust them all to Him! And if every sin that man has done in thought, word and deed since worlds were made, or time began, could meet upon my one guilty head—I dare say it—the precious blood of Jesus could wash them all away! Trust Him with one soul? Yes, indeed, it seems too little a thing!

He that goes on board a great Atlantic liner does not say, "I venture the weight of my body upon this vessel. I trust it to bear my ponderous frame." Yet your body is more of a load to the vessel than your soul is to the Lord Jesus. Did you ever hear of the gnat on the horn of the ox which feared that it might be an inconvenience to the huge creature? O Friend, you are but a gnat in comparison with the Lord Jesus! No, you are not so heavy to the ascended Savior as the gnat to the ox! You were a weight to Him once, but having borne that load once and for all, your salvation is no burden to Him now. Well may you say, "I am persuaded that He is able to keep that which I have committed unto Him."

What was this which Paul had committed to Christ? He committed to Him everything that he had for time and for eternity—his body, his soul, his spirit—all fears, cares, dangers, sins, doubts, hopes, joys. He just made a clean removal of his all from himself to his Lord. "I am persuaded that He is able to keep that which I have committed unto Him." See how the eyes of the Apostle light up as he tells his copyist to write down, "He is able to keep my deposit against that day." If he had little joy and rejoicing in his waiting time, he would, nevertheless, look to have his full of it in that day of days, that day in which his Lord would appear! He left everything with Jesus with a view to the Advent, the Judgment, and the eternal Glory! Then would he look for his Divine Keeper to produce the deposit entrusted to Him. There will be no need in that day to ask, "My Lord, is it all right?" Yes, we may picture Him as coming in all His Glory and majesty to be admired in all them that believe! He sits upon the Throne of His Glory and there are you among the countless multitude!

Suppose you could say, "My Lord, I trusted You with my soul. Am I safe? I trusted You with my eternal interests. Are they all secure?" How sweet will be His reply, as He says to His Father, "Of them which You gave Me have I lost none." And to us, "Come, you blessed of My Father, inherit the Kingdom prepared for you!" If any enquire of us in Glory, "How did you get here?" we will answer, "He brought us here." If they say, "How is it that you are on His right hand?" we will reply, "Because His own right hand brought us there." "But how is it that you are so bright in your apparel?" "We have washed our robes and made them white in His blood." "How is it that after you were converted you did not turn back?" "He kept us in the Way and preserved our lives, for He said, 'Because I live, you shall live also.'" "How is it that you have escaped the power of the enemy, since you were only a sheep, and a wolf was after you?" "It is because He said, 'I give unto My sheep eternal life and they shall never perish, neither shall any man pluck them out of My hand.'"

When the Lord shall make up His last account of His jewels in that Great Day, we shall be found in Christ, even as gems are found in a golden vault! In the Lord Jesus Christ, all His elect, all His blood-bought, all His called, all His justified, all His believing people shall be found in that day. None of His redeemed shall be absent in the day when the sheep shall pass, again, under the hand of Him that counts them. All who were marked with the blood-mark here below shall be folded in the pastures of Glory! "I know whom I have believed," says Paul, "and am persuaded that He is able to keep that which I have committed unto Him against that day."

Those of you who are acquainted with the original will follow me while I forge a link between my third division and my fourth. If I were to read the text, thus, it would be quite correct—"I am persuaded that He is able to keep my deposit against that day." Here we have a glimpse of a second meaning. If you have the Revised Version, you will find in the margin, "that which He has committed to me." And the original allows us to read the verse whichever way we choose—"He is able to keep that which I have committed unto Him"—or "that which He has committed unto me." This last expression, though I could not endorse it as giving the full sense of the text, does seem to me to be a part of its meaning. It is noteworthy that, in the 14th verse, the original has the same phrase as in this verse. It runs thus—"that good deposit guarded by the Holy Spirit which dwells in us."

Inasmuch as the words are the same—the Apostle speaking of "my deposit" in the 12th verse and, in the 14th verse speaking of "that good deposit"—I cannot help thinking that one thought dominated his mind. His soul and the Gospel were so united as to be, in his thought, but one deposit—and this he believed that Jesus was able to keep. He seemed to say, "I have preached the Gospel which was committed to my trust and now, for having preached it, I am put in prison, and am likely to die, but the Gospel is safe in better hands than mine." The demon of distrust might have whispered to him, "Paul, you are now silenced and your Gospel will be silenced with you! The Church will die out. The Truth of God will become extinct!" "No, no," says Paul, "I am not ashamed, for I know that He is able to guard my deposit against that day."

I cannot tell you what heart-cheer it often brings to my soul, in these evil days, to join in the confidence of this text! At the present moment it seems as if parts of the Church had almost forgotten the Gospel of the Grace of God. We hear on all hands, "another gospel, which is not another; but there are some that trouble you, and would pervert the

Gospel of Christ." We hear the noise of archers at every place of drawing of water and the wayfaring man almost ceases from the highways of Zion. Worldliness is growing over the Church, she is overgrown with the moss of it. The visible Church is honeycombed through and through with a baptized infidelity! Unholy living is following upon unbelieving thinking. They boast that they have nearly extirpated Puritanism—some of us are described as the last of the race! Have they quenched our coal? Far from it! The light of the Doctrines of Grace shall yet again shine forth as the sun!

Elijah was known to say, "As the Lord lives, before whom I stand." And this also is my confidence—the Truth of God lives because God lives! Though Truth were dead and buried, it would rise again. The day is not far distant when the old, old Gospel shall again command the scholarship of the age and shall direct the thoughts of men! Even if it were not so, it would be a small matter, for it signifies little, except to themselves, what men think, since God is true and with the Truth of God there is power. The fight is not over! The brunt of the battle is yet to come! They dreamed that the old Gospel was dead more than a hundred years ago, but they dug its grave too soon. Conformists and Nonconformists had, alike, gone over to a cold Socinianism and in the old sanctuaries, where holy men once preached with power, modern dreamers droned out their wretched philosophies! All was decorous and dead, but God would not have it so. All of a sudden, a voice was heard from Oxford, where the Wesleys and their companions had found a living Savior and were bound to tell of His love!

From an inn in Gloucester there came a youth who began to preach the Everlasting Gospel with a trumpet tongue. A new era dawned. Two schools of Methodists with fiery energy proclaimed the living Word of God. All England was awakened! A new springtide arrived—the time of the singing of birds had come—life rejoiced where once death withered all things! It will be so again. The Lord lives and the Gospel lives, too. Our charioteers are driving as fast as they can in the direction of Unitarianism and spiritual death, but the Lord will lay His hand upon the bridles of the horses, though Jehu himself drives them, and He shall turn them back by the way they came! "I know whom I have believed, and am persuaded that He is able to keep my deposit against that day."

IV. This leads me on to this fourth point—WHAT THE APOSTLE WAS CONCERENED ABOUT. The matter about which he was concerned was this deposit of his—this everlasting Gospel of the blessed God. He expresses his concern in the following words—

"Hold fast the form of sound words, which you have heard of me, in faith and love which is in Christ Jesus. That good thing which was committed unto you, keep by the Holy Spirit which dwells in us."

First, he is concerned for the steadfastness of Timothy and, as I think, for that of all young Christians and especially of all young preachers. What does he say? "Hold fast the form of sound words." I hear an objector murmur, "There is surely not much in words." Sometimes there is very much in words. Vital truth may hinge upon a single word. The whole Church of Christ once fought a tremendous battle over a syllable— but it was necessary to fight it for the conservation of the Truth of God. Only the unorthodox ridicule words and with them it is an affectation, for were they not impressed with the importance of words, they would not be so eager to alter them. "Surely we may change our terms." I have no objection if I know that your intentions are honest!

"Surely we may change the form of a creed, however sound it may be." Do so if you like. I will not contend for words to no profit. But as for some of you who ask for these changes, I shrewdly suspect that you would get rid of a phrase that you might be rid of that which the phrase means. You gentlemen who say, "Surely you will not stick out for a word," are, after all, neither so innocent nor so liberal as you appear to be. Brethren, it is not a word they would amend, but a Truth of God they would efface! I intend calling a rose a rose, even though I admit that by another name it might smell as sweet, for I perceive that there is an intent to inflict upon me a rank smelling weed which is no rose at all! When people rail at creeds as having no vitality, I suppose that I hear one say that there is no life in eggshells. Just so—there is no life in egg shells—they are just so much lime, void of sensation.

"Pray, my dear Sir, do not put yourself out to defend a mere shell." Truly, good Friend, I am no trifler, nor so litigious as to fight for a mere shell. But listen! I have discovered that when you break eggshells you spoil eggs! And I have learned that eggs do not hatch and produce life when shells are cracked! I have come to be rather tender about shells, now that I find that certain rogues are depriving me of chickens by cracking my eggshells! At certain periods when everybody is sound and right at heart, it may be wise to revise expressions, but we will have none of it when the very air is tainted with unbelief! If you walk round certain continental towns you will see bright lawns and gardens where once there stood grim walls. In times of peace we are glad to see fortifications demolished, but, mark you, when the Prussians are around Paris, no Frenchman will tolerate the proposition to throw down the forts! This is our case, today, and therefore we hold fast the form of sound words!

"We hate your narrowness—your nasty narrowness! You are shut in within your walls of creeds and beliefs!" Yes, gentlemen, so we are. And we mean to remain so, since we see how you hate the Gospel. If everything were in peace and we believed in you, we might, perhaps, think about turning bulwarks into boulevards—but at the present moment we will do nothing of the kind, but rather hear the voice of our old captain from his prison at Rome, crying—"Hold fast the pattern of wholesome words which you have heard from me." Brothers, do not change your posture nor shift your position! Stand fast on the Immutable Truth of God, trusting and loving your Lord. Hold the old faith and hold it in the old fashion, too. We are crossing the stream and can make no change of horses. Brothers, why should we change? Do these tempting novelties offer any real improvement on the old? Do they offer us anything to die upon? Can these new teachings afford us comfort in poverty, in sickness, in depression of spirit or in prospect of the Day of Judgment? They are only pretty flowers for the children of this world to play with. They suit well with minds that love frivolities, but they are not for men whose life is a warfare against sin! The eternal Truths revealed within this Book and grasped by the hands of our inner life—these are everything to us—therefore we shall stand by them even to the last with faith and love which is in Christ Jesus!

The Apostle was anxious not only that the men should stand, but that the Everlasting Gospel, itself, should be guarded. "That good thing which was committed unto you, keep by the Holy Spirit which dwells in us." O Friends, it were better for us that the sun were quenched than that the Gospel were gone! I believe that the moralities, the liberties and, perhaps, the very existence of a nation depend upon the proclamation of the Gospel in its midst! Have you not noticed that where the Gospel has been given up and various forms of infidelity have ruled, foul pollution has also boiled up from below! The very idea of morality seems to have departed from some men by whom belief in God has been rejected. The Lord save us from the general spread of this mischief! Let the sea, itself, cease to ebb and flow sooner than the Gospel fail to be preached among the sons of men! If the whole Church were to die for the defense of the Gospel, it were a cheap price to pay for the maintenance of it! I speak solemnly when I say that our main care in life should be to preserve this Gospel intact and hand it down to our descendants. God grant that future ages may not have to curse us for having been undecided or cowardly in the hour of conflict!

How are we to keep the faith? There is only one way. It is of little use trying to guard the Gospel by writing it down in a trust-deed—it is of small service to ask men to subscribe to a creed—we must go to work in a more effectual way. How is the Gospel to be guarded? "By the Holy Spirit which dwells in us." If, my dear Brothers and Sisters, the Holy Spirit dwells in you and you obey His monitions, are molded by His influences and exhibit the result of His work in the holiness of your lives, then the faith will be kept. A holy people are the true bodyguard of the Gospel. Only living people, in whom the Holy Spirit is the soul of their soul and the spirit of their spirit, are able to keep the Truth of God living and influential in the world! Let the power of the Gospel be missing where it may, it must be present where the Holy Spirit abides, for He makes the Word of God to be a living and incorruptible Seed which lives and abides forever! God send us, more and more, the Holy Spirit! May He be in us as rivers of Living Water! Oh for His heavenly Presence in this day of blasphemy and rebuke! Amen.

7

The Form of Sounds Words

(Sermon No. 79)

"Hold fast the form of sound words, which thou hast heard of me, in faith and love which is in Christ Jesus" (2 Timothy 1:13).

MY INCESSANT ANXIETY for you, dearly beloved in the faith of Jesus Christ, is that I may be able, in the first place, to teach you what God's truth is; and then, trusting that I have to the best of my ability taught you what I believe to be God's most holy gospel, my next anxiety is, that you should "hold fast the form of sound words;" that whatever may occur in the future, should death snatch away your pastor, or should anything occur which might put you in perilous circumstances, so that you were tempted to embrace any system of heresy, you might every one of you stand as firm and as unmoved as rocks, and as strong as mountains be, abiding in "the faith which was once delivered unto the saints," whereof ye have heard, and which we have proclaimed unto you. If the gospel be worth your hearing, and if it be a true gospel, it is worth your holding, and our anxiety is, that you should be so established in the faith, that you may, "hold fast the profession of your faith without wavering, for he is faithful that has promised."

The Apostle most earnestly admonished Timothy to "hold fast the form of sound words which he had heard of him in faith and love which is in Christ Jesus." I do not suppose that by this it is intended that Paul ever wrote out for Timothy a list of doctrines; or that he gave him a small abstract of divinity, to which he desired him to subscribe his name, as the articles of the church over which he was made a pastor. If so, doubtless the document would have been preserved and enrolled in the canons of Scripture as one of the writings of an inspired man. I can scarce think such a creed would have been lost, whilst other creeds have been preserved and handed down to us. I conceive that what the Apostle meant was this:—

"Timothy, when I have preached to you, you have heard certain grand outlines of truth; you have heard from me the great system of faith in Jesus Christ; in my writings and public speakings you have heard me continually insist upon a certain pattern or form of faith; now I bid you, my dearly beloved son in the gospel, "Hold fast the form of sound words, which thou hast heard of me, in faith and love which is in Christ Jesus."

This morning I shall first attempt to tell you what I conceive to be a *"form of sound words," which we are to hold fast.* In the second place, I shall endeavour to urge upon you *the strong necessity of holding fast that form.* In the third place, I shall *warn you of some dangers to which you will be exposed, tempting you to give up the form of sound words.* Then, in the last place I shall mention *the two great holdfasts, faith and love in Christ Jesus,* which are the great means of "holding fast the form of sound words."

1. What is a "FORM OF SOUND WORDS?" Ten thousand persons will quarrel upon this. One will say, "My creed is a form of sound words;" another will declare that his creed also is sound, if not infallible. We will not, therefore, enter into all the minutiae which distinguish creeds from each other, but just simply say, that no system can be a form of sound words unless it is *perfectly scriptural.* We receive no doctrines as the doctrines of men; whatever authority come to us which is not the authority of the Holy Spirit, and inspired by God, is no authority at all to us. We laugh to scorn all the dogmatism of men; we care for nothing they assert, however strongly they declare it, or however eloquently they plead for it; we utterly reject and discard it; we hold it a sin to "take for doctrines the commandments of men;" we give no heed to the traditions that are handed down to us. If our opponent cannot quote text or verse for anything he advances, we hold no argument with him. Scripture is the only weapon we can acknowledge.

But since it is said that texts may be found to prove almost everything, we must remark, that a form of sound words must be *one that exalts God and puts down man.* We dare not for a moment think that any doctrine is sound that does not put the crown upon the head of Jesus, and does not exalt the Almighty. If we see a doctrine which exalts the creature, we do not care one fig about what arguments may be brought to support it; we know that it is a lie, unless it lays the creature in the very dust of abasement, and exalts the Creator. If it does not do this, it is nothing but a rotten doctrine of pride; it may dazzle us with the brilliant malaria rising from its marshes, but it never can shed a true and healthful light into the soul; it is a rotten doctrine, not fit to be builded on the gospel, unless it exalts Jehovah Jesus, Jehovah the Father, and Jehovah the Holy Spirit.

We think, also, that we may judge of the soundness of doctrine *by its tendency*. We can never think a doctrine sound, when we see plainly upon its very surface that it has a tendency to create sin in men. Unless it be a doctrine according to godliness, we cannot conceive it to be a doctrine of God. Unless the believer of it, earnestly and truthfully believing it, doth give himself to virtue—unless that doctrine has in itself a natural tendency to promote in him a love to the right—we are at first sight suspicious of it; and if we find on examination that it is a licentious doctrine—it may have all the glitter and the glare of novelty, but we cast it away as not being the doctrine of Christianity, because it does not promote holiness in the soul.

We shall, perhaps, be asked what we *do* regard as a form of sound words, and what those doctrines are which are scriptural, which at the same time are healthful to the spirit and exalting to God. We answer, we believe a form of sound words must embrace, first of all, the doctrine of *God's being and nature*, we must have the Trinity in Unity, and the Unity in Trinity. Any doctrine, which hath not the Father, Son, and Holy Ghost, as equal persons in one undivided essence, we cast aside as being unsound, for we are sure that such doctrines must be derogatory to God's glory; and if they be so it is enough for us. If any man despise either Father, Son, or Holy Ghost, we despise him, and despise his teachings, and cannot even say to him, "I wish you God speed."

Now, we hold, that a form of sound words must *look upon man aright as well as upon God aright*; it must teach that man is utterly fallen, that he is sinful, and for his sin condemned, and in himself altogether hopeless of salvation. If it exalts man by giving him a character which is not a true one, and clothing him with a spurious robe of righteousness, woven by his own fingers, we reject and discard it utterly.

And next, we think that a doctrine that is sound *must have right views of salvation, as being of the Lord alone*; unless we find in it everlasting, unchanging love, working out a salvation for a people "who were not a people," but were made a people by special grace; unless we find discriminating love, others may say what they will—we cannot consider such a creed to be a form of sound words, unless we discern redeeming mercy openly and boldly taught; unless we see final perseverance, and all those great and glorious truths which are the very bulwarks of our religion, others may embrace the doctrine as being a form of sound words; but we cannot, and we dare not. We love the old system of our forefathers; we love the old truths of Scripture, not because they are old, but because we cannot consider anything to be truth which doth not hold the scriptural view of salvation. Methinks Paul himself, in this very chapter, gives us a form of sound words, where he speaks of

"God who hath saved us, and called us with an holy calling, not according to our works, but according to his own purpose and grace, which was given us in Christ Jesus before the world began."

I need not stop this morning to prove to you that which I have briefly hinted at as a form of sound words, because you believe it, and believe it firmly. I am not about to urge you to receive it, because I know you have already received it; but what I have to say is, "Hold fast," I beseech you, "the form of sound words, which thou hast heard of me in faith and love which is in Christ Jesus."

II. Now let me show you THE NECESSITY OF HOLDING FAST THIS FORM OF SOUND WORD, AND KEEPING IT FOR YOUR OWN SAKE, FOR THE CHURCH'S SAKE, FOR THE WORLD'S SAKE.

First, *for your own sake*, hold it fast, for thereby you will receive ten thousand blessings; you will receive the blessing of peace in your conscience. I protest, before God, that if at any time I ever doubt one of the great things I receive from God, instantly there comes an aching void which the world can never fill, and which I can never get filled until I receive that doctrine again, and believe it with all my heart. When at any time I am cast down and dejected, I always find comfort in reading books which are strong on the doctrines of the faith of the gospel; if I turn to some of them that treat of God's eternal love, revealed to his chosen people in the person of Christ; and if I remember some of the exceeding great and precious promises made to the elect in their covenant head, my faith at once becomes strong, and my soul, with wings sublime, mounts upwards towards its God. You cannot tell, beloved, if you have never tasted, how sweet is the peace which the doctrines of grace will give to the soul; there is nothing like them. They are—

> "A sovereign balm for every wound,
> A cordial for our fears."

They are God's sweet lullaby, wherewith he singeth his children to sleep, even in storms. They are God's sheet anchors, which are cast out into the sea, to hold our little vessels fast in the midst of tempests. There is a "peace of God which passeth all understanding," which accrues to a man who is strong believer, but you know the tendency of the day is to give up old land marks and to adopt new ones, and to avow anything rather than the old-fashioned divinity. Well, my dear friends, if any of you like to try new doctrines, I warn you, that if you be the children of God you will soon be sick enough of those new-fangled notions, those newly invented doctrines, which are continually taught. You may, for the first week, be pleased enough with their novelty; you may wonder at their transcendental spirituality, or something else, which entices you on; but you will not have lived on them long, before you will say, "Alas! alas! I have taken in my hands the apples of Sodom; they were fair to look upon, but they are ashes in my mouth." If you would be peaceful, keep fast to the truth, hold fast the form of sound words: so shall "your peace be like a river, and your righteousness like the waves of the sea."

"Hold fast the form of sound words," again, let me say, *because it will tend very much to your growth*. He who holds fast the truth will grow faster than he who is continually shifting from doctrine to doctrine. What a mighty number of spiritual weathercocks we have in this world now. We have men who in the morning hear a Calvinistic preacher, and say, "Oh, it is delightful;" in the evening they hear an Arminian, and they say, "Oh, it is just as good; and no doubt they are both true, though one contradicts the other!" The glorious charity of the present day is such, that it believes lies to be as good as truth; and lies and truth have met together and kissed each other; and he that telleth truth is called a bigot, and truth has ceased to be honourable in the world! Ah! beloved, we know better than to profess such unlimited, but false charity; the truth is, we know how to "hold fast the form of sound words," which has been given to us, because in this way we grow. Changeable people cannot grow much. If you have a tree in your garden plant it in one place to-day, and tomorrow place it somewhere else, how much bigger will it be in six months? It will be dead very likely; or if it does not die, it will not be very much grown; it will be marvellously stunted. So it is with some of you: you plant yourselves there; then you are persuaded that you are not quite right, and you go and plant yourself somewhere else. Why, there are men who are anything-arians; who go dodging about from one denomination to another, and cannot tell what they are; our opinion is, of these people, that they believe nothing, and are good for nothing, and anybody may have them that likes; we do not consider men to be worth much, unless they have settle principles, and "hold fast the form of sound words." You cannot grow unless you hold it fast. How should I know any more of my faith in ten years' time, if I allowed it to take ten forms in ten years? I should be but a smatterer in each, and know nothing thoroughly of one. But he that hath one faith, and knoweth it to be the faith of God, and holdeth it fast, how strong he becomes in his faith? Each wind or tempest doth but confirm him, as the fierce winds root the oaks, and make them strong, standing firmly in their places; but if I shift and change, I am none the better, but rather the worse. For your own peace sake then, and for your growth, "hold fast the form of sound words."

But, my beloved, I would beseech you to hold it fast for your own sakes, *from a remembrance of the great evils which will follow the contrary course*. If you do not "hold fast the form of sound words," listen to me while I tell you what you will do.

In the first place, *every deviation from truth is a sin*. It is not simply a sin for me to do a wrong act, but it is a sin for me to believe a wrong doctrine. Lately our ministers have absolved us all from obeying God in our judgments; they have told us point blank, many of them, in their drawing-rooms, and some of them in the pulpit, that we shall never be asked in the day of judgment what we believed. We have been told that for our acts we shall be responsible, but for our faith we shall be irresponsible, or something very much like it; they have told us plainly, that the God who made us, although he has authority over our hands, our feet, our eyes and our lips, hath but little authority over our judgments; they have told us, that if we make ever such blunders in divinity, they are no sins, so long as we can live right lives. But is that true? No; the whole man is bound to serve God; and if God gives me a judgment, I am bound to employ that judgment in his service; and if that judgment receive an untruth, it has received stolen goods, and I have sinned as much as if I put forth my hand to take my neighbour's goods. There may be degrees in the sin. If it be a sin of ignorance, it is nevertheless a sin; but it is not so heinous as a sin of negligence, which I fear it is with many. I tell you, beloved, if, for instance, baptism be not by immersion, I commit a sin every time I practice it; and if it be, my brother commits a sin who does not practise it. If Election be true, I am committing a sin if I do not believe it; and if Final Perseverance be true, I am committing a sin before Almighty God, if I do not receive it; and if it be not true, then I sin in embracing what is not scriptural. Error in doctrine is as much a sin as error in practice. In everything we are bound to serve our God with all our might, exercising those powers of judging and believing which he has given unto us; and I warn you, Christians, not to think it is a little thing to hold faith with a feeble hand: it is a sin every time you do aught which makes you waver in the faith of Jesus Christ. Remember, too, that error in doctrine is not only a sin, but a sin which has a great tendency to increase. When a man once in his life believes a wrong thing, it is marvellous how quickly he believes another wrong thing. Once open the door to a false doctrine—Satan says it is but a little one—ay, but he only puts the little one in like the small end of the wedge, and he means to drive in a larger one; and he will say it is only a little more, and a little more, and a little more. The most damnable heretics who ever perverted the faith of God erred by littles and littles; those who have gone the widest from truth have only gone so by degrees. Whence came the Church of Rome, that mass of abominations? Why, from gradual departures. It did not become abominable at first; it was not the "mother of harlots" all at once; but it first did deck itself in some ornaments, then in others, and by-and-bye it went on to commit its fornications with the kings of the earth. It fell by little and little, and in the same way it separated itself from the truth. For centuries it was a Church of Christ, and it is difficult to say, looking at history, when was the exact point in which it ceased to be numbered with Christian Churches. Take care, Christians, if you commit one error, you cannot tell how many more you will commit.

"Hold fast the form of sound words," *because error in doctrine almost inevitably leads to error in practice*. When a man believes wrongly, he will soon act wrongly. Faith has a great influence on our conduct. As a man's faith, so is he. If you begin to imbibe erroneous doctrines, they soon have an effect on your practice. Keep fast to the bulwarks of your fathers' faith. If you do not, the enemy will make sad havoc with you. "Hold fast the form of sound words which was delivered unto you."

2. And now, *for the good of the Church itself*, I want you all to "hold fast the form of sound words." Would you wish to see the Church prosperous? Would you wish to see it peaceful? Then "hold fast the form of sound words." What is the cause of divisions, schisms, quarrels, and bickerings amongst us? It is not the fault of the truth; it is the fault of the errors. There would have been peace in the Church, entire and perpetual peace, if there had been purity—entire and perpetual purity—in the Church. Going down to Sheerness on Friday, I was told by some one on board that during the late gale several of the ships there had their anchors rent up, and had gone dashing against the other ships, and had done

considerable damage. Now, if their anchors had held fast and firm, no damage would have been done. Ask me the cause of the damage which has been done to our churches by the different denominations, and I tell you, it is because all their anchors did not hold fast. If they had held fast by the truth, there would have been no disputing; disputing comes from errors. If there be any ill feeling, you must not trace it to the truth—you must trace it to the error. If the Church had always kept firm to the faith, and had always been united to the great doctrines of the truth, there would have been no disputes. Keep firm to you belief, and you will prevent discord in the Church.

Keep to your faith, I say again, for the Church's sake, *for so you will promote strength in the Church.* I saw lying between Chatham and Sheerness a number of ships that I supposed to be old hulks; and I thought how stupid Government was to let them remain there, and not chop them up for firewood, or something else; but some one said to me, those ships can soon be fitted for service; they look old now, but they only want a little paint, and when the Admiralty requires them, they will be commissioned and made fit for use. So we have heard some people say, "There are those old doctrines—what good are they?" Wait; there is not a doctrine in God's Bible that has not its use. Those ships that you may think are not wanted, will be useful by-and-bye. So it is with the doctrines of the Bible. Do not say, "Break up those old doctrines, you can do without them." Nay, we want them, and we must have them. Some people say, "Why do you preach against Arminians? We have not much to fear from them now." But I like to practice my men against the time comes for action. We are not going to burn our ships; they will be wanted by-and-bye, and when we sail out of harbour, the men will say, "Whence came these old ships?" "Why," we will reply, "they are just the doctrines you thought good for nothing; now we bring them out, and we will make good use of them." Now-a-days we are having new and marvellous hymn-books, full of perfect nonsense; and we are having new theories, and new systems; and they say, "Why be so stringent? our Christian brethren may believe what they like on those points just now;" but as certain as there is a church in this land, they will want our old ships to fight their battles; they may do very well in times of peace, but they will not do in the time of war. They will then need our broadside to support the faith of the gospel, though now they laugh at us. For the strength of the church, my brethren, I bid you "hold fast the form of sound words."

"Well," says one, "I think we ought to hold the truth firmly; but I do not see the necessity for holding *the form* of it; I think we might cut and trim a little, and then our doctrines would be received better." Suppose, my friends, we should have some valuable egg, and some one should say, "Well, now, the shell is good for nothing; there will never be a bird produced by the shell certainly, why not break the shell?" I should simply smile in his face and say, "My dear friend, I want the shell to take care of what is inside. I know the vital principle is the most important, but I want the shell to take care of the vital principle." You say, "Hold fast the principle, but do not be so severe about the form. You are an old Puritan, and want to be too strict in religion; let us just alter a few things, and make it a little palatable." My dear friends, do not break the shell; you are doing far more damage than you think. We willingly admit the form is but little; but when men attack the form, what is their object? They do not hate the form; they hate the substance. Keep the substance then, and keep the form too. Not only hold the same doctrines, but hold them in the same shape—just as angular, rough and rugged as they were, for if you do not, it is difficult to change the form and yet to keep fast the substance. "Hold fast *the form* of sound words, which thou has heard of me, in faith and love which is in Jesus Christ."

3. Again, I say, "hold fast the form of sound words," *for the world's sake*. Pardon me when I say that, speaking after the manner of men, I believe that the progress of the gospel has been awfully impeded by the errors of its preachers. I never wonder when I see a Jew an unbeliever in Christianity, for this reason, that the Jew very seldom sees Christianity in its beauty. For hundreds of years what has the Jew thought Christianity to be? Why, pure idolatry. He has seen the Catholic bow down to blocks of wood and stone; he has seen him prostrating himself before the Virgin Mary and all saints; and the Jew has said, "Ah! this is my watchword—hear, O Israel, the Lord thy God is our Lord; I could not be a Christian,

for to worship one God is the essential part of my religion." So the heathen, I believe have seen a false system of Christianity, and they have said, "What! is that your Christianity?" and they did not receive it. But I believe that when the gospel is purged from all the rudiments of men, and all the chaff and dust have been winnowed from it, and it is presented in all its naked simplicity, it will be sure to win the day; and I say again, speaking as a man, the gospel might have made a ten thousand fold greater progress, if it had been preached in all its simplicity, instead of that diluted or rather distorted form in which it is commonly proclaimed. If ye would see sinners saved, if ye would see God's elect gathered in, "Hold fast the form of sound words, which thou hast heard of me, in faith and love which is in Christ Jesus."

III. And now, very briefly, in the third place, LET ME WARN YOU OF TWO DANGERS.

One is, that you will be very much tempted to give up the form of sound words that you hold, *on account of the opposition you will meet with.* I do not prophesy that you will have corporeal persecution, though I know there are some poor creatures here that have to endure that from ungodly husbands, and such like; but you will all of you, in some measure, if you hold the truth, meet with the persecution of the tongue. You will be laughed at: your doctrine will be held up to ridicule, exhibited in a grotesque manner; you will be caricatured in all that you believe, and you will be sometimes tempted to say, "No I do not believe that," though all the while you do. Or if you do not positively say it, you will at times be led to turn a little, because the laughter you cannot stand, and the scoff of the worldly-wise is rather too hard for you. Oh! my beloved, let me warn you against being thus drawn aside. "Hold fast the form of sound words" in the midst of all ridicule. But the greatest obstacle you will have is a sort of slight and cunning, trying to pervert you to the belief, that your doctrine is the same with one which is just the very opposite. The enemy will try to persuade you that something he holds is quite harmless, though opposed to what you hold; and he will say, "You do not want to be broaching these things, that must bring forth controversy; there is a way of squaring your sentiments with mine." And you know we all like to be thought so liberal! The greatest pride in the world now is to be thought liberal in sentiment; and some of us would run a hundred miles, rather than be called a bigot or an Antinomian. I beseech you, be not drawn aside by those who are so ready to subvert your faith, not by openly attacking it, but by insidiously undermining every doctrine, saying, this does not signify, and that does not signify, while all the while they are trying to pull down every castle and fortress wherewith God has guarded his truth and his Church.

IV. And now, in the last place, I am to tell you of THE GREAT HOLDFASTS, WHEREBY YOU ARE TO HOLD FAST THE TRUTH OF THE GOSPEL.

If I might be allowed to mention one or two before coming to those in the text, I should say, in the first place, if you want to hold fast the truth, *seek to get an understanding of it.* A man cannot hold a thing fast, unless he has a good understanding of it. I never want you to have the faith of the collier who was asked what he believed; he said he believed what the Church believed. "Well, but what does the Church believe?" He said the Church believed what he believed, and he believed what the Church believed; and so it went all the way round. We do not want you to have that faith. It may be a very pertinacious faith, a very obstinate faith, but it is a very foolish faith. We want you to understand things, to get a true knowledge of them. The reason why men forsake truth for error is, that they have not really understood that truth; in nine cases out of ten they have not embraced it with enlightened minds. Let me exhort you, parents, as much as lieth in you, to give your children sound instruction in the great doctrines of the gospel of Christ. I believe that what Irving once said is a great truth. He said,

"In these modern times you boast and glory, and you think yourselves to be in a high and noble condition, because you have your Sabbath-schools and British-schools, and all kinds of schools for teaching youth. I tell you,"

he said,

119

"that philanthropic and great as these are, they are the ensigns of your disgrace; they show that your land is not a land where parents teach their children at home. They show you more is a want of parental instruction; and though they be blessed things, these Sabbath-schools, they are indications of something wrong, for it we all taught our children there would be no need of strangers to say to our children 'Know the Lord.'"

I trust you will never give up that excellent puritanical habit of catechising your children at home. Any father or mother who entirely gives up a child to the teaching of another has made a mistake. There is no teacher who wishes to absolve a parent from what he ought to do himself. He is an assistant, but he was never intended to be a substitute. Teach your children; bring up your old catechisms again, for they are after all blessed means of instruction, and the next generation shall outstrip those that have gone before it; for the reason why many of you are weak in the faith is this, you did not receive instruction in your youth in the great things of the gospel of Christ. If you had, you would have been so grounded, and settled, and firm in the faith, that nothing could by any means have moved you. I beseech you, then, understand truth, and then you will be more likely to hold fast by it.

But, then, Christian men, above all things, if you would hold fast the truth, *pray yourselves right into it.* The way to get a doctrine is to pray till you get it. An old divine says, "I have lost many things I learned in the house of God, but I never lost anything I ever learned in the closet." That which a man learns on his knees, with his Bible open, he will never forget. Well, have you ever bowed your knees, and said, "Open thou mind eyes, that I may behold wondrous things out of thy law?" If you have seen that wondrous thing you will never forget it. He that prays himself into a truth, will never be got out of it by the very devil himself, though he were to put on the garb of an angel of light. Pray yourselves into the truth.

But the two great holdfasts are here given—*faith and love.* If ye would hold the truth fast, put your faith in Jesus Christ, and have an ardent love towards him.

Believe the truth. Do not pretend to believe it, but believe it thoroughly. And he who does believe it, and fixes his faith first in Christ, and then in all Christ says, will not be likely to let it go. Why, we do not believe religion, most of us. We pretend to believe it, but we do not believe it with all our heart and all our soul, with all our might and all our strength—not with that "faith which is in Christ Jesus;" for if we did, come storms, come trials, like Luther of old, we should not flinch because of persecution, but stand fast in the evil day, having our faith fixed upon a rock.

And then the second holdfast is *love*. Love Christ and love Christ's truth because it is Christ's truth, for Christ's sake, and if you love the truth you will not let it go. It is very hard to turn a man away from the truth he loves. "Oh!" says one,

> "I cannot argue with you about it, but I cannot give it up: I love it, and cannot live without it; it is a part of myself, woven into my very nature; and though my opponent says that bread is not bread, and I cannot prove that it is, yet I know I go and eat it; it is wonderfully like it to me, and it takes away my hunger. He says that stream is not a pure stream; I cannot prove that it is, but I go and drink of it, and find it the river of the water of life to my soul."

And he tells me that my gospel is not a true one: well, it comforts me, it sustains me in my trials, it helps me to conquer sin and to keep down my evil passions, and brings me near to God, and if my gospel be not a true one, I wonder what sort of thing a true one is: mine is wonderfully like it, and I cannot suppose that a true gospel would produce better effects. That is the best thing to do, to believe the Word, to have so full a belief in it, that the enemy cannot pull you away. He may try to do it, but you will say,—

> "Amidst temptations sharp and long,
> My soul to the same refuge flies;
> Faith is my anchor, firm and strong
> When tempests blow or billows rise."

Hold on then, Christian, to "faith and love which are by Christ Jesus"—two blessed holdfasts, wherewith we grasp the truth.

And now, brethren and sisters. I pray that my Master will enable you to see the importance of what I have uttered. Perhaps you may not think it so important now, especially those of you who are young; but there are some here, the fathers of this church, who will tell you that the older they grow and the longer they live, the more they find truth to be valuable. They may perhaps in their youth have had a little radicalism in them with regard to truth, but they are conservative in their regard to the truth, we began to be conservative as soon as we believed it, and held it fast and never let it go. I think the chief fault of the present day is, that in seeking to be liberal we do not hold the truth firmly enough. I met some time ago with the case of an eminent minister in the gospel, a brother whom I respect and esteem, who preached a sermon from the text, "Prove all things." A young man was there who was professedly a believer in Christianity; but such was the style in which the subject was handled, that after hearing that sermon he went home and bought some infidel works, and the consequence is, that he has become entirely apostate even from virtue itself, and has forsaken everything that he once held to be true. I say, send your anchor right down, young Christian, and let whatever may come against you, hold on still by that truth; and you may yet even then "prove all things." But while you are doing it, remember to "hold fast that which is good." Do not "prove all things" by giving up that which is good to do it.

Now such of you as know not the Lord, if you ever are saved, let me tell you that the most likely place for you to meet with salvation is under a pure gospel ministry. Therefore there is a lesson for you. Attend where the gospel is preached.

Again: the most likely way for you ever to receive God's grace is to believe God's truths. Never kick against God's doctrines, but receive them. And I have one thing to say to thee this morning, if in thy heart, poor sinner, thou canst say, "I believe God's gospel to be a glorious gospel," thou art not far from something else. If thou canst say, "I submit to all its demands, I believe God just if he destroys me, and if he saves me, it will be of his sovereign mercy only," then, sinner, there are good hopes of thee; thou hast proceeded some way on the road to heaven. If thou canst but do one thing more, and say, "Though he slay me yet I trust in him," and if thou canst come to the cross of Christ, and say,

"Jesus, I love thy gospel and I love thy truth; if I perish, I will perish believing all thy truth, I will perish clasping thy cross; if I die, I will die owning that thou art a just and gracious God, and still in my poor way, holding fast the form of sound words,"

I tell thee, poor soul, God will never damn thee. If thou dost believe in Jesus Christ, and holdest fast his words, he will look upon thee in love, he will say,

"Poor soul! though he does not know that these truths are his, yet he thinks them precious; though he dares not hope that they belong to him, yet he will fight for them; though he does not know that he is really a soldier of the cross, chosen of me ere time began, yet see how valiantly he strives for me;"

and the Lord will say,

"Poor soul, thou lovest the things that thou thinkest are not thine own—I will make thee rejoice in them as thine own, by my grace; thou lovest election, though thou thinkest thou art not elect—that is an evidence that thou art mine."

"Believe on the Lord Jesus Christ, and be baptized, and thou shalt be saved."

And now, my brethren, stand fast, I beseech you. If my tears, if my bended knees, if my cries, yea, if my blood could prevail with you to lay to heart what I have said this morning, here should be tears, and cries, and blood too—if I could but make you all hold fast in these evil, perilous times. Hold fast, ah! with the tenacity of the dying hand of the sinking mariner—"Hold fast," I beseech you, "the form of sound words, which thou hast heard of me, in faith and love which is in Christ Jesus."

8

'That Day' and Its Disclosure

(Sermon No. 3531)

"The Lord grant unto him that he may find mercy from the Lord in that day" (2 Timothy 1:18).

GRATITUDE IS NEVER FAILING in Christians. When they have received a benefit, they are sure to acknowledge it. When Paul was at Rome, Onesiphorus found him out very diligently, and was not ashamed of his chains, but ministered to his necessities and, therefore, Paul felt bound to him and to his family in perpetual thankfulness. Let none of us ever be accused of ingratitude—it is one of the worst of sins. Paul, no doubt, would have done all he could for Onesiphorus in other ways, but he added to all other ways of showing his gratitude, that of praying for him—praying the prayer which we have here put on record in the Book of Inspiration. Learn hence that if we can do nothing else for our benefactors, we can bless them by our prayers. Let us be abundant in pouring out supplications before the Throne of God for all those who in any way have done us a service. We also learn from the text that the best of men have need to be prayed for. I cannot doubt but that Onesiphorus was saved. He seems to have been a most decided follower of Christ, for when others did not know Paul because he was a prisoner, Onesiphorus knew him. He sought him out—he sought him out diligently—even into the poorest quarters of that great city of Rome. He hunted him out, though probably the population at that time was not less, but perhaps far more than four millions of people. He found the Apostle and he ministered unto his need. He was a good man and yet Paul prayed for him—prayed for him a prayer which would be appropriate for a bad man, too, "The Lord grant that he may find mercy from the Lord in that day!" The best of us needs to be prayed for! Let us be thankful if we have anybody to pray for us. Let us count the prayers of the faithful to be our

124

truest riches. He is the happiest man who shall have the most of God's people lift up their hearts in prayer for him!

I call your attention, tonight, however, to none of these surrounding particulars. I want to fix your minds upon one thing. I desire, anxiously desire, that we may all be led to look forward to that day of which the Apostle here speaks. And our first point shall be that day. Then our second point shall be the mercy of that day. First, then—

I. "THAT DAY."

Paul speaks of the Day of Judgment here. He does not specify it, because it was so commonly believed in and expected among Christians, that it was quite sufficient for him to say, "that day." From the earliest times, wherever there has been Divine Light, that day has been expected. Enoch, also, the seventh from Adam, prophesied concerning the coming of the Lord. And his prophecy, though very early, was so clear that the Jew, who almost closes the Book of Inspiration, quotes it—feeling, I suppose, that he could not use words mode expressive than those which came from that ancient Prophet. All along the pages of Scriptural history you read of men raised up to tell of "that day." Asaph, in the Psalm we read just now, gave a most accurate description of that day when the Lord shall judge His people. And Daniel, when he saw the Throne of God set and the Ancient of Days come, perceived that day for which we also are now looking. Nothing, perhaps, is more often spoken of in Scripture than "that day." The New Testament teems with allusions to that Day of Judgment, when the Lord shall be revealed with flaming fire. I say it was so commonly understood that Paul had no need to say anything except, "that day." Questions will be asked tonight by some, "When will that day come?" to which I would answer, it were better for us to be prepared for it, come when it may, than to be anxious to fix its date! We can give you no information, because "of that day and of that hour knows no man— no, not even the angels of Heaven." After trying to discover what I can of the future, I arrive at this conclusion from Scripture, that the Lord would have us be in a state of perpetual vigilance and expectancy and, therefore, He has studded the Scriptures with phrases to the effect that He comes quickly. Truly His, "quickly," will not be the same as ours, but

I think the noontide of the world may have passed and these are the latter days—and we might to be looking for and hastening unto the coming of the Son of Man. He may come tomorrow! He may come tonight! He may delay His coming, but He shall come at such an hour as the mass of men think not, and at an hour when they are not aware! That day shall overtake them as a thief in the night, and come upon them as pain upon a woman in childbirth. Some may curiously ask whether the Day of Judgment will be a natural day or not. Will it be a day of twenty-four hours? To which we again reply, we have no information—but we know that one day is with the Lord as a thousand years, and a thousand years as one day. It will be a definite period. Whatever its length or brevity, it will suffice for an accurate judgment and a judgment of all mankind! Whether it shall occupy a thousand years or a single day, the work will be done—done thoroughly, done effectually, done forever—for all the race of Adam. Let us rest assured of that.

It is far more important for us to know these things about that day—first, that it will be ushered in as no other day has been. The day began in Eden with the rising sun. And when the sun's first beams had lit up the sky, the birds began to sing right joyously among the trees. But "that day" shall be ushered in, not by the rising sun, but by the Sun of Righteousness Himself! He shall arise with all the Glory of His Father and the holy angels shall come with Him. There will be sights and sounds on that tremendous morning such as never were seen or heard by mortal men before! Even Sinai's tremendous pomp, which made Moses fear and quake, shall be outdone in that dread day when the Lord shall descend from Heaven with a shout, with the trumpet of the archangel, and with the voice of God. It will be a day of days. Its dreadful surroundings are spoken of in Scripture, but, after all, words can but feebly describe them. It will be a day especially notable for the Revelation of our Lord and Savior, Jesus Christ! As yet He is hidden among the sons of men. He was as one concealed incognito. He traveled through this world and they counted Him a Man of Sorrows and acquainted with grief. He has gone into His Glory, but He is concealed at the right hand of God from the gaze of men below. They see Him not. They know Him not!

But in that day He shall sit upon the clouds of Heaven and every eye shall see Him—and they, also, who crucified Him. Then shall they say that He is Divine, and no longer shall they dare to dispute it! Then shall the Jew see that He is the Messiah who was to come and then shall the Gentile perceive that He is King of Kings and Lord of Lords! The flashings of His Glory shall convince all mankind—and the wicked shall stand speechless before His Judgment Seat! Pilate then shall not ask Him, "What is truth?" for he, alas, too late, shall perceive it! They shall bring no accusation against Him, then, for to their confusion they shall see that He was no traitor, but a King! Judas shall not sell Him, then, for he shall perceive, then, that he who sold Him was the son of perdition, to perish forever! Oh, what a day shall that be when, coming out of His chamber, rejoicing like a strong man to run a race, the Bridegroom of the Church shall appear, and all His saints shall appear with Him! It will be a day remarkable for its wonderful convictions. There will be a general assembly held on that day such as never has been held before! For, first, the Son of God shall be the center of all eyes, and around Him shall be His Father's angels. Heaven shall send her pomp to swell His train. He shall come and His saints, also, shall come with Him. The glorified shall come to sit with Him and then, as in a moment, the dead shall arise. I shall go into no minute questions or particulars, now, but certainly at that moment there shall stand upon the earth all the dead, both small and great—they that were on the earth buried in it and they that were in the sea shall all arise— and as the trumpet rings out clear and loud, the whole multitude of men that lived and died shall start up from their tombs to see their God upon His Throne! And those who are alive at that time—all shall come and live again—and the raised bodies of men and the spirits of the just! There shall come up from the infernal pit of Hell, lost spirits, too, and the chief foe of God and man, long scarred by Jehovah's lightning—he shall come and lift his brazen front once more, and the saints shall judge the fallen angel who long had persecuted them! He shall receive his final sentence and begin the utmost Hell which God had reserved for the devil and his angels, so that there on this poor planet, little compared with greater stars, and yet in God's sight most glorious of them all, there shall be a convocation of the three worlds! Heaven, Earth and Hell shall meet together, and Christ, in the midst of them all, shall judge the world in righteousness and the people with equity. Oh, what a day will that day be!

And it will be a day, in addition to the general convocation, of universal excitement. Next week the day of thanksgiving will move London from end to end, but there will be tens of thousands to whom it will be no day of thanksgiving, but perhaps of bitter sorrow. There will be nothing that could make them thankful in the pageantry of that day. So of all the days that have ever happened to the sons of men, there have been some unmoved thereby. Let us speak as though our soul were in every word—some of our Hearers will slumber, or their minds will wander. But on that day there will be no indifferent spectators of that tremendous pomp! The wicked shall wake up—their indifference shall have gone and they shall be filled with dismay and despair! They shall long for annihilation! They shall ask the rocks to cover them, and the mountains to conceal them. The righteous shall not be listless, either, for theirs shall be boldness in the Day of Judgment, and joy, and triumph, and acclamations of welcome with which they shall hail the King of Kings sitting upon His Throne! There will be a general excitement. Hell will howl its loudest howl and Heaven will resound with its loftiest songs on that closing day of the drama of time, that day of which the Apostle speaks!

And that will be a day of wondrous revelations. On that day we shall detect the hypocrite. See him yonder? The mask has fallen. See the leprosy on his brow? Then shall we see the men who were misrepresented, who were counted the off-scouring of all things, though of them the world was not worthy! The filth with which men pelted them in the pillory of scorn shall fall off and their garments shall be whiter than any fuller can make them in the Glory of the Righteousness which Christ shall put upon them! There will be a resurrection of reputations in that day. And at the same time there will be the judgment of mere profession. Perhaps in that hour we shall understand the Providence of God infinitely better than we do now. Then we shall see the evil of men's hearts as we never saw it, for every idle word that man has spoken shall be published there, and transgressions of midnight that were covered up with curtains of lies shall suddenly stand revealed as in the noonday sun—and the men who scorned the righteous and were themselves guilty of abominable sin! Oh, what a revealing day! The housetops, then, shall ring with secrets that have been hidden in the closet, and men shall read the writing, as it were, upon the sky, the dark sayings and the hidden things which were of old.

And then when the revealing shall have come, it will be a day of final judgment. From almost any court on earth there is an appeal. Even after the judge puts on the black cap and condemns the criminal, he yet appeals to public opinion and to the mercy from the nation, and perhaps an unworthy life may yet be spared. But from that Judgment Seat there shall be no appeal! Forever and forever fixed is the fate of men whom Christ has judged. "He that is filthy, let him be filthy, still, and he that is unrighteous let him be unrighteous still." No change can take place, and no appeal can ever be made. 'Tis done, 'tis sealed, 'tis inevitable. 'Tis over forever and forever—forever saved, or forever lost! That day, then, ought to be a matter of personal interest to everyone of my Hearers, yes, and to everyone beneath the sun. It will be the last day of time! Then there will be no more counting of rising and setting suns, no reckoning by waxing and waning moons. Then there will be no revolutions of the year to mark the period of time, nor will men count by centuries. It shall be eternity— one ocean of eternity without landmarks by which to say, "Thus far have we gone, and thus far have we yet to go." Oh, wondrous day! Oh! marvelous day! The last day of time, a day forever to be remembered— remembered by the wicked in Hell, to whom it shall be said, "Son, remember," and remembered, I think, by the righteous in Heaven forever, for they shall look back to that day when Christ appeared and they were declared to be the blessed of the Father to inherit the Kingdom prepared for them from before the foundation of the world! Oh, how I blame my tongue and chide myself that I cannot speak upon this theme as I would, but nevertheless may the solemn facts make up for my lack of speech and may they tell upon your souls! Now I must turn to the second point, and speak upon—

II. THE MERCY OF THAT DAY.

The mercy which is prayed for in this verse, "The Lord grant unto him that he may find mercy from the Lord in that day." Will that prayer be heard? Will that prayer be heard for me, for you, each one of you in this area, in these galleries? Will God have mercy on you in that day? I will tell you—

First, He will have no mercy in that day upon those who had no mercy upon others. If you cannot forgive, neither shall you be forgiven! If you cannot kneel down and sincerely pray, "Forgive us our debts as we forgive them that are indebted to us," then the gates of Heaven are fast barred against you! If you take your brother by the throat and say, "Pay me what you owe me," the great Master of us all will commit you to the tormentors, because your great debt has not been paid! Relentless, malicious, revengeful men, take heed of that! Lay it on your pillow tonight and let it pierce your heart—if you forgive not every man his brother, your heavenly Father will not forgive you!

Next, God will have no mercy in that day upon those who lived and died in wickedness. Here is the proof of it, "The wicked shall be turned into Hell," and Hell means not mercy, but misery! The men that have lied in the breaking of God's Law from day to day, from childhood to manhood, perhaps from manhood to old age, and have died still sinning—for them there shall be no mercy whatever! There shall be no mercy for those who neglect salvation. Again I give you God's words for it, "How shall we escape if we neglect so great a salvation?" These people had not done any particular mischief to anybody else. They had not persecuted Christ. They had not reviled His Gospel. They had not been heretics—they simply neglected the matter. "How shall you escape if you neglect so great a salvation?" You shall not escape at all! If you neglect His mercy, here, mercy will neglect you forever!

Then, again, they shall have no mercy who said they needed none. Are there not some here who fancy that they need no mercy from God? They do their best. They are excellent in character. They are well deserving and they expect to enter into Heaven through their good deeds. You seek no mercy, you shall have none! You proudly reject it. You trust to your own righteousness—you seek to have what you merit—you shall have what you merit—but that will be to be driven forever from the Presence of God! There cannot be mercy to those who will not confess that they need mercy. There shall be no mercy in that day for those who sought no mercy here. Prayer-less souls? You are graceless souls and mercy shall be denied you then! You will pray loudly enough then! Oh, how they pray in Hell! What tears and groans send they up to Heaven! They would gladly have mercy there, but Mercy's day is over—Justice has turned the key and hurled that key into the abyss where it can never be found! They are prisoners forever beneath the wrath of God! They who will not ask for it deserve not to have it. When mercy is to be had for the asking, if man turns upon his heels and refuses to ask, what shall God do but say, "Because I called and you refused—I stretched out My hand and no man regarded—I also will mock at your calamity. I will laugh when your fear comes"? There shall be no mercy for those who ask no mercy.

Further, there shall in that day be no mercy for those that scoffed at Christ, denied His dignity, railed at His people, broke His Sabbath and altogether abhorred His Gospel. Oh, Sirs, you fight a desperate battle against Him who made the heavens and the earth and who is the darling Son of God! In fighting against Christ, you dash yourselves upon the bosses of Jehovah's buckler! You cast yourselves upon the point of His spear! Be wise and stop your rebellion. "Kiss the Son lest He be angry, and you perish from the way when His wrath is kindled but a little." How shall the wax contend with the fire, or the thistles wage war with the flames? Yet you are doing this, O you that rebel against Christ! You shall either break or bow. Bow, I pray you, for if not, He shall break you with a rod of iron! He shall break you in pieces like a potter's vessel. Beware, you that despise Him, lest in the day of His coming He despises your image and you utterly perish.

There shall in that day be no mercy for those who refuse the Gospel. And I am sorry to say there are some here of that sort. Those cannot be said to refuse the Gospel who do not know it, but most of you do know it. I was thinking this afternoon, as I prayed God to let this subject get into my own soul, about some of you who do not lack for light and instruction, who do not need to know more about the way of salvation, or about the penalty of neglecting it. What you need is a new heart and a right spirit! You need your will subdued! You need decision of character! You need to be made thoughtful—you need to be made prayerful! I cannot do this for you, but I can warn you over and over and over again that they who go to Hell from under the shadow of the pulpit wherein there is an earnest ministry, go there with an emphasis! They that fall from the heights of privilege fall, indeed, into the Lake of Fire! God grant that not a solitary one of the many hearers who gather here may know what it is to have it said,

"It shall be more tolerable for Tyre and Sidon in the Day of Judgment than for you. They would have repented had they heard the gospel, but you heard it and repented not."

I must add to all this that there shall be no mercy in that day for those who have sold their Lord. "Where are they?" you ask. "Does there live on this earth a miscreant who has sold his Lord?" God have mercy on the man—he not only lives on earth, but he is here! He was once a professor, but he found it more profitable to cease from religion, and he has done so. He once came to the Communion Table, but he fell into lustful habits and he is no member of Christ. He has defiled the Temple of God—and God shall destroy him! He could sometimes pray in public—at the Prayer Meeting, but he dares not pray now—he has enough conscience left to let him cede from such hypocrisy! He sold his Lord for pleasure. He sold his Lord for money. He sold his Lord for the fear of man. "Verily I say unto you, he who is ashamed of Me and My Word, of him will I be ashamed when I shall come in the Glory of My Father and all My holy angels with Me." You know who spoke those words! They were spoken by Him whose hands were pierced! He has said it, and oh, note, you apostates, note it well, "He that denies Me before men, him will I deny before My Father who is in Heaven. Verily I say unto you, I never knew you! Depart from Me, you workers of iniquity." Oh, where is this unhappy man? May God have mercy on him, tonight, for He will have no mercy upon him in that day if he dies as he now is!

And I shall close that list by saying in that day God will have no mercy for false professors. He will have no mercy upon preachers who could talk glibly, but whose lives were not consistent with their own teaching. What a condemnation shall await me if I am not found in Christ after having preached so continuously to so many thousands! Oh, whatever a man shall be in Hell, may God grant he may never be an unfaithful minister of Christ, condemned out of his own mouth! But what shall I say of unfaithful deacons and Elders, and Church members? Their condemnation will be as just as it is terrible! Why needed they to add to their other sins the sin of a false profession? If they loved not Christ they need not have been traitors. There was no necessity for them to come forward and be baptized into the Triune name! There was no demand upon them to come to the Table in remembrance of Christ's death if they were not His! They voluntarily thrust themselves into a profession which was a lie and into the midst of a Church with which they were not akin. Surely if He begins first at the House of God, His judgments will be most terrible upon false professors! For this chaff there shall be the unquenchable fire, for it was once upon the Lord's threshing floor! For this dross there shall be consuming flames, for it was once in alliance with the precious gold which the King calls His own. I feel inclined to stop preaching and to pray for myself. The Lord have mercy upon me in that day! And then to take you all by name, if I could know you all, one by one, and kneel here and say, "The Lord have mercy upon this man—this woman—this child—in that day." But I beg you pray it for yourselves! Now, in the silence of your souls, let this prayer go up vehemently to Heaven, "O God, have mercy upon me! Have mercy upon me in that day and to that end have mercy upon me now."

I close, but I never like to close a sermon when it looks like Jeremiah's roll—written inside and outside with lamentations. Let us have a sweet word or two to finish with. We spoke of that day—for a moment let me speak of this day—of this day! You have not come to that day yet. Today it is not judgment, but love that rules the hour. Now the Great White Throne is not yet set, neither is there a trumpet that rings in your ears, but it is an affectionate voice which speaks to you and says, "Mercy is still to be had! Mercy is to be had by false professors! Mercy is to be had by apostates! Mercy is to be had by the very chief of sinners!" This is a night, this very night, in which prayer will be answered! God has said, "Seek and you shall find." This is a night in which Christ waits to be gracious! He is exalted on high on purpose to give repentance unto Israel, and remission of sins. This is a night in which sin may be forgiven! You are on praying ground—you are still on pleading terms! The sentence is not passed. The wax is still melted and it is not stamped and cold. There is hope for you! Better than that, there are kind invitations for you—there are loving exhortations! How long these may stand good, I cannot tell. As far as any one of us may be concerned, the Judgment Day may come tomorrow. It may come to all mankind—but as far as the practical fact is concerned—it may come in death to any one of us tonight. I look round me, now, and I remember a month ago certain seats in this place that were occupied by those that are now gone— gone to their account. If it were right, I think I could point my finger to some of you that are sitting in the places of dead men. They were their seats. They used to sit there, some of them, and they rejoiced in every word they heard! Is a sinner filling a saint's place?

There are some, again, that are gone out of this company who gave us no evidence of Grace. Alas, is there no sinner sitting in the place where one sat before him who forgot God? You are all passing away—I am passing with you. We are all shadows. We fly like an arrow through the air. We are a wind that passes and it is not. Oh, make sure of eternal things, Brothers and Sisters! Whatever you lose, lose not Christ! Whatever you miss, miss not salvation! May God impress you with this thought. May He impress you, moreover, with this thought—that, "today is the accepted time; today is the day of salvation"—and may some of you be unable to sleep tonight until you have found the Savior—

"For should swift death this night overtake you, And your couch become your tomb," then tomorrow, if unregenerate and unforgiven, you would be shut up where hope can never come to you! Oh, seek His face tonight! Dare not permit yourselves to feel the image of death upon you in sleep unless you have felt the scepter of Christ, touched by faith, communicate life and pardon to you! Seek Him! Oh, seek Him! Seek Him while He may be found! Call upon Him while He is near! The Lord bless you, everyone of you, and may we meet in Heaven without exception, for Christ's sake! Amen and Amen!

EXPOSITION OF 2 TIMOTHY 1:1-18

Verse 1. *Paul, an Apostle of Jesus Christ by the will of God, according to the promise of life which is in Christ Jesus.* Paul takes high ground. He is not an Apostle by the will of the Church, but an Apostle by the will of God! God's will is the great motive power in the Church of God. Some talk a great deal about man's will. What do you think of God's will, the will of the Almighty? Surely that shall stand! Paul felt that he had that at the back of him. "Paul, an Apostle of Jesus Christ by the will of God." Hence he always speaks very boldly. He never asks leave of anybody. If he is an Apostle by the will of God, he exercises his office without fear!

2. *To Timothy, my dearly beloved son Son in the faith.* When all the ties of natural descent shall be forgotten, son-ship in Christ will continue. I do not doubt that in Heaven Timothy is still Paul's son—Paul is still father to Timothy, for the relation is of the Spirit.

2. *Grace, mercy, and peace, from God the Father and Christ Jesus our Lord.* I think I have called upon you to notice that when Paul writes to a Church, it is, "Grace and peace." Whenever he writes to a minister, it is, "Grace, mercy, and peace." I have sometimes wondered whether we ministers need mercy more than other people, and I suppose that we do, or else the Apostle would not have said, "Grace, mercy, and peace." Oh, if a minister gets to Heaven, it will be a wonder!

His responsibilities are so great. "Who is sufficient for these things?" It will be a marvelous display of mercy if any of us shall be able to say at last, "I am clear of the blood of all men," for we have not only our own blood, but the blood of others to look to in this matter.

3. *I thank God, whom I serve from my forefathers with pure conscience, that without ceasing I have remembrance of you in my prayers night and day.* For this Paul

135

thanks God. He never forgot to pray for Timothy, and it is a matter of thankfulness. When we feel moved to pray, though it is for another, the spirit of prayer is essentially the same, whatever its object—and we ought to be thankful when we feel continually able to pray for a friend. "I thank God," he says, and he says that he had served God with a pure conscience all his days. So he had, but it was a blind conscience. At first, when he was a Pharisee, he still served God, though he then ignorantly persecuted the people of God! Oh, but it is a good thing sincerely to follow after God. May we be helped to do so. "I have remembrance of you in my prayers night and day."

4. *Greatly desiring to see you, being mindful of your tears, that I may be filled with joy.* What were those tears? Tears of holy men and women are as precious as diamonds! Paul had noticed the tears twinkling in brother Timothy's eyes—the tears of repentance, the tears of gratitude, the tears of fervent desire. He had noticed that and, being mindful of all this, he wished to see that dear face again! Christianity does not make us unsociable. It gives us new ties of love, fresh brothers, fresh sons.

5. *When I call to remembrance the unfeigned faith that is in you, which dwelt first in your grandmother Lois, and your mother Eunice: and I am persuaded that in you, also.* Happy son who has grandmother and mother before him in the faith! Unhappy young man who has quit the faith of his fathers and has turned aside altogether. If such are here, we would remember them in our prayers, but we cannot say that we can remember them with joy.

6. *Therefore I put you in remembrance that you stir up the gift of God which is in you by the putting on of my hands.* Stir up your gifts like a fire. It will not burn without sometimes poking. Stir it up! And every now and then it is a good thing to have the heart stirred up, awakened, quickened, brought to a higher diligence. We must try to do this. Perhaps there are some dear friends here who have a large measure of latent gifts, dormant faculties. Stir up the gift that is in you!

7. *For God has not given us the spirit of fear; but of power, and of love, and of a sound mind.* Neither Paul nor Timothy had a cowardly spirit. They were, neither of them, afraid. God had taught them His Truths and they knew them, and they held them, defying all opposition.

8. *Be not you, therefore, ashamed of the testimony of the Lord, nor of me, His prisoner.* What? Were people ashamed of Paul? Oh, yes, dear Friends. The great Apostle, because he was persecuted, found himself despised by some of the very people who owed their souls to him! It is the lot of those who are faithful to Christ to find even good men sometimes turning against them. But what of that? They are responsible to their Master, not to their fellow servants! Yet it is a hard thing when any come to be ashamed of you—ashamed of you, though you know that you have done right. I do not wonder that he puts it even to Timothy, "Be not you, therefore, ashamed of the testimony of our Lord, nor of me, His prisoner." Some of us know what it is to have trained and brought up those about us, who were to us what Timothy was to Paul—who have been ashamed of us and of the testimony of our Lord.

8. *But be you partaker of the afflictions of the Gospel according to the power of God.* You will need the power of God to do it, and mind you do it. Take your full share in whatever affliction the Gospel brings upon Christians. "According to the power of God."

9. *Who has saved us, and called us with an holy calling, not according to our works, but according to His own purpose and Grace, which was given us in Christ Jesus before the world began.* How plain it is that he earnestly believed in the eternal Election of Believers—in their being in Christ and in their possession of Grace in Christ. "Grace which was given us in Christ Jesus before the world began." God's love to His people is not a thing of yesterday! He loved them before the world was made and He will love them when the world has ceased to be. "It was given us in Christ Jesus before the world began."

10-12. *But is now made manifest by the appearing of our Savior Jesus Christ who has abolished death, and has brought life and immortality to light through the Gospel Whereunto I am appointed a preacher, and an Apostle and a teacher of the Gentiles. Indeed, for this cause I also suffer these things: nevertheless I am not ashamed: for I know whom I have believed, and am persuaded that He is able to keep that which I have committed unto Him against that day.* Paul knew that Grace could keep his soul, but I think that he here means that he could keep his own Gospel. Paul had kept it, kept the faith, but he committed it now into the hands of the Greater One, who would keep it when every Apostle was dead, and every faithful witness had passed away. "He is able to keep that which I have committed unto Him against that day."

13. *Hold fast thee form of sound words.* Many say they have no creeds, and there is hardly an Epistle in which there is not a distinct mention of a creed.

13. *Which you have heard of me, in faith and love which is in Christ Jesus.* Hold fast the Truth of God. Hold fast the very form and shape of it! If you are to keep the life that is in an egg, you must not break the shell. Take care of it all, and take care of it all the more when, with specious reasoning they say, "We will hold the same Truth of God, only in a different form." Why a different form at all, if they do not wish to hold a different Doctrine altogether? No, my Brothers, especially you that are like young Timothy, take this passage to heart. "Hold fast the form of sound words, which you have heard of me in faith and love which is in Christ Jesus."

14. *That good thing which was committed unto you keep by the Holy Spirit which dwells in us.* This is what we need! If the Holy Spirit is in us, we shall never trifle with the Truth. He is the lover and revealer of Truth, and we shall press the Doctrines of the Word of God and the Word of God, itself, nearer and nearer to our hearts in proportion as the Holy Spirit dwells in us!

15. *This you know, that all they who are in Asia have turned away from me;* What? Turned away from Paul? Some people think it is an awful thing because certain people turn away from a minister of Christ. It is not an awful thing at all, except for them! Paul stands fast—even he, the bravest of the brave—and they all turn aside from him. What of that? Does Paul flinch? No, not he! "This you know, that all they who are in Asia have turned away from me."

15. *Of whom are Phygellus and Hermogenes.* Two men who ought to have known better! Paul evidently fixed his eyes upon them—more bitter than others, more perverse, more cruel, more willfully guilty in turning aside from him.

16, 17. The Lord grant mercy unto the house of Onesiphorus; for he often refreshed me, and was not ashamed of my chains. But when he was in Rome, he sought me out very diligently, and found me. You could not tell in Rome where a prisoner was. The registers were not open to investigation. You had to go from prison to prison, and pay the guards to get admission, or to be told who might be there, but Onesiphorus was determined to find Paul. I suppose that he went to the Mamertine, a dungeon in which some of us have been—one dungeon under the bottom of another. The first one has no light, except through a round hole at the top. And the second has a round hole through which you drop into the lower one. We think that Paul was there. It is a tradition that he was. And then there is the Palatine prison, which was at the guard house of the Praetorian guards, near the palace on the Palatine Hill. There Paul certainly was, and Onesiphorus went from one jail to another. "Have you seen a little Jew with weak eyes?" I daresay that was his description of him. "He is a friend of mine. I want to speak with him." "What? That Paul?—the man that is chained to one or another of us every morning? We have twelve hours of it and he preaches to us most of the time! And we know it by the time we are let go again!" "Oh, that is the man," said Onesiphorus. "That is the man! Does he talk about Jesus Christ?" "Oh, nothing else but that. He will not let any soldier go from being bound to him without hearing about Jesus Christ." "That is my man," said Onesiphorus. He sought him out very diligently, and he found him!

18. The Lord grant unto him that he may find mercy from the Lord in that day: and in how many things he ministered unto me at Ephesus, you know very well.

9

A Good Soldier of Jesus Christ

(Sermon No. 938)

"A good soldier of Jesus Christ" (2 Timothy 2:3).

MANY MEN, MANY MIND. IN reference to what a Christian is there have been very many and diverse opinions. According to the notions of some, a Christian is an exquisite of remarkably delicate tastes. He cannot worship except it be in a place whose architecture is correctly Gothic, otherwise his dainty soul will be shocked. He is unable to offer prayer aright unless his devotions are uplifted upon the wings of the choicest music. And, even then, scarcely will he be successful unless he is aided by sundry gentlemen, whose pedigree, like that of racehorses, can be clearly traced, and whose garments the tailor has fashioned according to the directions of the ecclesiastical fashion book for the various seasons of the year.

If this is to be a Christian in these days, it must be confessed that Paul has said little concerning this delicate and artistic sort of creature, unless, indeed, he had reference to it in Galatians 4:9, 10, 11, which read at your leisure—neither would Paul's Master acknowledge it.

With some a Christian is a spiritual gourmet. He attends upon the ministry of the Word for no purpose but to be fed. He strongly denounces every sermon that is aimed at the conversion of sinners, for he looks even upon the Bible itself as a book solely intended to yield him personal consolation. The more any doctrinal teaching promises him a monopoly of good things, and the more it excludes others, the better he enjoys it— it being to him a particular part of the sweetness of the feast to believe that but a very slender company may dare to partake of it.

For him to live is to enjoy and not to serve. To gratify his selfishness he would blot out the free invitations of the Gospel. He is not a hearer only, but certainly he is not also a doer. He is a hearer and a feeder, in a certain coarse sense, upon the Word of God, and nothing more. That is not Paul's ideal of a Christian. He does not picture him with his napkin in his hand, sitting at a banquet table, but rather with a sword girt upon his thigh, ready for the conflict.

To some, the highest form of Christian is a great reader—a profound student of the best of books—for the purpose of composing spiritual riddles. He reads for no practical end. He is a picker-out of words, a speller-over of syllables, a magnifier of microscopic points, a proficient in biblical hair-splitting. The more a passage perplexes others the more sure he is of its meaning. He cares most for things which have the least practical bearing. He is a peeper through spiritual spyglasses, fancying that he can interpret what wiser men leave to God to expound. He is a hunter after spiritual conies, which, if caught, would never pay the huntsman for his toil, while the weightier matters he holds in small esteem. This does not seem to have been Paul's conception of a Christian. For the Apostle was no lover of foolish and unlearned questions which gender strife.

And I am afraid I must add that with some the ideal of a Christian is that of a man who can sleep out his existence in blissful serenity—a man who, having believed, or professed to believe in Christ—has settled his lifework forever, and from now on can say,

"Soul, take your ease, you have from now on much goods laid up for many years in your own security. Eat, drink, be merry in the Gospel. But as for feeding the hungry or clothing the naked, are you your brother's keeper? What is that to you? See you to yourself, and if you, yourself are right, let fate, or Providence, or Sovereignty, take care of the rest."

Paul does not appear to have pictured true Believers as sluggards sound asleep upon the downiest beds. His description of a Christian in the text is that of a soldier. And that means something far different either from a religious fop, whose best delight is music and millinery, or a theological critic who makes a man an offender for a word. Or a spiritual glutton who cares for nothing but a lifelong enjoyment of the fat things full of marrow. Or an ecclesiastical slumberer who longs only for peace

141

for himself. Paul represents him as a soldier and that, I say, is quite another thing.

For what is a soldier? A soldier is a practical man, a man who has work to do, and hard, stern work. He may sometimes, when he is at his ease, wear the fineries of war, but when he comes to real warfare he cares little enough for them. The dust and the smoke, and the garments rolled in blood—these are for those who go soldiering. And swords all hacked, and dented armor, and bruised shields—these are the things that mark the good, the practical, soldier. Truly to serve God, really to exhibit Christian graces, fully to achieve a lifework for Christ, actually to win souls—this is to bear fruit worthy of a Christian.

A soldier is a man of deeds, and not of words. He has to contend and fight. In war times his life knows little of luxurious ease. In the dead of night, perhaps, the trumpet sounds to boot and saddle—just at the time when he is most weary—and he must hurry to the attack just when he would best prefer to take his rest in sleep. The Christian is a soldier in an enemy's country always needing to stand on his watchtower, constantly to be contending, though not with flesh and blood—with far worse foes—namely, with spiritual wickedness in high places.

The Christian is a self-sacrificing man as the soldier must be. To protect his country, the soldier must expose his own bosom. To serve his King, he must be ready to lay down his life. Surely he is no Christian who never felt the spirit of self-sacrifice. If I live unto myself I am living unto the flesh, and of the flesh I shall reap corruption. Only he who lives to his God, to Christ, to the Truth of God, to the Church, and to the good old cause—only he is the man who can reckon himself at all to be a soldier of Jesus Christ.

A soldier is a serving man. He does not follow his own pleasure. He is under law and rule. Each hour of the day has its prescribed duty. And he must be obedient to the word of another and not to his own will and whim. Such is the Christian. We serve the Lord Jesus Christ. Though no longer the slaves of man so as to dread his frown, we are servants of Christ who has loosed our bonds.

The soldier is full often a suffering man. There are wounds, there are toils, there are frequent stays in the hospitals—there may be ghastly cuts which let the soul out with the blood. Such the Christian soldier must be ready to suffer, enduring hardship, not looking for pleasure of a worldly kind in this life, but counting it his pleasure to renounce his pleasure for Christ's sake. Once again, the true soldier is an ambitious being. He pants for honor, seeks for glory. On the field of strife he gathers his laurels, and amidst a thousand dangers he reaps renown.

The Christian is fired by higher ambitions than any earthly warrior ever knew. He sees a crown that can never fade. He loves a King who best of all is worthy to be served. He has a motive within him which moves him to the noble deeds—a Divine spirit impelling him to the most self-sacrificing actions. Thus you see the Christian is a soldier, and it is one of the main things in Christian life to contend earnestly for the faith, and to fight valorously against sin.

Paul does not exhort Timothy to be a common, or ordinary soldier, but to be a "good soldier of Jesus Christ." For all soldiers, and all true soldiers may not be good soldiers. There are men who are but just soldiers and nothing more. They only need sufficient temptation and they readily become cowardly, idle, useless and worthless. But he is the good soldier who is bravest of the brave, courageous at all times. He is zealous, does his duty with heart and earnestness. He is the good soldier of Jesus Christ who, through Divine Grace, aims to make himself as able to serve his Lord as shall be possible.

He tries to grow in Grace and to be perfected in every good word and work that he may be in his Master's battles fit for the roughest and sternest service, and ready to bear the very brunt of the fray. David had many soldiers, and good soldiers, too, but you remember it was said of many, "These attained not unto the first three." Now Paul, if I read him rightly, would have Timothy try to be of the first three, to be a good soldier. And surely I would, this morning, say to my dear comrades in the little army of Christ meeting here—let each one of us try to attain unto the first three. Let us ask to be numbered among the King's mighties, to do noble work for Him and honorable service, that we may bring to our

Master's cause fresh glory. Be it ours to covet earnestly the best gifts, and as we have had much forgiven, let us love much, and prove that love by action.

Before I proceed fully to open up this metaphor, let me say that though we shall use military terms this morning, and stirring speech, it should ever be remembered that we have no war against persons, and that the weapons which we use are not such as are forged for the deadly conflicts of mankind. The wars of a Christian are against principles, against sins, against the miseries of mankind, against that Evil One who has led man astray from his Maker. Our wars are against the iniquity which keeps man an enemy to himself. The weapons that we use are holy arguments and consecrated lives, devotion and prayer to God, teaching and example among the sons of men.

Ours is battling for the peace, and fighting for rest. We disturb the world to make it quiet, and turn it upside down to set it right. We pull down strongholds that they may not pull down the Zion of God. We dash down the mighty that the humble and the meek may be established. We have no sympathy with any other war, but count it an evil of the direst sort, let it be disguised as it may. Now with that caution, whatever I shall seem to say will not sound as though I loved or excused ordinary warfare—for nothing can be more abhorrent to the Christian man than wholesale slaughter. Nothing can be more desired by us than the promised era when men shall beat their swords into ploughshares, and their spears into pruning hooks.

Now let us come to the work of this morning. First, we shall describe a good soldier of Jesus Christ, and when we have done so, we shall exhort you to be such.

I. First, then, this morning, we shall endeavor TO DESCRIBE A GOOD SOLDIER OF JESUS CHRIST. We must begin with this fundamental—he must be loyal to his King. A soldier of Jesus Christ owns the Divine Redeemer as his King, and confesses His sole and undivided sovereignty in the spiritual kingdom. He abhors Antichrist in all its forms, and every principle that opposes itself to the reign of the Beloved Prince of Peace. Jesus is to him both Lord and God. The day when he enlisted, he did, as it were, put his finger into the print of the nails, and said with Thomas, "My Lord and my God."

This was his enlistment declaration, and he remains true to it. "Christ is All," is his motto, and to win all men to obedience to Immanuel is his lifework. Till he sheathes his sword in the last victory, the Crucified is sole monarch of his soul. For Him he lives, for Him he would even dare to die. He has entered into solemn league and covenant, to maintain against all comers that Jesus Christ is Lord to the glory of God the Father.

Moreover, the Christian soldier not only acknowledges Jesus to be his King, but his heart is full of loving devotion to Him as such. Nothing can make his heart leap like the mention of that august, that more than royal name. He remembers who Jesus is, the Son of God, "the Wonderful, the Counselor, the Mighty God." He remembers what Jesus did, how He loved him, and gave Himself for him. He looks to the Cross and remembers the streams of blood whereby the elect were redeemed, even when they were enemies of God. He remembers Christ in Heaven, enthroned at the right hand of the Father.

He loves Him there, and it ravishes his heart to think that God has highly exalted the once-despised and rejected One, and given Him a name that is above every name, that at the name of Jesus every knee shall bow, of things in Heaven, and things in earth, and things under the earth. He pants for the time when the Crucified shall come in His Glory, and rule the nations as their liege Lord. He loves Jesus so that he feels he belongs to Him altogether, bought with His blood, redeemed by His power, and comforted by His Presence. He delights to know that he is not his own, for he is bought with a price. And since he loves his King, and loves Him with an ardor unquenchable—for many waters cannot drown his love, neither can the floods quench it—he loves all the King's Brethren and servants for the King's sake.

He hails his Brethren in arms with hearty affection. He loves the grand old banner of the Gospel. He prays for the wind of the Holy Spirit to expand its furls, that all eyes may behold its beauties. He is steadfast in the faith once delivered to the saints, and rejoices so much at every doctrine of the Gospel that he would gladly lay down his life to preserve it to the world. Above all, he loves the crown of his King, and the cause of his Master. Oh, could he set the Captain of his salvation higher among men, he would be content to die in the ditch of neglect and scorn! Could he but see the King come to His own, and the Heir of all things loyally acknowledged by His revolted provinces, he would be satisfied whatever might become of himself. His heart is more than loyal, it is full of personal affection for the Chief among ten thousand.

I ask you, Brethren, whether it is so with you? Believing, yes, knowing that it is so with many, I would to God it were thus with all. Brethren, I know you love Jesus well, no music sounds to your ears so sweetly as His charming name. No song of choicest minstrel is half so sweet. The very thought of Him with rapture fills your breasts. Assuredly you have one of the first marks of good soldiers—go on, I pray you, to that which lies beyond.

The next characteristic of a good soldier is that he is obedient to his captain's commands. He would be no soldier at all who would not take his marching orders from his leader, but must needs act after his own mind. He would soon be dismissed from service, if not shot by order of a court martial for crimes which military rule cannot tolerate. Now, without enlarging on that illustration, let me ask every Christian here, and myself first of all, are we doing all the Master's will? Do we wish to know the Master's will? I should not like that any part of the Scripture should be distasteful to me. I would tremble if there were portions of my Lord's Testimony which I feared to read, or found it convenient to forget.

It is terrible when men are obliged to pass over certain texts, or else to cut and square them to make them agree with their beliefs. We should not practice an ordinance merely because our Church teaches it, or our parents believed in it. We must read the Scriptures and search the question for ourselves, or we are not respectful to our Lord. The soldier who did not take the trouble to read the orders of his superior might justly be suspected of mutinous intentions. Disobedience rankles in any heart where there is carelessness about knowing the Lord's will. Be courageous enough always to look Scripture in the face—it is, after all, nothing more than your bare duty.

Better for us that we changed our sentiments every day in order to be right, than that we held to them obstinately while we had some fear that perhaps we were wrong. To live a life of obedience is a greater matter than some suppose. Obedience is no second-rate virtue—"to obey is better than sacrifice, and to hearken than the fat of rams." "If you love Me"—what does Jesus say, "Go to the stake for Me," or, "Preach before kings for Me"? No, neither of these things is expressly selected, but "If you love Me, keep My commandments," as though this were the surest and most accepted test of love. May you thus, then, being loyal to the King, be in the second place obedient to His commands.

The third matter for a good soldier to mind is this—if he is, indeed, a first-class soldier, worthy of the service—to conquer will be his ruling passion. The fight is on, and the soldier's blood is up, and now he feels,

"I must drive the enemy from his entrenchment, I must take yonder redoubt. I must plant our conquering standard on the castle of the foe, or I must die. Accursed be the sun if he goes down this day and sees me turn my back upon the enemy."

He is resolved that he will win or lie cold and stark upon the battlefield. The Christian man, in order that he may win for Christ the souls of others, may make known Christ's Truth, may establish Christ's Church on fresh ground, is quite as ready to suffer or die as is the boldest member of the most renowned regiment.

To do this he disentangles himself as much as he can from all other ambitions and aims, "for he that wars, entangles not himself with the affairs of this life." With a good soldier of Christ the master passion is to spread the Gospel, to save souls from perishing—and he would sooner do this and be poor than be rich and neglect it. He would sooner be useful and live unknown than rank among the great ones of the earth and be useless to his Lord. A truly good soldier of Jesus Christ knows nothing about difficulties except as things to be surmounted. If his Master bids him perform exploits too hard for him, he draws upon the resources of Omnipotence, and achieves impossibilities.

Wellington sent word to his troops one night, "Ciudad Rodrigo must be taken tonight." And what do you think was the commentary of the British soldiers appointed for the attack? "Then," said they all, "we will do it." So when our great Captain sends round, as He does to us, the Word of command, "Go you into all the world and preach the Gospel to every creature," if we were all good soldiers of the Cross, we should say at once, "We will do it." However hard the task, since God Himself is with us to be our Captain, and Jesus the Priest of the Most High is with us to sound the trumpet, we will do it in Jehovah's name. May such dauntless resolution fire your breasts, my Brothers and Sisters, and may you thus prove yourselves "good soldiers of Jesus Christ."

The passion for victory with the soldier often makes him forget everything else. Before the battle of Waterloo, Picton had had two of his ribs smashed in at Quartre Bras, but he concealed this serious injury, and, though suffering intense agony, he rode at the head of his troops, and led one of the great charges which decided the fortunes of the day. He never left his post, but rode on till a ball crushed in his skull and penetrated to his brain. Then in the hot fight the hero fell. How few among us could thus endure hardness for Jesus? O that we felt we could suffer anything sooner than be turned aside from accomplishing our lifework for Him we love!

In that same battle one of our lieutenants, in the early part of the day, had his left forearm broken by a shot. He could not, therefore, hold the reins in his hand, but he seized them with his mouth and fought on till another shot broke the upper part of the arm to splinters, and it had to be amputated. But within two days there he was, with his arm still bleeding, and the wound all raw, riding at the head of his division. Brave things have been done among the soldiers of our country—O that such brave things were common among the armed men of the Church militant!

Would to God that in the teeth of suffering we could all persevere in living the holy life He bids us live, and in zealously spreading abroad that glorious Gospel which has saved our souls and which will save the souls of others. Great Master, by Your own example inspire us with this valor! I desire to see in this, our Beloved Church, more of you who are resolved that Christ's Gospel shall conquer this South of London. That it shall conquer the world! That Christ shall see of the travail of His soul and be satisfied. I long to witness more of that dogged perseverance among Christians which would make them work on and on, even without success, and persevere under every discouragement, until at last their Master shall give them their reward on earth, or else take them away to their reward in Heaven. To be a good soldier of Jesus Christ there must be a passion for victory, an insatiable greed for setting up the Throne of Jesus in the souls of men.

Fourthly, a good soldier is very brave at a charge. When the time comes and the orders are given for the good soldier to advance to the attack, he does not wish himself away. Though a perfect hail of hurtling shot whistles all around, and the ranks of the army are thinned, he is glad to be there—for he feels the stern joy that flushes the face in the light of battle—and he only wants to be within arm's length of the foe and to come to close quarters with him. So is it with the genuine Christian when his heart is right with God. If he is bid to advance, let the danger be what it may, he feels he is honored by having such a service allotted to him.

But are we all such? I fear not. How many of us are silent about Jesus Christ in private conversation? How little do we show forth our light before men. If we were good soldiers, such as we ought to be, we should select every favorable opportunity in private as well as in public communion with our fellow men, and prudently but yet zealously press the claims of Jesus Christ and His Gospel upon them. Oh, do this, Beloved, and good will come of it! We should each one be seeking to have his own special work for Jesus, and if no one else were attempting the task, we should, like the brave men who rush in to the storming of a battery, carry the flag first and plant it, knowing that there are hundreds of others who will follow the first brave man, who might not be able perhaps to lead the way themselves.

My Beloved, may you and I be ready for anything, and bold to bear witness for Christ before a scoffing world. In the pulpits where we preach, in the workshops where we labor, in the markets where we trade, in every company amidst which we are called to move—wherever we may be, may we be brave enough to own our Lord and to uphold His cause.

But this is not all that goes to make a good soldier. A good soldier is like a rock under attack. So British soldiers have been. They have stood in solid squares against the enemies' cavalry until their foes have dashed upon them madly, gnashed their teeth, fired in their faces, thrown their guns at them, and yet might just as well have ridden against granite rocks. For our soldiers did not know how to yield, and would not retreat. As fast as one fell another filled up the gap, and there stood the square of iron defying the rush of the foe.

We want this kind of fixed, resolved, persevering godliness in our Churches, and we shall have it if we are good soldiers of Jesus Christ. Alas, too many are exhausted by the zeal at first exhibited. For a time they can reach the highest point, but to continue on, and on, and on—this is too difficult a task for them. How many young people will join the Church and for awhile seem very zealous and then grow cold! Alas, it is not always the young, there are some among yourselves who were once most diligent in your various forms of service. What hinders you that you are not diligent in your Master's business now? Has Christ given you leave to retire into inglorious ease? Does He exempt you from service?

Take heed lest you are also exempt from reward. No, we must through all our Christian life maintain our integrity, resist temptation, tread the separated path, and seek the souls of men with undying ardor— with indefatigable earnestness—wrestling with God for men and with men for God. Oh, for more of this stern determination to stand, and having done all—to still stand!

The last mark of a really good soldier of Jesus Christ is that he derives his strength from on High. This has been true even of some common soldiers, for religious men, when they have sought strength from God, have been all the braver in the day of conflict. I like the story of Frederick the Great. When he overheard his favorite general engaged in prayer, and was about to utter a sneering remark, the fine old man, who never feared a foe, and did not even fear his majesty's jest, said, "Your

Majesty, I have just been asking aid from your Majesty's great Ally." He had been waiting upon God.

This is how Christians get the victory. They seek it from the Church's great Ally, and then go to the conflict sure that they shall win the day. He is the best Christian who is the best intercessor. He shall do the most who shall pray the best. In the battle of Salamanca, when Wellington bade one of his officers advance with his troops and occupy a gap which the Duke perceived in the lines of the French, the general rode up to him, and said, "My lord, I will do the work, but first give me a grasp of that conquering right hand of yours." He received a hearty grip, and away he rode to the deadly encounter.

Often has my soul said to her Captain, "My Lord, I will do that work if You will give me a grip of Your conquering right hand." Oh, what power it puts into a man when he gets a grip of Christ, and Christ gets a grip of him! Fellowship with Christ is the fountain of the Church's strength. Her power did never lie in her wealth, nor in the eloquence of her preachers, nor in anything that comes of man. The strength of the Church is Divine, and if she fails to draw strength from the Everlasting Hills, she becomes weak as water. Good soldiers of Jesus Christ, watch unto prayer, "praying in the Holy Spirit," for so shall you be strong in the Lord, and in the power of His might.

II. Thus I have in a very poor way described a good soldier of Jesus Christ. Give me a few minutes while I EXHORT YOU TO BE SUCH. And, mark you, I shall speak especially to the members of this Christian Church. I exhort you, dear Brethren, who are soldiers of Christ, to be good soldiers, because many of you have been so. Paul was likely to commend the Churches when he could, and I feel I may honestly and from my heart commend many of you, for you have served your Lord and Master well.

I know you have nothing whereof to glory, for when you have done all, you are unprofitable servants. But still I rejoice, and will rejoice when I see the work of the Holy Spirit in you. And I will venture to say that I have seen here instances of Apostolic ardor and self-sacrifice such as I have read of in ancient records, but hardly ever expected to see. There are those in this House this day who will shine as stars forever and ever, for they have turned many to righteousness. Dishonor not your past, I beseech you! Fall not from your high standing. "Forward" is your motto! Never think of declining, but rather advance in love to God, and in the ardor of your zeal.

Be good soldiers still, and depart not from your first love. I am sure there is greater need of good soldiering now than ever. Ten years ago, or sixteen years ago, when first I addressed you, the power of popery in this land was nothing compared to what it is now. In those days the Church of England was more generally Protestant. Now it is so frequently popish that I may broadly say that now we are afflicted with two popish churches—that of Rome and that of Oxford. The second one is not one whit better than the first—only more crafty and insidious—inasmuch as it attracts to itself a number of godly and gracious men who protect the villains who bear a Protestant name and who are doing the Pope's work.

I grieve to know that the evangelical clergy of England, by their continued union with the Church of England are acting as a shield to the ritualistic or popish party, and giving them every opportunity to work out their schemes for leading the nation back to popery *en masse*. Around this very spot a battle will have to be fought between the Sacramentarians and the lovers of the Gospel. At your very doors the battle is come at last. It was not so till but lately, but here it is—and you that are men must show your colors, and serve your Master against innumerable and constantly active foes. You have never failed me, you have always been bold and steadfast, and laborious, and so let it be, for the time requires it.

I can see on all hands that many of you young men are being attracted by the worldly amusements which surround us, for our dangers are not only those of popery, but those of the world, the flesh, and the devil. There must be greater earnestness and a deeper piety among you, or the next generation will become unworthy of yourselves—your grief—and not your joy. I pray you see to this. Be good soldiers, for much depends upon it. Your country will be blessed in proportion as you are earnest. Nonconformity in England will lose all its power if it loses its godliness. I do not care much for our political strength—I was about to say I am almost indifferent to our political rights—I care for them, but only so much as to occupy a very minor place in my consideration.

Our spirituality is the main matter. It is this, alone, that can make us a blessing to our country. Sons of the Puritans, you must walk with God, or your day is past—you will be swept away as Esther would have been, who came to the kingdom for the salvation of her nation—if she had not fulfilled the office for which God had exalted her. You have grown in numbers, grown in strength. O that you may grow in Grace, love the Gospel better, and love Christ better, for your country needs it, your children need it, you, yourselves need it! The times are perilous, and yet they are hopeful! By their peril, and by their hopefulness, I beseech you, be good soldiers of Jesus Christ! Good soldiers we ought to be, for it is a grand old cause that is at stake. It is the kingdom of God, it is the Church of Christ, it is the Word of God, the Truth, the doctrine of the Gospel, the crown of Jesus, that are all at stake.

I grant you that none shall ever shake the Throne of Jesus, for though "the heathen rage, and the people imagine a vain thing," yet shall His Throne be established. But we now speak according to the manner of men. God has been pleased to leave this matter to His Church, which is the pillar and ground of the Truth. Oh then! Stand up manfully, and fight earnestly when so much rests upon it! God grant that you may not be as the children of Ephraim, who being armed and carrying bows turned their backs in the day of battle.

I implore you, my Brethren, and mostly myself, to be good soldiers of Jesus when you consider the fame that has preceded you. A soldier, when he receives his colors, finds certain words embroidered on them to remind him of the former victories of the regiment in which he serves. Look at the eleventh chapter of Hebrews and see the long list of the triumphs of the faithful. Remember how Prophets and Apostles served God. Remember how martyrs joyfully laid down their lives. Look at the long line of the reformers and the confessors. Remember your martyred sires and covenanting fathers, and by the Grace of God I beseech you, walk not unworthy of your noble lineage.

Be good soldiers because of the victory which awaits you. Oh, it will be a grand thing to share in the ultimate triumph of Christ, for triumph He will! When all His soldiers shall come back from the war, and the King Himself at their head with the spoils of the victory. When they shall come back to the metropolitan city, to the ivory palaces of the great Captain. When the song is heard,

"Lift up your heads, O you gates, and be you lifted up, you everlasting doors."

When the question shall be answered, "Who is the King of Glory?" by the reply, "The Lord of Hosts, the Lord mighty in battle, He is the King of Glory," it will be a glorious thing to have shared the fight, for so surely you shall share the honors of that coronation day!

A crown is prepared for that head though it is now made to ache with care for the cause. There is a palm branch for that hand which now toils in the fight. There are silver sandals for those feet which have now to march over weary miles for Christ's sake. Honor and immortality not to be imagined till they are enjoyed await every faithful soldier of the Cross!

Besides, and lastly, if I want another argument to make you good soldiers, remember your Captain, the Captain whose wounded hands and pierced feet are tokens of His love to you. Redeemed from going down to the pit, what can you do sufficiently to show your gratitude? Assured of eternal Glory by-and-by, how can you sufficiently prove that you feel your indebtedness? Up, I pray you! By Him whose eyes are like a flame of fire, and yet were wet with tears—by Him on whose head are many crowns, and who yet wore the crown of thorns—by Him who is King of kings and Lord of lords, and yet bowed His head to death for you—resolve that to life's latest breath you will spend and be spent for His praise. The Lord grant that there may be many such in this Church—good soldiers of Jesus Christ.

Two or three words and I will close. At this present time I contemplate exhorting you to engage in fresh efforts for Christ. I do not know that you are relaxing, neither have I complaints to make of any. But

I would wish that we would commence with renewed vigor this day, if God so wills it. As I myself commence a new year of Sundays as to my own age, I desire to see a new era of greater exertion in the cause of Jesus Christ. And, in order that it may be successful, let not a single man or woman on the Church-roll be missing from his or her post in the spiritual conflict.

It is a remarkable fact that on the eve of a great battle in the Peninsular War the officers read the muster-roll, and noted that "not a man was missing." They had all good stomach for the fight, and were all there. You that are in the Sunday school, you that distribute your tracts, you that preach in the streets—every man to his post! And if you have no post as yet, find one—let there not be one idler, not one single loiterer, for a single sluggard may mar the work. Then if we are to be successful let nothing divide us. The motto of one of our most famous regiments embroidered on their banner is, "*Quis separabit.*" Who shall separate us?

We are but mortals, and, therefore, little jealousies may spring up. And among us there may be little causes of personal vexation, but brave warriors in the olden times who had fallen out have been known to come together on the eve of battle and say, "Come, let us be reconciled, we may die tomorrow. Besides, we join in common hatred of the foe and love to the king." Let your peace be unbroken, your union indissoluble, and God will bless you.

To help us to succeed now, let us lay down this one rule—let no low standard of work, or virtue, or spiritual attainment, content any one of us. Let us resolve to be as good Christians as can be found beneath the stars, as fond of Christ as human hearts can be, doing and giving as much for Christ as we can do or give consistently with other duties. Let us spare nothing, and keep back no part of the price. Let there be no Ananias and Sapphira among us, but all be as John, who loved his Lord. And Paul, who counted all things but loss for the excellency of Christ Jesus his Lord.

Next, let me say let the present moment be seized. I should like to saturate this district with a mass of tracts simply teaching the Gospel and protesting against the bastard popery around us. Heaven and earth are being raised around us just now. Our poor are being bribed, the houses of our members are being systematically visited with the view of decoying them from our worship. We are told that a certain small building used by the Episcopal body is the parish Church, and we ought to attend it. I might far more truthfully assert this to be the Church of the parish by the choice of a far more numerous body, but I care not to make pretensions which prove nothing.

The true question is—do we follow Christ, and uphold the teachings of Scripture? If so, our standing is unassailable. Doubtless the word has gone forth that Dissent must be crushed, but if we live near to God, and maintain our zeal, Dissent will rise invincible from every attack. Foreseeing the gathering storm, it is our consolation that we know where He dwells who is Master of the tempest, and can walk the waters for our help, and calm the sea around the weather-beaten boat. It becomes us now at this present moment to be indefatigable, to put forth all our strength for the Truth of God, even the Lord's pure Word in doctrine and in ordinance.

Let no man's heart fail him. There is no fear of defeat. Lo, these many years the Lord of Hosts has been with us as a Church, and He will still be our Helper. We have seen the rise and fall of many who blazed for awhile—but are now quenched in darkness—while we have increased from a handful to this mass, and God who has been our trust, and is still our stay, will not forsake us now. He has not drawn you together, and held you in one body by cords of love, that after all you may prove to be a powerless unwieldy mass of associated Christians. He intends to direct and strengthen you for nobler ends and purposes!

God, even our own God, will bless us! Immanuel, God with us, leads the van. The Truth, like the virgin daughter of Zion, shakes her head at boastful error, and laughs it to scorn. Let Falsehood put on her tawdry garments and think herself a queen, and say that she shall sit alone, and see no sorrow. Let Error come forth in her panoply and wave her flaunting banner before the sun. She draws near her end. Her armor— what is it? It is but pasteboard, and the lance of Truth shall pierce it through and through. Her banner, what is it but a foul rag of the Roman harlot? It shall be laid in the dust.

No, let Error bring forth all her hosts, and let them stand in their serried ranks, and through them the faithful soldiers of Jesus will ride and bow the columns like reeds in the wind. In these days, the doctrines and traditions of men compass us about, yes, like bees they compass us about, but in the name of the Lord will we destroy them. Only let us have confidence in God, and the victory is sure. As for the thought of turning back, that can never be endured. A message came to Sir Colin Campbell at the Alma, that Her Majesty's Guards were falling thick and fast beneath the shot, had they not better retire for a little while into safe quarters? The answer was, "It were better, Sir, that everyone of Her Majesty's Guards should lie dead on this battlefield than turn their backs on the enemy."

And it is so. Let us die, yes—it were to be devoutly wished rather than we lived a coward's life! Let the preacher first of all be carried to his grave. Let him never live to see the shame of this Israel. Let these eyes be sealed in death rather than behold "Ichabod" written on these walls! No, Brethren, it shall not be! You will serve Jesus, you will love Him, and "Onward to victory" shall be your watchword from today on. Be more in PRAYER—for this is the great matter. Seek out, each one, your own sphere of action—give yourselves wholly to it. And if any grow cold or careless, let him remember Jesus says,

"I stand at the door, and knock: if any man hear My voice, and open the door, I will come in to him, and will sup with him, and he with Me."

This blessed supping with Jesus will restore you! Though you are like Laodicea, "neither cold nor hot," fellowship with Jesus will renew the love of your espousals. Oh, then, my Brethren, in Jesus' name I bid you be strong in the Lord, and in the power of His might!

I have not preached to sinners, but you will do that if you catch the spirit of this sermon. There will be many thousands of words to sinners spoken as the result of this exhortation, if God, the Holy Spirit, makes it answer my design. Only this word to those who are not soldiers of Jesus Christ—trust Him now! Come now and kiss His silver scepter of Divine

Grace. He will forgive the rebel, and take him to be His servant. God bless you. Amen.

10

The Resurrection of Our Lord Jesus

(Sermon No. 1653)

"Remember that Jesus Christ of the seed of David was raised from the dead according to my Gospel" (2 Timothy 2:8).

ROM LONG SICKNESS my mind is scarcely equal to the work before me. Certainly, if I had ever sought after brilliance of thought or language, I should have failed, today, for I am almost at the lowest stage of incapacity. I have only been comforted in the thought of preaching to you this morning by the reflection that it is the doctrine, itself, which God blesses, and not the way in which it may be spoken—for if God had made the power to depend upon the speaker and his style, He would have chosen that the Resurrection, grandest of all the Truths of God, would have been proclaimed by angels rather than by men! Yet He set aside the seraph for the humbler creature.

After angels had spoken a word or two to the women, their testimony ceased. The most prominent testimony to the Resurrection of the Lord was, at first, that of holy women, and afterwards that of each one of the guileless men and women who made up the 500 or more whose privilege it was to have actually seen the risen Savior and who, therefore, could bear witness to what they had seen, though they may have been quite unable to describe with eloquence what they had beheld! Upon our Lord's rising I have nothing to say! And God's ministers have nothing to say beyond bearing witness to the fact that Jesus Christ of the seed of David was raised from the dead.

Put it in poetry. Proclaim it in sublime Miltonic verse—it will come to no more! Tell of it in monosyllables and write it so that little children may read it in their first spelling books and it will come to nothing less— "The Lord is risen, indeed!" is the sum and substance of our witness when we speak of our risen Redeemer. If we do but know the Truth of this

Resurrection and feel the power of it, our mode of utterance is of secondary consequence, for the Holy Spirit will bear witness to the Truth of God and cause it to produce fruit in the minds of our hearers.

Our present text is found in Paul's second letter to Timothy. The venerable minister is anxious about the young man who has preached with remarkable success and whom he regards, in some respects, as his successor. The old man is about to put off his tabernacle and he is concerned that his son in the Gospel should preach the same Truths of God as his father has preached—and should by no means adulterate the Gospel. A tendency showed itself in Timothy's day and the same tendency exists at this very hour—to try to get away from the simple matters of fact upon which our religion is built—to something more philosophical and hard to be understood.

The Word of God which the common people heard gladly is not fine enough for cultured sages and so they must surround it with a mist of human thought and speculation. Three or four plain facts constitute the Gospel, even as Paul puts it in the 5th chapter of his first Epistle to the Corinthians—

"For I delivered unto you, first of all, that which I also received, how that Christ died for our sins according to the Scriptures; and that He was buried, and that He rose again the third day according to the Scriptures."

Upon the Incarnation, life, death and Resurrection of Jesus, our salvation hinges. He who believes these Truths of God, aright, has believed the Gospel and, believing the Gospel, he shall without doubt find eternal salvation!

But men want novelties. They cannot endure that the trumpet should give forth the same certain sound! They crave some fresh fantasia every day. "The Gospel with variations" is the music for them! Intellect is progressive, they say; they must, therefore, march ahead of their forefathers. Incarnate Deity, a holy life, an atoning death and a literal Resurrection—having heard these things, now, for nearly nineteen centuries, they are just a little stale—and the cultivated mind hungers for a change from the old-fashioned manna. Even in Paul's day this tendency was manifest and so they sought to regard facts as mysteries or parables—and they labored to find a spiritual meaning in them till they went so far as to deny them as actual facts!

Seeking an ambiguous meaning, they overlooked the fact, itself, losing the substance in a foolish preference for the shadow. While God set before them glorious events which fill Heaven with amazement, they showed their foolish wisdom by accepting the plain historical facts as myths to be interpreted or riddles to be solved. He who believed as a little child was pushed aside as a fool, that the disputer and the scribe might come in to mystify simplicity and hide the light of the Truth of God! Hence there had arisen a certain Hymenaeus and Philetus, "Who concerning the truth have erred, saying that the Resurrection is already past; and overthrow the faith of some." Turn to verse 17 and read for yourselves. They spirited away the Resurrection! They made it to mean something very deep and mystical—and in the process they took away the actual Resurrection altogether.

Among men there is still a craving after new meanings, refinements upon old doctrines, and spiritualization of literal facts. They tear out the heart of the Truth of God and give us the carcass stuffed with hypotheses, speculations and larger hopes. The golden shields of Solomon are taken away and shields of brass are hung up in their place—will they not answer every purpose—and is not the metal more in favor with the age? It may be so, but we never admired Rehoboam and we are old-fashioned enough to prefer the original shields of gold! The Apostle Paul was very anxious that Timothy should stand firm to the old witness and should understand, in their plain meaning, his testimonies to the fact that Jesus Christ of the seed of David rose again from the dead.

Within the compass of this verse several facts are recorded and, first, there is here the great Truth of God that Jesus, the Son of the Highest, was anointed of God. The Apostle calls Him "Jesus Christ," that is, the Anointed One, the Messiah, the Sent of God. He calls Him, also, "Jesus," which signifies a Savior, and it is a grand Truth that He who was born of Mary; He who was laid in the manger at Bethlehem; He who loved and lived and died for us, is the ordained and anointed Savior of men! We have not a moment's doubt about the mission, office and design of our Lord Jesus! In fact, we hang our soul's salvation upon His being anointed of the Lord to be the Savior of men!

This Jesus Christ was really and truly Man, for Paul says He was "of the seed of David." True He was Divine and His birth was not after the ordinary manner of men, but still, He was, in all respects, partaker of our human nature and came of the stock of David. This, also, we believe. We are not among those who spiritualize the Incarnation and suppose that God was here as a phantom, or that the whole story is but an instructive legend. No, in very flesh and blood did the Son of God abide among men! He was bone of our bone and flesh of our flesh in the days of His sojourn here below. We know and believe that Jesus Christ has come in the flesh. We love the Incarnate God and in Him we fix our trust.

It is implied, too, in the text, that Jesus died, for He could not be raised from the dead if He had not first gone down among the dead and been one of them! Yes, Jesus died—the Crucifixion was no delusion, the piercing of His side with a spear was most clear and evident proof that He was dead—His heart was pierced and the blood and water flowed from them. As a dead Man, He was taken down from the Cross and carried by gentle hands and laid in Joseph's virgin tomb. I think I see that pale corpse, white as a lily! Mark how it is stained with the blood of His five wounds which make Him red as the rose. See how the holy women tenderly wrap Him in fine linen with sweet spices and leave Him to spend His Sabbath all alone in the rock-hewn sepulcher.

No man in this world was ever more surely dead than He. "He made His grave with the wicked and with the rich in His death." As dead they laid Him in the place of the dead, with napkin and grave clothes fit for a grave. Then they rolled the great stone at the grave's mouth and left Him, knowing that He was dead. Then comes the grand Truth of God, that as soon as the third sun commenced, Jesus rose again! His body had not decayed, for it was not possible for that Holy Thing to see corruption! But still, it had been dead and, by the power of God, by His own power, by the Father's power, by the power of the Spirit—for it is attributed to each of these in turn—before the sun had risen, His dead body was quickened!

The silent heart began to beat, again, and through the stagnant canals of the veins, the life-flood began to circulate. The soul of the Redeemer again took possession of the body and it lived once more! There He was within the sepulcher, as truly living as to all parts of Him as He had ever been! He literally and truly, in a material body, came forth from the tomb to live among men till the hour of His Ascension into Heaven! This is the Truth of God which is still to be taught, refine it who may, spiritualize it who dare! This is the historical fact which the Apostles witnessed! This is the Truth of God for which the confessors bled and died! This is the doctrine which is the keystone of the arch of Christianity! And they that hold it not have cast aside the essential Truth of God. How can they hope for salvation for their souls if they do not believe that "the Lord is risen, indeed"?

This morning I wish to do three things. First, let us consider the bearings of the Resurrection of Christ upon other great Truths of God. Secondly, let us consider the bearings of this fact upon the Gospel, for it has such bearings, according to the text—"Jesus Christ of the seed of David was raised from the dead according to my Gospel." And thirdly, let us consider its bearings on ourselves, which are all indicated in the word, "Remember."

I. First, then, Beloved, as God shall help us, let us CONSIDER THE BEARINGS OF THE FACT THAT JESUS ROSE FROM THE DEAD. It is clear at the outset that the Resurrection of our Lord was a tangible proof that there is another life. Have you not quoted a great many times certain lines about, "That undiscovered country from whose journey no traveler returns"? It is not so! There was once a Traveler who said, "I go to prepare a place for you, and if I go away I will come again and receive you unto Myself; that where I am there you may be also."

He said, "A little time and you shall see Me, and again a little time and you shall not see Me because I go to the Father." Do you not remember these words of His? Our Divine Lord went to the undiscovered country and He returned! He said that at the third day He would be back, again, and He was true to His Word! There is no doubt that there is another state for human life, for Jesus has been in it and has come back from it! We have no doubt as to a future existence, for Jesus existed after death! We have no doubt as to a Paradise of future bliss, for Jesus went to it and returned! Though He has left us, again, yet that coming back to tarry with us forty days assures us that He will return a second time, when the hour is due, and then pledge with us for a thousand years and reign gloriously on earth amongst His ancients!

His return from among the dead is a pledge to us of existence after death and we rejoice in it! His Resurrection is also a pledge that the body will surely live, again, and rise to a superior condition, for the body of our blessed Master was no phantom after death any more than before. "Handle Me, and see." Oh wondrous proof! He said, "Handle Me, and see"! And then to Thomas, "Reach here your finger, and behold My hands; and reach here your hand, and thrust it into My side." What deception is possible here? The risen Jesus was no mere spirit! He promptly cried, "A spirit has not flesh and bones, as you see I have." "Bring Me," He said, "something to eat." And as if to show how real His body was, though He did not need to eat, yet He did eat—and a piece of a broiled fish and honeycomb were proofs of the reality of the act!

Now, the body of our Lord in its risen state did not exhibit the whole of His glorification, for otherwise we should have seen John falling at His feet as dead! And we should have seen all His disciples overcome with the Glory of the vision! But, still, in a great measure, we may call the 40 days' sojourn—"The life of Jesus in His Glory upon earth." He was no longer despised and rejected of men, but a Glory surrounded Him. It is evident that the raised body passed from place to place in a single moment; that it appeared and vanished at will and was superior to the laws of matter. The risen body was incapable of pain, of hunger, thirst, or weariness during the time in which it remained here below—fit representative of the bulk of which it was the first fruits.

Of our body, also, it shall be said before long, "It was sown in weakness, it is raised in power: it was sown in dishonor, it is raised in Glory." Let us, then, as we think of the risen Christ, rest quite sure of a future life and quite sure that our body will exist in it in a glorified condition! I do not know whether you are ever troubled with doubts in connection with the world to come—as to whether it can be true that we shall live eternally. Here is the point which makes death so terrible to doubters, for while they have realized the grave, they have not realized the life beyond it! Now, the best help to that realization is a firm grip of the fact that Jesus died and Jesus rose again.

This fact is proved better than any other event in history! The witness to it is far stronger than to anything else that is written either in profane or sacred records. The rising of our Lord Jesus Christ being certain, you may rest assured of the existence of another world! That is the first bearing of this great Truth of God. Secondly, Christ's rising from the dead was the seal to all His claims. It was true, then, that He was sent of God, for God raised Him from the dead in confirmation of His mission. He had said, Himself, "Destroy this body, and in three days I will raise it up." Look, there He is—the Temple of His body is rebuilt! He had even given this as a sign, that as Jonas was three days and three nights in the whale's belly, so should the Son of Man be three days and three nights in the heart of the earth—and should then come forth to life again.

Behold His own appointed sign fulfilled! Before men's eye the seal is manifest! Suppose He had never risen? You and I might have believed in the truth of a certain mission which God had given Him, but we could never have believed in the truth of such a commission as He claimed to have received—a commission to be our Redeemer from death and Hell! How could He be our Ransom from the grave if He had, Himself, remained under the dominion of death? Dear Friends, the rising of Christ from the dead proved that this Man was innocent of every sin! He could not be held by the bands of death, for there was no sin to make those bands fast! Corruption could not touch His pure body, for no original sin had defiled the Holy One! Death could not keep Him a continual prisoner because He had not actually come under sin! And though He took sin of ours and bore it by imputation and, therefore, died, yet He had no fault of His own and must, therefore, be set free when His imputed load had been removed.

Moreover, Christ's rising from the dead proved His claim to Deity. We are told in another place that He was proved to be the Son of God with power by the Resurrection from the dead. He raised Himself by His own power and though the Father and the Holy Spirit were cooperative with Him and, therefore, His Resurrection is ascribed to them, too, yet it was because the Father had given Him to have life in Himself that, therefore, He arose from the dead! Oh, risen Savior, Your rising is the seal of Your work! We can have no doubt about You now that You have left the tomb! Prophet of Nazareth, You are, indeed, the Christ of God, for God has loosed the bands of death for You! Son of David, You are, indeed, the elect and precious One, for You live forever! Your Resurrection life has set the sign-manual of Heaven to all that You have said and done, and for this we bless and magnify Your name.

A third bearing of His Resurrection is this—and it is a very grand one—the Resurrection of our Lord, according to Scripture, was the acceptance of His Sacrifice. By the Lord Jesus Christ rising from the dead, evidence was given that He had fully endured the penalty which was due to human guilt. "The soul that sins, it shall die"—that is the determination of the God of Heaven! Jesus stands in the sinner's place and dies—and when He has done that, nothing more can be demanded of Him, for he that is dead is free from the Law of God. You take a man who has been guilty of a capital offense. He is condemned to be hanged. He is hanged by the neck till he is dead—what more has the Law to do with him? It has done with him, for it has executed its sentence upon him.

If he can be brought back to life, he is clear from the Law. No writ that runs in Her Majesty's dominions can touch him—he has suffered the penalty. So when our Lord Jesus rose from the dead, after having died, He had fully paid the penalty that was due to Justice for the sin of His people and His new life was a life clear of penalty, free from liability. You and I are clear from the claims of the Law of God because Jesus stood in our place and God will not exact payment both from us and from our Substitute! It were contrary to justice to sue both the Surety and those for whom He stood! And now, joy upon joy! The burden of liability which once did lie upon the Substitute is removed from Him, also, seeing He has, by the suffering of death, vindicated Justice and made satisfaction to the injured Law of God!

Now both the sinner and the Surety are free! This is a great joy, a joy for which to make the golden harps ring out a loftier style of music. He who took our debt has now delivered Himself from it by dying on the Cross. His new life, now that He has risen from the dead, is a life free from legal claims and it is the token to us that we whom He represented are also free! Listen! "Who shall lay anything to the charge of God's elect? It is God that justifies, who is he that condemns? It is Christ that died, yes, rather, that is risen again." It is a knockdown blow to fear when the Apostle says that we cannot be condemned because Christ has died in our place, but he puts a double force into it when he cries, "Yes, rather, that is risen again!"

If Satan, therefore, shall come to any Believer and say, "What about your sins?" Tell him Jesus died for them and your sins are put away. If he come a second time and says to you, "What about your sins?" Answer him, "Jesus lives, and His life is the assurance of my justification; for if our Surety had not paid the debt, He would still be under the power of Death." Inasmuch as Jesus has discharged all our liabilities and left not one farthing due to God's Justice from one of His people, we live and are clear—and we live in Him and are clear, also, by virtue of our union with Him. Is not this a glorious doctrine, this doctrine of the Resurrection, in its bearing upon the justification of the saints? The Lord Jesus gave Himself for our sins, but He rose again for our justification!

Bear with me while I notice, next, another bearing of this Resurrection of Christ. It was a guarantee of His people's resurrection. There is a great Truth of God that never is to be forgotten, namely, that Christ and His people are one, just as Adam and all his seed are one. That which Adam did, he did as a head for a body—and as our Lord Jesus and all Believers are one—that which Jesus did, He did as a Head for a body. We were crucified together with Christ! We were buried with Christ! And we are risen together with Him! Yes, He has raised us up together and made us sit together in the heavenly places in Christ Jesus! He says, "Because I live, you shall live also."

If Christ is not raised from the dead, your faith is in vain and our preaching is in vain! And you are yet in your sins! And those that have fallen asleep in Christ have perished—and you will perish, too! But if Christ has been raised from the dead, then all His people must be raised, also—it is a matter of Gospel necessity! There is no logic more imperative than the argument drawn from union with Christ. God has made the saints one with Christ—and if Christ has risen, all the saints must rise, too! My soul takes firm hold on this and as she strengthens her grasp, she loses all fear of death!

Now we bear our dear ones to the cemetery and leave them, each one in his narrow cell, calmly bidding them farewell and saying—

"So Jesus slept—God's dying Son,
Passed through the grave and blest the bed!
Rest here, dear saint, till from His throne,
The morning breaks and pierces the shade."

It is not merely ours to know that our Brothers and Sisters are living in Heaven, but also that their mortal parts are in Divine custody, securely kept till the appointed hour when the body shall be reanimated and the perfect man shall enjoy the adoption of God! We are sure that our dead men shall live—together with Christ's dead body they shall rise! No power can hold in durance the redeemed of the Lord. "Let My people go" shall be a command as much obeyed by Death as once by the humbled Pharaoh who could not hold a single Israelite in bonds! The day of deliverance comes quickly—

"Break from His throne, illustrious morn! Attend, O earth, His sovereign Word! Restore your trust, a glorious form He must ascend to meet His Lord."

Once more, our Lord's rising from the dead is a fair picture of the new life which all Believers already enjoy. Beloved, though this body is still subject to bondage like the rest of the visible creation, according to the Law of God stated in Scripture, "the body is dead because of sin," yet, "the spirit is life because of righteousness." The regeneration which has taken place in those who believe has changed our spirit and given to it eternal life! But it has not affected our body further than this—that it has made it to be the Temple of the Holy Spirit and thus it is a holy thing—and cannot be obnoxious to the Lord, or swept away among unholy things.

But the body is still subject to pain and weariness, and to the supreme sentence of death. Not so the spirit! There is already within us a part of the resurrection accomplished, since it is written, "And you has He quickened who were dead in trespasses and sins." You once were like the ungodly—under the Law of sin and death—but you have been brought out of the bondage of corruption into the liberty of life and Grace, the Lord, having worked in you gloriously, "according to the working of His mighty power, which He worked in Christ, when He raised Him from the dead, and set Him at His own right hand in the heavenly places."

Now, just as Jesus Christ led, after His Resurrection, a life very different from that before His death, so you and I are called upon to live a high and noble spiritual and heavenly life, seeing that we have been raised from the dead to die no more! Let us joy and rejoice in this! Let us behave as those who are alive from the dead—the happy children of the Resurrection of Christ! Do not let us be money-grubbers, or hunters after worldly fame. Let us not set our affections on the foul things of this dead and rotten world, but let our hearts fly upward, like young birds that have broken loose of their shells—upward towards our Lord and the heavenly things upon which He would have us set our minds! Living truth, living work, living faith—these are the things for living men—let us cast off the grave clothes of our former lusts and wear the garments of light and life! May the Spirit of God help us in further meditating upon these things at home.

II. Now, secondly, LET US CONSIDER THE BEARINGS OF THIS FACT OF THE RESURRECTION UPON THE GOSPEL, for Paul says, "Jesus Christ was raised from the dead according to my Gospel." I always like to see what way any kind of statement bears on the Gospel. I may not have many more opportunities of preaching and I have made up my mind to this one thing—that I will waste no time upon secondary themes—and when I do preach, it shall be the Gospel, or something very closely bearing upon it.

I will endeavor, each time I preach, to strike under the fifth rib and never beat the air. Those who have a taste for the superfluities may take their fill of them—it is for me to keep to the great necessary Truths of God by which men's souls are saved! My work is to preach Christ Crucified and the Gospel which gives men salvation through faith! I hear, every now and then, of some preaching sermons about some bright new nothing or another. Some preachers remind me of the emperor who had a wonderful skill in carving men's heads upon cherry stones! What a multitude of preachers we have who can make wonderfully fine discourses out of a mere passing thought of no consequence to anyone!

But we need the Gospel! We have to live and die—and we must have the Gospel! Certain of us may be cold in our graves before many weeks are over and we cannot afford to toy and trifle—we need to see the bearings of all teachings upon our eternal destinies and upon the Gospel which sheds its light over our future! The Resurrection of Christ is vital because, first it tells us that the Gospel is the Gospel of a living Savior. We have not to send poor penitents to the crucifix, the dead image of a dead man!

We say not, "These are your gods, O Israel!" We have not to send you to a little baby Christ nursed by a woman! Nothing of the sort! Behold the Lord that lives and was dead and is alive forevermore! Behold our Master who has the keys of Hell and of death! Behold in Him a living and accessible Savior who, out of Glory still cries with loving accents, "Come unto Me, all you that labor and are heavy laden, and I will give you rest." "He is able also to save them to the uttermost that come unto God by Him, seeing He ever lives to make intercession for them." I say we have a living Savior—and is not this a glorious feature of the Gospel?

Notice, next, that we have a powerful Savior in connection with the Gospel that we preach, for He who had power to raise Himself from the dead has all power now that He is raised! He who in death vanquishes death, can much more conquer by His life! He who being in the grave did, nevertheless, burst all its bonds, can assuredly deliver all His people! He who, coming under the power of the Law of God, did, nevertheless, fulfill the Law, and thus set His people free from bondage, must be mighty to save! You need a Savior strong and mighty, yet you do not need one stronger than He of whom it is written that He rose again from the dead! What a blessed Gospel we have to preach—the Gospel of a living Christ who has returned from the dead leading captivity captive!

And now notice that we have the Gospel of complete justification to preach to you. We do not come and say, "Brethren, Jesus Christ, by His death, did something by which men may be saved, if they have a mind to be, and diligently carry out their good resolves." No, no! We say Jesus Christ took the sins of His people upon Himself and bore the consequences of them in His own body on the Cross—so that He died— and having died and paid the penalty, He lives again! And now all for whom He died, all His people whose sins He bore, are free from the guilt of sin! You ask me, "Who are they?" and I reply, as many as believe on Him!

Whoever believes in Jesus Christ is as free from the guilt of sin as Christ is! Our Lord Jesus took the sins of His people and died in the sinner's place—and now being, Himself, set free, all His people are set free in their Representative! This doctrine is worth preaching! One may well rise from his bed to talk about perfect Justification through faith in Christ Jesus! One might as well stay asleep as rise to say that Jesus accomplished little or nothing by His passion and His Resurrection! Some seem to dream that Jesus made some little opening by which we have a slight chance of reaching pardon and eternal life if we are diligent for many years. This is not our Gospel! Jesus has saved His people! He has performed the work entrusted to Him! He has finished transgression and made an end of sin! And He has brought in everlasting righteousness— and whoever believes in Him is not condemned and never can be!

Once again, the connection of the Resurrection and the Gospel is this—it proves the safely of the saints, for if when Christ rose, His people rose, also, they rose to a life like that of their Lord—and therefore they can never die. It is written, "Christ being raised from the dead dies no more; death has no more dominion over Him," and it is so with the Believer! If you have been dead with Christ and are risen with Christ, death has no more dominion over you! You shall never go back to the beggarly elements of sin! You shall never become what you were before your regeneration! You shall never perish, neither shall any pluck you out of Jesus' hands. He has put within you a living and incorruptible Seed which lives and abides forever! He says, Himself, "The water that I shall give him shall be in him a well of living water springing up unto everlasting life." Therefore hold fast to this and let the Resurrection of your Lord be the pledge of your own final perseverance!

Brothers and Sisters, I cannot stop to show you how this Resurrection touches the Gospel at every point, but Paul is always full of it. More than thirty times Paul talks about the Resurrection and, occasionally, at great length, giving whole chapters to the glorious theme! The more I think of it, the more I delight to preach Jesus and the Resurrection! The glad tidings that Christ has risen is as truly the Gospel as the doctrine that He came among men and for men presented His blood as a ransom! If angels sang Glory to God in the highest when the Lord was born, I feel impelled to repeat the note, now, that He is risen from the dead!

III. And so I come to my last head and to the practical conclusion— THE BEARING OF THIS RESURRECTION UPON OURSELVES. Paul expressly bids us to, "Remember" it. "Why?" asks one, "we don't forget it." Are you sure you don't? I find myself far too forgetful of Divine Truths. We ought not to forget, for this first day of the week is consecrated for Sabbatical purposes to remind us to think of the Resurrection. On the seventh day men celebrated a finished creation. On the first day we celebrate a finished redemption. Bear it, then, in mind!

Now, if you will remember that Jesus Christ of the seed of David rose from the dead, what will follow? First, you will find that most of your trials will vanish. Are you tried by your sin? Jesus Christ rose again from the dead for your justification! Does Satan accuse? Jesus rose to be your Advocate and Intercessor! Do infirmities hinder? The living Christ will show Himself strong on your behalf! You have a living Christ and in Him you have all things! Do you dread death? Jesus, in rising again, has vanquished the last enemy! He will come and meet you when it is your turn to pass through the chilly stream and you shall ford it in sweet Company! What is your trouble? I care not what it is, for if you will only think of Jesus as living, full of power, full of love and full of sympathy—having experienced all your trials, even unto death—you will have such a confidence in His tender care and in His boundless ability that you will follow in His footsteps without a question! Remember Jesus and that He rose again from the dead—and your confidence will rise as on eagles' wings!

Next, remember Jesus, for then you will see how your present sufferings are as nothing compared with His sufferings, and you will learn to expect victory over your sufferings even as He obtained victory. Kindly look at the chapter and you will find the Apostle saying in the third verse, "You therefore endure hardness, as a good soldier of Jesus Christ," and further on in the 11th verse, "It is a faithful saying: For if we are dead in Him, we shall also live in Him: if we suffer, we shall also reign with Him." Now, then, when you are called to suffer, think—"Jesus suffered, yet Jesus rose again from the dead. He came up out of His baptism of griefs the better and more glorious for it and so shall I!"

Therefore go into the furnace at the Lord's bidding and do not fear that the smell of fire shall pass upon you. Go down into the grave and do not think that the worm shall make an end of you any more than it did of Him! Behold, in the Risen One, the type and model of what you are and are to be! Fear not, for He conquered! Stand not trembling, but march boldly on, for Jesus Christ of the seed of David rose from the dead—and you who are of the seed of the promise shall rise again from all your trials and afflictions—and live a glorious life!

We see here, dear Brothers and Sisters, in being told to remember Jesus, that there is hope even in our hopelessness! When are things most hopeless in a man? Why, when he is dead! Do you know what it is to come down to that, so far as your inward weakness is concerned? I do. At times it seems to me that all my joy is buried like a dead thing and all my present

173

usefulness and all my hope of being useful in the future are in a coffin and laid underground like a corpse. In the anguish of my spirit and the desolation of my heart, I could count it better to die than to live. You say it should not be so. I grant you it should not be so, but so it is!

Many things happen within the minds of poor mortals which should not happen. If we had more courage and more faith they would not happen. Yes, but when we go down, down, down, is it not a blessed thing that Jesus Christ of the seed of David died and was raised from the dead? If I sink right down among the dead, yet will I hold to this blessed hope— that as Jesus rose again from the dead, so, also, shall my joy, my usefulness, my hope, my spirit rise! "You, which have showed us great and sore troubles shall quicken us, again, and bring us up from the lowest depths of the earth."

This casting down and slaying is good for us. We take a deal of killing and it is by being killed that we live. Many a man will never live till his proud self is slain. O proud Pharisee, if you are to live among those whom God accepts, you will have to come to the slaughterhouse and be cut in pieces as well as killed. "This is dreadful work," says one, "this dividing of joints and marrow, this spiritual dismemberment and destruction." Assuredly, it is painful, and yet it were a grievous loss to be denied it! Alas, how many are so good and excellent, strong and wise, clever and all that, that they cannot agree to be saved by Grace through faith! If they could be reduced to less than nothing, it would be the finest thing that ever happened to them.

Remember what Solomon said might be done with the fool, and yet it would not answer—he was to be ground in a mortar among wheat with a pestle—pretty hard dealing that, and yet his folly would not depart from him. Not by that process alone, but through some such method, the Holy Spirit brings men away from their folly. Under His killing operations, this may be their comfort that, if Jesus Christ rose literally from the dead, (not from sickness, but from death), and lives again, even so will His people! Did you ever get, where Bunyan pictures Christian as getting—right under the old dragon's foot? He is very heavy and presses the very breath out of a fellow when he makes him his footstool!

Poor Christian lay there with the dragon's foot on his chest, but he was just able to stretch out his hand and lay hold on his sword, which, by God's Grace, lay within his reach. Then he gave Apollyon a deadly thrust which made him spread his dragon wings and fly away. The poor crushed and broken pilgrim, as he gave the stab to his foe, cried, "Rejoice not over me, O my enemy; though I fall, yet shall I rise again!" Brothers and Sisters, do the same! You that are near despair, let this be the strength that nerves your arm and steels your heart. "Jesus Christ of the seed of David was raised from the dead according to Paul's Gospel."

Lastly, this proves the futility of all opposition to Christ. The learned are going to destroy the Christian religion. Already, according to their boasting, it has pretty nearly come to an end! The pulpit is infertile—it cannot command public attention. We stand up and preach to empty benches! As you see—or do not see—nothing remains for us but to die decently, so they insinuate. And what then? When our Lord was dead, when the clay-cold corpse lay watched by the Roman soldiers, and with a seal upon the enclosing stone—was not the cause in mortal jeopardy? But how fared it? Did it die out? Every disciple that Jesus had made forsook Him and fled—was not Christianity then destroyed?

No, that very day our Lord won a victory which shook the gates of Hell and caused the universe to stand astonished! Matters are not worse with Him at this hour! His affairs are not in a sadder condition, today, than then. No, see Him today and judge! On His head are many crowns and at His feet the hosts of angels bow! Jesus is the master of legions, today, while the Caesars have passed away! Here are His people—needy, obscure, despised, I grant you, still—but assuredly somewhat more numerous than they were when they laid Him in the tomb! His cause is not to be crushed! It is forever rising! Year after year, century after century, bands of true and honest hearts are marching up to the assault of the citadel of Satan! The prince of this world has a stronghold, here on earth, and we are to capture it! But as yet we see small progress, for rank after rank the warriors of the Lord have marched to the breach and disappeared beneath the terrible fire of death. All who have gone before seem to have been utterly cut off and destroyed, and still the enemy holds his ramparts against us.

Do you think nothing has been done? Has death taken away those martyrs, and confessors, and preachers, and laborious saints, and has nothing been achieved? Truly if Christ were dead, I would admit our defeat, for they that are fallen asleep in Him would have perished! But as Christ lives, so the cause lives, and they that have fallen are not dead—they have vanished from our sight for a little while—but if the curtain could be withdrawn, every one of them would be seen to stand in his lot unharmed, crowned and victorious! "Who are these arrayed in white robes, and whence came they?" These are they that were defeated! Why, then, their crowns? These are they that were dishonored! Why, then, their white robes? These are they who clung to a cause which is overthrown! Why, then, their long line of victories, for there is not a vanquished man among them all?

Let the Truth of God be spoken! Defeat is not the word for the cause of Jesus, the Prince of the house of David! We have always been victorious, Brothers and Sisters! We are victorious now. Follow your Master on your white horses and be not afraid! I see Him in the front with His blood-stained vesture around Him, fresh from the winepress where He has trod down His foes. You have not to present atoning blood, but only to conquer after your Lord! Put on your white raiment and follow Him on your white horses, conquering and to conquer! He is nearer than we think and the end of all things may be before the next jibe shall have come forth from the mouth of the last new skeptic. Have confidence in the Risen One and live in the power of His Resurrection!

11

Not Bound Yet

(Sermon No. 1998)

"Wherein I suffer trouble, as an evil doer, even unto bonds; but the Word of God is not bound" (2 Timothy 2:9).

YOU WILL OBSERVE, if you read the preceding verse, which, indeed, it would be wrong to sever from the text, that the doctrine of the Resurrection of our Lord Jesus Christ was the sheet anchor of Paul's comfort, as it was the great substance of his preaching. "Remember that Jesus Christ, of the seed of David, was raised from the dead according to my Gospel: wherein I suffer trouble, as an evildoer, even unto bonds; but the Word of God is not bound." Perhaps we do not give sufficient prominence to the doctrine of the Resurrection of Jesus Christ from the dead. Possibly, also, for this reason we do not fully grasp the idea of "the power of His Resurrection." Our Lord's death was not the close of His career—He still passed onward. From the Cross to the sepulcher was still forward. With weeping and mourning they laid Him in the tomb—surely that was the finis of His course. Ah, no, He passed into the grave, it is true, but He also passed through it! The grave had hitherto seemed a cul-de-sac—a blind alley from which there was no exit. All the footsteps pointed to entrance, but none to return. It looked like a dread abyss swallowing all and offering passageway to none.

Look what our Lord Jesus has done! He has made a tunnel of it for all His redeemed to pass into the Kingdom of God—we enter at the grave to emerge in the resurrection into eternal life! In this lies part of the power of His Resurrection, that He has opened the Kingdom of Heaven to all Believers. It looked like an iron door or gate of death, but He has unhinged it, yes, He has taken it quite away. The grave was once "a charnel house to fence the relics of lost innocence," but it is so no longer—the imprisoning stone is rolled away! By passing through death, our Lord has made a thoroughfare for us. We take death and the grave in transit, now—they do not hinder our advance to Glory, immortality and eternal life! Our course is always onward, whatever may lie in the way!

In the strength of that Truth of God, Paul, when he found himself in prison, expected to come out of it. When he saw great difficulties in the way to Heaven, he expected to go through those difficulties and to come out with gain at the further end thereof. This helped to cheer him in his darkest moments. His brave heart thus spoke within him and said, "What if I should be even dead and buried, I shall rise again! And if the Gospel should seem dead and buried, yet it will rise again! And if the particular cause which I am advocating in Rome should seem dead and buried, yet it must come to life again. I take courage from the great Truth of God that the Lord Jesus Christ rose from the dead according to my Gospel."

Friends, I think we, too, may encourage ourselves in our hour of sorrow. From the tomb of our Lord, we may gather gems of comfort! Though He died, yet He is dead no longer! And though He was buried, yet the sepulcher could not hold Him—and that same victorious power which brought again from the dead our Lord Jesus Christ, that great Shepherd of the sheep, will also bring all His sheep with Him in due time—though they, also, shall descend into the same darkness of the tomb—

"Vain the stone, the watch, the seal Christ has burst the gates of Hell! Death in vain forbids His rise, Christ has opened Paradise. Lives again our glorious King! 'Where, O death, is now your sting?' Once He died our souls to save! 'Where's your victory, boasting grave?'

"Soar we now where Christ has led,
Following our exalted Head;
Made like He, like He we rise;
Ours the cross, the grave, the skies."

I like much this self-forgetting sentence of the Apostle, "I suffer trouble, as an evildoer, even unto bonds; but the Word of God is not bound." He is shut up in the gloomy dungeon at Rome. No hideous cells could be worse than Roman dungeons usually were. No prison is a desirable place, but a Roman prison was a very vestibule of death. Paul is not only in prison, but in bonds! His right arm is chained to the left hand of a soldier. He cannot do anything except under the inspection of his enforced companion, who, kindly as he may be disposed, cannot be so closely bound to him without causing him much discomfort. One would not like to be chained to the best man that ever lived, but much less to a rough Roman soldier! Paul is in bonds as he writes. His fetters clank, but he makes light of them and finds more than sufficient comfort in the reflection, "I suffer as an evildoer, even unto bonds; but the Word of God is not bound."

I am going to talk to you upon that point with as much brevity as I can. First, I call your attention to this grand Truth, that the Word of God is not bound—in what sense is this true? And, secondly, for what reasons is this true? And, thirdly, what other facts run parallel to this fact, that though the preacher is bound, yet the Word he preaches is not bound?

I. First, then, IN WHAT SENSE IS IT TRUE that, "the Word of God is not bound"? Possibly a meditation upon this text may revive the spirits of some who are cast down. May the Holy Spirit, Himself, bless the subject to us!

That the Word of God is not bound, is, at this time, true in many senses. And, first, it is not bound so that it cannot be preached. Paul could preach it even when in bonds and he did preach it, so that the Gospel was made known throughout Caesar's palace—and there were saints in the imperial household! Many came to and fro into the Praetorian guard-room and heard the Word from the mouth of the Apostle. You may be quite sure that he never neglected to make known the message of the Gospel to all that visited him in his prison, so that the Word of God was not bound, even, with respect to himself!

And, dear Friends, whatever saddens us at this hour, we rejoice that the Word of God still finds a tongue and a voice with which to speak to the multitudes. That Word of God which, when there was nothing, spoke everything into existence, would still be able to speak for itself if not a single tongue voluntarily yielded itself to give forth speech for God! But, at the same time there are many tongues which gladly proclaim the glorious Grace of God, the Word of God is not bound by reason of the lack of men to make it known—the true Apostolic succession continues among us and, "Christ is preached." That everlasting Gospel will never be silenced! It will still be proclaimed to the ends of the earth and to the end of time. It shall never cease to bless the world so long as the sea pulses with tides and time is checkered with night and day—

> **"Nor shall Your spreading Gospel rest,**
> **Till through the world Your truth has run;**
> **Till Christ has all the nations blest,**
> **That see the light, or feel the sun."**

"The Word of God is not bound." Nineteen centuries after Paul, we still have an open Bible and a free pulpit. Blessed be God for this!

There have been a great many attempts to bind the Word of God, but yet it has not been bound. The preachers of the holy faith of Christ have been hunted to death. They have "wandered about in sheepskins and goatskins, destitute, afflicted, tormented"—but, "the Word of God has not been bound." When Hamilton was burned in Scotland, there was such an impetus given to the Gospel through his burning that the adversaries of the Gospel were known to say, "Let us burn no more martyrs in public, for the smoke of Hamilton's burning has made many eyes to smart until they were opened." So, no doubt, it always was! Persecution is a red hand which scatters the white wheat far and wide. I need not remind you how the ashes of God's martyred servant, cast into a brook, were borne onward to a river and afterwards to the sea—and by the sea they were carried to every shore! The Word of God is not bound by the binding of the preachers, but it happens to the persecuted as to Israel in Egypt— "The more they afflicted them, the more they multiplied." Probably the Church of God has never had better times, certainly she has never had happier times, than during periods of persecution! These were the days of her purity and, consequently, her glory. When she has been in the dark,

God has been her light—and when she has been driven to and fro by the cruelties of men—then has she most effectually rested under the shadow of the Almighty!

"The Word of God is not bound" so as to be no longer a living, working power among men. Sometimes the enemies of the Truth of God have thought that they had silenced the last witness and then there has been an unexpected outburst—and the old faith has been to the front again. When in Scotland, under the reign of Moderates, the Gospel seemed to have died out, one earnest man, by Providence, fell in with a little book, Fisher's, "Marrow of Divinity." He was enlightened as to the pure Truth of God, began, at once, to preach it and found thousands to rejoice in it! That marrow has never been taken away from Scotland's bones ever since, nor can it, nor shall it, let the devil do what he may! A desperate and subtle attempt is now being made, but it will be assuredly foiled through the Wisdom of God. Yet, if it should come to this, that they should get rid of all the preachers of the Gospel—of the men who would thunder out God's Word like Boanerges, or speak it out in tender tones as Barnabas—if the last of the faithful testifiers were consigned to the tomb, God would be sure to raise up another generation to publish His Truth, so that the Word of God would not lack a spokesman in the midst of the earth! The devil's work is never done—one word from the Lord—and it is all undone in an instant!

The enemies of the Gospel have also attempted to bind it by the burning of books. I have in my possession an early copy of Luther's sermons and I was told how very rare it was because, at first, the circulation was forbidden, and afterwards they were bought up and burned as soon as they were met with. And what did they do? They only put fire into Luther when they burned his sermons—they drove him to be more outspoken than he otherwise might have been—and so they helped the cause they thought to destroy! It is impossible that the Truth of God can die. It has about it the Immortality of God. It is utterly impossible that the Truth of the Gospel shall die, since it is wrapped up in the work of the Lord Jesus Christ who lives and reigns forever! He must see of the travail of His soul and must be satisfied for all the scoffs and agonies He has endured. Neither will less content Him than a Kingdom in which all others shall be merged.

"The Word of God is not bound." It will still be preached despite the scoffs of philosophers and the roaring of devils. Do not, therefore, at any time sit down in despair because of evil times, for the times are always evil in one respect or another! Do not imagine that the Truth of God will become extinct and that the simple Gospel will be forgotten. Heaven and earth shall pass away, but God's Word shall never pass away! If the Gospel which we hold is of men, it will be over-thrown—and let it be—let us see it die without regret! But if it is of God, none can overcome it and woe unto those who set themselves to do so! If these things are so, why are we so timorous? If our Gospel is, as some think, only man's voice, it shall die down into the eternal silences. But if it come from Heaven, it shall increase into the everlasting chorus of Heaven! Error shall be blown away like smoke from the chimney, or like March dust in the north wind—but God's own Word is as eternal as God Himself! As the sun is not blown out by the tempest, nor the moon quenched by the damp of the night, so is not the Gospel destroyed by the sophistries of perverse minds! Therefore, let us comfort one another with these words, "The Word of God is not bound." It will be preached till doomsday!

Another sense must be remembered—the Word of God is not bound so that it cannot reach the heart. You may have, perhaps, dear Friend, some very obdurate relative about whose salvation you have very great concern. You have prayed long and have used the means within your reach perseveringly. You have also used extraordinary means and you have looked for an immediate result. But as yet the hard heart does not melt. As yet you see no tear of repentance and hear no cry of faith and, moreover, it may be that your friend refuses to go and hear the Gospel and appears to be more opposed to it than before! I see that you are beginning to be bound in spirit, for the hot tears force up your eyelids and scald their way down your cheeks while I mention the painful subject. You are hardly able to speak a good word, however much you desire it, for you have so often been repulsed. I think I hear you complaining to the Lord in prayer and saying—

"But feeble my compassion proves,
And can but weep where most it loves;
Your own all-saving arm employ,
And turn these drops of grief to joy."

But oh, remember that "the Word of God is not bound!" God has ways of reaching the hardest hearts and melting them—and He can do it in a moment when such a work is least expected! He has ways of making His servants draw the bow at what to them is a venture, but to Him is an absolute certainty—and between the joints of the harness the shaft of conviction finds its way! Do not give anybody up in despair! While God is almighty, have hope for the chief of sinners! Hope on, hope always, even when your last argument seems to have failed and your last instruction has been refused. It is well that it should be so, that in the work of salvation God may have all the glory and you may learn to love Him and trust Him all the better in years to come. "The Word of God is not bound."

Sometimes it happens to those whom we love that they are removed from the means of Grace, but even then the Word of God is not bound. We thought full surely, while we could take them to hear the minister whom God blessed to us, that they were within the reach of God's Grace. But now they have gone away and our spirit sinks. At this hour, perhaps, they are on the sea, or you have had a letter telling you that they live in a place remote from Gospel preaching. You sigh within your soul and think, "Oh, now they cannot be saved!" But the Word of God is not bound! Had we not, a little while ago, an instance of one whom we were praying for at a Prayer Meeting and that night, while we were praying, it was a moonlight night, and as he was walking the deck of the ship, the Lord met with him? When no tongue was able to reach him, the memory of what he had heard at home came over his soul and he was humbled before God!

I was telling, just a little while ago, at our Prayer Meeting, a very singular instance of how, just lately, three or four sermons on Sunday evenings have been made most useful to a young friend. He was going away to Australia unconverted and without God. He went on board to depart and when the vessel steamed out of dock, it ran into another ship and he was obliged to wait and spend almost a month here while the vessel was being repaired. The Lord met with him on those Sunday nights and he has gone, now, leaving in his mother's heart the sweet persuasion that he has found his mother's God! The God of all Grace has ways of getting at human hearts when, to our thinking, every avenue is fast closed! He can reach the poor in the slums of London. He can reach the harlot in her chambers of iniquity. He can touch the most debauched man in town in his lordly mansion. There is not a soldier who has gone into the ranks for the sake of hiding away from God and indulging his passions, but what the Lord can conquer him! There is not a runaway thief but what the Lord can find him when the police cannot! He knows just where His fugitives are—His warrants are out against them and when the time comes, His Grace will arrest them—

"Thus the eternal counsel ran, 'Almighty Grace, arrest that man'!"

And he was arrested, though he never thought that he should be made to turn to God and seek eternal life. "The Word of God is not bound." It goes forth conquering and to conquer!

But sometimes we are apt to think a case is more hopeless, still, when, in addition to natural depravity and the absence of the means of Grace, there springs up a skepticism, perhaps a downright derision of the Word of God and of things sacred. One is apt to think, then, "It is all over now. It is of no further use praying for such an one." I am not so sure that the case is any the worse for being openly declared and honestly described. Nothing is more deadly than absolute indifference and, sometimes, when a man begins to avow himself an infidel, it is only that his conscience is troubling him and he is obliged to take some drug with which to stifle it—no drug is more handy for his use than avowed infidelity. A profession of skepticism is often nothing more than the whistling of the boy as he goes through the churchyard and is afraid of ghosts and, therefore, "whistles hard to keep his courage up." They try to get rid of the thought of God because of that ghost of conscience which makes cowards of them all! They might have professed to be believers if it had not become too barefaced an inconsistency to live as they do and yet acknowledge God.

I think it would be a good rule for all Christians to immediately pray whenever they hear a man swear. Pray for that particular man and keep him in your mind's eye as far as you can, hoping that he may be converted to God. "The Word of God is not bound." Even blasphemy and infidelity yield to the conquering touch of Sovereign Grace. I knew a man who had lived a life of carelessness and indifference, with occasional outbursts of drunkenness and other vices. This man happened, one day, on Peckham Rye, to hear a preacher say that if any man would ask anything of God, He would give it to him. The assertion was much too broad and might have done harm, but this man accepted it as a test and resolved that he would ask and thus would see if there really was a God. On the Saturday morning of that week, when he was going early to his work, the thought came upon him, "Perhaps there is a God, after all." He was ready to swoon as the possibility struck him and then and there he offered the test petition, concerning a matter which concerned himself and his fellow workmen!

His prayer was granted in a remarkable manner and he came, then, to be a believer in God! He is more than that, now, and has found his way to be a believer in all that God has spoken and has found peace through believing in Jesus Christ. It struck me as wonderful that this man, who never had any religious care at all, should, all of a sudden, be turned to serve the living God! The preacher at Peckham Rye never had a more unlikely hearer and yet he succeeded with him! Oh, pray for them! Pray for them till the doors of death enclose them, till the bolts of the gates of eternal destiny are driven home! Pray for them! Pray for them! Never cease to cry to God for those who go to the utmost extremity of sin, for though you cannot reach them, "the Word of God is not bound." It is not bound, then, as to the preaching of it, nor as to its power to reach the heart!

Still further, it is not bound as to its power to comfort the soul. I have—perhaps you have in your measure—to deal with persons under conviction of sin; with others who are suffering through ill health, or mental decline; with some who groan under Satanic temptation and various forms of mental trial causing awful depression of spirits. We have spoken to certain of them many times without being able to bring them the Light of God and comfort. We put the Gospel very plainly to them and try to place it in different lights, hoping that somehow or other they may see hope. Alas, we are often unable to touch the wound of their spirit. And, oh, how they baffle us! How frequently have we had to cry out, "O God, help us!" We cannot comfort these poor people. The man in the iron cage, described by Bunyan, is repeated many times over in our observation. We bring the promises. We bring the doctrines. We bring our own experience to bear upon such persons, but their despair defies our consolation! The darkness is too dense for our poor rushlight to remove. The captive is too closely shut up in prison for us to set him free.

But here is a blessed Truth of God—"The Word of God is not bound." By-and-by that blessed Word of God will break into the midnight darkness! Let us, therefore, continue to ply the afflicted with the Word of God, searching out its most cheering assurances and giving them full and free scope. Perhaps we put too much of our own explanation with the Lord's own Words—perhaps we have thought that clever illustrations were necessary—and so have overlaid the Truth of God with our poor imagination! When we have come to the end of our explanations and our illustrations, it may be that the Word which is not bound will come in and give liberty to the captives! Wonderful cases have we seen of persons driven to despair and ready to lay violent hands upon themselves, who have been raised up and set at joyful liberty by the Word of God, of itself, alone! Oh, that some may prove its Divine power tonight!

One Scripture has set many at liberty—"Him that comes to Me I will in no wise cast out." Hear it, think of it, believe it and be at peace. I think a second passage has been fruitful above all other texts—"God so loved the world, that He gave His only begotten Son, that whoever believes in Him should not perish, but have everlasting life." Let a man muse on that verse till he sees his fetters turn to cobwebs and his prison walls dissolve like dreams! You are bound, poor sinner, but the Word of God is not bound! You are bound, poor preacher, but the Word of God is not bound! You are bound, dear mother, dear father—bound up in your weakness and unable to do anything for your wayward child—but the Word of God is not bound! It wears no bonds but it is able to take them from all who groan under them.

Thus I have given you several senses of the text. There is another one. The Word of God is not bound in the sense that it cannot be fulfilled. I now allude principally to the promises and prophecies of God's Word. If there is a promise of deliverance to you and you cannot see the way in which you are to be delivered, you may not, therefore, doubt the promise, for that would dishonor the Lord who spoke it. The Word of God is not bound! The Word of God will cleave its own way and reach its own destination. Who makes a path for the lightning? The lightning burns its own instant way. Who shall make a path for the Word of God? It will effect its own design. Jehovah speaks and it is done. He said to the primeval darkness, "Let there be light!" And there was light. Now, if God has given a promise to you, He will as readily fulfill His Word of promise to the least of His people, as He will make His own Word effective for His own designs in Nature, Providence, or Judgment. The Word of God is not bound!

You are come, perhaps, to your last penny, but He has said, "I will never leave you, nor forsake you." You have come to your last grain of strength, but He faints not, neither is He weary, and He has said, "As your days, so shall your strength be." And so shall it be. Oh, that we could believe the promises of God! We do not half believe them, Brothers and Sisters. We have never yet pressed the best of the wine out of them because we have let them lie like uncrushed bunches of grapes! Truly they are beautiful to look upon, like the clusters of Eshcol, but that is not the way to know all that is in them. Oh, that we had but faith to tread them in the winepress, that the ruddy juice might run out and we might drink and be refreshed!

Remember that God has promised nothing beyond His strength, nothing beyond His will. God carries out His promise to the full! He may sometimes exceed it, but He certainly never falls short of it. Therefore, let us be comforted tonight with the recollection that God's Word is free to effect its own accomplishment. His decree is Omnipotence resolving and His Providence is Omnipotence acting. "The Word of God is not bound."

There is yet one other sense. "The Word of God is not bound" so that it cannot endure and prevail unto the end. I know that there are those who think it dead and, therefore, they are anxious to attend its funeral and bury it out of sight, while the new theology shall dance on its grave. They call us poor old fogies for believing in the old Gospel—and tell us to go home and order our coffins—and leave the world to these wiser men. They begin to crow as if their work of defeating us had been unquestionably done. We are out of date. We are dead. We are extinct! Perhaps so! Perhaps so! But we think they will be mistaken in their imagination, for the Word of God is not defeated, after all. And if it were—if it were bound like the Lord Jesus and were taken before priests and princes to be scourged and spit upon. And if it were crucified among thieves and taken down from the Cross and laid in the tomb. And if the grave were sealed and watched by mighty men, yet the story would not be ended! Because the Lord lives, it would live again and its Resurrection power would be testified in the midst of its adversaries! For this Gospel, on which we have rested our souls, and on which our fathers rested throughout their generations, this is not bound!

Who is to bind it? With what will they bind it? Green willow branches, ropes and bars of brass cannot hold this greater than Samson! It shall snap them in pieces as twigs! There is no overcoming the free Gospel! They dreamed that they had bound it many times before and they cried in mockery, "The Philistines are upon you, Samson," but they have had to learn its might when least they expected it and so they shall yet again! Philosophy and heresy are in league and they gather their armies in haste. The Lord shall make them as the sheaves of the threshing floor. Therefore, let us be of good comfort, Brothers, and rest quite sure that, though we are beaten, the Word of God is not beaten! And though we are in a minority and our preaching at a discount, it does not matter—"The Word of God is not bound."

II. For a moment or two I have further to enquire, WHAT ARE THE REASONS WHY THE WORD OF GOD IS NOT BOUND? It is not bound because it is the voice of the Almighty. If the Gospel is, indeed, the Gospel of God, and these Truths are Revelations of God, Omnipotence is in them! It is not possible that the Omnipotent Word can be bound. Who will attempt the deed? Go bit the tempest! Put a chain about the hurricane, control the winds and bridle the raging sea! And when you have done these, you are but at the beginning of your task—you cannot, even then, hinder the Omnipotence of God which finds a chariot for itself in the Word of God and rides forth conquering and to conquer!

Moreover, the Holy Spirit puts forth His power in connection with the Word of God and, as He is Divine, He is unconquerable! He comes as a rushing, mighty wind—who can stop Him? He comes as fire—who can stand before His flaming vehemence? The Holy Spirit's being with the Gospel is the reason of its great power. It is not that Truth, alone, is mighty and will prevail, but that the Spirit of Truth works mightily by it and causes it to subdue the minds of men. If we had no Holy Spirit, what could we do? But as He has promised to take of the things of Christ, and to show them to His people, while He reproves the world of sin, of righteousness and of judgment, we know that "the Word of God is not bound." The Holy Spirit manifests His own Sovereign will, doing what He pleases, even as the wind blows where it wishes—and this is the surest proof that His Word "is not bound."

If you needed another reason less strong than these two, I should say, "How can it be bound while it is so necessary to men?" There are certain things which, if men need, they will have. I have heard say that in the old Bread Riots, when men were actually starving for bread, no word had such a terribly threatening and alarming power about it as the word, "Bread!" when shouted by a starving crowd. I have read a description by one who once heard this cry—he said he had been startled at night by a cry of, "Fire!" but when he heard the cry of, "Bread! Bread!" from those that were hungry, it seemed to cut him like a sword. Whatever bread had been in his possession, he must, at once, have handed it out.

So it is with the Gospel—when men are once aware of their need of it, there is no monopolizing it. None can make "a ring" or "a corner" over the precious commodity of heavenly Truth. Neither can anyone put this candle under a bushel so as to conceal its light. It cannot be hidden because there are so many that need it. They are pining, these myriads of London, these myriads all over the world—and though they hardly know it—yet there is a cry coming up forever from them for something which they can never find except in Christ! You may depend upon it—you cannot stop the Gospel being preached while there is this awful hunger after it in the souls of men. They must have it! You cannot cheat them into enduring a substitute for it.

You may set up your altars and put up your gimcrackeries,[5] but they won't have them instead of the Gospel! You may preach your speculations and tell them "modern thought" has done away with the old Gospel, but as soon as the Holy Spirit shows them their state by nature and their future danger, they sweep all this rubbish away! As the mower lays the grass in swaths to dry in the sun when he has passed up and down the field, so will the nations of the earth sweep away the green and flowery growths of human philosophy—and either give them to beasts to eat, or cast them into the oven! When men once know what they need, they will have it, despite priests or princes, scientists or skeptics. Oh, it must be so! This dire need of men must be met—the Word of the Lord cannot be bound.

I have one thing else to tell you. The Word of God is not bound because, when once it gets into men's hearts, it works such an enthusiasm in them that you cannot bind it. You cannot silence lips which have been touched by a live coal from off the Altar of Christ! When the humblest woman gets to know the Gospel, you may say, "There, hold your tongue about it!" But you charge her in vain! She cannot but speak of what the Lord has done for her. The converted man must talk to his work mates about it. You may say, "It would be very irregular for you to hold a meeting. It would be out of all character for a mere working man to stand

---

[5] **Gimcrack**; *noun*: a showy object of little or no value.

up on the village green." But he is very likely to do it. You let the man alone—he cannot help it!

Look at the many that gathered together in the desert in the South of France in the old persecuting times! Why did they thus risk their lives? Why did they expose themselves to be ridden down by dragoons? They could not help it! They were eager for the Gospel! They were in danger of being broken on the wheel if they preached, or listened to preaching, but they could not help it—they must hear the Word of the Lord! The preacher said, "Woe is unto me if I preach not the Gospel." Their adversaries tortured them and sent them to the galleys. They threatened them with banishment and death, but all in vain. You had better let them go on, for you cannot stop them! In our own land there was no binding the Word of God, for those who knew it felt compelled to spread it.

There is Master Bunyan. They have put him in prison and his family is nearly starving. They bring him up and they say, "You shall go out of prison, John, if you won't preach. Go home and tag your laces, that is what you have to do, and leave the Gospel alone. What have you got to do with that?" But honest John answers, "I cannot help it. If you let me out of prison today, I will preach again tomorrow, by the help of God. I will lie here till the moss grows on my eyelids, but I will never promise to cease preaching the Gospel." They could sooner bind the sweet influences of the Pleiades, or loose the bands of Orion, than govern the movements of the Spirit of God in men! The love of Christ is such that when it once pours into a man's heart, it must run out at his lips in loving testimony! Has He not put rivers of Living Water into the midst of those who once drink of the life-giving stream? And they must speak of it, even till they die!

III. Now I come to the close. ONE OR TWO OTHER FACTS RUN PARALLEL TO THE TEXT. Paul is bound, but the Word of God is not bound. Read it thus—the preacher has had a bad week. He is full of aches and pains. He feels ill, but the Word of God is not ill. Oh, what a blessing that is! We preach a healthy Gospel even though we are unhealthy ourselves. In this, let the invalid rejoice! Dear suffering worker, your work shall not suffer, for it is a sound Gospel which you preach, though you, yourself, are hampered by a poor, weak body!

"What will become of the congregation when a certain minister dies?" Well, he will be dead, but the Word of God is not dead. God buries His workmen, but His work goes on. One light goes out, but another torch flames forth. Star by star sinks beneath the horizon, but another star appears on the other side to make glad the night. The Word of God is not dead when the preacher is dead!

"Oh, but the worker is so feeble!" The Word of God is not feeble. "But the worker feels so stupid." But the Word of God is not stupid. "But the worker is so unfit." But the Word of God is not unfit. You see it all comes to this—the preacher is bound, but the Word of God is not bound! The worker is feeble, but the Word of God is not feeble! You are nothing and nobody, but the Word of God cannot be said to be nothing and nobody—it is everything and everybody—it is girt about with All Power.

But you bitterly and truthfully lament that Christian men are, nowadays, very devoid of zeal. "All hearts are cold in every place." The old fire burns low. But the Word of God is not cold, nor lukewarm, nor in any way losing its old fire! "Such and such a congregation is as frozen as the North Pole." Yes, but the Word of God is not frozen! Divine Truth is not turned into an iceberg. Do not fret yourself into despair as to the condition of the Church, since the Lord lives! Things are bad, indeed, without His power, but then in the dark hour the Glory of the Lord will shine out.

"Yes," says one, "but I am disgusted with the cases I have lately met with of false brethren." Yes, but the Word of God is not false. "But they walk so inconsistently." I know they do, but the Word of God is not inconsistent. "But they say they have disproved the faith." Yes, they have disproved their own faith, but they have not disproved the Word of God for all that! The Word of God is not affected by the falsehood of men. "If we believe not, He abides faithful; He cannot deny Himself." And till He denies Himself we need not make much account of who else denies Him.

"Oh, but," says one, "it is an awful thing to think of the spiritual ruin of so many that are round about us, who hear the Gospel and yet, after all, willfully refuse it, and die in their sins." Truly this is a grievous fact. They appear to be bound by their sins like beasts for the slaughter, but the Word of God is not bound or injured. It was said of old that it would be a sweet savor unto God in them that are saved, and in them that perish—in the one a savor of life unto life, and in the other a savor of death unto death.

Is not the fact as the Lord, Himself, forewarned us? The ungodly reject the Gospel, but the Gospel has not, therefore, failed. O Sinners, you cannot overcome God's Word! You have defeated its influence of love upon yourselves, but it is not defeated, after all. If you will not come to Christ, others will—the Spirit of the Lord shall bring them. Christ shall see of the travail of His soul. If you turn away from His precious blood and refuse the redemption that He has worked, Christ shall not be disappointed as to the result of His passion. He shall see His seed and shall prolong His days. You may bite at the Gospel, but it shall be as when the viper in the fable gnawed at the file and destroyed his teeth. You may seek to put out the Gospel light, but you will be thrusting your hand into the fire and your own flesh shall be consumed!

Do not try to war against the Gospel! Choose some other adversary than the Lord God Almighty and His invincible Gospel. I pray you, cease to fight against the Lord, for the Word of God is not bound! However much you may try to bind it, you shall find that it has its liberty and it will, in the next world, have liberty to accuse and to condemn if you will not now give it liberty to persuade and to save you! God bless you, dear Friends, for Christ's sake! Amen.

12

Suffering and Reigning with Jesus

(Sermon No. 547)

"If we suffer, we shall also reign with Him: if we deny Him, He also will deny us" (2 Timothy 2:12).

MY VERNERABLE FRIEND who has up to now sent me a text for the New Year, still ministers to his parish the Word of Life and has not forgotten to furnish the passage for our meditation today. Having preached from one of a very similar character a short time ago, I have felt somewhat embarrassed in preparation. But I will take courage and say with the Apostle, "To write the same things to you, to me, indeed, is not grievous, but for you it is safe." If I should bring forth old things on this occasion, be you not unmindful that even the wise householder does this at times. For oft-recurring sickness the same wine may be prescribed by the most skillful physician without blame. No one scolds the contractor for mending rough roads again and again with stones from the same quarry. The wind which has borne us once into the haven is not despised for blowing often from the same quarter, for it may do us good service yet again. And therefore I am assured that you will endure my repetitions of the same Truths of God, since they may assist you to suffer with patience the same trials.

You will observe that our text is a part of one of Paul's faithful sayings. If I remember rightly, Paul has four of these. The first occurs in 1 Timothy 1:15, that famous, that chief of all faithful sayings, "This is a faithful saying and worthy of all acceptation, that Christ Jesus came into the world to save sinners; of whom I am chief." A golden saying, whose value Paul himself had most marvelously proved. What shall I say of this verse, but the same—the lamp of a lighthouse, it has darted its ray of comfort through leagues of darkness and guided millions of tempest-tossed spirits to the port of Peace.

194

The next faithful saying is in the same Epistle, at the fourth chapter and the ninth verse. "Godliness is profitable unto all things, having the promise of the life that now is and of that which is to come. This is a faithful saying and worthy of all acceptation." This, too, the Apostle knew to be true, since he had learned in whatsoever state he was in to be content. Our text is a portion of the third faithful saying. And the last of the four you will find in Titus 3:8,

"This is a faithful saying and these things I will that you affirm constantly, that they which have believed in God might be careful to maintain good works. These things are good and profitable unto men."

We may trace a connection between these faithful sayings.

The first one, which speaks of Jesus Christ coming into the world to save sinners, lays the foundation of our eternal salvation in the Free Grace of God, as shown to us in the mission of the great Redeemer. The next affirms the double blessedness which we obtain through this salvation—the blessings of the upper and nether springs—of time and of eternity. The third faithful saying shows one of the duties to which the chosen people are called. We are ordained to suffer for Christ with the promise that "if we suffer, we shall also reign with Him." The last faithful saying sets forth the active form of Christian service, bidding us diligently to maintain good works.

Thus you have the root of salvation in Free Grace. You have next the privileges of that salvation in the life which now is and in that which is to come. And you have also the two great branches of suffering with Christ and service of Christ loaded with the fruits of the Spirit of all Divine Grace. Treasure up, dear Friends, those faithful sayings, "Lay up these words in your heart; bind them for a sign upon your hand that they may be as frontlets between your eyes." Let these choice sayings be printed in letters of gold and set up as tablets upon the doorposts of our house and upon our gates. Let them be the guides of our life, our comfort and our instruction. The Apostle of the Gentiles proved them to be faithful. They are faithful still, not one word shall fall to the ground. They are worthy of all acceptation—let us accept them now and prove their faithfulness—each man for himself.

This morning's meditation is to be derived from a part of that faithful saying which deals with suffering. We will read the verse preceding our text. "It is a faithful saying: For if we are dead with Him, we shall also live with Him." All the elect were virtually dead with Christ when He died upon the tree—they were on the Cross—crucified with Him. In Him, as their representative, they rose from the tomb and live in newness of life. Because He lives, they shall live also. In due time the chosen are slain by the Spirit of God and so made dead with Christ to sin, to self-righteousness, to the world, the flesh and the powers of darkness.

Then it is that they live with Jesus! His life becomes their life and as He was, so are they also in this world. The Spirit of God breathes the quickening Grace into those who were once dead in sin and thus they live in union with Christ Jesus. When Believers die, though they may be sawn in sunder, or burnt at the stake, yet, since they sleep in Jesus, they are preserved from the destruction of death by Him and are made partakers of His immortality. May the Lord make us rooted and grounded in the mysterious but most consolatory doctrine of union with Christ Jesus.

We must at once advance to our text—"If we suffer, we shall also reign with Him: if we deny Him, He also will deny us." The words naturally divide themselves into two parts—suffering with Jesus and its reward—denying Jesus and its penalty.

I. SUFFERING WITH JESUS AND ITS REWARD. To suffer is the common lot of all men. It is not possible for us to escape from it. We come into this world through the gate of suffering and over death's door hangs the same escutcheon. We must suffer if we live, no matter in what style we spend our existence. The wicked man may cast off all respect for virtue and riot in excess of vice to the utmost degree, yet, let him not expect to avoid the well-directed shafts of sorrow. No, rather let him look for a tenfold share of pain of body and remorse of soul. "Many sorrows shall be to the wicked."

Even if a man could so completely degrade himself as to lose his intellectual powers and become a brute, yet even then he could not escape from suffering. For we know that the brute creation is the victim of pain as much as more lordly man. Only, as Dr. Chalmers well remarks, the brutes have the additional misery that they have no mind endowed with reason and cheered by hope to fortify them under their bodily affliction.

Understand, O Man, that however you may degrade yourself, you are still under the yoke of suffering—the loftiest bow beneath it nor the meanest can avoid it. Every acre of humanity must be furrowed with this plow. There may be a sea without a wave but never a man without sorrow. He who was God as well as Man had His full measure pressed down and running over! Let us be assured that if the Sinless One was not spared the rod, the sinful will not go free. "Man that is born of woman is of few days and full of trouble." "Man is born unto trouble as the sparks fly upward."

If then, a man has sorrow, it does not necessarily follow that he shall be rewarded for it since it is the common lot brought upon all by sin. You may smart under the lashes of sorrow in this life but this shall not deliver you from the wrath to come. Remember, you may live in poverty and drag along a wearisome existence of ill-requited toil. You may be stretched upon a bed of sickness and be made to experience an agony in every single member of your body. And your mind, too, may be depressed with fears, or plunged in the depths of despair. And yet, by all this you may gain nothing of any value to your immortal spirit, for, "Except a man be born again, he cannot see the kingdom of God."

And no amount of affliction upon earth can alter that unchanging rule so as to admit an unregenerate man into Heaven. To suffer is not peculiar to the Christian—neither does suffering necessarily bring with it any recompense of reward. The text implies most clearly that we must suffer with Christ in order to reign with Him. The structure of the preceding verse plainly requires such a reading. The words, "with Him," may be as accurately supplied at the close of the one clause as the other. The suffering which brings the reigning with Jesus must be a suffering with Jesus.

There is a very current error among those poor people who are ignorant of true religion that all poor and afflicted people will be rewarded for it in the next state. I have heard working men refer to the parable of the rich man and Lazarus with a cruel sort of satisfaction at the pains of Dives because they have imagined that, in the same manner, all rich people would be cast into the flames of Hell without a drop of water to cool their tongue—while all poor persons like Lazarus would be triumphantly carried into Abraham's bosom.

A more fearful mistake could not be made! It was not the suffering of Lazarus which entitled him to a place in Abraham's bosom. He might have been licked by all the dogs on earth and then have been dragged off by the dogs of Hell! Many a man goes to Hell from a dunghill. A drunkard's hovel is very wretched—is he to be rewarded for bringing himself to rags? Very much of the beggary we see abroad is the result of vice, extravagance, or folly—are these things so meritorious as to be passports to Heaven?

Let no man deceive himself so grossly! On the other hand the rich man was not cast into Hell because he was rich and fared sumptuously. Had he been rich in faith, holy in life and renewed in heart, his purple and fine linen would have done him no hurt. Lazarus was carried above by the angels because his heart was in Heaven—and the rich man lifted up his eyes in Hell, because he had never lifted them up towards God and heavenly things. It is a work of Free Grace in the heart and character which shall decide the future—not poverty or wealth. Let intelligent persons combat this notion whenever they meet with it.

Suffering here does not imply happiness hereafter. It is only a certain order of suffering to which a reward is promised—the suffering which comes to us from fellowship with the Lord Jesus and conformity to His image. A few words here, by way of aiding you in making the distinction. We must not imagine that we are suffering for Christ and with Christ if we are not in Christ. If a man is not a branch of the Living Vine, you may prune and cut until the sap flows and the branch bleeds but he will never bring forth heavenly fruit. Prune the bramble as long as ever you like. Use the knife until the edge is worn away—the brier will be as sharp and fruitless as ever!

You cannot by any process of pruning translate it into one of the vines of Eshcol. If a man remains in a state of nature, he is a member of the earthly Adam—he will not, therefore, escape suffering—but ensure it. He must not, however, dream that because he suffers he is suffering with Christ! He is plagued with the old Adam. He is receiving with all the other heirs of wrath the sure heritage of sin. Let him consider these sufferings of his to be only the first drops of the awful shower which will fall upon him forever—the first tingling cuts of that terrible whip which will lacerate his soul forever.

If a man is in Christ, he may then claim fellowship with the second Man, who is the Lord from Heaven and he may expect to bear the image of the heavenly in the Glory to be revealed. O my Hearers, are you in Christ by a living faith? Are you trusting in Jesus only? If not, whatever you may have to mourn over on earth, you have no hope of reigning with Jesus in Heaven. Supposing a man to be in Christ—it does not even follow, then, that all his sufferings are sufferings with Christ. If a good man were, out of mistaken views of mortification and self-denial, to mutilate his body, or to flog his flesh as many a sincere enthusiast has done, I might admire the man's fortitude, but I should not allow for an instant that he was suffering with Christ!

Who called men to such austerities? Certainly not the God of Love! If, therefore, they torture themselves at the command of their own fancies, fancy must reward them, for God will not. If I am rash and imprudent and run into positions for which neither Providence nor Grace has fitted me, I ought to question whether I am not rather sinning than communing with Christ. Peter drew his sword and cut off the ear of Malchus. If somebody had cut his ear off, what would you say? He took the sword and he feels the sword! He was never commanded to cut off the ear of Malchus and it was his Master's gentleness which saved him from the soldiers' rage.

If we let passion take the place of judgment, and let self-will reign instead of Scriptural authority, we shall fight the Lord's battles with the devil's weapons! And if we cut our own fingers we must not be surprised. On several occasions, excited Protestants have rushed into Romish cathedrals, have knocked down the priest and dashed the wafer upon the ground, trod upon it and in other ways exhibited their hatred of idolatry.

Now when the Law has interposed to punish such outrages, the offenders are hardly to be considered as suffering with Christ! This I give as one instance of a class of actions to which overheated brains sometimes lead men under the supposition that they will join the noble army of martyrs.

The martyrs were all chosen to their honorable estate. And I may say of martyrdom as of priesthood, "No man takes that honor upon himself but he that is called thereunto as was Aaron." Let us mind we all make a distinction between things which differ and do not pull a house down on our heads and then pray the Lord to console us under the trying Providence.

Again, in troubles which come upon us as the result of sin, we must not think we are suffering with Christ. When Miriam spoke evil of Moses and the leprosy polluted her, she was not suffering for God. When Uzziah thrust himself into the temple and became a leper all his days, he could not say that he was afflicted for righteousness' sake. If you speculate and lose your property, do not say that you are losing all for Christ's sake! When you unite with bubble companies and are duped, do not whine about suffering for Christ—call it the fruit of your own folly. If you will put your hand into the fire and it gets burned, why, it is the nature of fire to burn you or anybody else! Be not so silly as to boast as though you were a martyr.

If you do wrong and suffer for it, what thanks have you? Go behind the door and weep for your sin, but come not forth in public to claim a reward. Many a hypocrite, when he has had his deserts and has been called by his proper name, has cried out, "Ah, I am persecuted!" It is not an infallible sign of excellence to be in bad repute among men. Who feels any esteem for a cold-blooded murderer? Does not every man reprobate the offender? Is he, therefore, a Christian because he is spoken against and his name cast out as evil? Assuredly not! He is a heartless villain and nothing more. Brethren, truthfulness and honesty should stop us from using expressions which involve a false claim. We must not talk as if we suffered nobly for Jesus when we are only troubled as the result of sin. O, to be kept from transgression! Then it matters not how rough the road of obedience may be—our journey shall be pleasant because Jesus walks with us.

Be it observed, moreover, that suffering such as God accepts and rewards for Christ's sake must have God's Glory as its end. If I suffer that, I may earn a name, or win applause among men. If I venture into trial merely that I may be respected for it, I shall get my reward—but it will be the reward of the Pharisee and not the crown of the sincere servant of the Lord Jesus. I must mind, too, that love to Christ and love to His elect is ever the mainspring of all my patience, remembering the Apostle's words, "Though I give my body to be burned and have not charity, it profits me nothing."

If I suffer in bravado, filled with proud defiance of my fellow men. If I love the dignity of singularity and out of dogged obstinacy hold to an opinion, not because it is right—but because I choose to think as I like, then I suffer not with Jesus. If there is no love to God in my soul. If I do not endure all things for the elect's sake, I may bear many a cuff and buffeting, but I miss the fellowship of the Spirit and have no recompense.

I must not forget, also, that I must manifest the Spirit of Christ or I do not suffer with Him. I have heard of a certain minister, who, having had a great disagreement with many members in his Church, preached from this text, "And Aaron held his peace." The sermon was intended to portray himself as an astonishing instance of meekness. But as his previous words and actions had been quite sufficiently violent, a witty hearer observed that the only likeness he could see between Aaron and the preacher, was this, "Aaron held his peace and the preacher did not."

It is easy enough to discover some parallel between our cases and those of departed saints, but not so easy to establish the parallel by holy patience and Christ-like forgiveness. If I have, in the way of virtue, brought down upon myself shame and rebuke. If I am hot to defend myself and punish the slanderer. If I am irritated, unforgiving and proud—I have lost a noble opportunity of fellowship with Jesus. I must have Christ's Spirit in me, or I do not suffer acceptably. If like a sheep before her shearers, I can be dumb. If I can bear insult and love the man who inflicts it. If I can pray with Christ, "Father, forgive them, for they know not what they do." If I submit all my case to Him who judges righteously and count it even my joy to suffer reproach for the cause of Christ—then and only then, have I truly suffered with Christ.

These remarks may seem very cutting and may take away much false but highly-prized comfort from some of you. It is not my intention to take away any true comfort from the most humble Believer who really suffers with my Lord. But God grant we may have honesty enough not to pluck flowers out of other men's gardens, or wear other men's honors. Truth will only be desired by true men.

I shall now very briefly show what are the forms of real suffering for Jesus in these days. We have not now to rot in prisons, to wander about in sheepskins and goatskins, to be stoned, or to be sawn in sunder—though we ought to be ready to bear all this if God wills it. The days of Nebuchadnezzar's furnace are past, but the fire is still upon earth. Some suffer in their estates. I believe that to many Christians it is rather a gain than a loss, so far as pecuniary matters go, to be Believers in Christ. But I meet with many cases—cases which I know to be genuine—where persons have had to suffer severely for conscience sake.

There are those present who were once in very comfortable circumstances, but they lived in a neighborhood where the majority of the business was done on a Sunday. When Divine Grace shut up their shop, trade left them. And I know some of them are working very hard for their bread, though once they earned abundance without any great toil. They do it cheerfully for Christ's sake, but the struggle is a hard one. I know other persons who were employed as servants in lucrative positions involving sin, but upon their becoming Christians they were obliged to resign their former post and are not at the present moment in anything like such apparent prosperity as they were.

I could point to several cases of persons who have really suffered to a very high degree in pecuniary matters for the Cross of Christ. Brethren, you may possess your souls in patience and expect as a reward of Grace that you shall reign with Jesus your Beloved! Those feather-bed soldiers who are broken-hearted if fools laugh at them should blush when they think of those who endure real hardship as good soldiers of Jesus Christ.

Who can waste his pity over the small griefs of faint hearts when cold, hunger, and poverty are cheerfully endured by the true and brave?

Cases of persecution are by no means rare. In many a country village squires and priests rule with a high hand and smite the godly villagers with a rod of iron. "No blankets, no coals, no almshouse for you if you venture into the Meeting House. You cannot live in my cottage if you have a Prayer Meeting in it. I will have no religious people on my farm." We who live in more enlightened society little know the terrorism exercised in some of the rural districts over poor men and women who endeavor conscientiously to carry out their convictions and walk with Christ.

True Christians of all denominations love each other and hate persecution, but nominal Christians and ungodly men would make our land as hot as in the days of Mary if they dared. To all saints who are oppressed, this sweet sentence is directed—"If we suffer, we shall also reign with Him." More usually, however, the suffering takes the form of personal contempt. It is not pleasant to be pointed at in the streets and have opprobrious names shouted after you by vulgar tongues. Nor is it a small trial to be saluted in the workshop by opprobrious epithets, or to be looked upon as an idiot or a madman.

And yet this is the lot of many of the people of God every day of the week. Many of those who are of the humbler classes have to endure constant and open reproach. And those who are richer have to put up with the cold shoulder and neglect and sneers as soon as they become true disciples of Jesus Christ. There is more sting in this than some dream. And we have known strong men who could have borne the lash brought down by jeers and sarcasms, even just as the wasp may more thoroughly irritate and vex the lion than if the noblest beast of prey should attack him. Believers have also to suffer slander and falsehood. It is not expedient for me, doubtless, to glory, but I know a man who scarcely ever speaks a word which is not misrepresented and hardly performs an action which is not misconstrued.

The press at certain seasons, like a pack of hounds, will get upon his track and worry him with the most bases and undeserved abuse. Publicly and privately he is accustomed to be sneered at. The world whispers, "Ah, he pretends to be zealous for God, but he makes a fine thing of it!" Mark you, when the world shall learn what he does make of it, maybe it will have to eat its words! But I forbear such is the portion of every servant of God who has to bear public testimony for the Truth of God.

Every motive but the right one will be imputed to him. His good will be evil spoken of. His zeal will be called imprudence—his courage, impertinence—his modesty, cowardice. It is impossible for the true Believer in Christ who is called to any eminent service to do anything right. He had better at once learn to say with Luther, "The world hates me and there is no love lost between us, for as much as it hates me, so heartily do I hate it." He meant not the men in the world, for never was there a more loving heart than Luther's. But he meant the fame, the opinion, the honor of the world he trod beneath his feet. If in your measure you bear undeserved rebuke for Christ's sake, comfort yourselves with these words, "If we suffer, we shall also reign with Him: if we deny Him, He also will deny us."

Then again, if in your service for Christ you are enabled to sacrifice yourself—bearing upon yourself inconvenience and pain, labor and loss—then I think you are suffering with Christ. The Missionary who tempts the stormy deep—the herald of the Cross who penetrates into unknown regions among savage men—the tract distributor toiling up the mountainside—the teacher going wearily to the class—the village preacher walking many toilsome miles—the minister starving on a miserable pittance—the evangelist content to break down in health—all these and their like suffer with Christ.

We are all too much occupied with taking care of ourselves. We shun the difficulties of excessive labor. And frequently behind the entrenchments of taking care of our constitution we do not half as much as we ought. A minister of God is bound to spurn the suggestions of ignoble ease—it is his calling to labor! And if he destroys his constitution, I for one, thank God that He permits us the high privilege of so making ourselves living sacrifices. If earnest ministers should bring themselves to the grave, not by imprudence, for that we would not advocate—but by honest labor, such as their ministry and their consciences require of them—they will be better in their graves than out of their graves if they come there for the cause of Christ. What? Are we never to suffer? Are we to be carpet-knights? Are God's people to be put away in padding, perfumed with lavender and boxed up in quiet softness? No! Not unless they would lose the reward of true saints!

Let us not forget that contention with inbred lusts, denials of proud self, resistance of sin and agony against Satan are all forms of suffering with Christ. We may, in the holy war within us, earn as bright a crown as in the wider battlefield beyond us. O for Grace to be ever dressed in full armor, fighting with principalities and powers and spiritual wickedness of every sort! There is one more class of suffering which I shall mention and that is, when friends forsake, or become foes. Father and mother forsake sometimes. The husband persecutes the wife. We have known even the children turn against the parents. "A man's foes are they of his own household." This is one of the devil's best instruments for making Believers suffer. And those who have to drain this cup for the Lord's sake shall reign with Him.

Brethren, if you are thus called to suffer for Christ, will you quarrel with me if I say, in adding all up, what a very little it is compared with reigning with Jesus? "For our light affliction, which is but for a moment, works for us a far more exceeding and eternal weight of Glory." When I contrast our sufferings of today with those of the reign of Mary, or the persecutions of the Albigenses on the mountains, or the sufferings of Christians in Pagan Rome—why ours are scarcely a pin's prick—and yet what is the reward? We shall reign with Christ!

There is no comparison between the service and the reward. Therefore it is all of Grace. We do but little and suffer but little—and even that little, Grace gives us! And yet the Lord grants us, "A far more exceeding and eternal weight of Glory." We are not merely to sit with Christ, but we are to reign with Christ. All that the pomp imperial of His Kingship means. All that the treasure of His wide dominions can yield. All that the majesty of His everlasting power can bestow—all this is to belong to you—given to you of His rich, Free Grace, as the sweet reward of having suffered for a little time with Him!

Who would draw back, then? Who among you will flinch? Young man, have you thought of flying from the Cross? Young woman, has Satan whispered to you to shun the thorny pathway? Will you give up the crown? Will you miss the Throne? O Beloved, it is so blessed to be in the furnace with Christ, and such an honor to stand in the pillory with Him that if there were no reward, we might count ourselves happy! But when the reward is so rich, so super-abundant, so eternal, so infinitely more than we had any right to expect—will we not take up the Cross with songs and go on our way rejoicing in the Lord our God?

II. DENYING CHRIST, AND ITS PENALTY. "If we deny Him, He also will deny us." Dreadful "if," and yet an "if" which is applicable to every one of us. If the Apostles, when they sat at the Lord's Supper, said, "Lord, is it I?" surely we may say as we sit here, "Lord, shall I ever deny You?" You who say most loudly, "Though all men shall deny You, yet I will not"—you are the most likely to do it!

In what way can we deny Christ? Some deny Him openly, as scoffers do, whose tongue walks through the earth and defies Heaven. Others do this willfully and wickedly in a doctrinal way, as the Arians and Socinians do who deny His deity—those who deny His Atonement, who rail against the inspiration of His Word—these come under the condemnation of those who deny Christ. There is a way of denying Christ without even speaking a word and this is the more common.

In the day of blasphemy and rebuke, many hide their heads. They are in company where they ought to speak up for Christ. But they put their hands upon their mouths. They come not forward to profess their faith in Jesus. They have a sort of faith, but it is one which yields no obedience. Jesus bids each Believer to be baptized. They neglect His ordinance. Neglecting that, they also despise the weightier matters of the Law. They will go up to the House of God because it is fashionable to go there. But if it were a matter of persecution, they would forsake the assembling of themselves together.

In the day of battle they are never on the Lord's side. If there is a parade, and the banners are flying and the trumpets are sounding, if there are decorations and medals to be given away, there they are. But if the shots are flying, if trenches have to be carried and forts to be stormed, where are they? They have gone back to their dens and there will they hide themselves till fair weather shall return.

Mind, mind, mind, for I am giving a description, I am afraid, of some here. Mind, I say, you silent ones, lest you stand speechless at the bar of Judgment. Some, after having been long silent and so practically denying Christ, go farther and apostatize altogether from the faith they once had. No man who has a genuine faith in Christ will lose it, for the faith which God gives will live forever. Hypocrites and formalists have a name to live while yet they are dead—and after a while they return like the dog to its vomit and the sow which was washed to her wallowing in the mire. Certain professors do not run this length, yet practically deny Christ by their lives, though they make a profession of faith in Him.

Are there not some here who have been baptized and who come to the Lord's Table but what is their character? Follow them home. I would to God they never had made a profession because in their own houses they deny what in the House of God they have avowed. If I see a man drunk. If I know that a professor indulges in lasciviousness. If I know a man to be harsh and overbearing and tyrannical to his servants. If I know another who cheats in his traffic and another who adulterates his goods. And if I know that such men profess allegiance to Jesus—which am I to believe—their words or their deeds? I will believe that which speaks loudest! And as actions always speak louder than words, I will believe their actions—I believe that they are deceivers whom Jesus will deny at the last.

Should we not find many present this morning belonging to one or other of these grades? Does not this description suit at least some of you? If it should do so, do not be angry with me but stand still and hear the Word of the Lord. Know, O Man that you will not perish even if you have denied Christ, if now you fly to Him for refuge. Peter denied, but yet Peter is in Heaven. A transient forsaking of Jesus under temptation will not bring on everlasting ruin, if faith shall step in and the Grace of God shall intervene. But persevere in it—continue still in a denial of the Savior and my terrible text will come upon you—"He also will deny you."

In musing over the very dreadful sentence which closes my text, "He also will deny us," I was led to think of various ways in which Jesus will deny us. He does this sometimes on earth. You have read, I suppose, of the death of Francis Spira. If you have ever read it, you never can forget it to your dying day. Francis Spira knew the Truth of God. He was a reformer of no mean standing, but when brought to death, out of fear, he recanted. In a short time he fell into despair and suffered Hell upon earth. His shrieks and exclamations were so horrible that their record is almost too terrible for print. His doom was a warning to the age in which he lived.

Another instance is narrated by my predecessor, Benjamin Keach, of one whom, during Puritanical times, was very earnest for Puritanism but afterwards, when times of persecution arose, forsook his profession. The scenes at his deathbed were thrilling amid terrible. He declared that though he sought God, Heaven was shut against him. Gates of brass seemed to be in his way. He was given up to overwhelming despair. At intervals he cursed. At other intervals he prayed and so perished without hope.

If we deny Christ, we may be delivered to such a fate. If we have stood highest and foremost in God's Church and yet have not been brought to Christ—if we should become apostates—a high soar will bring a deep fall. High pretensions bring down sure destruction when they come to nothing. Even upon earth Christ will deny such. There are remarkable instances of persons who sought to save their lives and lost them. One Richard Denton, who had been a very zealous Lollard and was the means of the conversion of an eminent saint, when he came to the stake, was so afraid of the fire that he renounced everything he held and went into the Church of Rome.

A short time after, his own house took fire, and going into it to save some of his money, he perished miserably, being utterly consumed by that fire which he had denied Christ in order to escape. If I must be lost, let it be any way rather than as an apostate. If there is any distinction among the damned, those have it who are wandering stars, trees plucked up by the roots, twice dead, for whom Jude tells us, is "reserved the blackness of darkness forever." Reserved! As if nobody else were qualified to occupy that place but themselves. They are to inhabit the darkest, hottest place because they forsook the Lord.

Let us, my dear Friends, rather lose everything than lose Christ. Let us sooner suffer anything than lose our ease of conscience and our peace of mind. When Marcus Arethusus was commanded by Julian the apostate to subscribe towards the rebuilding of a heathen temple which his people had pulled down upon their conversion to Christianity, he refused to obey. And though he was an aged man, he was stripped naked and then pierced all over with lancets and knives. The old man still was firm.

If he would give but one halfpenny towards the building of the temple, he could be free—if he would cast in but one grain of incense into the censer devoted to the false gods, he might escape. He would not countenance idolatry in any degree. He was smeared with honey and while his innumerable wounds were yet bleeding, the bees and wasps came upon him and stung him to death. He could die, but he could not deny his Lord. Arethusus entered into the joy of his Lord, for he nobly suffered with Him!

In the olden time when the Gospel was preached in Persia, one Hamedatha, a courtier of the king, having embraced the faith, was stripped of all his offices, driven from the palace and compelled to feed camels. This he did with great content. The king, passing by one day, saw his former favorite at his ignoble work, cleaning out the camel's stables. Taking pity upon him he took him into his palace, clothed him with sumptuous apparel, restored him to all his former honors and made him sit at the royal table. In the midst of the dainty feast, he asked Hamedatha to renounce his faith.

The courtier, rising from the table, took off his garments with haste, left all the dainties behind him, and said, "Did you think that for such silly things as these I would deny my Lord and Master?" And away he went to the stable to his ignoble work. How honorable is all this! How shall I denounce the meanness of the apostate—his detestable cowardice to forsake the bleeding Savior of Calvary to return to the beggarly elements of the world which he once despised and to bow his neck again to the yoke of bondage? Will you do this, O followers of the Crucified?

You will not! You cannot! I know you cannot if the Spirit of the Lord dwells in you and it must dwell in you if you are the children of God. What must be the doom of those who deny Christ, when they reach another world? Perhaps they will appear with a sort of hope in their minds and they will come before the Judge, with, "Lord, Lord, open to us." Who are you? He says,

"Lord, we once took the Lord's Supper—Lord, we were members of the Church, but there came very hard times. My mother bade me give up religion. Father was angry. Trade went bad. I was so mocked at, I could not stand it. Lord, I fell among evil acquaintances and they tempted me—I could not resist. I was Your servant—I did love You—I always had love towards You in my heart, but I could not help it—I denied You and went to the world again."

What will Jesus say? I know you not! "But, Lord, I want You to be my Advocate." I know you not! "But, Lord, I cannot get into Heaven unless You should open the gate—open it for me." I do not know you! I do not know you! "But, Lord, my name was in the Church Book." I know you not—I deny you. "But will You not hear my cries?" You did not hear Mine—you did deny Me and I deny you. "Lord, give me the lowest place in Heaven, if I may but enter and escape from wrath to come." No, you would not brook the lowest place on earth and you shall not enjoy the lowest place here. You had your choice and you did choose evil. Keep to your choice. You were filthy, be you filthy still. You were unholy, be you unholy still.

O, Sirs, if you would not see the angry face of Jesus! O, Sirs, if you would not behold the lightning flashing from His eyes and hear the thunder of His mouth in the day when He judges the fearful and the unbelieving and the hypocrite. If you would not have your portion in the lake which burns with fire and brimstone, cry this day mightily unto God, "Lord, hold me fast, keep me, keep me. Help me to suffer with You, that I may reign with You. But do not, do not let me deny You, lest You also should deny me."

13

Eternal Faithfulness Unaffected by Human Unbelief

(Sermon No. 1453)

"If we believe not, yet He abides faithful: He cannot deny Himself" (2 Timothy 2:13).

THIS IS ONE OF THE FIVE faithful sayings which the Apostle mentions. All those faithful sayings are weighty and important. I suppose that they may have come into the possession of the Church by having been uttered by some of those Prophets who were raised up to cherish the infancy of the Church, such as Agabus and the daughters of Philip and others. These may have been some of their more remarkable sayings which laid hold upon the minds of good men; were quoted by the preachers and teachers and so became current throughout the Church. Such golden sayings were minted into proverbs and passed from hand to hand, enriching all who received them. To the saints they became "familiar in their mouths as household words" and were specially named faithful or true sayings.

No doubt the Apostle Paul gave his endorsement to many of these holy proverbs, but five of them he has encased in the amber of Inspiration and handed down for our special note. Perhaps it may interest you to notice them as they occur. The first one, probably the best one, is in the First Epistle of Timothy, first chapter, and the 15th verse, "This is a faithful saying, and worthy of all acceptation, that Christ Jesus came into the world to save sinners; of whom I am chief." I can suppose that the good news was frequently conveyed by humble-minded Christians to the outside world in that short and compact form—"Jesus Christ came into the world to save sinners," so that it was commonly known to be a saying among Christians. It was the way in which those who could not preach a sermon and, perhaps, could scarcely compose a sentence for themselves, learned the pith and marrow of the Gospel and had it in a concise and simple form for instructing others. Converts were in the habit of telling this to their heathen friends and acquaintances wherever they went, that they might know what Jesus Christ had come to do and might be led to believe on His name.

The next faithful or true saying is in the First Epistle of Timothy, the third chapter and the first verse. "This is a true saying, If a man desire the office of a bishop, he desires a good work." Any man who desires to oversee the Church of God and to be in the midst of the people as a shepherd, desires a good work. He will bring himself great anxiety, labor and travail, but the work is honorable and has so large a spiritual reward that a man is wise to choose it and to give his whole life to it. Another of these faithful sayings will be found in the First Epistle of Timothy, the fourth chapter, and the eighth verse, for so the words run,

"For bodily exercise profits a little: but godliness is profitable unto all things, having promise of the life that now is and of that which is to come. This is a faithful saying and worthy of all acceptation. For therefore we both labor and suffer reproach, because we trust in the living God, who is the Savior of all men, specially of those that believe."

Godliness has the profit of this life and the next and, therefore, godly men are content to suffer, because they expect and receive an abundant blessing as the result thereof at the hand of God. Such a proverb as this was greatly needed in persecuting times and it is still valuable in these greedy days when men find godliness a hindrance to their hasty snatching at wealth and, therefore, turn aside unto ways of dishonesty and falsehood. The next is the one which constitutes our text. We will not, therefore, read it again till we come to handle it. But the fifth is in Titus, the third chapter, and the eighth verse—"This is a faithful saying, and these things I will that you affirm constantly, that they which have believed in God might be careful to maintain good works. These things are good and profitable unto men." That those who believe in Jesus should manifest the holy character of their faith by their lives is another one of these faithful sayings which comes with all the greater force from

Paul because he, above all men, was free from any suspicion of legality, or the putting of human merit into the place of the Grace of God which is received by faith.

And now, coming to the faithful saying before us, it may not strike you at first, but scholarly men have observed that the 11th , 12th and 13th verses assume the form of a hymn. The Hebrew hymns were written in parallelisms, not, of course, in rhymes, and these three verses are thought to have been one of the oldest of Christian hymns—

> "It is a faithful saying:
> For if we are dead with Him,
> We shall also live with Him:
> If we suffer, we shall also reign with Him:
> If we deny Him, He also will deny us:
> If we believe not, yet He abides faithful:
> He cannot deny Himself."

This is a miniature Psalm—one of those Psalms and hymns and spiritual songs with which the saints of God were known to edify one another. I am sure this last part of this brief hymn is well worthy to be regarded as a faithful saying among ourselves. Brethren, we may often mention it. We may frequently quote it. We may roll it under our tongue as a sweet morsel. We may pass it from one to another as a classic saying of Christian wisdom—"If we believe not, yet He abides faithful: He cannot deny Himself."

In handling it at this time I would divide it into two folded parts. The first double portion is, the sad possibility, with the consoling assurance. "If we believe not"—sad possibility, "yet He abides faithful"—consoling assurance. The second part of our subject is the glorious impossibility and the sweet inference that we may draw from it. The glorious impossibility is—"He cannot deny Himself" and the inference we draw from it is the obverse or converse of our text—If we believe, He abides faithful: He cannot deny Himself.

I. To begin, then, with THE SAD POSSIBILITY AND THE CONSOLING ASSURANCE—"If we believe not, yet He abides faithful." I must take the sad possibility first—"if we believe not," and I shall read this expression as though, first of all, it concerned the world in general, for I think it may so be fairly read. If we believe not—if mankind believes not, if the race believes not, if the various classes of men believe not—yet He abides faithful. The rulers believe not and there are some that make this a very great point. They said concerning Jesus, "Have any of the rulers believed on Him?"

If Lord So-and-So hears the preacher, there must be something in what he says. Englishmen are wonderfully impressed with the judgment of a duke or an earl and even with that of titled folk of lower degree. If any of the rulers believe in Him, who among worshippers of rank would raise a question? Is it published under authority? Do the great ones subscribe to it? "Oh, then," says one, "it must be good and it must be true." Now, I venture to say that all history proves that the Truth of God has very seldom been accepted by the rulers of this world and, for the most part, the poorest of the poor have been more able to perceive the Truth than the greatest of the great have ever been!

There would have been no Christianity in the world at the present moment if it had not found a shelter in workshops and in cottages. It has flourished among the despised poor when it has been condemned by the great ones of the earth. Well, Sirs, if we believe not—that is, if our greatest men, if our senators and magistrates, princes and potentates, believe not—it does not affect the Truth of God in the smallest conceivable degree—"yet He abides faithful." Many, however, think it more important to know on which side the leaders of thought are enlisted and there are certain persons who are not elected to that particular office by popular vote, who, nevertheless, take it upon themselves to consider that they are dictators in the republic of opinion.

They are advanced men and far ahead of the old school of Divines. Some of us think that they are advancing in the direction of going backwards and that they are putting ignorant guess-work into the room of proved doctrine and solid, experimental, Scriptural teaching. Still, as in their own opinion they are our superiors and pioneer the way of progress, we will, for a moment, think of them as such. Now, in our Lord's day the advanced thinkers were not on His side at all—they were all against Him—and after He had departed, the greatest peril of the Church of God arose from the advanced thought of the period. The Gnostics and other Grecian thinkers came forward and threw their philosophical mud into the pure stream of the Gospel till there was no plain statement which was not rendered mythical, mystical, confused, or clouded, so that only the initiated could possibly understand it.

The Gospel of Jesus Christ was meant to be the most plain Truth that ever shone upon the sons of men. It was meant to be legible in its own light by the young, the unlearned and the simple. But the advanced thinkers took the Gospel and twisted it, colored it, adorned it and bedaubed it till by the time it came through their various processes you would not have known it to be the same thing at all! And, in fact, Paul said that it was not the same thing, for he called it, "another gospel," and then he corrected himself and said it was not another—"But there are some," he said, "that trouble you."

However, we need not care because of these wise men, for if they believe not, but becloud the Gospel, yet God abides faithful!

If over there in the groves where Socrates and Plato gathered disciples by their philosophy; if over there, I say, there should not be found a single philosopher who believes in God, so much the worse for the philosophers! It does not affect the Gospel or our faith in it—if they believe not, He abides faithful! If Paul at the Areopagus gets no sympathy except from two or three and, in fact, they have only asked him there to "hear what this babbler says" and though they all, as they go home, say that Paul is beside himself and mad—and a setter forth of strange gods— yet Paul is right and the Lord abides faithful! Yes, and I venture to enlarge this thought a little more. If the rulers do not believe and if the philosophical minds do not believe—and if, in addition to this, public opinion, so called, rejects it—yet the Gospel is still the same eternal Truth of God.

Public opinion is not the test and gauge of the Truth of God, for public opinion has continually altered and it will continue to alter. The aggregate thinking of fallible men is less than nothing when set against the one solitary mind of God, who is Infallible, as He reveals it to us by the Holy Spirit in the Words of Truth in the Scriptures. But some think that the old Gospel cannot be right because, you see, everybody says that it is out of date and wrong. That is one reason for being the more sure that it is right, for the world lies in the Wicked One and its judgment is under his sway. What are multitudes when they are all under the influence of the Father of Lies?

The greatest majority in the world is a minority of one when that man is on God's side. Count heads, do you? Well, count by the millions if you like, but I shall rather weigh, than count—and if I speak the Truth of God—I have more weight on my side than can be found in a million who believe not! I wish we all partook of the spirit of Athanasius when he said, defending the Deity of his great Master, "I, Athanasius, against the world." You must learn to stand alone! When you know that you have a grip on revealed Truth, you may not set all the judgments of men in comparison with the eternal and Infallible judgment of the mighty God! No, though we believe not, that is, the mass of us and nations of us, "yet He abides faithful: He cannot deny Himself."

I want to ask your thoughtful attention to one consideration here. Have you not often heard it said that ministers ought to be abreast of the times; that theology should be always toned and varied so as to suit the advanced thought of the wonderful period in which we live? And as this is a time when infidelity appears to be in the very air, we are told that we ought to sympathize with it very earnestly and heartily, for it is a form of struggling for the Light which we ought to encourage. Now, this is another sort of talk from what I hear from the Apostle Paul. He has no sympathy with it! He put his foot on it. "Let God be true and every man a liar"—that is the style in which he speaks! As to going in to study the philosophies in order to tune the Gospel to their note, he says, "I determined not to know anything among you save Jesus Christ and Him crucified."

When he finds that this style of doctrine does not please the Jew and that it is a stumbling block to him and that it does not please the Greek, but makes him sneer and call it foolishness, does the Apostle, therefore, say, "Come here, dear Jewish Friend. I have a way of putting this which will show you that I do not quite mean what you thought I did. I used the word, 'Cross,' in a certain sense not at all objectionable to Judaism"? Does he gently whisper, "Come to me, my learned Greek Friend and I will show you that your philosophers and I mean the same thing"? Not a bit! No, he stands fast and firm to Christ crucified and salvation by His blood, as, by God's Grace, I trust we are resolved to do. Though we believe not— that is, though the whole world believe not—yet God's Gospel is not to be altered to suit human whims and fancies, but in all its forms, in all its Divine authority, unpaved, uncut, worked out as a whole, it is still to be proclaimed, for, "He abides faithful: He cannot deny Himself."

Now, having spoken of our text as referring to the world in general, it is, perhaps, a more sorrowful business to look at it as referring to the visible Church in particular. The Apostle says, "Though we believe not," and surely he must mean the visible Church of God. And does the Church of God ever fall into such a state that we may say of it, "It believes not"? Yes, the visible Church has many and many a time fearfully turned aside. Go back for a type of it to the wilderness. The children of Israel were brought up out of Egypt with a high hand and an outstretched arm. They were fed in the wilderness with angels' food and made to drink of water from the Rock—but they were continually doubting their God—

> "Now they believe His word,
> While rocks with rivers flow.
> But soon with sin they grieve the Lord,
> And judgments lay them low."

And what happened? Did God depart from His purpose to give the land that flowed with milk and honey to the seed of Abraham? Did He break up the Covenant and grow weary of it? No—Abraham's seed inherited the land and they dwelt therein, every man under his own vine and fig tree. Though the visible people of God rejected Him full often, so that for their unbelief they died in the wilderness, yet He remained faithful—He did not, He could not deny Himself. Well, now, it comes to pass, sometimes, according to this type, that the visible Church of God apostatizes from the Truth of God. The Doctrines of Grace, the Truths of the Gospel are obscured, beclouded, scarcely preached—preached with gaudy words or hid behind ceremonies and rites and all sorts of things.

And what happens? Are the foundation Truths removed? Is the eternal verity reversed? Has God recalled His promises? Oh no! "He abides faithful: He cannot deny Himself." Alas, the Church of God seems to lose, sometimes, her faith in prayer! Her pleading assemblies become scarce. Her prayer for men's conversion is scarcely raised. Few come together to supplicate the Lord and besiege the Mercy Seat. But what then? Does God change? Does He forsake His cause? Oh, no: "He abides faithful: He cannot deny Himself." At such times the Church almost loses her faith in the Holy Spirit and looks upon preaching as, perhaps, a necessary evil to be borne with—not as the vehicle by which the Holy Spirit saves men. They have small confidence in God's Word that, "By the foolishness of preaching" He will "save them that believe."

They do not expect the kingdom of Christ to be predominant, but they say, "Since the fathers fell asleep what long ages have dragged along and what slow progress Christianity has made! It is a hopeless cause. Let us be content to let the heathen world alone." At such time they lose all heart and all faith in God! Have we not seen large portions of the visible Church of God decline into such a state as this till we have been ready to ask with our Master, "When the Son of Man comes, shall He find faith on the earth?" But, what then, my Brothers and Sisters? Suppose we should live to see a degenerate Church everywhere? Suppose it should become like Laodicea, till the Lord should seem to spew the visible Church out of His mouth because she has become neither hot nor cold?

Suppose He should say of the professing Church of today as He did of Shiloh of old—"Go now to Shiloh where My place was at the first and see if there is one stone left upon another that is not cast down"? He took the candlestick away from Rome and He may take that candlestick away from other Churches, too. But would that prove that God was unfaithful, or that He had denied Himself? No, Beloved, no! His faithfulness would then be seen in the judgment with which He would visit an unfaithful Church. Yes, and it is seen today. You shall see a Church which does not believe in the simple Gospel grow few and feeble. According as the Churches cease to be evangelical, they are diminished and brought low. A Church that neglects prayer becomes disunited, scattered, lethargic, all but dead.

A Church that has no faith in the Holy Spirit may carry on her ordinances, but it will be with barren formality and without power from on high—all of which proves the faithfulness of Him who said, "If you walk contrary to Me, I will walk contrary to you." If they cast away from them that which is their strength, it is but faithfulness on God's part that they should become weak. All the history of the Church, if you read it, from the days of Christ till now, will go to show that He deals with His Church in such a way as to make her see that He is faithful, whatever she may be. He will help her when she turns to Him. He will bless her when she trusts Him. He will crown her when she exalts Him. But He will bring her low and chasten her when she turns, in any measure, aside from the simplicity of her faith. Thus does He prove that He is still faithful.

Once more, my Brethren, I will read the text in a somewhat narrower circle. "If we believe not"—that is to say, if the choicest teachers, preachers and writers believe not, yet He abides faithful. One of the most shocking trials to young Christians is the fall of an eminent teacher. I have known some that have been almost ready to give up their faith when someone who appeared to be very earnest and faithful has suddenly apostatized. Such things have happened in our memory, to our intense grief and I want, therefore, to put it very, very plainly. If it should come to pass that anyone whom you revere as having been blest to your soul—whom because you have received from him the Word of Life—if such a one upon whom you may, perhaps, have learned much, should, in the future, turn out not to be true and faithful and should not believe, do not follow his unbelief, for "if we believe not, yet He abides faithful: He cannot deny Himself."

Peter denies his Master—do not follow Peter when he is doing that, for he will have to come back weeping and you will hear him preaching his Master again. Worse still, Judas sells his Master—do not follow Judas, for Judas will die a wretched death and his destruction shall be a warning to others to cling more closely to the King. You may see the man who stood like a cedar in Lebanon fall by one stroke of the devil's axe, but do not, therefore, think that the trees of the Lord, which are full of sap, will fall, too. He will keep His own, for He knows them that are His.

Pin not your faith to any man's sleeve. Let not your confidence rest on any arm of flesh, neither say, "I believe because of the testimony of such a one and I hold to the form of sound words because my minister has held it," for all such props may be pulled away and all of a sudden may fail you! Let me put this very, very plainly. If we believe not—if those that seem to be the choice teachers of the age, the most successful evangelists of the period—if those who seem to stand the highest in the esteem of God's people, should, in an evil hour, forsake the eternal verities and begin to preach to you some other gospel which is not the Gospel of Jesus Christ, I beseech you follow us not, whoever we may be or whatever we may be!

Suffer no teachers, however great they may be, to lead you to doubt, for God abides faithful! Keep to the revealed will and mind of God—for "He cannot deny Himself." Here, then, is the fearful possibility and side by side with it rims this most blessedly consoling assurance—"He abides faithful." Jesus Christ abides—there are no shifts and changes in Him. He is a rock and not a quicksand! He is the Savior whether the rulers and the philosophers believe in Him or refuse Him; whether the Church and her ministers are true to Him or desert Him. He is the same Savior, God-Man, sitting supreme upon the Truth of God. "Why do the heathens rage and the people imagine a vain thing? The kings of the earth set themselves and the rulers take counsel together against the Lord and against His anointed? He that sits in the heavens shall laugh: the Lord shall have them in derision. Yet," says He, "have I set My king upon My holy hill of Zion."

They cannot affect the imperial throne of our immortal Lord! He is still "the blessed and only Potentate" and so He must be, let them say what they will! And as Christ remains the same Savior, so we have the same Gospel. They have improved upon it, they tell us! Well, well, I feel so satisfied with the Gospel as I get it from Paul and the Inspired Apostles that I would rather not have this improved gospel if they will allow me to keep to the old original. But so it is, like babies pleased with new toys, they cry their "modern thought" and culture and advanced ideas! He that has once tasted the old wines does not desire the new, because he says, "The old is better."

Our Savior and His Gospel abide the same! The Gospel of Paul, the Gospel of Augustine, the Gospel of Calvin, the Gospel of Whitefield, the Gospel of any succession of faithful men you like to mention suffices us. He abides faithful! And as the Gospel is the same, so does Christ remain faithful to His engagements to His Father. He has promised to keep those whom the Father gave Him and He will keep them even to the end. And when the sheep shall pass again under the hands of Him that counts them, He will say, "Of all whom You gave me I have lost none." "He abides faithful." To sinners all over the world He says that if they come to Him, He will not cast them out and He is faithful to that. He graciously promises that "whoever calls upon the name of the Lord shall be saved." And He will be faithful to that.

He is also faithful to His saints. He has promised to preserve them to His eternal kingdom and Glory and He will preserve them. He says, "I give unto My sheep eternal life and they shall never perish, neither shall any pluck them out of My hands"—and He has held them in His loving grasp and He will hold them even to the end! And all this, though all the unbelief in the world should rise against Him! He will stand to every Word He has spoken and carry out every promise He has declared, though all should distrust and deny. "Yes and amen in Christ Jesus" are all the promises, henceforth and forever—and we shall find it so.

II. And now we have but a little time to spend upon the second very important part of our text, which is A GLORIOUS IMPOSSIBILITY WITH A SWEET INFERENCE THAT MAY BE DRAWN FROM IT. "He cannot deny Himself." Three things God cannot do. He cannot die. He cannot lie. And He cannot be deceived. These three impossibilities do not limit His power, but they magnify His majesty, for these would be infirmities, and infirmity can have no place in the Infinite and Ever-Blessed God. Here is one of the things impossible with God—"He cannot deny Himself." What is meant by that?

It is meant, first, that the Lord Jesus Christ cannot change as to His Nature and Character towards us, the sons of men, for if He were to change He could only change from one state to another—from a better to a worse or from a worse to a better. If from a better to a worse, that were to deny Himself, indeed, by ceasing to be as good as He is by Nature.

And if from a worse to a better, that were to deny Himself by proving that He was not, before, so good as He might have been! In no one point can Jesus Christ be changed, for He is "Jesus Christ, the same yesterday, today and forever." If in any point He changed, He would, in that point, deny Himself. But He cannot do this, for being God He changes not.

His Word cannot alter. I want you to notice this, because His Word is so conspicuously Himself. His name shall be called the Word of God. Yes, He is Himself the Logos, the Eternal Word, and that Word cannot change. "The grass withers, and the flower falls away, but the Word of the Lord endures forever and this is the Word which by the Gospel is preached unto you." O servant of the Lord, the assurance which Paul and Peter gave, you may give! That same Word of mercy which those first messengers of Heaven went forth to declare, you may declare, for it still stands the same! He cannot deny His Word since that Word is Himself and He cannot deny Himself. He cannot, beloved Friends, withdraw the salvation which He has presented to the sons of men, for that salvation is, indeed, Himself.

Jesus is the salvation of Israel. If a sinner wants to know where salvation lies, we point him to the Christ of God. He is not only a Savior, but He is Salvation itself! And His salvation cannot be changed, for if it were changed He would be Himself changed or denied and He cannot deny Himself. There is still the same pardon for the chief of sinners; still the same renewing for the hardest hearts; still the same generous response to those who have strayed most; still the same adoption into the family for aliens and foreigners. His salvation, as Peter preached it at Pentecost, is the salvation which we preach to sinners today. "He cannot deny Himself." And then the Atonement is still the same, for that, too, is Himself—He has, by Himself, purged our sins.

He Himself is the Sacrifice. Well did the poet say—

"Dear dying Lamb, Your precious blood shall never lose its power."

Because it is His blood, it must be unchanged in efficacy. He cleanses away our sins by Himself. His blood is His life and He always lives. And since He always lives, He is "able to save to the uttermost them that come unto God by Him." Blessed be His name, the atoning Sacrifice has not, even in the smallest degree, lost its efficacy! It is just as mighty as when it washed the dying thief from the foulness of Hell into the purity of Heaven and carried him from the gallows to a throne! Oh, how blessed must its power be to have cleansed so foul a wretch and to have placed him with the Master Himself in Paradise the same day! The Atonement cannot change, for that would involve that Jesus had denied Himself.

And the Mercy Seat, the place of prayer, still remains, for if that were altered He would have denied Himself, for what was the Mercy Seat, or propitiatory, but that golden lid upon the Covenant Ark? What was it but Christ Himself, who is our Propitiatory, the true Mercy Seat? You may always pray, Brothers and Sisters, for if prayer were denied its efficacy, God would have denied Himself! This is His memorial, "The God that hears prayer," and if He does not hear prayer He has denied Himself and ceased to be what He was. Jehovah will never so deny Himself as to become like Baal, a deaf God—to imagine it would be blasphemy!

And here is another sweet thought—Christ's love to His Church and His purpose towards her cannot change, because He cannot deny Himself and His Church is Himself. I mean not that visible Church of which I spoke just now, which is a mixed multitude, but I mean that invisible Church, that spiritual people, that bride of Christ which no man sees, for she is prepared in darkness and curiously worked in the lowest parts of the earth—and her Lord Himself will never actually see her till she is perfected, even as Adam never saw Eve, but slept until the great God had finished His bride and presented her in all her matchless beauty to be His sister and spouse. The day comes when the Lord Jesus Christ shall thus receive His perfected bride—and meanwhile He cannot change towards her, but His espousals shall be confirmed. She was taken out of His side when He lay in deep sleep of death and she is fashioned to be like He, so that when in joy He shall behold her, His joy and her joy shall be full. No, He will never, never deny her, for He cannot deny Himself. His plan of love shall be carried out and all His thoughts of Grace fulfilled.

Nor will any of His offices towards His Church and people ever fail. The Prophet shall be Prophet forever—"He cannot deny Himself." The Priest shall be a Priest forever after the order of Melchisedec and will never refuse to offer our prayers and praises and to cleanse our souls, for He cannot deny Himself. The King will never cease to reign, or doff His crown, or lay down His scepter, for He cannot deny Himself. The Shepherd will forever keep the flock. The Friend will eternally stick closer than a brother. The Husband will still love His spouse. All that He is in relation to His people shall continue and abide, for He abides faithful. "He cannot deny Himself."

Now, my last word is about an inference. The text says, "If we believe, not, yet He abides faithful." It runs on that supposition. Now, Brethren, take the other supposition—suppose we do believe? Will He not be faithful in that case, too? And will it not be true that He cannot deny Himself? I will suppose that a sinner is, at this moment, saying, "I believe that Christ can save me. I will go and ask Him, I will go and trust Him." Ah, He will not deny Himself by rejecting your cry! I tell you, if He were to shut you out, dear Soul, whoever you may be, if you go to Him, He would deny Himself! He never did deny Himself yet. Whenever a sinner comes to Him, He becomes his Savior. Whenever He meets a sick soul, He acts as his physician.

Now, I have heard of persons who have been physicians who were ill, or weary and needed rest—an accident has happened and they have felt inclined to get out of the way, if they could, because they were very hard-worked and worn out. They have told their servant to say, "My master is not at home!" But my Master never denied Himself! He will never get out of the way of a sinner! If you go to Him, you will find Him at home and on the look-out for you! He will be more glad to receive you than you will be to be received, for He "waits to be gracious." As Matthew sat at the receipt of custom, waiting for the people to pay their dues, so does Christ sit at the receipt of sinners waiting for them to mention their needs!

He is watching for you. I tell you again that He cannot reject you— that would be to alter His whole Character and "un-Christ" Himself! To spurn a coming sinner would un-Jesus Him and make Him to be somebody else, and not Himself any longer. "He cannot deny Himself." Go and try Him! Go and try Him. I wish some trembling soul would, at this moment, go and cast Himself upon Christ and then report to us the result. Come, poor quivering Seekers, sing in your heart, unbelieving as you are, that hymn of ours—

> **"I can but perish if I go, I am resolved to try!**
> **For if I stay away, I know I must forever die."**

Oh, but if you were to perish at His feet, you would be the first that ever did so out of all those who have ever come to Him! And that first man has never been seen yet! Go and try my Lord and see for yourselves.

Well now, you Christian people, I want you to come, also. If you believe your Lord, He will be faithful to you. Suppose it is a time of trouble with you? He will be faithful to you—go and cast your burden upon Him. Suppose at this time you are much exercised with spiritual distress? Go to the Lord as you did at first, as poor, guilty, rebellious sinners—and cast yourself upon Him and you will find Him faithful. "He cannot deny Himself." If my Lord were not kind to me tonight when I go to Him with my burdens, I should think that I had knocked at the wrong door because the Lord has been so good and so faithful to me up to now that it would take my breath away if I found Him changed! Oh, how good, how exceedingly good is my Lord! Did not we sing just now—

"He by my side has always stood:
His loving kindness, oh, how good!"?

I could sing that with all my heart and I hope many of you could earnestly join with me. You have a dear mother, or a fond wife, or a choice friend and none of them has ever spoken anything but kindness to you—if, therefore, in some dark hour you were to go to them and, instead of showing sympathy, they gave you sharp words and you could evidently see that they did not love you, how surprised you would be! So should I be if I were to meet anything but love from my dear Lord after all these years of tenderness! There is no fear of it, for "He cannot deny Himself."

So I finish by saying that we shall find it so in connection with the things of His kingdom and the concerns of His Truth. There is a great uproar just now about the God of Providence and they call me, I know not by what names, for speaking the Truth for my Master. Well, what comes of it? Shall we, therefore, be afraid? No! If we believe, we shall find Him faithful—He will not deny Himself. Is the good old cause really in danger from skepticism and superstition? Speaking after the manner of men, it may seem so, but it never really is so. Even if it were tottering, we must not put our hand upon the Ark of the Lord to steady it.

God's cause is always safe! I do not know whether we may live to see it, but as surely as the Lord lives the Truth of God will be triumphant in England! They may tell us that Puritanism is thrust to the wall, but it will take the crown of the causeway yet. The old cause goes back a little to take a breath, but she will make such a leap in this land as shall utterly surprise the soothsayers, for the Lord will make the Diviners mad and they that count the towers and say that Zion is utterly fallen shall not know where to hide their heads! The devil once flew all over Europe and said, "It is all mine. Here they are, selling indulgences and the Pope and I are master of it all."

But there was a poor monk who had not, himself, seen the Light of God but for a short time, who nailed his theses on the door of a Church and from that hour the Light of Christ began to spread all over Europe! And do you think the Lord is short of Luthers? Do you imagine that He has no sword or spear left in His armory? I tell you He has as many instruments within reach as there are stars in the sky! When the influence of the Gospel appears to recede, it is like the tide when it is ebbing out. Steadily it goes back and if we did not know better, we should begin to think that the silver waves would all give place to mire and shingle—yet when the hour comes, at the very minute—the waters pause and remain at one point awhile.

Then up comes the first wave of the wash and another and another and another and another, rising, advancing, conquering the shore till the set has come to her fullness again! So must it be and so shall it be with the ocean of the Truth of God! Only let us have faith and we shall see the Gospel at the flood, again, and old England covered with it! Doubt what you like, Brothers and Sisters, but do not doubt Divine Truth or doubt God! Hold on to the side that is most disgraced and dishonored—that has the worst word from men—for Christ and His Church usually have the bleak side of the hill. Be content to breast the stream with courage learned from your Redeemer and Lord, for the day comes when to have stood with the Truth and with the Son of the Highest will be the grandest honor that a creature can have worn. May that honor be ours, for Jesus' sake. Amen.

14
Rightly Dividing the Word of Truth
(Sermon No. 1217)

"Rightly dividing the word of truth" (2 Timothy 2:15).

TIMOTHY WAS TO DIVIDE rightly the Word of God. Every Christian minister must do this if he would make full proof of his ministry and if he would be clear of the blood of his hearers at the Last Great Day. Of the whole twenty years of my printed sermons, I can honestly say that this has been my aim—rightly to divide the Word of Truth. Wherein I have succeeded, I magnify the name of the Lord. In which I have failed I lament my faultiness. And now once more we will try, again, and may God the Holy Spirit, without whose power nothing can be done aright, help us rightly to divide the Word of Truth.

The expression is a very remarkable one because it bears so many phases of meaning. I do not think that any one of the figures by which I shall illustrate it will be at all strained, for they have been drawn from the text by most eminent expositors, and may be fairly taken as honest comments, even when they might be challenged as correct interpretations of the text. "Rightly dividing the word of truth" is our authorized version, but we leave it for a little to consider other renderings. Timothy was neither to mutilate, nor twist, nor torture, nor break in pieces the Word of God, nor keep on the outside of it, as those do who never touch the soul of a text, but rightly to divide it, as one taught of God to teach others.

I. The Vulgate version translates it—and with a considerable degree of accuracy—"Rightly *handling* the word of truth." What is the right way, then, to handle the Word of Truth? It is like a sword and it was not meant to be played with. That is not rightly to handle the Gospel. It must be used in earnest and pushed home. Are you converted, my Friends? Do you believe in Jesus Christ? Are you saved, or not? Swords are meant to cut and hack, wound and kill—and the Word of God is for pricking men in the heart and killing their sins. The Word of God is not committed to God's ministers to amuse men with its glitter, nor to charm them with the jewels in its hilt, but to conquer their souls for Jesus!

Remember, dear Hearers, if the preacher does not push you to this—that you shall be converted, or he will know the reason why. If he does not drive you to this—that you shall either willfully reject, or cheerfully accept Christ—he has not yet known how rightly to handle the great "sword of the Spirit, which is the Word of God." Now, then, where are you personally at this moment? Are you unbelievers, upon whom the wrath of God abides, or are you Believers who may lay claim to that gracious Word, "Verily, verily, I say unto you, he that believes in Me has everlasting life"? Oh that the Lord would make His all-discerning Word go round this place and strike at every conscience and lay bare every heart with its mighty power!

He that rightly handles the Word of God will never use it to defend men in their sins, but to slay their sins! If there is a professing Christian here who is living in known sin, shame upon him! And if there is a non-Christian man who is living in sin, let his conscience upbraid him! What will he do in that day when Christ comes to judge the hearts of men? Remember, the books shall be opened and every thought shall be read out before an assembled universe! I desire to handle the Word of God so that no man may ever find an excuse in my ministry for his living without Christ and living in sin, but may know clearly that sin is a deadly evil and unbelief the sure destroyer of the soul! He has, indeed, been made to handle the word aright who plunges it like a two-edged sword into the very heart of sin!

The Gospel ought never to be used for frightening sinners from Christ. I believe it is so handled sometimes. Sublime doctrines are rolled like rocks in the sinner's way and dark experiences set up as a standard of horror which must be reached before a man may believe in Jesus—but to rightly handle the Word of Life is to frighten men to Christ rather than from Him—yes, to woo them to Him by the sweet assurance that He will cast out none that come! That He asks no preparations of them, but if they come at once, as they are, He will assuredly receive them. Have I not handled the Word of Truth in this way hundreds of times in this house? Has it not been a great magnet attracting sinners? As a magnet has two poles, and with one pole it repels, so, no doubt, the Truth of God repels the prejudiced, rebellious heart—and thus it is a savor of death unto death. But our object is so to handle it that the attractive pole may come into operation through the power of the Spirit of God—and men may be drawn to Christ.

Moreover, if we rightly handle the Word of God we shall not preach it so as to send Christians into a sleepy state. That is easily done. We may preach the consolations of the Gospel till each professor feels "I am safe enough. There is no need to watch, no need to fight, no need for any exertion whatever! My battle is fought, my victory is won. I have only to fold my arms and go to sleep." No, no! This is not how we handle the Word of God, but our cry is,

"Work out your own salvation with fear and trembling; for it is God which works in you both to will and to do of His good pleasure. Watch and pray that you enter not into temptation. Reckon not yourselves to have attained unto perfection, but forget the things that are behind, and reach forward to that which is before, looking unto Jesus."

This is rightly to handle the Word of God. And, oh, Beloved, there is one thing that I dread above all others—that I should ever handle the Word of God so as to persuade some of you that you are saved when you are not. To collect a large number of professors together is one thing. But to have a large number of true saints built together in Christ is quite another. To get up a whirl of excitement and to have people influenced by that excitement so that they think, full surely, that they are converted, has been done a great many times. But the bubble, has, by-and-by, vanished. The balloon has been filled until it has burst. God save us from that! We want sure work—lasting work—a work of Divine Grace in the heart.

If you are not converted, do not pretend that you are. If you have not known what it is to be brought down to see your own nothingness and then to be built up by the power of the Spirit upon Christ as the only foundation, O, remember that whatever is built upon the quicksand will fall with a crash in the hour of trial! Do not be satisfied with anything short of a deep foundation, cut in the solid rock of the work of Jesus Christ. Ask for real vital godliness, for nothing else will serve your turn at the Last Great Day. Now, this is rightly to handle the Word of God—to use it to push the Truth of God home upon men for their present conversion, to use it for the striking down of their sins—to use it to draw men to Christ, to use it to arouse sinners and to use it to produce, not mere profession, but a real work of Grace in the hearts of men

May the Holy Spirit teach all the ministers of Christ after this fashion to handle the two-edged sword of the Spirit, which is the Word of God.

II. But now, secondly, my text has another meaning. It has an idea in it which I can only express by a figure. "Rightly dividing, or STRAIGHT CUTTING. A plowman stands here with his plow and he plows right along from this end of the field to the other, making a straight furrow. And so Paul would have Timothy make a straight furrow right through the Word of Truth. I believe there is no preaching that God will ever accept but that which goes decidedly through the whole line of Truth from end to end, is always thorough, honest and downright. As the Truth of God is a straight line, so must our handling of the Truth be straightforward and honest, without shifts or tricks.

There are two or three furrows which I have labored hard to plow. One is the furrow of free Grace. "Salvation is of the Lord"—He begins it, He carries it on, He completes it. Salvation is not of man, neither by man, but of Grace alone. Grace in election, Grace in redemption, Grace in effectual calling, Grace in final perseverance, Grace in conferring the perfection of Glory—it is all Grace from beginning to end! If we say, at any time, anything which is really contrary to this distinct testimony that salvation is of Grace, do not believe us! This furrow must be plowed fairly, plainly and beyond all mistake.

Sinner, you cannot be saved by any merit, penance, preparation, or feeling of your own! The Lord, alone, must save you as a work of gratis mercy, not because you deserve it, but because He wills to do it to magnify His abundant love. That is the straight furrow of the Word. We endeavor always to make a straight furrow upon the matter of human depravity—to preach that man is fallen, that every part and passion of his nature is perverted, that he has gone astray altogether, is sick from the crown of his head to the sole of his feet—yes, is dead in trespasses and sins, and corrupt before God. "There is none that does good, no, not one."

I have noticed some preachers plowing this furrow very crookedly, for they say, "There are still some very fine points about man and many good things in him which only need developing and educating." You may have read, in the history of Mr. Whitfield's time, what a howl was made at him because he once said that man was half beast and half devil. I do not think he ever got nearer the truth than when he said that—only I would beg the beast's pardon—for a beast would scarcely become so evil and vile as human nature becomes when it is left alone to fully develop itself! O pride of human nature, we plow right over you!

The hemlock stands in your field and must be cut up by the roots. Your weeds smile like fair flowers, but the plow must go right through them till all human beauty is shown to be a painted Jezebel, and all human glorying a bursting bubble. God is everything, man is nothing! God in His Grace saves man, but man by his sin utterly ruins himself until God's Grace interposes. I like to plow a straight furrow here. Another straight furrow is that of faith. We are sent to tell men that he that believes and is baptized shall be saved, and our duty is to put it so. "Salvation is not of works"—works is not the furrow. Not of prayers—that is not the furrow. Not of feelings—that is not the Gospel Arrow. Not of preparations and amendments and reforms—but by faith in Jesus Christ. He that believes on Him is not condemned.

As we begin the new life by faith, we must abide in it by faith. We are not to be saved by faith up to a certain point and then to rely upon ourselves. Having begun in the Gospel we are not to be perfected by the Law. "The just shall live by faith." We live by faith at the wicket gate and we live by faith until we enter into our eternal rest. Believe!—that is the grand Gospel precept and we trust we have never gone out of this furrow, but have tried to plow right across the Gospel field from end to end, crying, "Look unto Me and be you saved, all you ends of the earth, for Jehovah is God, and beside Him there is none else."

Another furrow which some do not much like to plow, but which must be distinctly marked if a man is an honest plowman for God, is that of repentance. Sinner, you and your sins must part! You have been married long and you have had a merry time of it, perhaps, but you must part. You and your sins must separate, or you and your God will never come together! You may not keep one sin. They must all be given up! They must be brought out like the Canaanite kings from the cave and hanged up before the sun. Not one darling must be spared. You must forsake them, loathe them, abhor them and ask the Lord to overcome them. Do you not know that the furrow of repentance runs right through the Christian's life? He sins, and as long as he sins he repents of his sin. The child of God cannot love sin—he must loathe it as long as he sees any of it in existence!

There is the furrow of holiness, that is the next turn the plowman takes. "Without holiness no man shall see the Lord." We have preached salvation by Grace, but we do not preach salvation to those who still continue in sin. The children of God are a holy people—washed, purged, sanctified and made zealous for good works. He who talks about faith, and has no works to prove that his faith is a living faith, lies to himself and lies before God. It is faith that saves us, not works—but the faith that saves us always produces works. It renews the heart, changes the character, influences the motives and is the means in the hand of God of making the man a new creature in Christ Jesus. No nonsense about it, Sirs—you may be baptized and re-baptized, you may attend to sacraments, or you may believe in an orthodox creed—but you will be damned if you live in sin.

You may become a deacon, or an elder, or a minister, if you dare, but there is no salvation for any man who still harbors his sins. "The wages of sin is death"—death to professors as well as to non-professors. If they hug their sins in secret, God will reveal those sins in public and condemn them according to the strict justice of His Law. These are the furrows we have tried to plow—deep, sharp cut and straight. O, that God might plow them, Himself, in all your hearts, that you may know, experimentally, how the Truth of God is rightly divided!

III. There is a third meaning to the text. "Rightly dividing the word of truth" is, as some think, an expression taken from the priests dividing the sacrifices. When they had a lamb or a sheep, a ram or a bullock to offer, after they had killed it, it was cut in pieces, carefully and properly. And it requires no little skill to find out where the joints are, so as to cut up an animal discreetly. Now, the Word of Truth has to be taken to pieces wisely—it is not to be hacked or torn as by a wild beast—but rightly divided.

There has to be DISCRIMINATION AND DISSECTION. It is a great part of a minister's duty to be able to dissect the Gospel—to lay one piece there, and another there, and preach with clearness, distinction and discrimination. Every Gospel minister must divide between the Covenant of Works and the Covenant of Grace. It is a very nice point, that, and many fail to discern it well, but it must always be kept clear, or great mischief will be done. Confusion worse confounded follows upon confusing Grace and Law. There is the Covenant of Works—"This do, and you shall live," but its voice is not that of the Covenant of Grace which says, "Hear and your soul shall live." "You shall, for I will"—that is the Covenant of Grace.

It is a covenant of pure promise unalloyed by terms and conditions. I have heard people put it thus—"Believers will be saved if, from this time forth, they are faithful to Grace given." That smells of the Covenant of Works! "God will love you"—says another—"if you—." Ah, the moment you get an "if" in it, it is the Covenant of Works and the Gospel has evaporated! Oil and water will sooner mix than merit and Grace! When you find the Covenant of Works anywhere, what are you to do with it? Why, do what Abraham did and what Sarah demanded, "Cast out the bondwoman and her son, for the son of the bondwoman shall not be heir with my son, even with Isaac."

If you are a child of the Free-Grace promise, do not suffer the Hagar and Ishmael of legal bondage and carnal hope to live in your house. Out with them! You should have nothing to do with them. Let Law and

Gospel keep their proper places. The Law is master to bring us to Christ, but when we have come to Christ we are no longer under a schoolmaster. Let the Law principle go its way to work conviction in sinners and destroy their ill-grounded hopes, but you abide in Christ Jesus even as you have received Him. If you are to be saved by works then it is not of Grace, otherwise work is no more work. And if saved by Grace, then it is not of human merit, otherwise Grace is no more Grace. To be absolutely clear, here, is of the first importance, for on the rocks of legality many a soul has been cast away.

We need, also, to keep up a clear distinction between the efforts of nature and the work of Grace. It is commendable for men to do all they can to improve themselves, and everything by which people are made more sober, more honest, more frugal, better citizens, better husbands, better wives is a good thing. But that is nature and not Grace. Reformation is not regeneration. "You must be born again," still stands for the good as well as for the bad. To be made a new creature in Christ Jesus is as necessary for the moral as for the debauched, for when flesh has done its best, "that which is born of the flesh is flesh"—and men must be born of the Spirit or they cannot understand spiritual things, or enter into Heaven.

I have always tried to keep up this distinction and I trust none of you will ever mistake the efforts of nature for the works of Divine Grace. Do what you can for human reformation, for whatever things are honest and of good repute you are to foster, but, still, never put the most philanthropic plan, or the most elevating system in the place of the work of Sovereign Grace, for, if you do, you will do ten times as much mischief as you can possibly do good. We must rightly divide the Word of Truth.

It is always well, too, for Christian men to be able to distinguish one Truth of God from another. Let the knife penetrate between the joints of the work of Christ for us and the work of the Holy Spirit in us. Justification, by which the Righteousness of Christ is imputed to us, is one blessing. Sanctification, by which we, ourselves, are made personally righteous, is another blessing. I have known some describe Sanctification as a sort of foundation, or at least a buttress for the work of Justification. Now, no man is justified because he is sanctified—he is justified because he believes in Him that justifies the ungodly. Sanctification follows Justification. It is the work of the Spirit of God in the soul of a Believer, who, first of all, was justified by believing in Jesus while as yet he was unsanctified. Give Jesus Christ all the glory for His great and perfect work and remember that you are perfect in Christ Jesus and accepted in the Beloved. But, at the same time, give glory to the Holy Spirit and remember that you are not yet perfect in holiness, but that the Spirit's work is to be carried on and will be carried on all the days of your life.

One other point of rightly dividing should never be forgotten—we must always distinguish between the root and the fruit. He is a very poor botanist who does not know a bulb from a bud—but I believe that there are some Londoners who do not know which are roots and which are fruits, so little have they seen of anything growing! And I am sure there are some theologians who hardly know which is the cause and which is the effect in spiritual things. Putting the cart before the horse is a very absurd thing, but many do it. Hear how people will say—"If I could feel joy in the Lord I would believe." Yes, that is the cart before the horse, for joy is the result of faith, not the reason for it! "But I want to feel a great change of heart, and then I will believe." Just so—you wish to make the fruit the root. "Believe in the Lord Jesus Christ," that is the root of the matter! Change of life and joy in the Lord will spring up as gracious fruits of faith and not otherwise. When will you discriminate?

Thus I have given you three versions of my text—rightly handling, straightly furrowing, and wisely discriminating.

IV. The next interpretation of the Apostle's expression is practically CUTTING OUT the Word for holy uses. This is the sense given by Chrysostom. I will show you what I mean here. Suppose I have a skin of leather before me and I want to make a saddle. I take a knife and I begin cutting out the shape. I do not want those parts which are dropping off on the right and round this corner—they are very good leather—but I cannot, just now, make use of them. I have to cut out my saddle and I make that my one concern.

Or, suppose I have to make a pair of reins out of the leather. I must take my knife round and work away with one object, keeping clearly before me what I am aiming at. The preacher, to be successful, must also have his wits about him. And when he has the Bible before him he must use those portions which will have a bearing upon his grand aim. He must make use of the material laid ready to his hand in the Bible. Every portion of the Word of God is very blessed and exceedingly profitable, but it may not happen to be connected with the preacher's immediate subject and, therefore, he leaves it to be considered another time. And, though some will upbraid him for it, he is much too sensible to feel bound to preach all the doctrines of the Bible in each sermon!

He wants to have souls saved and Christians quickened and, therefore, he does not forever pour out the vials and blow the trumpets of prophecy. Some hearers are crazy after the mysteries of the future. Well, there are two or three Brothers in London who are always trumpeting and vialing. Go and hear them if you want to! I have something else to do. I confess I am not sent to decipher the apocalyptic symbols—my errand is humbler but equally as useful—I am sent to bring souls to Jesus Christ!

There are preachers who are always dealing with the deep things, the very deep things. For them the coral caves of mystery and the far descending shafts of metaphysics have a mighty charm. I have no quarrel with their tastes, but I do not think the Word of God was given us to be a riddle book. To me the plain Gospel is the part which I cut out and rightly cut out of the Word of God. There is a soul that needs to know how to find peace with God. Some other Brother can tell him where predestination falls in with free agency, I do not pretend to know. But I do know that faith in Jesus brings peace to the heart. My business is to bring forth that which will save souls, build up saints and set Christians to work for Christ. I leave the mysteries, not because I despise them, but because the times demand that we, first, and above all other things, seek the souls of men!

Some Truths of God press to be heard. They must be heard now, or men will be lost. The other Truths they can hear tomorrow, or by-and-by, but now escape from Hell and fitness for Heaven are their immediate business! Fancy the angels sitting down with Lot and his daughters, inside

Sodom, and discussing predestination with them, or explaining the limits of free agency! No, no! They cry, "Come along," and they take them by the arm and lead them out, saying, "Flee, flee, flee, for fire is coming down from Heaven and this city is to be destroyed!"

This is what the preacher has to do—leaving certain parts of the Truth of God for other times, he is now rightly dividing the Word of Truth when he brings out that which is of pressing importance. In the Bible there are some things that are essential, without which a man cannot be saved at all. There are other things which are important, but still, men are saved, notwithstanding their ignorance of those things. Is it not clear that the essentials must have prominence? Every Truth ought to be preached in its turn and place, but we must never give the first place to a second Truth, or push that to the front which was meant to be in the background of the picture.

"We preach Christ," said the Apostle, "Christ and Him crucified." And I believe that if the preacher is rightly to divide the Word, he will say to the sinner,

"Sinner, Christ died, Christ rose again, Christ intercedes. Look to Him. As for the difficult questions and nice points, leave them for awhile. You shall discuss them by-and-by, so far as they are profitable to you, but just now, believing in the Lord Jesus Christ is the main matter."

The preacher must, thus, separate the vital from the secondary, the practical from the speculative and the pressing and immediate from that which may be lawfully delayed. And in that sense he will rightly divide the Word of Truth.

V. I have given you four meanings. Now I will give you another, leaving out some I might have mentioned. One thing the preacher has to do is to ALLOT TO EACH ONE HIS PORTION. And here the figure changes. According to Calvin, the intention of the Spirit, here, is to represent one who is the steward of the house and has to apportion food to the different members of the family. He has rightly to divide the loaves so as not to give the little children and the babes all the crust. He has to rightly supply each one's necessities, not giving the strong men milk, nor the babes hard diet—not casting the children's bread to the dogs, nor giving the swine's husks to the children—but placing before each his own portion.

Let me try and do it. Child of God, your portion is the whole Word of God. Every promise in it is yours! Take it. Feed on it. Christ is yours. God is yours. The Holy Spirit is yours. This world is yours and worlds to come. Time is yours. Eternity is yours. Life is yours. Death is yours. Everlasting Glory is yours! There is your portion! It is very sweet to give you your royal meat. The Lord gives you a good appetite. Feed on it! Feed on it! Sinner, you who believe not in Jesus, none of this is yours! While you remain as you are, only the threats are yours. If you refuse to believe in Jesus, neither this life nor the next is yours, nor time, nor eternity. You have nothing good.

O, how dreadful is your portion now, for the wrath of God abides on you! O, that you were wise, that your character might be changed, for until it is, we dare not flatter you. There is not a promise for you, nor a single approving sentence! You get your food to eat and your raiment to put on, but even that is given to you by the abounding long-suffering of God and it may become a curse to you unless you repent. I am sorry to bring you such a portion but I must be honest with you. That is all that I can give you. God has said it—it is an awful sentence—"I will curse their blessings." O, Sinner, the curse of the Lord is in the house of the wicked!

We have also to divide a portion to the mourners, and O, how sweet a task that is, to say to those that mourn in Zion that the Lord will give them beauty for ashes. "Blessed are they that mourn, for they shall be comforted." The Lord will restore peace unto His mourners! Fear not, neither be dismayed, for the Lord will help you! But when we have given the mourners their sweet meats we have to turn round upon the hypocrites and say to them,

"You may hang your heads like bulrushes. You may rend your garments and pretend to fast, but the Lord, who knows your heart, will suddenly come and unmask you! And if you are not sincere before Him—if you are weighed in the balances and found wanting—He will deal out

the gall of bitterness to you forever! For his mourners there is mercy, but for the deceiver and the hypocrite there is judgment without mercy."

It is a very pleasant thing, moreover, to deal out a portion to the seeker—when we say, "He that seeks finds, and to him that knocks it shall be opened." "Come unto Me all you that labor and are heavy laden," says Christ, "for I will give you rest." Take your portion and be glad! We have to turn round and say to others who think they are seekers, but who are delaying, "How long will you wait between two opinions?" How is it that you continually hesitate and refuse to believe in Jesus, and stay in the condition of unbelief, when the Gospel mandate is, "Believe—believe now and live"? So we have to give to one comfort, to another counsel—to one reproof, to another encouragement. We have to give to one the invitation—to another the warning. This is to rightly divide the Word of Truth.

Yes, and sometimes God enables His servants to give the Word very remarkably to some men. I believe that if I were to tell a few of the things which have happened to me during the last twenty-one years they would not be believed. Or if I were to tell you of passages of history which are known to me that have occurred in this Tabernacle to people who have come here and to whom I have spoken the exact Word, not knowing them for a moment, the facts would sound like fictions. I will give you one instance. Some of you may remember my preaching from the text, "What if your father answers you roughly?" There came into the vestry, after that sermon, a venerable Christian gentleman, bringing with him a young foreigner whom he was anxious to satisfy upon one point.

He said, "Sir, I want you kindly to answer this question—have you seen me, concerning this young gentlemen?" "No, Sir, certainly not," I said. And assuredly, though I knew the gentleman who addressed me, he had never spoken to me about the foreign stranger whose very existence was, up to that moment, unknown to me. Said he, "This young gentleman is almost persuaded to be a Christian. His father is of quite another faith and worships other gods. And our young friend knows that if he becomes a Christian he will lose his father's love." I said to him, when he conversed with me, come down and hear Mr. Spurgeon this morning. "Here he came, and your text was, 'What if your father answers you roughly?' Now, have you ever heard a word from me about this young gentleman?" "No, never," I said. "Well," said the young man, "it is the most extraordinary thing I ever heard in my life." I could only say, "I trust it is the voice of God to your soul. God knows how to guide His servants to utter the Word most fitted to bless men."

Some time ago a town missionary had, in his district, a man who never would suffer any Christian person to come into his house. The missionary was warned by many that he would get a broken head if he ventured on a visit. He therefore kept from the house though it troubled his conscience to pass it by. He made a matter of prayer of it, and one morning he boldly ventured into the lion's den and the man said, "What have you come here for?" "Well, Sir," he said, "I have been conversing with people in all the houses along here, but I have passed you by because I heard you objected to it. But somehow I thought it looked cowardly to avoid you and therefore I have called."

"Come in," the man said. "Sit down, sit down. Now, you are going to talk to me about the Bible. Perhaps you do not know much about it yourself. I am going to ask you a question and if you can answer me you shall come again. If you do not answer it, I will bundle you downstairs. Now," he said, "do you understand me?" "Yes," said the other, "I do understand you." "Well, then," he said, "this is the question—where do you find the word, 'girl,' in the Bible, and how many times do you find it?" The city missionary said, "The word, 'girl,' occurs only once in the Bible, and that is in the Book of Joel, the third chapter and the third verse. 'They sold a girl for wine.'"

"You are right," he said, "but I would not have believed you knew it, or else I would have asked you some other question. You may come again." "But," said the missionary, "I should like you to know how I came to know it. This very morning I was praying for direction from God and when I was reading my morning chapter I came upon this passage, 'And they sold a girl for wine,' and I took down my Concordance to see whether the word, 'girl,' was to be found anywhere else. I found that the word, 'girls,' occurs in the passage, 'There shall be girls and boys playing in the streets of Jerusalem,' but the word did not occur as, 'girl,' anywhere but in Joel."

The result, however, of that story, however odd it seems, was that the missionary was permitted to call and the man took an interest in his visits. And the whole family were the better—the man and his wife, and one of his children becoming members of a Christian Church some time afterwards. What an extraordinary thing it seems, yet, I can assure you that such extraordinary things are as commonplaces in my experience. God does help His servants rightly to divide the Word, that is to say, to allot a special portion to each special case, so that it comes upon the man as if everything about him was known.

Before I came to London, a man met me one Sunday, in a dreadful state of rage. He vowed he would horsewhip me for bullying him from the pulpit. What had I said, I asked. "What have you said? You looked me in the face and said, 'What more can God do for you? Shall He give you a good wife? You have had one—you have killed her by bad treatment! You have just got another and you are likely to do the same by her.'" "Well," I said, "did you kill your first wife by your bad treatment?" "They say so, but I was married on Saturday," said he. "Did you not know it?" "No, I did not, I assure you," I replied. "I have no knowledge whatever of your family matters, and I am sure I wish you joy with your new wife." He cooled down a great deal but I believe that I had struck the nail on the head that time—that he had killed his wife with his unkindness and he scarcely liked to bring his new wife to the place of worship to be told of it.

The cap fit him. And if any cap fits you, I pray you wear it, for so far from shrinking from being personal, I do assure you I try to be as personal as I can, for I long to see the Word go home to every man's conscience, and convict him and make him tremble before God and confess his sin and forsake it!

VI. You must give me a few more minutes while I take the last point, which is this. Rightly to divide the Word of Truth means to TELL EACH MAN WHAT HIS LOT AND HERITAGE WILL BE IN ETERNITY. Just as when Canaan was conquered, it was divided by lot among the tribes, so the preacher has to tell of Canaan, that happy land, but he has to also tell of the land of darkness and of death-shade, and to let each man know where his last abode will be. You know it. You who come here know it.

Need I repeat a story that we have gone over and over a thousand times? As many as believe in Jesus and are renewed in heart, and are kept by the Grace of God through faith unto salvation, shall inherit eternal life. But as for those who believe not on God, who reject His Son, who abide in their sins—there remains nothing for them but "a fearful looking for of judgment and of fiery indignation." "The wicked shall be turned into Hell with all the nations that forget God." "These shall go away into everlasting punishment; but the righteous into life eternal." "Beware," says God—"Beware, you that forget God, lest I tear you in pieces and there be none to deliver." O, the wrath to come! The wrath to come!

Believer, there is your portion—in the blessed land! Sinner, unless you repent, there is your portion—in the land of darkness and of weeping—of wailing and of gnashing of teeth! I take a religious newspaper from America and the last copy I had of it bore on it these words at the end, in good large type, printed in a practical, business-like, American way—

"If you do not want to have this paper, discontinue it NOW. If you wish to have it for the year 1876, send your subscription NOW. If you have any complaint against it, send your complaint NOW. If you have removed, send a notice of your change of residence NOW."

There was a big "NOW" at the end of every sentence! As I read it, I thought, well, that is right. That is common sense. And it struck me that I would say to you on this last Sunday night of the year, if you wish to forsake your sins, forsake them NOW. If you would have mercy from God through Jesus Christ, believe on Him NOW. What fitter time than before the dying year is gone—NOW, NOW, NOW? In that very paper I read a story concerning Messrs. Moody and Sankey on the same point.

The story is that while they were preaching in Edinburgh, there was a man sitting opposite to them who was very deeply interested, and was drinking it all in. There was a pause in the service and the man went out with his friend, but when he reached the door he stopped and his friend said, "Come away, Jamie." "No," he said, "I will go back. I came here to get good to my soul and I have not taken it all in yet, I must go back again." He went back, and sat in his old place and listened again. The Lord blessed him. He found Christ and so found salvation. Being a miner, he went down the pit the next day, to his work, and a mass of rock fell on him. He was taken out, but he could not recover. He said to the man who was helping him out, "O, Andrew, I am so glad it was all settled last night. Oh, mon," said he, "it was all settled last night."

Now, I hope those people who were killed in the railway accident on Christmas Eve could say—"It was all settled the night before." What a blessed thing it will be for you, if you should meet with an accident tomorrow, to say, "Blessed be God, it was all settled last night. I gave any heart to Jesus, I yielded myself to His Divine Love and Mercy, and I am saved." O Holy Spirit, grant it may be so, and You shall have the praise. Amen and amen!

15

The Foundation and Its Seal

(Sermon No. 1854)

"Nevertheless the foundation of God stands sure, having this seal, 'The Lord knows them that are His,' and, 'Let everyone that names the name of Christ depart from iniquity'" (2 Timothy 2:19).

P AUL HAD MET WITH MANY difficulties in his earnest career, but his most painful trials came from false brethren. It is battle, enough, for the Church to contend with the world, but what is she to do when she has to contend with herself? To go forth weeping, bearing precious seed and, in due time, to reap it in the heat of the sun is toil enough for the farmer—but what is he to do when the tares are sown among the wheat and they spring up and well-near choke the growing grain? He is distressed and knows not what to do! At first he is eager to root up the tares; then he fears that he might root up the wheat with them and so, at his Master's command, he lets both grow together until the harvest. This he does with tears in his eyes, for he foresees that those growing tares must do fearful mischief to the good seed and, in the end, where he looked for much, he will gather little.

A compact army of brave spirits, every man in health and every man a hero, can march across a continent and strike at the foe, time after time—and every stroke shall fall as from the hammer of Thor. But if you have the leadership of a great and motley host—and there are many sick folk to be carried in the ambulances, while others are faint-hearted, cowardly and cold in the cause and, yet another company are half suspected of a design to go over to the adversary—then the captain's hair may well turn gray in a night at the thought of what may be the result of a battle! Paul was full of somewhat similar anxieties when about to leave the field of conduct to receive his crown. He was handing over his commission of Watchman of the Churches to Timothy and, as he did so, it was with a trembling hand, as he thought of the evil influences which were at work within the Church, itself. Outside persecution seemed light enough to him, but internal dissension, heresy and ungodliness weighed upon his spirit.

When I read this Second Epistle to Timothy, it reminds me, somewhat—only it is a great improvement upon it—of David's addressing Solomon and reminding him of those who had given him trouble in his lifetime. He exhorted him how to deal wisely with them lest his kingdom should be disturbed by them. You notice that throughout the Epistle, the Apostle makes more mention of troublesome individuals than in any other letter. In the first chapter there is Phygellus and Hermogenes. And now we come upon Hymenaeus and Philetus. These dogs generally hunt in couples. A little further on you get Demas and Alexander, the coppersmith, who had done much evil to the Apostle. The departing saint, harboring no resentment, yet has great anxiety of spirit as to what these mischief-makers might do with a young man like Timothy, since they had been such thorns in his own side.

It is a cheering thing to note that while Paul mentions these things with a gracious anxiety, they do not disturb the serenity of his faith, nor make him question, for a moment, the success of the cause, nor doubt the success of the work which the Lord had worked by his own hands. These are his words—

> "For I am now ready to be offered, and the time of my departure is at hand. I have fought a good fight, I have finished my course, I have kept the faith: therefore there is laid up for me a crown of righteousness, which the Lord, the Righteous Judge, shall give me at that day: and not to me only, but unto all them, also, that love His appearing."

Courage, then, servant of God! Whatever may be your trials because of an apostatizing church, your faith will give you victory! Be faithful to the Word of the Holy Testimony and the Truth of God shall yet prevail. Live much in communion with your Master, for by His name shall you triumph!

Project yourself into the eternal future. Feel the crown already upon your head when it is aching under many sorrows! Hear the Master's word, "Well done," when you are weary with the noise of them that oppose the Cross. Stand fast! Having done all, still stand! The campaign is not lost. Despite all that has happened, or ever shall happen, not one jot the less does, "the foundation of God stands sure." The work of God goes on and the reward which God gives to the workers is not diminished, nor even placed in danger. Therefore, in patience, possess your soul.

This morning, with deep solemnity of soul, I approach this text and pray that the Spirit of God may bless it to us all. I see in it, three things. The first, perhaps, is rather in the context, it is the lamentable overthrow of which the Apostle has been speaking. He says that these two men, Hymenaeus and Philetus, overthrew the faith of some. Secondly, we shall survey the abiding foundation—"the foundation of God stands sure." And then, thirdly, the instructive inscription upon the foundation stone, "The Lord knows them that are His." And, "Let everyone that names the name of Christ depart from iniquity."

I. First, let us think, for a little, of THE LAMENTABLE OVERTHROW which the Apostle so much deplored.

The Apostle observed with sorrow a general coldness. It was, in some respects, coldness towards himself, but in reality it was a turning away from the simplicity of the Doctrine of Salvation by Grace through faith. He says in the 15th verse of the previous chapter, "This you know, that all they which are in Asia are turned away from me; of whom are Phygellus and Hermogenes," two men, I suppose, of whom he had hoped better things—perhaps persons who had professed a warm attachment to him. Their departure was the unkindest cut of all.

A great lack of spiritual life and zeal for the Truth of God is our trial, today. Laodicea is not the only Church that is neither cold nor hot. I am, at this moment, unwillingly compelled to believe that a very serious blight is upon many of our Churches. From a wide correspondence, I gather that a wintry chill is just now upon the Church—possibly it is not to such an extent as in certain terrible periods—but still to a very saddening degree. There is not that firmness in the faith, that holiness of life and that enthusiasm for the Cross of Christ that one would wish to see. I view the immediate prospect with serious anxiety. Yet, I was reading Mr. Bunyan's words concerning the age in which he lived and I find that he had similar apprehensions in his time. And I notice that before his day, each loyal-hearted man of God was troubled with similar fears.

Nor were those fears childish—they were not a presumptuous trembling for the Ark of the Lord, but a godly jealousy lest the enemy should get an advantage over the hosts of God. It is a mercy that there should be somebody to complain; somebody to express the longing of the Church for better things. I am sure that there is grave reason for regret at this moment. Though we look with the greatest gratitude upon all the things that are good, we still have to look with heavy hearts upon much that is grievous to the Spirit of God in the Churches of the present day.

Furthermore, the Apostle saw with much alarm that teachers were erring. He names two especially, Hymenaeus and Philetus, and he mentions the doctrine that they taught—not needlessly explaining it, but merely giving a hint at it. They taught, among other things, that the Resurrection was already past. I suppose they had fallen into the manner of certain in our day who spiritualize or rationalize everything. They say, "This is mythical! This death of Christ is to be understood as the triumph of self-sacrifice. This Resurrection of Christ means the revival of forgotten principles." Thus they hold an atonement which is no Atonement and a resurrection which is no Resurrection. They appear to accept the great historical fact and yet they reduce it to fiction! This is the subtlety of the old serpent! Somehow or other, these men manage to extract from the Gospel an attractive philosophy, but it is not the Gospel which God intended to be preached! They seek, rather, the wisdom of man's thought than the Revelation of God's thoughts. You need not that I go into particulars, for all around us men are dealing craftily with the Truth of God—adulterating it and in heart denying it. These are, by no means, persons to be trifled with—many of them are keen, acute, and thoughtful—and it is the great peril of the Church, at this moment, that she numbers such among her teachers. These can stab under the shield. We care not for the besiegers outside, but we are distressed because of the traitors within! God grant that this thing may go no further, but may His people become alarmed by the growing decline of the Church and resolve to be rid of this destructive influence which eats as does a canker.

In Paul's day, many professors were apostatizing from the faith because of the evil leaders. Sheep are such creatures to follow something, that, when they do not follow the shepherd, they display great readiness to follow one another. When Hymenaeus and Philetus taught a highly intellectual doctrine, many people who fancied themselves to be cultured, must necessarily be of their mind. Hymenaeus had discovered a method of being abreast of the times, so that the Christian teacher could figure in the heathen academy and be complimented for his liberal views. These "cultured" teachers looked down with contempt upon those uncouth fishermen who were so unlearned and ignorant as to believe that the teaching of Jesus meant what it said, for they, themselves, gave the Gospel a more rational meaning! They thought themselves profound and eclectic men who could see the soul of things and, therefore, they rejected the simplicity of the Cross and put in its place the theories of the philosophers. They took away the foundation facts under the pretence of building higher and thus the faith of many was overthrown.

Take away the Resurrection and what remains of the Gospel? The Resurrection of Christ and the consequent resurrection of His people is the keystone of the arch of the Christian system! And if that is removed as a myth, the whole building falls. The Apostle saw numbers of persons led astray by this error as, alas, we see many in these times deluded with kindred falsehoods! It becomes Christian men, nowadays, to carefully discriminate as to what they hear. I read, the other day, a complaint as to small towns having many chapels where one might have sufficed. Truly, one might suffice if the Gospel were faithfully preached in it, but a score would not be enough if, in them all, there was an absence of the Gospel of Jesus Christ and of the life and power of the Holy Spirit! When another Gospel is introduced, those who love the Truth of God are bound to enter their earnest protest and to form another congregation. I am for unity in the life and Truth of God, and for our coming closer and closer together—spiritual men to spiritual men—but that is quite another thing from making an aggregate of this great motley mass of Christian profession and unchristian teaching, since it has so little of the true life of Christ within it! Would to God that in every place where Christ is preached professedly, He were preached truthfully! Oh that you who profess to follow Christ were really doing so! But what is the chaff to the wheat? How much of chaff is mixed with every heap that lies upon our Lord's threshing floor!

Paul also deplored that ungodliness increased. He says that the profane and vain babblings of his time increased unto more ungodliness. O Brothers and Sisters, it is godliness that we need—the living of the soul with God, in God and to God. We need a holy fear of God, a sacred sense of God, a true delight in God! We need less of man and more of God! Less of mere creed-repeating and more of vital faith in God. Less following of men and more following of God in Christ Jesus. More of union with God, living in God and likeness to God. Oh that He would work this in us! The world grows dark with accursed lusts and the Christian Church grows more conformed to the ungodly world. Persecutions unto death have ceased—it is easy and respectable to bear the Christian name—and, therefore, the separation from the world, which is the glory of Christians, becomes less and less apparent!

My heart is sorely wounded with the sight of some who will come into God's house and undertake God's service during the Sabbath and yet, during the week they are unjust, oppressive, graceless and greedy— not servants of God, but servants of self and sin! By unholy professors, the Cross is dishonored, the Holy Spirit is grieved and Christ is put to an open shame! All this vexed the heart of the Apostle in his day and it is our cross and burden at this hour. "Lord have mercy upon us! Christ have mercy upon us!"

II. Now let us turn to the subject which supplied Paul with consolation. He speaks of the ABIDING FOUNDATION—"Nevertheless the foundation of God stands sure." It is a joy to quit the ever-moving flood for the firm, substantial rock. It is bliss to feel that there is something under your feet, something substantial, abiding, sure. "Nevertheless, the foundation of God stands sure." Though the earth is removed and though the mountains are carried into the midst of the sea—though the waters thereof roar and are troubled and though the mountains shake with the swelling thereof—yet will we not fear, for the Lord Jehovah changes not!

What is this foundation which stands sure? Those who have interpreted the passage have given many meanings to it, but I believe that all those meanings are really one. For the sake of clearness, I would give three answers to the enquiry—the foundation is, secretly, the purpose of God; doctrinally, the Truth of God; effectively, the Church of God—in all, the system of God whereby He glorifies His Grace. The foundation is the Divine purpose. Though men prove fickle, false, wicked and the Church is sorely grieved, "nevertheless" God's purpose is carried out! The Covenant of Grace is fulfilled and the Glory of God is revealed. God has a grand design from which He has never swerved, no, not by so much as a hair's breadth! His purpose shall stand! He will do all His pleasure. It is incumbent upon us to believe in the responsibility of men and to feel the weight of that Truth, for as a Truth of God, it is of the most solemn importance. It is our duty to give ourselves up with all our might to the doing of that which is right, as if all things depended on us. Yet when we are baffled by matters which are beyond our control, it is a blessed thing to fall back upon the purpose and Providence of the Almighty—and feel that though we are defeated—He cannot be! There is a power high over all which works for righteousness. The Messiah "shall not fail nor be discouraged till He has set judgement in the earth and the isles shall wait for His Law." The Divine design in creation shall be effected and in redemption and in Providence, it shall be the same. The Lord shall be, at the last, victor all along the line! The good shall glorify Him and even the evil shall be compelled to magnify the greatness of His majesty. "The Lord reigns; let the earth rejoice; let the multitude of isles be glad thereof." God Himself, who is in very deed the Foundation of all things, stands sure!

The Apostle also meant the Divine Truth, which is the foundation of the Gospel. He had been speaking about certain Truths of God which were spirited away by those two unworthies, Hymenaeus and Philetus, and he says, "Nevertheless the foundation of God stands sure."

Interpreters have thought that Paul points at the doctrine of the Resurrection. No doubt he does, but he includes every other doctrine which is a foundational Truth of the Gospel of Jesus Christ. Yonder is a man who has proved that Jesus is not truly God. Let him prove what he likes, since Jesus is God for all that! Another man has disproved the substitutionary Atonement of Christ—let him disprove it if he pleases, for it is just as true! Rhetoric and logic can do wonders in appearance, but they do nothing in reality. The orator's thunder has not shaken the unchangeable Truth of God! He is proud of his triumphs, but as we look into the Book and look into the dear Master's face, we feel that, "nevertheless the foundation of God stands sure."

No Truth of God has ever been destroyed by all the fires through which it has passed! The fire which tried the bush in the wilderness was a much more potent element than any that men can kindle, for it was God's own Presence and He is, emphatically, "a consuming fire." Yet the bush was not consumed by such a fire! What, then, can destroy it? Even so, since the Truth can stand the test of God, the All-Trying One, depend upon it, it can endure the test of such poor fires as man can bring to bear upon it! In a broad Scotch version I read, "The bush lowe'd and was nane the waur"—that is to say, "it was none the worse." Brethren, the Gospel is none the worse for all the opposition which has surrounded it, though it has been as fierce as a devouring flame! Only the additions of men have been burnt out of it. Everything that can be consumed ought to be consumed and only that which cannot be burned is really God's eternal Truth. All that has happened by all the controversy of all the ages, is that man's fiction has been separated from God's foundation—man's speculation has been purged out of God's Revelation! The foundation of God stands sure and, oh, the joy of this fact to every heart that loves the Lord!

But, further, I think Paul meant, here, not only the purpose of God and the Truth of God, but God's Divine work in the world in the salvation of His own. The Divine Election of God has been fulfilled so far—and those whom God has really saved—in whom there has been a real work of Grace, stand sure when all others are overthrown. You look upon the

Church and lament that so many have turned aside; that so many others are very poor specimens of Christians; that so many more are sadly questionable and that a certain company are evidently false. Well, it is very sad, but there is a remnant according to the election of Grace—"the foundation of God stands sure." Those who were really laid upon the foundation by the Spirit of God—those who are vitally united to Christ—these still stand firm in faith and character! Those who are truly born of God live unto God! The righteous hold on their way. The choice spirits endure unto the end. Does not Jesus say, "My sheep hear My voice, and I know them, and they follow Me"? Does He not declare that, "A stranger will they not follow, but will flee from him, for they know not the voice of strangers"?

The teachers of error would, if it were possible, have deceived the very elect, but the chosen detect the deception by the spiritual discernment which is in them and by the teaching of the Holy Spirit! They love the Truth and live the Truth—and the Truth lives in them. Thus in their persons, "the foundation of God stands sure." Brothers and Sisters, let us take great joy in this foundation of God, this faithful Church of God which is steadfast and immovable in the day of blasphemy and rebuke. Blessed be the name of the Lord, He still has a quickened people! He still has a Church in the world—in all communities of professing Christians, there is a secret seed of faithful ones—and while the floods and the winds have driven down the stream, the many towering houses that were built upon the sand, yet the house of God still stands upon the Rock!

It is not yet complete so as to be fully built as the great House of God is to be. At the present it wears, rather, the aspect of a foundation, or basement, than of a house—but it will rise by degrees to be a fair palace—and even now the King, Himself, deigns to dwell in it! What there is of the true Church is a sure prophecy of what there shall be before long. "The foundation of God stands sure." Let us take courage from this and be not sorely moved nor dismayed in the day of apostasy. "They went out from us, but they were not of us." The hireling flees because he is an hireling. Let us not dwell exclusively upon the mournful side, lest we lose that joy of the Lord which is our strength. Our Master wept over

Jerusalem, once, but He also rejoiced in spirit when His mind looked another way. In His heart He always mourned over the woes of ungodly men, but still, He thought and spoke of more cheering themes—and so must we. It would not become us to let any one form of thought penetrate our hearts through and through with painful monotony. You can contemplate the sad side of things till you become so wretched as to be unable to do good! Have a brave and hopeful heart. When you see a black cloud, look for its silver lining. When you see that which looked like substantial material consumed in the fire, be thankful that if the wood and hay are gone, the gold and silver remain. God is laying a foundation for the future, a foundation so sure that it cannot be moved! And He will build upon it, course after course of jeweled stones till its walls, great and high, appear unto all men!

Soon shall we see its windows of agate and its gates of carbuncle. Soon shall the glittering pinnacles of "the terrible crystal" shine in the eternal light and, best of all, we shall inhabit the house forever and go no more out, for the Lord God and the Lamb shall be the Glory of that House and His faithful ones shall be built into it as living stones! Pluck up courage, then, and stand in your place, O you who are trembling! Let, "Onward!" be your watchword! Victory is not so far away as we fear. The retreat of yonder cowards is nothing—the turning back of the men of Ephraim is according to their nature. But be strong and quit yourselves like men, for the Lord of Hosts is with us, the God of Jacob is our refuge!

III. Now, we are, in the third place, as we may be helped of the Holy Spirit, to look at this foundation and observe THE INSTRUCTIVE INSCRIPTION. I think this figure best expresses the Apostle's intent. He represents the foundation stone as bearing an inscription upon it, like the stone mentioned by the Prophet Zechariah, of which we read, "I will engrave the graving thereof, says the Lord of Hosts, and I will remove the iniquity of that land in one day." The custom of putting inscriptions upon foundation stones is ancient and general. In the days of the Pharaohs, the royal cartouche was impressed upon each brick that was placed in buildings raised by royal authority. The structure was thus known to have been erected by a certain Pharaoh. Here we have the royal cartouche, or seal, of the King of Kings set upon the foundation of the great palace of the Church. The House of Wisdom bears, on its forefront and foundation, the seal of the Lord. The Jews were known to write texts of Scripture upon the doorposts of their houses—in this, also, we have an illustration of our text.

The Lord has set upon His purpose, His Gospel, His Truth, the double mark described in the text—the Divine Election and the Divine Sanctification. This seal is placed to declare that it belongs to the Lord, alone, and to set it apart for His personal habitation. Does not the Lord thus say, "This is My rest forever: here will I dwell; for I have desired it"? By His choice and by His sanctifying Grace, He has formed a people for Himself and they shall show forth His praise. The inscription, moreover, is put upon the foundation stone, that every man may take heed how he builds on it. We cannot be sure, when we build, that every stone we place upon the foundation is well and truly laid there—"The Lord knows them that are His." But we have this mark to guide us—those who truly name the name of Christ depart from all iniquity. "By their fruits you shall know them."

We are to use judgement in our building and this is the rule of it—we must look for holiness in every real convert, for, "without holiness no man shall see the Lord." It is labor in vain to build those into the visible Church who are not sanctified in the spirit of their minds. In doctrine, also, it is in vain to preach unless our doctrine is according to godliness. A holy God will not dwell with an unholy people! If the foundation is holy, so must the building be. The seal upon the foundation is the mark of the builder and the indication of the object of that which is built. It is intended to denote the character of the entire edifice, for God's building is all of one piece and of one nature throughout. On each individual Christian, who is truly so, there is the private seal of Divine knowledge and the public seal of Divine likeness. God knows and approves each true Believer and each true Believer proves his knowledge of God and his delight in Him by departing from iniquity.

My inmost soul vehemently desires to aid in building up a Church that shall be composed of men approved of God—God-fearing, God-loving men and women in whom God lives and who, therefore, live unto Him! What a Church this will be! Upon such a people will be seen the second mark, for they will hate all sin and flee from it. They love that which is good, true, loving and God-like. In us these two things must meet—God's free and sovereign Grace towards us and our hearty and practical obedience to His will, or else we are not His sealed ones and are not built on His sealed foundation.

If I might use another illustration, I can suppose that when the stones for the Temple were quarried in the mountains, each one received a special mark from Solomon's seal, marking it as a Temple stone and, perhaps, denoting its place in the sacred edifice. This would be like the first inscription, "The Lord knows them that are His." But the stone would not long lie in the quarry. It would be taken away from its fellows, after being marked for removal. Here is the transport mark in the second inscription—"Let everyone that names the name of Christ depart from iniquity." The first seal marked it for the Lord, the second secured its removal from the common stones around it. First comes election and then sanctification follows. I want every professing Christian to have that double mark and so to be Christ's man, known of all to be such by coming out from the unclean and being separated unto the Lord. Remember the words of the Prophet Isaiah—

"Depart you, depart you, go you out from them, touch no unclean thing; go you out of the midst of her; be you clean, that bear the vessels of the Lord."

Carefully follow me while I notice that the first mark is concerning God and us, and the second mark is concerning us and God.

The first is concerning God and us. "The Lord knows them that are His." He knows, that is, He foresees and predestinates, for, "whom He did foreknow He also did predestinate." Those that are His, He always has known to be His, for they were His from before the foundation of the world! They are His known ones when He deals with them in Grace and comes into their hearts by His powerful operations. He watches over them by a special Providence, knowing the way that they take and never losing sight of them.

The text teaches us that the Lord discriminates—"The Lord knows them that are His." Some who bear His name are not His and He knows them not. He will say of them at the last, "I never knew you." They are supposed to be His. They suppose themselves to be His—they are taken into His Church as His, they continue throughout a long life nominally His—but they are discovered at the last. There is another and severer test than that of ministers, elders and Church votes—the Lord knows the secret things of the heart. Be not deceived, God is not mocked! There is an eye that has no failure in its vision, but sees to the very soul of things and reads the hypocrite despite his pretended sanctity! This discernment on the part of God should make us walk very truthfully before Him. Let none of us profess to be the Lord's unless we are such—nor ever pretend to an experience which we have not truly felt, for the Lord cannot be, in any measure, deceived—He searches the heart and tries the reins of the children of men.

"The Lord knows them that are His," signifies that He is familiar with them and communes with them. They that are really the Lord's property are also the Lord's company—He has conversation with them. They know Him and He knows them. He makes Himself known to them and they make themselves known to Him. O Brothers and Sisters, do you know God? Does God know you? Will He ever say, "I never knew you"? When I have been cast down, I have said unto the Lord—

"Lord, You cannot say You do not know me, for I have knocked at Your door by the hour together! I have burdened You with my needs and haunted You with my groans. I have been Your daily beggar, receiving large alms at Your hands."

It is a blessed thing to be sure that we are not unknown in Heaven. At least we have the fellowship of asking and receiving, if no more.

Further, the words imply God's preservation of His own, for when God knows a man, He approves him and, consequently, preserves him. "The Lord knows them that are His" and He will keep such to the end.

This man, Hymenaeus, and his fellow, Philetus, may deceive many, but the Lord, who is the true Pastor of the Church, will keep His own sheep according to His word—"I give unto My sheep eternal life and they shall never perish, neither shall any man pluck them out of My hand." This is the first seal of the sure foundation. Be not afraid of it. "The Lord knows them that are His."

The second seal is concerning us and God—"Let everyone that names the name of Christ depart from iniquity." Observe how the practical always goes with the doctrinal in holy Scripture. Those whom Free Grace chooses, Free Grace cleanses. We are not chosen because we are holy, but chosen to be holy and, being chosen, the purpose is no dead letter, but we are made to seek after holiness. Note that the word is universal as to Believers—"Let everyone that names the name of Christ depart from iniquity." You expect ministers to be careful in their conduct and so they should be. But are not their people under the same obligation? Elders and deacons are expected to be gracious. This, indeed, is as it should be, but why not those of whom they are the servants? Let everyone that is called a Christian, or trusts Christ, or preaches Christ, or teaches Christ, flee far from the ways of unrighteousness!

This is a sweeping precept as to the thing to be avoided—let him, "depart from iniquity"—not from this or that crime or folly, but from iniquity, itself, from everything that is evil, from everything that is unrighteous or unholy! O you Christian people, be holy, for Christ is holy! Do not pollute that holy name by which you are named. O you people of God, if you are, indeed, the Lord's, let no sin dwell with you! Do not say, "It is a constitutional sin." You are born again, what have you to do with the old constitution but to mortify it? Do not say, "Oh, but others do it." What have you to do with others?—to their own master they stand or fall! Depart from iniquity on your own account, even as Israel departed out of Egypt. Let your family life, your personal life, your business life be as holy as Christ, your Lord, would have it to be.

The text is very decisive—it does not say, "Let him put iniquity on one side," but, "Let him depart from it." Get away from evil. All your lives long travel further and further from it.

Do you know where my text originally came from? I believe it was taken from the Book of Numbers. Read in the 16th chapter the story of Korah, Dathan and Abiram. In the Septuagint, almost the same words occur as those now before us. Moses and Aaron were the servants of God and they were, so to speak, the foundation of the building of the Jewish Commonwealth. Moses was faithful in all his house. Korah, Dathan and Abiram rebelled and sought to overthrow that foundation—and Moses replied to them, "The Lord will show who are His, and who are holy; and will cause him to come near unto Him; even him whom He has chosen will He cause to come near to Him." So Moses bids them come and bring their censers and officiate as priests, if they dare to do so. There they stand and there stands Aaron and the Lord knows and shows who are His!

Now, turn to the 26th verse of the same chapter and read, "Depart, I pray you, from the tents of these wicked men, and touch nothing of theirs, lest you be consumed in all their sins." Then the faithful fled away from their tents on every side and, before long, the ground split asunder that was under them and the earth opened her mouth and swallowed them up. What a parallel is the whole chapter with my text! And what a warning to all who teach false doctrine within the Church of God! Judgment will surely overtake them. The Lord shall "gather out of His Kingdom all things that offend, and them which do iniquity and shall cast them into a furnace of fire." The Lord Jesus is exercising discipline in His Church every day. It is no trifling matter to be a Church member and no small business to be a preacher of the Gospel. If you name the name of Christ, you will either be settled in Him or driven from Him! There is continually going on an establishment of living stones upon the foundation and a separating from it of the rubbish which gathers.

Come to Christ, we say, and oh that you would come! But still do not come to Him pretendedly and nominally, for, "His fan is in His hand and He will thoroughly purge His floor." To and fro goes that great winnowing fan and every breath of the wind drives away chaff that looks like wheat! Who can tell, by sight, what it is? The good grain falls to the ground, but lo, the chaff is blown away! Yonder fire that is burning outside the threshing floor destroys it. Judgment must begin at the House of God! The Lord may let the wicked remain in this world unpunished for many a day, but if you come near to Him, He will be sanctified in you, or upon you. There is discipline within my Master's house and if you come under His roof, you must come under that discipline. For this cause in olden times many were sick in the Churches and many died prematurely— and it is still so, for within His great house a jealous God maintains a strict rule. Thus says the Lord, "You only have I known of all the families of the earth: therefore I will punish you for all your iniquities." Look how He dealt with Ananias and Sapphira within the Church, while many a liar outside of it grows gray in falsehood! Nadab and Abihu died before the Lord because they offered strange fire, while many another man has lived on in the blackest iniquities. For Achan's sin, the whole nation of Israel was sorely troubled! What a solemn thing is iniquity in the Church of God!

Brothers and Sisters, I conclude with a brief but earnest appeal. Let us seek after the highest degree of holiness. Let us not be satisfied with being nominal Christians! Let us aim at the greatest measure of godliness. Let us plunge into the stream of Grace, immersing ourselves wholly into the life of God. How many professors appear to know nothing of the real force and energy of the Spirit of God in subduing sin and creating holiness! Theirs is a shallow life. Alas, how much they lose! They come under the obligations of the House of God, but they do not know the infinite privileges of that house. It is for the truly spiritual that God reserves the choicest of His dainties. Be half a Christian and you shall have enough religion to make you miserable—be wholly a Christian and your joy shall be full! Walk with God in the light as He is in the light and you shall have fellowship with Him, such as shall make earth akin to Heaven!

But take a little light and a little darkness and attempt to make a mixture of them—seek to join the Church and the world—and you shall have neither the pleasures of the world nor the comforts of the Spirit. It is a pity for a man to miss joys which an angel might covet! What an injury such professors are to the Church! Each one pulls his companions up or drags them down. Every man in the Church is either a help or a hindrance. No Christian man can live to himself. He may attempt to confine himself within his own ribs, button up his coat and fancy that what he does is to himself, alone, and that his tongue and his heart are his own, but it is not so. A smell steals forth from every man's life and it is either like the spikenard of the alabaster box, or like the reeking of a dung-hill. God help us to remember our influence upon others!

Think, also, how much the world is injured by Christians who are not Christians! Oh Friends, we need, nowadays, a sterling Christianity! We cannot do with German silver, now! We must have the real metal. I was about to say I would sooner you had no religion and made no pretence to having any, than to have the imitation of it. Sin is real today. We have heard enough of how far sinners will go—they venture not only to the brink of Hell, but they snatch the accursed fire out of the pit, itself, and bring it into our city! Shall saints be shams, when sinners are so real? Shall Baal have worshippers that cut themselves with knives and leap upon his altar in the frenzy of their lust—and shall Jehovah have only a faithless company who, as yet, are halting between two opinions and do not know whether He is God or not? Oh for a Church of God that will shake itself loose from the world! If we had but one such Church, there would be hope for our age. God send it!

Last of all, how is Christ shamed and dishonored when we are not holy, but worldly, covetous, proud and unloving! Oh, Sirs, it seems to me that since the foundation of God was laid in agony and bloody sweat and, since God Himself became Incarnate that He might lay the foundation of holiness in the world, we ought to take heed how and what we build thereon! We must come to it, for, "other foundation can no man lay." And it behooves us to come very solemnly to it and to know what we mean by building thereon. True godliness is not to say, "I believe," but to believe! Not to talk of repentance, but to repent! It is not to speak of regeneration, but to be born again! It is not to talk about consecration, but really to live to God! It is not to speak about the Holy Spirit, but to have Him dwelling in you!

Be it ours to have the Truth of God in the inward parts and Grace in the core of the heart. Oh, may God bring us to this! We ask it for our Lord Jesus Christ's sake. Amen.

16

The Great House and the Vessels in It

(Sermon No. 1348)

"But in a great house there are not only vessels of gold and of silver, but, also, of wood and of earth; and some to honor and some to dishonor. If a man, therefore, purges himself from these, he shall be a vessel unto honor, sanctified, and meet for the Master's use, and prepared unto every good work" (2 Timothy 2:20-21).

ONE OF THE MOST SERIOUS calamities which can befall a Church is to have her own ministers teaching heresy. Yet this is no new thing—it has happened from the beginning. Paul and Peter and James and John, in their Epistles, had to speak of seducers in the Churches, even in those primitive days, and ever since then there have arisen in the very midst of the House of God those who have subverted the faith of many and led them away from the fundamental Truths of God into errors of their own inventing.

The Apostle compares this to gangrene which is one of the most dangerous and deadly mischiefs which can occur to the body. It is within the body—it eats deeper and deeper into the flesh, festering and putrefying—and if it is not stopped it will continue its ravages till life is extinguished by "black mortification." False doctrine and an unchristian spirit in the midst of the Church, itself, must be regarded as such a gangrene—a silent wolf ravenously gnawing at the heart—the vulture of Prometheus devouring the vitals. No external opposition is one-half so much to be dreaded!

Yet here is our comfort when distressed at the evils of the present age, among which this is one of the chief, that the Truth of God abides forever the same! "The foundation of God stands sure." There is no moving that. Whether 10,000 oppose it or promulgate it, the Truth of God is still the same in every jot and tittle. Even as the sun shines evermore, as well when clouds conceal its brightness as when, from a clear sky, it pours abroad a flood of glory, the lovers of profane and vain babblings have not taken away from us, nor can they take from us, the eternal Truths of God!

The Lord lives, though they have said, "There is no God." The precious blood of Jesus has not lost its efficacy, though divines have beclouded the Atonement. The Spirit of God is not less mighty to quicken and to console though men have denied His personality. The Resurrection is as sure as if Hymenaeus and Philetus had never said that it is passed already. And the eternal Covenant of Grace abides forever unbroken though Pharisees and Sadducees unite to revile it! The foundation of God stands sure and, moreover, the foundation of the Church remains sure, also, for, blessed be God, "the Lord knows them that are His."

All that God has built upon the foundation which He, Himself, has laid, keeps its place—not one living stone that He ever laid upon the Foundation has been lifted from its resting place. Earthquakes of error may test the stability of the building and cause great searching of heart, but sooner shall the mountains which are round about Jerusalem start from their seats than the work or Word of the Lord be frustrated! The things which cannot be shaken remain unaltered in the very worst times. "After all," says the Apostle, in effect, though in fewer words,

"it is not such a very great wonder that there should be persons in the Church who are not of the sterling metal of sincerity, nor of the gold and silver of Truth which endures the fire. You must not look at Hymenaeus and Philetus as if they were prodigies. There have been many like they are and there will be many more. These ill weeds grow in all ages and they multiply and increase."

Where, dear Brothers and Sisters, beneath the skies shall we find absolute purity in any community? The very first family had a Cain in it and there was a wicked Ham even in the select few within the Ark. In the household of the father of the faithful there was an Ishmael. Isaac, with all his quiet walk with God, must be troubled with an Esau. And you know how, in the house of Jacob, there were many sons that walked not as they should. When the Church of God was in the wilderness and had a barrier of desert between it and the outer world, yet you know how Korah, Dathan and Abirain were there, beside many other troublers in Israel!

Yes, even amidst the most select part of the visible Church of God, in the priesthood, there were found those that dishonored it. Nadab and Abihu were slain with fire before the Lord and Hophni and Phineas died in battle because they had made themselves vile, though God's anointed priests. Even when our Divine Master had formed for Himself—

"A little garden, walled around, Chosen, and made peculiar ground," in which there were but 12 choice trees, yet one of them bore evil fruit. "I have chosen you 12, and one of you is a devil." In the great field which Christ has sown, tares will spring up among the wheat, for the enemy takes pains to sow them. Neither is it possible for us to root them up. In the king's garden, briars will grow—thorns, also—and thistles will the most sacred soil yield us.

Even the lilies of Christ grow among thorns. You cannot keep the best of Churches altogether pure, for though the Lord Himself has prepared a vineyard and make a winepress and built a wall about it, yet the foxes come and spoil the vines. And though our great Lord has an orchard which yields rare fruit, yet when He comes to visit it, He finds a barren fig tree, dug about and fed, it is true, but still barren! Look to Christ's fold on earth and behold there are wolves in sheep's clothing there! Look to the net which His servants draw to shore and there are both good and bad fish in it. Yes, lift your eyes to the skies and though there are myriads of stars, yet you shall mark wandering stars among them—and meteors which are and are not—and are quenched in the blackness of darkness forever. Until we shall come to the Heaven of the Most High we must expect to find chaff mixed with the wheat, dross with the gold, goats with the sheep and dead flies in the ointment. Only let us see to it that we are not of that ill character, but are precious in the sight of the Lord.

Coming to the text, the Apostle suggests the encouragement I have already given, under a certain metaphor. He says that in a great house there will naturally be varieties of furniture. And there will be vessels and utensils of many kinds—some of them will be of wood and of earthenware, for meaner purposes—but others of gold and silver, for state occasions—when the honor and glory of the great proprietor are to be displayed. There are vessels of precious metal in a great house and these are its honor, decking the tables on high festivals when the Master is at home. But there are others of baser stuff kept in the background, never displayed at times of rejoicing, but meant for common drudgery.

There are cups and flagons of solid silver prized as perpetual heirlooms of the family which are carefully preserved. And there are plates and pots which are soon worn out and are only of temporary use. There are many sets of them being broken up in the lifetime of a family. The same is true in the Church of God which, being in the world, has its common side and its common vessels. But being, also, a heavenly house, the Church has its nobler furniture, far more precious than gold which perishes though it is tried with fire.

For our instruction, may the Holy Spirit help us while we look, first, at the great house. Secondly, at the meaner vessels, peeping into the kitchen. Thirdly, at the nobler vessels, going into the china cabinet to look at the silver and gold. And then, fourthly, before we leave the house, let us ask for an interview with the Master, Himself.

I. First, let us consider THE GREAT HOUSE. The Apostle compares the Church to a great house. We feel sure he is not speaking of the world. It did not occur to him to speak about the world and it would have been altogether superfluous to tell us that in the world there are all sorts of people—everybody knows that! The Church is a great house belonging to a great Person, for the Church is the House of God, according to the promise—"I will dwell in them, and walk in them."

The Church is the temple in which the Lord is worshipped, the palace in which He rules. It is His castle and place of defense for His Truth. It is the armory out of which He supplies His people with weapons. The Church is God's mansion in which He abides—"This is My rest forever. Here will I dwell for I have desired it." There it is that He rests in His love and, in infinite condescension, manifests Himself as He does not unto the world. King Solomon built a house for himself in the forest of Lebanon, and behold, the Lord has, of living stones, built for Himself a far more glorious house where He may abide! It is a great house because it is the house of the great God! Who can be so great as He? It is a great house because planned and designed upon a great scale.

I fear that some who live in the house have no idea how great it is. They have a very faint notion of its length and breadth. The great thoughts of God are far beyond their most elevated conception, so that He might say to them as He has said to others, "My thoughts are not your thoughts, neither are My ways your ways, says the Lord." The palace of the King of kings is "exceedingly magnificent," and for spaciousness far excels all the abodes of earthly princes. We read of the golden palace of Nero, that it reached from hill to hill and enclosed lakes and streams and gardens beneath its wondrous roof. But behold, the Lord has stretched the line of His electing Grace over nations and kindreds even to the ends of the earth!

His house takes in a mighty sweep of humanity. Many are the rooms in the house and there are dwellers in one room who have never yet seen any part of the great house but the little chamber in which they were born! They have never walked through the marvelous corridors, or moved in the vast halls which God has built with cedar pillars and cedar beams and carved work of heavenly workmanship. Some good men hardly care to see the long rows of polished columns, quarried by Grace from the rough mass of Nature which now shine resplendent as monuments of Divine Love and Wisdom! Colossal is the plan of the Eternal—the Church of God is worthy of the infinite mind!

Angels and principalities delight to study the stupendous plan and well they may—as the great Architect unrolls His drawings, piece by piece, to let them see the various sections of the complete design, they are struck with admiration and exclaim, "Oh the riches of the wisdom and the knowledge of God!" The Church is no narrow cottage wherein a few may luxuriate in bigotry, but it is a great house, worthy of the infinite heart of Jehovah, worthy of the blood of Jesus, the Incarnate God, and worthy of the power of the ever-blessed Spirit!

It is a great house because it has been erected at great cost and with great labor. Who can tell the cost of this mansion? It is a price beyond price, for God has given His only-begotten Son—He had but one, and Heaven could not match Him—that He might redeem unto Himself a people who should be His dwelling place forever. Solomon's temple, now that they have laid bare a part of the foundations, even though it is in utter ruin, astonishes all beholders as they mark the enormous size and accurate adjustment of the stones—what must it have been in its glory? What cost was lavished on that glorious house!

But think of the labor and the skill, the Divine art and engineering with which Jehovah has hewn out of the rock of sinful nature the stones with which He builds up His spiritual house! What energy has the Holy Spirit displayed! What resurrection power! Harder than any granite we were by nature, yet has He cut us away from the rock of which we formed a part and fashioned and squared us—and made us to be built together for an habitation of God through the Spirit. Tell it to the praise of the glory of His Grace, that the Lord's Omnipotent power and boundless wealth of love are revealed in His Church!

When our eyes shall see the Church of God, at last, in all her beauty descending out of Heaven from God, having the Glory of God and her light like unto a stone most precious, even like unto a jasper stone—when we shall see, I say, that the length and the breadth and the height of it are equal—when we shall see its deep foundations laid in the eternal purpose and its walls built up with lofty pinnacles of glory, high as the Divine Person of her Lord. And when we shall mark its wondrous compass, broad enough to hold the glory and honor of the nations—then shall we shout for joy as we behold the riches and the power and the splendor of the great King of kings who has built for Himself this great house!

It is a great house, again, because its household arrangements are conducted on a great scale. You know how country people, when there is some rich lord living in the village, speak always of his mansion as "the great house." It is the great house for which those bullocks are being fattened and those sheep and lambs will be consumed at the great house, for there are many in the family and none are allowed to go hungry. Solomon kept a great house. When you read the account of the daily provision for his table, you see that it was a great house, indeed—a vast and truly royal establishment!

Yes, but neither for quality nor quantity could Solomon's palace match the great house of God in its plenty. Speak of fine flour—behold, He has given us angels' food! Speak of royal dainties—behold, the Lord has given us fat things full of marrow, wines on the lees well-refined! What a perpetual feast does the Lord Jesus keep up for all His followers! If any of them hunger it is not because their rations are stinted. If there are any complaints, it is not because the Master's oxen and fatlings are not freely provided! Ah, no, to every man there is a good piece of meat and a flagon of wine dealt out, even as David dealt it out in the day when he removed the Ark unto the hill of Zion.

Glory be to God! He has said, "Eat, O Friends! Drink, yes, drink abundantly, O Beloved!" In this mountain shall the hand of the Lord rest and He will make unto all nations a feast of fat things. Behold, His oxen and fatlings are killed, all things are ready. It is a great house, where great sinners are fed on great dainties and filled with the great goodness of the Lord! It is a great house for the number of its inhabitants. How many have lived beneath that roof tree for ages. "Lord," they say like a great host, "You have been our dwelling place throughout all generations." God is the home of His people, and His Church is the home of God!

And what multitudes are dwelling there now! Not only the companies that we know of, with whom it is our delight to meet for solemn worship, but all over the world the Lord has a people who dwell in the midst of His Church! And, though men have disfigured their Master's house by chalking up odd signs over some of the rooms and calling them by other names than those of the Owner, yet the Lord's people are all one Church—and to whatever part or party they may seem to belong, if Christ is in them they belong to Him of whom the whole family in Heaven and earth is named—and they make up but one spiritual house. What a swarm there is of the Lord's children and yet not one of the family remains unfed. The Church is a great house wherein thousands dwell, yes, a number that no man can number!

Once more, it is a great house because of its importance. People speak of "the great house" in our remote counties because to the whole neighborhood it bears a special relationship, being connected with some of its most vital interests—county politics and police—dignity and wealth find their center at "the great house." The Church is a great house because it is God's hospice where He distributes bread and wine to refresh the weary and entertains wayfarers that otherwise had been lost in the storm. It is God's hospital into which He takes the sick and there He nourishes them till they renew their youth like the eagle's.

It is God's great lighthouse with its lantern flashing forth a directing ray so that wanderers far away may be directed to the haven of peace. "Out of Zion, the perfection of beauty, God has shined." It is the seat of God's magistracy, for there are set thrones of judgment, the thrones of the house of David. Behold, the Lord has set His King upon His holy hill of Zion and therefore shall the power of His scepter go forth to the ends of the earth! The great house of the Church is the university for teaching all nations! It is the library wherein the sacred oracles are preserved! It is the treasury wherein His Truth is deposited and the registry of new-born heirs of Heaven!

It is important to Heaven as well as to earth, for its topmost towers reach into Glory and there is in it a ladder, the foot of which rests on earth, but the top reaches to Heaven—up and down which the angels come and go continually. Said I not well that the Apostle had wisely chosen the figure when he called the Church a great house?

II. We will now go inside the great house and we at once observe that it is well furnished. Our text, however, invites us to note that it contains a number of MEANER VESSELS, articles of the coarser kind for ordinary and common uses. Here are plates, wooden buckets, pitchers and pots and various vessels of coarse pottery. Some have thought that this figure of vessels to dishonor relates to Christians of a lower grade, persons of small Grace and of less sanctified conversation. Now, although Believers may, from some points of view, be comparable to earthen vessels, yet I dare not look upon any child of God, however low in Grace, as a vessel to dishonor!

269

Moreover, the word, "these," refers to the earthen and wooden vessels—surely they cannot represent saints—or we should never be told to purge ourselves from them! If a man is God's child, into whatever state and condition he may fall it is our business to look after him and endeavor to restore him, remembering ourselves, also, lest we be tempted. But it cannot be right to purge ourselves from even the least of our believing Brothers and Sisters! Besides, that is not the run of the chapter at all.

The real meaning is that in the Church of God there are unworthy persons serving inferior and temporary purposes who are vessels to dishonor. They are in the Church, but they are like vessels of wood and vessels of earth—they are not the treasure of the mansion, they are not brought out on state occasions and are not set much store by—for they are not "precious in the sight of the Lord." The Apostle does not tell us how they came there, for it was not his intent to do so and no parable or metaphor could teach everything. Neither will I stay to describe how some professors have come into the Church of God—some by distinct falsehood and by making professions which they knew were untrue—others through ignorance and others, again, by being self-deceived and carried away with excitement.

The parable does not say how they got there, but they are there—yet they are only vessels of wood and vessels of earth. It is no credit to them that they are where they are, for they are not vessels to honor, though in an honorable place. It is no honor to any man to be a member of a Christian Church if he is, in himself, intrinsically worthless though they make a minister of him, or elect him deacon! It is no honor to him to be in office if the metal he is made of does not fit him for so honorable a purpose. He is an intruder in an honorable position and it is a dishonor to him to be where he is. It is no honor to a weed to grow in the best part of the garden. It is no honor to a barren fig tree to cumber the finest ground in the vineyard.

Ah, dear Friend, if you are in the Church of God, but not truly one of the Lord's people, it is a dishonorable thing of you to have come there! And it is equally dishonorable for you to remain there without fulfilling that great requisite which is demanded of everyone who names the name of Jesus—that he departs from all iniquity! The vessels in the great house are, however, of some use, even though they are made of wood and earth. And so there are persons in the Church of God whom the Lord Jesus will not acknowledge as His treasure, but He, nevertheless, turns them to some temporary purpose. Some are useful as the scaffold to a house, or the dogshores to a ship, or the hedges to a field. I believe that some unworthy members of the Church are useful in the way of watch dogs to keep others awake, or knives to let blood, or burdens to try strength. Some quarrelsome members of the Church help to scour the other vessels lest they should rust through being peaceful.

The Church is made up of men who are yet in the body and it has to deal with the outside world. And sometimes the worldly men who are in her serve some purpose in connection with this, her lowest need. Judas made a good treasurer, for his economy saved more than he stole. Joab was a good warrior for David, though he was by no means a saint. False professors do not make the Gospel untrue and sometimes, when they have spoken it, God has blessed it. You may see, if you go down the Kennington Park road today, a row of young trees planted by the road—how are they kept up while yet they are slender? Why, small posts of dead timber hold them up! And even so, a dead Sunday school teacher may yet be useful to a genuine Christian child—and a dead deacon may be the financial support of a living Church! Yes, and there are dead preachers, too, who, nevertheless, serve to fill up a space—but what vessels to dishonor they are!

It is a dreadful thing, however, for those who are like the posts I just mentioned, because the quicker the young tree grows, the sooner will the post be taken away, having no participant in the life which it helped to support. You see, then, that the base professors who get into the Church are turned to some good for His Church by our great Master. The servants of the great house can use the wooden ware and the earthenware, for a while, for rough everyday purposes, even as mere formalists can be employed in some scullery work or another.

There is one thing noticeable—the wooden and earthen vessels are not for the Master's use. When He holds high festival His cups are all of precious metal! "All King Solomon's drinking vessels were of gold." Would you have the King of kings set an earthen pot upon His royal table? Shall the guests at His table eat from wooden bowls? False professors are only useful to the servants, not to the Master—they serve base purposes and are not to be seen on those great days when He manifests His Glory. The Great Master overrules all things, being the Master of the servants and, as far as that which answers the purpose of His servants, is serviceable to Him. But personally, between the King at His table and the wooden vessel, there is no congruity—it would be an insult to hand Him wine in any but a sumptuous cup of precious metal, or to bring Him butter in any but a lordly dish!

How sad it is that many Christians are useful to the Church in various ways, but as for personal service rendered to the Lord Jesus Christ, Himself, they have no share, whatever, and never can have till Grace changes them from wood to silver, or from earth to gold. Note that in these vessels of which the Apostle speaks the substance is base. They are wood, or they are earth, nothing more. So are we all, by nature, of base material. Grace must make us into silver or into golden vessels or the Master cannot, Himself, use us, nor can our use in the Church ever be to honor. The wooden vessels in the Church are very easily hacked and carved and spoiled—if a man is inclined to mischief, he can put his knife to them and can cut great notches in them. He can ruin their character and render them worthless. Cunning teachers can soon take away from merely nominal Christians what they professed to believe, for they are very readily cut and hacked by those who play at such games.

As for the earthen vessels, how soon they are broken! Outside of any great house there are the remains of many broken pots which fell to the ground and shattered to pieces. And, I am sorry to say, we, also, can find enough of such relics to sadden us all. There were some in this house, once, who were comely to look upon. But there came a temptation and brushed them from the table—and they were shattered in a moment! Others of precious metal have endured far more shocks and tests of a severer kind. But those being only of earth were broken at once. Heaps of crockery accumulate outside every great house and certainly outside the great house of Christ. These vessels unto dishonor, though turned to some account, require a great deal of care on the part of the servants.

When our forefathers used to eat from wooden plates, the time the good wives used to spend in scalding and cleaning them to keep them at all sweet to eat upon was something terrible! And there are members of the Church who take a world of time from pastors and elders to keep them at all decent—we are continually trying to set them right, or keep them right in the common relationships of life. There are quarrels in their families which must be settled lest they become scandals—and these occupy the careful thought of their fellow Christians who have to watch for their good. Or they get lax in their doctrines, or foolish in their habits, or loose in their business transactions and we have to be scouring and cleaning them times without number!

Certain sorts of earthen vessels you have to be very particular in handling. Like egg-shell china, you may hardly look at them. Thank God I have not many in this Church—perhaps none of that sort as far as my handling is concerned—but other people's touches, though quite as wise, are not so welcome. Certain earthen vessels get dreadfully chipped unless they have dainty handling. If a Brother does not take his hat off to them in very lowly style and behave very reverently, they are ready to take offense! They feel themselves hurt and slighted when no such thing was intended. They stand upon their dignity and expect the fullest recognition of it. These are real earthen pots, very apt to be chipped, perhaps a little cracked already and needing a great deal of care and trouble on the part of the Lord's servants, lest they should go to pieces and spill everything that is put into them.

There are such in all great houses, and in the Master's great house there are, I fear, not just a few. They are useful up to a certain point, but they bring no honor to the house because there are plenty as good as they in other houses—every cottage can have common earthen pitchers in it. They are vessels in which is no pleasure. They are not peculiar, or precious. Nobody ever sounds abroad the Master's fame because He has so many thousands of wooden bowls or earthen pots. No, the king's honor comes from the plates—the gold and silver vessels, the peculiar treasure of kings. People speak about these rich goods and say,

"You should see the sideboards loaded down with the massive services of gold and silver! You should see how the tables groan beneath the splendor of the royal feast when the king brings forth his treasures."

True Christians are the glory of Christ, but false professors bring, at their very best, only dishonor. Better the smallest silver vessel than the largest earthen one! Better the least of all the saints than the greatest of vain professors! So much upon the vessels of dishonor.

III. We are now going into the treasury, or plate room, and will think of THE NOBLER VESSELS. These are, first of all, of solid metal—vessels of silver and vessels of gold. They are not all equally valuable, but they are all precious. Here is weight for you—here is something that is worth treasuring—something which will last for ages and at any time will endure the fire. Now, in real Christians, those who really love the Lord, there is something substantial and weighty. When you get hold of them, you know the difference between them and the wooden professor. Even those who do not like them—strange taste, that which does not appreciate silver and gold—are nevertheless compelled to say, "That is a genuine article, worth a great deal, weighty and substantial."

Now, we shall, none of us, ever be vessels of silver and gold unless the Lord makes us so by Divine Grace. Vessels of earth are things of nature—any potter can make them. Vessels of wood are common enough. Copper soon produces a pail. But a vessel of silver or of gold is a rarer thing! It costs mining and searching, furnace work and fashioning, toil and skill. On each vessel unto honor, Jesus Himself has put His hand to mold and fashion it—and to cause it to be "prepared unto glory." Did you ever hear how vessels come to be golden? Listen to this, and you shall know. One very dear to me has put the story into rhyme—

"'Oh that I were a cup, a golden cup,
Meet for the Master's use!

Brimming and trembling with that draught of joy,
    (The love of His beloved and purchased ones)
Which fills His heart with gladness.'

"So spoke a poor, vile, broken, earthy thing,
    A worthless castaway.
The Master heard and when He passed that way
    He stooped and touched it with His wounded hand—
When lo! Its baseness vanished, and instead
    There stood a golden chalice wondrous fair,
And overflowing with deep love for him!
    He raised it to His gracious lips, and quaffed
'The wine that makes glad the heart of God,'
    Then took the cup to Heaven."

On the vessels of honor you can see the hallmark. What is the hallmark which denotes the purity of the Lord's golden vessels? Well, He has only one stamp for everything. When He laid the foundation what was the seal He put upon it? "The Lord knows them that are His, and let everyone that names the name of Christ depart from all iniquity." That was God's seal! That was the impress of the great King upon the foundation stone. Do we find it here? Yes, we do. "If a man, therefore, purges himself from these, he shall be a vessel unto honor." You see, then, that the man who is the golden or silver vessel, departs from all iniquity—and that is the token of his genuine character.

The man who is truly the Lord's, seeks to be cleansed, not only from the open sin of the world, but from the common sin of professing Christians. He labors to be purged from that which the wooden vessel and the earthen vessel would delight in. He wants to be pure within and without. He desires perfection. He labors daily to conquer every sin and strives with all his might to serve his Lord. He is not content to have a fair appearance, as wood and earth may have—he wishes to be solid, substantial metal, purged and purified to the utmost possible degree and fit for the highest purposes. Now, this seeking after purity is the hallmark of the King's vessels of gold and silver.

Notice, however, that they are purged, for the Lord will not use filthy vessels no matter what they may be. He will only use those that are clean. And He would have His true people purged, as I have said before, not only from gross sin, but from doctrinal error and from association with the perverse-minded. We are to be purged from Hymenaeus and Philetus and from the vain babblings of which the Apostle has been speaking in the previous part of the chapter. I fear that Christian men do a great deal of mischief by their complicity with those who are teaching what is downright falsehood. If we are to serve the Lord in the matter of advancing His Truth, we must be true to the Truth of God ourselves. If we join hand in hand with others and so form a confederacy when the very pillars of the temple are being pulled down by rude hands, it may be we shall be partakers of other men's sins. We must be clean-handed in this matter!

And then notice that these gold and silver vessels are reserved as well as purged. They are made meet for the Master's use. Nobody is to drink out of them but the King, Himself. This is the blessedness of the child of God when he comes to be what he should be, that he can sing as we did just now—

> "I am Yours and Yours, alone,
> This I gladly, fully own!
> And in all my works and ways,
> Only now would seek Your praise."

As Joseph had a cup out of which he, alone, drank, so the Lord takes His people to be His peculiar treasure, vessels for His personal use. Brethren, I count it an honor to be useful to the meanest child of God, but I confess that the honor lies mainly in the fact that I am thereby serving the Master, Himself. Oh, to be used by God! This is to answer the end of our being. If you can feel that God has used you, then may you rejoice, indeed!

There are some Christians whom the Lord cannot much use, because, first of all, they are not cleansed from selfishness. They have an eye to their own honor or aggrandizement. The Lord will not be in complicity with selfish aims! Some men are self-confident—there is too much of the "I" about them—and our Master will not use them. He will have our weakness, but not our strength! And if we are great somebodies, He will pass us by and take some little nobody and make use of him. The Lord cannot use other men because they are too apt to be proud. If He were to give them a little success, it would be dangerous to their Christian existence! Their poor brains would begin to swim and they would think the Lord could hardly do without them! Indeed, when they meet with a little encouragement they swell into such wonderful people that they expect everybody to fall down and worship them!

God will not use them, neither will He set upon His table vessels which are in any way defiled. There must be purity! A man may work his heart out in the ministry or the Sunday school, but if he is practicing some secret sin he cannot prosper—it is not possible that God should honor him! There may be a measure of apparent success for a time and, in God's Sovereignty, He may use His Truth, itself, in spite of the man, but the man himself will not be useful to the Master. Littleness of Grace and contentedness with that spiritual poverty, also puts many a man aside. We must be full if God is to pour out of us to the thirsty! We must be full of His Light if we are to illuminate the darkness of others! We cannot reveal to the world what the Lord has not revealed to us.

Oh, for a holy character and holy communion with God! Then we shall be golden vessels fit for the Master's use and so, according to the text, we shall be ready for every good work—ready for the work when it comes and ready at the work when it has come—because completely consecrated to God and subject to His hand. In this readiness for whatever comes we shall be honored. Men may despise us, as they will, but what does it matter if God honors us? This height of Grace may cost us a sharp experience, but must not gold be tried with fire? As thieves are most anxious to steal not the pots and wooden vessels, but the gold and the silver, so we may expect to be exposed to greater temptations and greater persecutions than others.

More Grace involves more trials, but then we shall have the delight of glorifying God more. Oh, to be vessels unto honor! Beloved members of this Church, aspire to this! You have acknowledged in your names, that you are Christians! You have been baptized into the sacred name of the Divine Trinity! You have borne, up to now, a consistent moral character, but oh, see to it that the inner substance is the real metal—the gold and silver! See to it that you are reserved for the Lord's own special use! Be as consecrated to Him as were the bowls before the altar. Never let the world drink out of you, as Belshazzar did out of the vessels taken at Jerusalem. May the Lord grant that you may never be defiled, but may be kept, by His Grace, pure and consecrated to Him.

IV. Fourthly, for a moment we must speak about THE MASTER. He is introduced here, you see, as having certain vessels meet for His use—and this shows that He is in the house. There would be no need to reserve vessels for His use if He were not there—He is in the midst of His Church by His indwelling Spirit. How this ought to make us wish to be purged, sanctified and ready for Him! Your Master is not far away. His Presence in the Church is promised—"Lo, I am with you always, even to the end of the world." What manner of persons, therefore, ought you to be?

Secondly, the Master knows all about the house and knows the quality of all the vessels. There is no deceiving Him with the wooden plate—He knows it is not gold. And as for that earthen cup, though it may be gilt all over, He knows it is not gold. He reads the heart of everyone here present—wood or earth, silver or gold—the Master understands us. And then reflect that the Master will use us all as far as we are fit to be used. We are in God's house and if we are wood, He will put us to wooden use.

There are many wooden preachers. If we are earth and earthly-minded He may put us to earthly uses, as He did Judas, who carried the bag, but had no Grace. If you are silver He will give you silver use. And if you are gold He will give you golden service in which you shall be happy, honored and blessed. What comes of this, then, lastly? Why, Brothers and

Sisters, let us bestir ourselves that we be purged, for the text says, "If a man therefore purges himself." It throws this business upon each one of us personally—a man must purge himself from ill company! And when we have confessed the responsibility, let us turn to God in prayer and feel that thorough purging is a work which we cannot achieve and, therefore, we cry, "Cleanse me, O God! Sanctify me! Make me meet for Your service and prepared for every good work."

Beloved, finish with earnest prayer. Pray God that you may not be hypocrites! Beseech the Lord to search you and try you, that you not be found deceivers. And when you are sure that you are His, then ask Him to make you not merely silver, for it is very apt to tarnish, but rather the precious gold which, when exposed to the worst influences, scarcely shows a trace of dullness. Pure unalloyed gold may we be! And then may the Master, both in secret and public, use us to His own joy. May He refresh Himself with our love and faith, yes, may His joy be fulfilled in us, that our joy may be full. God grant it may be so, for Christ's sake.

17

The Form of Godliness Without the Power

(Sermon No. 2088)

"Having a form of godliness but denying the power thereof: from such turn away" (2 Timothy 3:5).

PAUL WARNS US OF CERTAIN characters which will appear in the last times. It is a very terrible list. The like have appeared in other days but we are led by his warning to apprehend that they will appear in greater numbers in the last days than in any previous age.

> "Lovers of their own selves, covetous, boasters, proud, blasphemers, disobedient to parents, unthankful, unholy, without natural affection, trucebreakers, false accusers, incontinent, fierce, despisers of those that are good, traitors, heady, high-minded, lovers of pleasures more than lovers of God."

These will swarm like flies in the decay of the year and will make the times exceeding perilous. We are nearing that period at this very time. That these people would, some of them, be within the Church is the most painful part of it. But they will be so, for they are comprehended in this last clause of the black catalog, which we have taken for our text—"Having a form of godliness but denying the power thereof."

Paul does not paint the future with rose-colored glasses—he is no smooth-tongued Prophet of a golden age into which this dull earth may be imagined to be glowing. There are sanguine Brothers and Sisters who are looking forward to everything growing better and better and better, until, at last, this present age ripens into a millennium. They will not be able to sustain their hopes, for Scripture gives them no solid basis to rest upon. We who believe that there will be no millennial reign without the

King and who expect no rule of righteousness except from the appearing of the righteous Lord, are nearer the mark.

Apart from the second Advent of our Lord, the world is more likely to sink into a pandemonium than to rise into a millennium. A Divine interposition seems to me the hope set before us in Scripture and, indeed, to be the only hope adequate to the occasion. We look to the darkening down of things. The state of mankind, however improved politically, may yet grow worse and worse spiritually. Certainly, we are assured in verse 13 that "evil men and seducers shall wax worse and worse, deceiving and being deceived." There will spring up in the Christian Church and round about it, a body of faithless men who profess to have faith—ungodly men who will unite with the saints—men having the form of godliness but denying the power.

We may call these hard times, if we will, but we have hardly yet come to the border of those truly harder times when it will go hard with the Church and she shall need, even more than today, to cry mightily unto the Lord to keep her alive. With this cloud upon our spirit, we come to the text itself. Let us consider it carefully and may the Holy Spirit help us!

True religion is a spiritual thing but it necessarily embodies itself in a form. Man is a spiritual creature but the human spirit needs a body in which to enshrine itself. And thus, by this need, we become allied to materialism. And if not "half dust, half Deity," as one has said, we are certainly both matter and soul. In each of us there is the form or body and the soul or power. It is so with religion—it is essentially a spiritual thing but it requires a form in which to embody and manifest itself.

Christian people fall into a certain outward method of procedure, a peculiar outward mode of uttering their faith, which becomes to true godliness what the body is to the soul. The form is useful, the form is necessary, the form ought to be vitalized—just as the body is useful and is necessary and is vitalized by the soul. If you get both the form, as modeled in the Word of God and the power, as bestowed by the Spirit of God, you do well and are living Christians. If you get the power alone, without the ordained form, you somewhat maim yourself. But if you get the form without the power, then, you dwell in spiritual death.

The body without the spirit is dead. And what follows upon death with flesh? Why, corruption—corruption so horrible that even love itself has to cry, "Bury my dead out of my sight." So that if there is in any the body of religion without the life of religion, it leads to decay and thus to corruption—and that has a tendency to decompose the character. The raw material of a devil is an angel bereft of holiness. You cannot make a Judas except out of an Apostle. The eminently good in outward form, when without inward life, decays into the foulest thing under Heaven. You cannot wonder that these are called "perilous times," in which such characters abound.

One Judas is an awful weight for this poor globe to bear but a tribe of them must be a peril, indeed. Yet, if not of the very worst order, those are enough to be dreaded who have the shadow of religion without its substance. Of such I have to speak at this time—from such may God give you Divine Grace to turn away! May none of us ever be spots in our feasts of love, or clouds without water carried about of winds. But this we shall be if we have the form of godliness without the power thereof.

With great solemnity of soul I approach this subject, seeking from the Lord the aid of His Spirit, who makes the Word to be a discerner of the thoughts and intents of the heart. First, I shall speak of the men, and secondly, of their folly. And when I am done with that, I shall have some words of instruction to give by way of conclusion.

I. First, let us talk awhile of THE MEN. They had the form of godliness but denied the power thereof. Note what they had and then observe what they had not. They had a form of godliness. What is a form of godliness? It is, first of all, attention to the ordinances of religion. These, so far as they are Scriptural, are few and simple. There is Baptism, wherein, in figure, the Believer is buried with Christ, that he may rise into newness of life. And there is the Lord's Supper, wherein, in type and emblem, he feeds upon Christ and sustains the life which came to him by fellowship with Christ's death. Those who have obeyed the Lord in these two ordinances have exhibited in their own persons the form of godliness. That form is every way instructive to others and impressive to the man himself.

Every baptized person and every communicant at the Lord's Table, should be godly and gracious. But neither Baptism nor the Lord's Supper will secure this. Where there is not the life of God in the soul, neither holiness or godliness follow upon the ordinances. And thus we may have around us baptized worldlings and men who go from the table of the Lord to drink the cup of devils. It is sad that it should be so. Such persons are guilty of presumption, falsehood, sacrilege and blasphemy. Ah me, we sit beside such every Sabbath!

The form of godliness involves attendance with the assemblies of God's people. Those who have professed Christ are accustomed to come together at certain times for worship and, in their assemblies, they join in common prayer and common praise. They listen to the testimony of God by His servants whom He calls to preach His Word with power. They also associate together in Church fellowship for purposes of mutual help and discipline. This is a very proper form—full of blessing both to the Church and to the world—when it does not die down into mere form. A man may go to Heaven alone but he will do better if he travels there with Mr. Great-Heart and Father Honest and Christiana and the children.

Christ's people are called sheep for one reason—they love to go in flocks. Dogs do very well separately but sheep do best in company. The sheep of Christ love to be together in the same pasture and to follow in a flock the footsteps of the Good Shepherd. Those who constantly associate in worship, unite in Church fellowship and work together for sacred purposes have the form of godliness and a very useful and proper form it is. Alas, it is of no value without the power of the Holy Spirit.

Some go further than public worship. They use a great deal of religious talk. They freely speak of the things of God in Christian company. They can defend the doctrines of Scripture, they can plead for its precepts and they can narrate the experience of a Believer. They are fondest of talking of what is doing in the Church—the tattle of the streets of Jerusalem is very pleasant to them. They flavor their speech with godly phrases when they are in company that will relish it. I do not censure them—on the contrary, I wish there were more of holy talk among professors. I wish we could revive the old habit, "They that feared the Lord spoke often one to another."

Holy conversation causes the heart to glow and gives to us a foretaste of the fellowship of the glorified. But there may be a savor of religion about a man's conversation and yet it may be a borrowed flavor—like hot sauces used to disguise the staleness of ancient meat. That religion which comes from the lips outward but does not well up from the deep fountains of the heart is not that living water which will spring up unto eternal life. Tongue godliness is an abomination if the heart is destitute of Divine Grace.

More than this—some have a form of godliness upheld and published by religious activity. It is possible to be intensely active in the outside work of the Church and yet to know nothing of spiritual power. One may be an excellent

Sunday school teacher after a fashion and yet have need to be taught what it is to be born again. One may be an eloquent preacher, or a diligent officer in the Church of God and yet know nothing of the mysterious power of the Spirit of Truth upon the heart. It is well to be like Martha in service. But one thing is needful—to sit at the Master's feet and learn as Mary did.

When we have done all the work our position requires of us, we may only have displayed the form of godliness. Unless we hearken to our Lord and from His Presence derive power, we shall be as a sounding brass and a tinkling cymbal. Brethren, I speak to myself and to each one of you in solemn earnestness. If much speaking, generous giving and constant occupation could win Heaven, we might easily make sure of it. But more than these are needed. I speak to each one of you. And if I singled out anyone more than another to be the pointed object of my address, it would be the best among us—the one who is doing most for his Master and who, in his inmost soul, is thinking, "That warning does not apply to me."

O my active and energetic Brother, remember the word, "Let him that thinks he stands take heed lest he fall." If any of you dislike this searching sermon, your dislike proves how much you need it. He that is not willing to search himself should stand self-incriminated by that unwillingness to look at his affairs. If you are right, you will not object to be weighed in the balances. If you are, indeed, pure gold, you may still feel anxiety at the sight of the furnace but you will not be driven to anger at the prospect of the fire. Your prayer will always be, "Search me, O God and know my heart: try me and know my thoughts: and see if there is any wicked way in me and lead me in the way everlasting."

I need not enlarge further. You all know what a form of godliness is and most of us who are here present hold fast that form—may we never dishonor it! I trust we are anxious to make that form accurate according to Scripture so that our form of godliness may be that into which the earliest saints were delivered. Let us be Christians of a high type, cast in our Lord's own mold. But do not become sticklers for the form and neglect the inner life—that will never do. Shall we fight about a man's clothes and allow the man, himself, to die?

But now, as these people had not the power of godliness, how did they come to hold the form of it? This needs several answers. Some come by the form of godliness in an hereditary way. Their ancestors were always godly people and they almost naturally take up with the profession of their fathers. This is common and where it is honest, it is most commendable. It is a great mercy when, instead of the fathers, shall be the children. And we may hopefully anticipate that our children will follow us in the things of God, if by example, instruction and prayer, we have sought it before the Lord.

We are unhappy if we do not see our children walking in the God's Truth. Yet the idea of birthright membership is an evil one and is as perilous as it is unscriptural. If children are taken into the Church simply because of their earthly parentage, surely this is not consistent with that description of the sons of God which is found in the inspired Scripture— "Which were born, not of blood, nor of the will of the flesh, nor of the will of man but of God." Not generation but *regeneration*, makes the Christian. You are not Christians because you can trace a line of fleshly descent throughout twenty generations of children of God.

You must, yourselves, be born again. For except a man is born from above, he cannot see the kingdom of God. Many, no doubt, lay hold naturally on the form of godliness because of family ties—this is poor work. Ishmael is a sorry son of Abraham and Esau of Isaac and Absalom of David. Grace does not run in the blood. If you have no better foundation for your religion than your earthly parentage, you are in a wretched case.

Others have accepted the form of godliness by the force of authority and influence. They were, as lads, put apprentice to godly men. As girls, they were under the guidance of pious teachers. And as they grew up, they came under the influence of persons of superior intelligence and character who were on the Lord's side. This accounts for their form of godliness. Many persons are the creatures of their surroundings—religion or irreligion is with them the result of circumstances. Such persons were led to make a profession of faith in Christ because others did so and friends encouraged them to do the same.

The deep searching of heart, which they ought to have exhibited, was slurred over and they were found among the people of God without having to knock for entrance at the wicket gate. I do not wish anyone to condemn himself because he was guided to the Savior by godly friends—far from it. But, nevertheless, there is danger lest we fail to have personal repentance and personal faith and are content to lean upon the opinions of others.

I have seen the form of godliness taken up on account of friendships. Many a time courtship and marriage have led to a formal religiousness, but a lacking heart. The future husband is induced to make a profession of religion for the sake of gaining one who was a sincere Christian and would not have broken her Lord's command to be unequally yoked together with an unbeliever. Godliness should never be put on in order that we may put a wedding ring upon the finger—this is a sad abuse of religious profession.

Other kinds of friendship, also, have led men and women to profess a faith they never had and to unite themselves visibly with the Church, while in spirit and in truth they were never truly a part of it. I put these things to you that there may be a great searching of heart among us all and that we may candidly consider how we have come by our form of godliness. Certain persons assume the form of godliness from a natural religious disposition. Do not suppose that all unconverted people are without religion. Much religiousness is found in the heathen and there are races which have naturally more of reverence than others.

The German, with his profound philosophy, is often free, not only from superstition but from reverence. The Russian is by race naturally religious, not to say superstitious. I am speaking after the manner of men—the usual Russian takes off his hat to Holy Places, pictures and persons—and he is little inclined to disbelieve or scoff. We perceive like differences among our own acquaintances—one man is readily fooled by skeptics, while another is ready, with open mouth, to believe every word. One is naturally an infidel, another is as naturally credulous.

I mean, then, that to some the form of godliness commends itself because they have a natural leaning that way. They could not be happy unless they were attending where God is worshipped, or unless they were reckoned among the Believers in Christ. They must play at religion even if they do not make it their life business. Let me remind you of the questionable value of that which springs out of fallen human nature. Assuredly it brings no one into the spiritual kingdom, for "that which is born of the flesh is flesh." Only "that which is born of the Spirit is spirit." "You must be born again." Beware of everything which springs up in the field without the sowing of the husbandman, for it will turn out to be a weed. O Sirs, the day will come when God will try us as with fire and that which comes of unregenerate nature will not stand the test but will be utterly consumed!

I do not doubt that, in these silken days, many have a form of godliness because of the respect it brings them. Time was when to be a Christian was to be reviled, if not to be imprisoned and, perhaps, burned at the stake. Hypocrites were fewer in those days for a profession cost too much. Yet, strange to say, there were some who played the Judas even in those times. Today religion walks forth in her velvet slippers. And in certain classes and ranks, if men did not make some profession of religion, they would be looked upon with suspicion and therefore men will take the name of Christian upon them and wear religion as a part of full dress.

The cross is at this day worn as a necklace. The cross as the instrument of our Savior's shame and death is forgotten, and instead thereof, it is made the badge of honor, a jewel wherewith ungodly men may adorn themselves. Is this indicative of the deceitfulness of the age? Beware of seeking respect by a hypocritical godliness. Honor gained by a heartless profession is, in God's sight, the greatest disgrace. The actor may strut in his mimic royalty, but he must take off his crown and robes when the play is over. And what will he then be?

From the days of Iscariot until now, some have taken up the form of godliness to gain thereby. To make gain of godliness is to imitate the son of perdition. This is a perilous road and yet many risk their souls for the lucre which they find therein. Apparent zeal for God may really be zeal for gold. The Emperor Maximilian showed great zeal against idolatry and published a decree that images of gold and silver should be melted down. He was extremely zealous about this. The images were all to be melted down and the metal forfeited to the emperor.

It was shrewdly suspected that this great iconoclast was not altogether swayed by unselfish motives. When a business brings grist to the mill, it is not hard to keep to it. Some love Christ because they carry His money bag for Him. Beware of that kind of godliness which makes a man hesitate until he sees whether a duty will pay or not and then makes him eager because he sees it will answer his purpose.

Once more—I do not doubt that a form of godliness has come to many because it brings them ease of conscience and they are able, like the Pharisee, to thank God that they are not as other men are. Have they not been to Church? Have they not paid for their pew? They can now go about their daily business without those stings of conscience which would come of neglecting the requirements of religion. These people profess to have been converted and they are numbered with Believers. But, alas, they are not of them.

Of all people these are the hardest to reach and the least likely to be saved. They hide behind the earthworks of a nominal religion. They are out of reach of the shot and shell of Gospel rebukes. They fly among the sinners and they have taken up their quarters among the saints. Sad is that man's plight who wears the name of life but has never been quickened by the Holy Spirit. Thus, I have very feebly tried to show what these men had and why they had it.

Let us now remember what they did not have. They had "the form" of godliness. But they were denied "the power." What is that power? God Himself is the power of godliness, The Holy Spirit is the life and force of it. Godliness is the power which brings a man to God and binds him to Him. Godliness is that which creates repentance towards God and faith in Him. Godliness is the result of a great change of heart in reference to God and His Character. Godliness looks towards God and mourns its distance from Him. Godliness hastens to draw near and rests not till it is at home with God.

Godliness makes a man like God. Godliness leads a man to love God and to serve God. It brings the fear of God before his eyes and the love of God into his heart. Godliness leads to consecration, to sanctification, to concentration. The godly man seeks first the kingdom of God and His righteousness and expects other things to be added to him. Godliness makes a man commune with God and gives him a partnership with God in His glorious designs. And so it prepares him to dwell with God forever.

Many who have the form of godliness are strangers to this power and so are in religion worldly, in prayer mechanical, in public one thing and in private another. True godliness lies in spiritual power and they who are without this are dead while they live.

What is the general history of those who have not this power? Well, dear Friends, their course usually runs thus—they do not begin with denying the power but they begin by trying to do without it. They would like to become members of the Church and as they fear that they are not fit for it, they look about for something which looks like conversion and the new birth. They try to persuade themselves that they have been changed—they accept emotion as regeneration and a belief of doctrine for belief in Christ.

It is rather hard at first to reckon brass as gold but it grows easier as it is persisted in. Patching up a conversion and manufacturing a regeneration, they venture forward. At the first they are a good deal suspicious of themselves but they industriously kill every question by treating it as a needless doubt. Thus, by degrees, they believe a lie.

The next step is easy—they deceive themselves and come to believe that they are surely saved. All is now right for eternity, so they fancy. And they fold their arms in calm security. Meeting with godly people, they put on a bold front and speak up as bravely as if they were the true soldiers of King Jesus. Good people are charmed to meet with fresh Brethren and at once take them into their confidence. Thus they deceive others and help to strengthen themselves in their false hope.

They use the choice phrases of earnest Christians. Mixing with them, they pick up their particular expressions and pronounce Shibboleth in the most approved fashion. At last they take the daring step of denying the power. Being without it themselves, they conceive that others are without it, also. Judging from their own case, they conclude that it is all an affair of words. They get on very well without any supernatural power and others, no doubt, do the same—only they add a little cant to it to please the very godly folk.

They practically deny the power in their lives, so that those who see them and take them for Christians say, "There really is nothing in it. For these people are as we are. They have a touch of paint here and a little varnish there but it is all the same wood." Practically, their actions assure the world that there is no power in Christianity. It is only a name. Very soon, privately, in their hearts they think it is so and they invent doctrines to match. Looking about them they see inconsistent Christians and faulty Believers and they say to themselves, "There is not much in faith, after all. I am as good as any of these Believers and perhaps better, though I am sure there is no work of the Spirit in me."

Thus, within their own hearts they believe, what, at first, they dare not speak—they count godliness an empty thing. By-and-by, in some cases, these people profanely deny the Divine power of our holy faith and then they become the greatest enemies of the Cross of Christ. These traitors, nourished in the very House of God, are the worst foes of the Truth of God and righteousness. They ridicule that which once they professed to reverence. They have measured Christ's corn with their own bushel. And because they never felt the powers of the world to come, they imagine that no one else has done so either.

Look at the Church of the present day. The advanced school, I mean. In its midst we see preachers who have a form of godliness but deny the power thereof. They talk of the Lord Jesus but they deny His Godhead, which is His power. They speak of the Holy Spirit but deny His personality, wherein lies His very existence. They take away the substance and power from all the doctrines of Revelation, though they pretend still to believe them. They talk of redemption but they deny substitution, which is the essence of it.

They extol the Scriptures but deny their infallibility, wherein lies their value. They use the phrases of orthodoxy and believe nothing in common with the orthodox. I know not which to loathe the more—their teachings or their spirit—surely they are worthy of each other. They burn the kernel and preserve the husk. They kill the truth and then pretend to reverence its sepulcher—"they say they are Jews and are not but do lie."

This is horrible, but the evil is widely spread and in the presence of it the children of God are framing compromises, selling their Lord and becoming partakers with the despisers of His Truth. "Having a form of godliness but denying the power thereof." It is the sin of the age—the sin which is ruining the Churches of our land.

II. In the second place, we are to observe THE WICKED FOLLY of this hypocritical conduct. Those who rest in the mere show of godliness are acting in a shameless manner and I will try to expose it.

First, they degrade the very name of Christ. Brethren, if there is no spiritual power in godliness, it is worth nothing. We want no clouds without rain. Of shams and mere pretences we have more than enough. Those who have not the power of godliness show us a very damaging picture of religion. They make out our Lord's religion to be comparable to a show at a country fair, with fine pictures and loud drumming on the outside and nothing within worth a moment's consideration. The best of the show is on the outside.

Or if there is anything within, it is a masquerade where all act borrowed parts but no one is what he seems to be. Gracious Lord, never suffer us so to act as to make the world think that our Redeemer is nothing more than the clever manager of a theater, where nothing is real but all is pantomime. Brothers and Sisters, if you pray at all, pray God to make you real through and through. May you be made of true metal! It were better for you that you had never been born than that you should make Christ dishonorable among the sons of men by leading them to conclude that religion is all a piece of acting.

The folly of this is illustrated by the fact that there is no value in such a dead form. The form of godliness without the power is not worth the trouble it takes to put it together and keep it together. Imitation jewels are pretty and brilliant. But if you take them to the jeweler he will give you nothing for them. There is a religion which is all paste gems—a godliness which glitters but is not gold. And in that day when you will want to realize something from it, you will be wretchedly disappointed.

A form of godliness joined to an unholy heart is of no value to God. I have read that the swan was not allowed to be offered upon the altar of God because, although its feathers are as white as snow, yet its skin is black. God will not accept that external morality which conceals internal impurity. There must be a pure heart as well as a clean life. The power of godliness must work within, or else God will not accept our offering. There is no value to man or to God in a religion which is a dead form.

Next, there is no use in mere formality. If your religion is without spiritual life, what is the use of it? Could you ride home on a dead horse? Would you hunt with dead dogs? Would anyone like to go into battle with a pasteboard helmet? When the sword fell on it, what use would such a helmet be? What an outcry has been raised about bad swords! Is false religion any better? In the depth of winter can you warm yourself before a painted fire? Could you dine off the picture of a feast when you are hungry?

There must be vitality and substantiality—or else the form is utterly worthless. And worse than worthless, for it may flatter you into deadly self-conceit. Moreover, there is no comfort in it. The form without the power has nothing in it to warm the heart, to raise the spirits, or to strengthen the mind against the day of sickness, or in the hour of death. O God, if my religion has been a mere form, what shall I do in the swelling of Jordan? My fine profession will all disappear and nothing will come of it wherewith I may face the last enemy.

Peter called hypocrites "wells without water." You are thirsty and you gladly spy a well. It is well surrounded with a curb and provided with a windlass and bucket. You hasten to draw water. What? Does the bucket come up empty? You try again. How bitter is your disappointment! A well without water is a mockery. It is a mere pit of destruction—a deadly delusion. Are some of you possessors of a religion which never yields you a drop of comfort? Is it a bondage to you? Do you follow Christ as a slave follows his master? Away with such a religion!

The godliness which is worth having is a joy to a man—it is his choice, his treasure, his all. When it does not yield him conscious joy, yet he prizes it as the only source from which joy is expected of him. He follows after Christ with love, out of his heart's desire after Him and not from the force of fashion, or the power of fear.

To have the form of godliness without the power of it is to lack constancy in your religion. You never saw a mirage, perhaps. But those who have travel in the East, when they come home, are sure to tell you about them. It is a very hot and thirsty day and you are riding on a camel. Suddenly there rises before you a beautiful scene. Just a little from you are brooks of water, flowing between beds of osiers and banks of reeds and rushes. Yonder are palm trees and orange groves. Yes, and a city rises on a hill, crowned with minarets and towers.

You are rejoiced and ask your guide to lead you nearer to the water which glistens in the sun. He grimly answers, "Take no notice, it is a mirage. There is nothing yonder but the burning sand." You can scarce believe him. It seems so real! But lo, it is all gone, like a dream of night. And so is the hope which is built upon the form of godliness without the power. The white ants will eat up all the substance of a box and yet leave it standing till a touch causes the whole fabric to fall in dust—beware of a profession of which the substance has been eaten away. Believe in nothing which has not the stamp of eternity upon it.

Be careful, poor Child—you may blow your bubble and the sunlight may paint it with rainbows. But in an instant it is gone and not a trace of it remains. Your transient globe of beauty is for you and your fellow children and not for men.

In reality, this kind of religion is in opposition to Christ. It is Jannes and Jambres over again—the magician of hypocrisy is trying to work miracles which belong to God only. In appearance he would produce the same marvels as the finger of God. But he fails. God grant we may never be guilty of resisting the Truth of God by a lying profession. False men do serious injury to true godliness. For, like Ehud, they come with a pretended message from God and with their dagger sharpened at both edges, they strike vital godliness in its very heart. Nobody can do so much damage to the Church of God as the man who is within its walls but not within its life.

This nominal godliness, which is devoid of power, is a shameful thing. I close with that. It is a shameful thing for this life, for the Lord Jesus loathes it. When He passed by the fig tree, which was so early with its leaves but so empty of fruit, He saw therein the likeness of the vainglorious professor who has no real holiness and He said, "Henceforth let no fruit grow on you forever." His Word withered it at once—it stood a terrible emblem of the end of a false profession.

How shameful will such a fruitless, lifeless professor be in eternity, when the secrets of all hearts shall be revealed! What shame and everlasting contempt will await him when his falsehood shall be detected and his baseness shall fill all holy minds with horror! O, beware of the Hell of the false professor!

I have done when I have added a few words of instruction. The form of godliness is most precious. Let those who feel the power of godliness honor it and use it. Do not despise it because others have damaged it. Come forth and make an open profession of religion. But see that you have the power of it. Cry to God that you may never wear a sleeve which is longer than your arm—I mean may never go beyond what is really and truly your own. It will be better for you to go to God as a lost soul and cry for mercy, than to profess yourself saved when you are not.

Yet confess Christ without fail or fear. Do not be ashamed of Jesus because of the ill manners of His disciples. Regard the ill savor of false professors as a part of the cross which you will have to bear for your Lord. To be associated with some who are not true seems inevitable in this life—however carefully we choose our company.

My next is a word of discrimination. Those to whom my text has nothing to say will be the first to take it home to themselves. When I discharge my heart with a faithful sermon, certain trembling souls whom I would gladly comfort are sure to think that I mean them. A poor woman, in deep distress, comes to me, crying, "Sir, I have no feeling." Dear heart, she has ten times too much feeling. Another moans out, "I am sure I am a hypocrite." I never met with a hypocrite who thought himself one. And I never shall.

"Oh," said another, "I feel condemned." He that feels himself condemned may hope for pardon. If you are afraid of yourselves I am not afraid of you. If you tremble at God's Word, you have one of the surest marks of God's elect. Those who fear that they are mistaken are seldom mistaken. If you search yourselves and allow the Word of God to search you, it is well with you. The bankrupt trader fears to have his books examined. The sound man even pays an accountant to overhaul his affairs. Use discrimination and neither acquit nor condemn yourself without reason.

If the Spirit of God leads you to weep in secret for sin and to pray in secret for Divine Grace. If He leads you to seek after holiness. If He leads you to trust alone in Jesus, then you know the power of godliness and you have never denied it. You who cry, "Oh, that I felt more of the power of the Holy Spirit, for I know that He could comfort and sanctify me and make me live the life of Heaven on earth!" You are not aimed at either by the text or the sermon. For you have not denied the power. No, no, this text does not belong to you but to quite another class of people.

Let me give you a word of admonition. Learn from the text that there is something in godliness worth having. The "form" of godliness is not all—there is a blessed "power." The Holy Spirit is that power and He can work in you to will and to do of God's good pleasure. Come to Jesus Christ, dear Souls. Do not come to the minister, nor to the Church, in the first place. But come to Jesus. Come and lay yourselves at His feet and say, "Lord, I will not be comforted unless You comfort me." Come and take everything at first hand from your crucified Lord. Then shall you know the power of godliness.

Beware of second-hand religion, it is never worth the carrying home. Get your godliness direct from Heaven by the personal dealing of your own soul with your Savior. Profess only what you possess and rest only in that which has been given you from above. Your heavenly life, as yet, may be very feeble but the grain of mustard seed will grow. You may be the least in Israel but that is better than being the greatest in Babylon.

The Lord bless these words and apply them to each one in his own way by His Holy Spirit. You can make either a blister of them or a plaster of them, as conscience shall direct. God guide you, for Jesus Christ's sake. Amen.

18

The Sunday School and the Scriptures

(Sermon No. 1866)

"And that from childhood you have known the Holy Scriptures, which are able to make you wise unto salvation through faith which is in Christ Jesus" (2 Timothy 3:15).

HOW VERY REMARKABLY the times repeat themselves! As I said just now, in the reading of the chapter, the warning which Paul gave concerning his own times is quite as necessary for this present age. Again darkness thickens and the mists hang heavily around our footsteps. Evil men and seducers wax worse and worse and very many have turned away their ears from the Truth of God to listen to fables. Nor do we wonder that it is so. History must repeat itself so long as we have the same human nature to deal with, the same sins to ensnare mankind, the same Truth to be trifled with and the same devil to stir men up to the same mischief.

But, Brothers and Sisters, when the same evils come, we must apply to them the same remedies. When a disease appears which has done deadly mischief in past times, physicians inquire for medicines which, on a former occasion, curbed the enemy. We are bound to do the same in spiritual matters. We must see what Paul did in his day when the malaria of false doctrine was in the air. It is remarkable how very simple, as a rule, everything is that is really effective. If a discovery is made in science or machinery, it is complicated, at first, and that for the very reason that it is imperfect. But all improvements are in the direction of simplicity. It is just the same with spiritual teachings. When we get at reality, we cut off superfluity. Let us not talk of inventing wise measures for the present distress in the spiritual world, but let us use the great remedy which was so effectual in Paul's day! Paul, himself, taught young Timothy the Gospel—he made him not only hear his doctrine, but see his practice. We cannot force the Truth of God upon men, but we can make our own teaching clear and decided—and make our lives consistent therewith. Truth and holiness are the surest antidotes to error and unrighteousness. The Apostle said to Timothy, "Continue in the things which you have learned and have been assured of, knowing from whom you have learned them."

He then dwelt upon another potent remedy which had been of great service to the young preacher, namely, the knowing of the Holy Scriptures from his earliest childhood. This was, to young Timothy, one of his best safeguards. His early training held him like an anchor and saved him from the dreadful drift of the age. Happy young man, of whom the Apostle could say, "From childhood you have known the Holy Scriptures, which are able to make you wise unto salvation through faith which is in Christ Jesus!"

Brothers and Sisters, to be prepared for the coming conflict, we have only to preach the Gospel and to live the Gospel—and also to take care that we teach the children the Word of the Lord! This last is especially to be attended to, for it is by the mouth of babes and sucklings that God will still the enemy. It is idle to dream that human learning must be met by human learning, or that Satan must cast out Satan. No! Lift up the bronze serpent wherever the fiery serpents are biting the people and men shall look to it and live. Bring the children out and hold them up—and turn their little eyes towards the divinely ordained remedy, for still there is life in a look—life as against the varied venoms of the serpent which are now poisoning the blood of men! There is no cure, after all, for midnight but the rising sun. No hope remains for a dark world but in that Light of God which lightens every man. Shine forth, O Sun of Righteousness, and mist, cloud and darkness must disappear. Brothers, keep to the Apostolic plans and rest assured of Apostolic success! Preach Christ! Preach the Word in season and out of season—and teach the children. One of God's chief methods for preserving His fields from tares is to sow them early with wheat. Upon that I am going to speak, this morning, as the Holy Spirit shall help me.

In tracing the gracious work of God upon the heart of Timothy and upon others who are favored as he was, I shall notice that this work commenced with early instruction—"From childhood you have known the Holy Scriptures." And secondly, it was quickened and made effectual by saving faith—"The Holy Scriptures which are able to make you wise unto salvation through faith which is in Christ Jesus." Then we shall notice that the effect of this early teaching upon Timothy was that it created a solid character and, furthermore, that it produced great usefulness.

I. The work of God's Grace in Timothy COMMENCED WITH EARLY INSTRUCTION—"From childhood you have known the Holy Scriptures."

Note the time for instruction. The expression, "from childhood," might be better understood if we read it, "from a very child" or, as the Revised Version has it, "from a babe." It does not mean a well-grown child, or youth, but a child just rising out of infancy. From a very child Timothy had known the sacred writings. This expression is, no doubt, used to show that we cannot begin too early to imbue the minds of our children with Scriptural knowledge. Babes receive impressions long before we are aware of the fact. During the first months of a child's life, it learns more than we imagine. It soon learns the love of its mother and its own dependence—and if the mother is wise, it learns the meaning of obedience and the necessity of yielding its will to a higher will. This may be the keynote of its whole future life. If it learns obedience and submission early, it may save a thousand tears from the child's eyes and as many from the mother's heart. A special vantage ground is lost when even babyhood is left uncultured.

The Holy Scripture may be learned by children as soon as they are capable of understanding anything. It is a very remarkable fact which I have heard asserted by many teachers, that children will learn to read out of the Bible better than from any other book. I scarcely know why. It may, perhaps, be on account of the simplicity of the language—and I believe it is so. A Biblical fact will often be grasped when an incident of common history is forgotten. There is an adaptation in the Bible for human beings of all ages and, therefore, it has a fitness for children. We make a mistake when we think that we must begin with something else and lead up to the Scriptures. The Bible is the book for the peep of day. Parts of it are above a child's mind, for they are above the comprehension of the most advanced among us. There are depths in it where leviathan may swim—but there are also brooks in which a lamb may wade. Wise teachers know how to lead their little ones into the green pastures beside the still waters.

I was noticing, in the life of that man of God whose loss presses very heavily upon many of our hearts, namely, the Earl of Shaftesbury, that his first religious impressions were produced by a humble woman. The impressions which made him Shaftesbury, the man of God and the friend of man, were received in the nursery! Little Lord Ashley had a godly nurse who spoke to him of the things of God. He tells us that she died before he was seven years of age—clear proof that early in life his heart had been able to receive the seal of the Spirit of God—and to receive it by humble instrumentality. Blessed among women was she whose name we know not, but who worked incalculable service for God and man by her holy teaching of the chosen child! Young nurses, note this.

Give us the first seven years of a child, with God's Grace, and we may defy the world, the flesh and the devil to ruin that immortal soul! Those first years, while yet the clay is soft and plastic, go far to decide the form of the vessel. Do not say that your office, you who teach the young, is in the least degree inferior to ours, whose main business is with older folks. No, you have the first of them and your impressions, as they come first, will endure last—oh that they may be good and only good! Among the thoughts that come to an old man before he enters Heaven, the most plentiful are those that before visited him when he sat upon his mother's knee. That which made Dr. Guthrie ask for a "bairn's hymn" when he was dying is but an instinct of our nature which leads us to complete the circle by folding together the ends of life. Childlike things are dearest to old age! We shuffle off a portion of the coil that surrounds and hampers us and go back, again, to our more natural selves and, therefore, the old songs are on our lips and the old thoughts are in our minds! The teachings of our childhood leave clean cut and sharp impressions upon the mind which remain after 70 years have passed. Let us see that such impressions are made for the highest ends.

It is well to note the admirable selection of instructors. We are not at a loss to tell who instructed youthful Timothy. In the first chapter of this Epistle, Paul says, "When I call to remembrance the unfeigned faith that is in you, which dwelt first in your grandmother Lois, and your mother Eunice; and I am persuaded that in you, also." No doubt grandmother Lois and mother Eunice united in teaching the little one. Who should teach the children but the parents? Timothy's father was a Greek and probably a heathen, but his child was happy in having a venerable grandmother, so often the dearest of all relatives to a little child. He had also a gracious mother, once a devout Jewess and afterwards, also, a firmly believing Christian who made it her daily pleasure to teach her own dear child the Word of the Lord.

O dear mothers, you have a very sacred trust reposed in you by God! He has, in effect, said to you, "Take this child and nurse it for Me and I will give you your wages." You are called to equip the future man of God, that he may be thoroughly furnished unto every good work. If God spares you, you may live to hear that pretty boy speak to thousands and you will have the sweet reflection in your heart that the quiet teachings of the nursery led the man to love his God and serve Him! Those who think that a woman detained at home by her little family is doing nothing, think the reverse of what is true! Scarcely can the godly mother quit her home for a place of worship, but dream not that she is lost to the work of the Church—far from it—she is doing the best possible service for her Lord! Mothers, the godly training of your offspring is your first and most pressing duty! Christian women, by teaching children the Holy Scriptures, are as much fulfilling their part for the Lord as Moses in judging Israel, or Solomon in building the Temple!

Nowadays, since the world has in it, alas, so few of Christian mothers and grandmothers, the Church has thought it wise to supplement the instruction of home by teaching held under her fostering wing. Those children who have no such parents, the Church takes under her maternal care. I regard this as a very blessed institution. I am thankful for the many of our Brothers and Sisters who give their Sabbaths—and many of them a considerable part of their week evenings, also—to the teaching of other people's children who somehow grow to be very much their own. They endeavor to perform the duties of fathers and mothers, for God's sake, to those children who are neglected by their own parents—and therein they do well. Let no Christian parents fall into the delusion that the Sunday school is intended to ease them of their personal duties. The first and most natural condition of things is for Christian parents to train up their own children in the nurture and admonition of the Lord.

Let holy grandmother's and gracious mothers, with their husbands, see to it that their own boys and girls are well taught in the Book of the Lord. Where there are no such Christian parents, it is well and wisely done for godly people to intervene. It is a Christly work when others undertake the duty which the natural doers of it have left undone. The Lord Jesus looks with pleasure upon those who feed His lambs and nurse His babes, for it is not His will that any of these little ones should perish. Timothy had the great privilege of being taught by those whose natural duty it is, but where that great privilege cannot be enjoyed, let us all, as God shall help us, try to make up to the children the terrible loss which they endure. Come forward, earnest men and women, and sanctify yourselves for this joyful service!

Note the subject of the instruction. "From childhood you have known the Holy Scriptures"—he was led to treat the Book of God with great reverence. I lay stress upon those two words, "Holy Scriptures." One of the first objects of the Sunday school should be to teach the children great reverence for these holy writings, these Inspired Scriptures. The Jews esteemed the Old Testament beyond all price and though, unfortunately, many of them fell into a superstitious reverence for the letter and lost the spirit of it, yet were they much to be commended for their profound regard to the Holy Oracles. Especially is this feeling of reverence needed nowadays. I meet with men who hold strange views, but I do not care one-half so much about their views, nor about the strangeness of them, as I do about a certain something which I spy out at the back of this novel thinking. When I find that, if I prove their views to be unscriptural, I have, nevertheless, proved nothing to them, for they do not care about Scripture—then I have found out a principle far more dangerous than mere doctrinal blundering!

This indifference to Scripture is the great curse of the Church at this hour! We can be tolerant of divergent opinions, so long as we perceive an honest intent to follow the Statute Book. But if it comes to this, that the Bible, itself, is of small authority to you, then we have no need of further parley—we are in different camps and the sooner we recognize this, the better for all parties concerned. If we are to have a Church of God at all in the land, Scripture must be regarded as holy and to be had in reverence. This Scripture was given by Holy Inspiration and is not the result of dim myths and dubious traditions! Neither has it drifted down to us by the survival of the fittest as one of the best of human books. It must be given to my children and accepted by ourselves as the Infallible Revelation of the Most Holy God! Lay much stress upon this—tell your children that the Word of the Lord is a pure Word, as silver tried in a furnace of earth, purified seven times. Let their esteem for the Book of God be carried to the highest point!

Observe that Timothy was taught not only to reverence holy things in general, but especially to know the Scriptures. The teaching of his mother and his grandmother was the teaching of Holy Scripture. Suppose we get the children together on the Sabbath and then amuse them and make the hours to pass away pleasantly? Or instruct them, as we do in the weekdays, in the elements of a moral education—what have we done? We have done nothing worthy of the day, or of the Church of God! Suppose that we are particularly careful to teach the children the rules and regulations of our own Church and do not take them to the Scriptures? Suppose that we bring before them a book which is set up as the standard of our Church but do not dwell upon the Bible—what have we done? The aforesaid standard may or may not be correct and we may, therefore, have taught our children the Truth of God or have taught them error! But if we keep to Holy Scripture, we cannot go aside. With such a Standard we know that we are right. This Book is the Word of God and if we teach it, we teach that which the Lord will accept and bless.

O dear teachers—and I speak here to myself, also—let our teaching be more and more Scriptural! Fret not if our classes forget what we say, but pray them to remember what the Lord says. May Divine Truths about sin, righteousness and judgement to come be written on their hearts! May revealed Truths of God concerning the love of God, the Grace of our Lord Jesus Christ and the work of the Holy Spirit never be forgotten by them! May they know the virtue and necessity of the atoning blood of our Lord, the power of His Resurrection and the Glory of His Second Coming! May the Doctrines of Grace be engraved as with a pen of iron upon their minds and written as with the point of a diamond upon their hearts—never to be erased! Brothers and Sisters, if we can secure this, we have not lived in vain. The generation now ruling seems bent on departing from the eternal Truths of God, but we shall not despair if the Gospel is impressed upon the memory of the rising race.

Once more upon this point—it appears that young Timothy was so taught as a child that the teaching was effectual. "You have known the Holy Scriptures," says Paul. It is a good deal to say of a child that he has "known the Holy Scriptures." You may say, "I have taught the children the Scriptures," but that they have known them is quite another thing. Do all of you who are grown up, know the Scriptures? I fear that although knowledge in general increases, knowledge of the Scriptures is far too rare! If we were now to hold an examination, I am afraid that some of you would hardly shine in the lists at the end. But here was a little child who knew the Holy Scriptures! That is to say, he had a remarkable acquaintance with them. Children can get that—it is by no means an impossible attainment. God blessing your efforts, dear Friends, your children may know all of Scripture that is necessary to their salvation. They may have as true an idea of sin as their mother has. They may have as clear a view of the Atonement as their grandmother can have. They may have as distinct a faith in Jesus as any of us can have!

The things that make for our peace require no length of experience to prepare us for receiving them—they are among the simplicities of thought. He may run that reads them—and a child may read them as soon as he can run! The opinion that children cannot receive the whole Truth of the Gospel is a great mistake, for their child-condition is a help rather than a hindrance! Older folk must become as little children before they can enter the Kingdom of Heaven. Do lay a good groundwork with the children. Let not Sunday school work be slurred, nor done in a slovenly manner. Let the children know the Holy Scripture! Let the Scriptures be consulted rather than any human book.

II. Our second need was to be that this work was QUICKENED BY SAVING FAITH. The Scriptures do not save, but they are able to make a man wise unto salvation. Children may know the Scriptures and yet not be children of God. Faith in Jesus Christ is that Grace which brings immediate salvation. Many dear children are called of God so early that they cannot precisely tell when they were converted—but they were converted—they must, at some time or other, have passed from death to life. You could not have told this morning, by observation, the moment when the sun rose, but it did rise—and there was a time when it was below the horizon and another time when it had risen above it. The moment, whether we see it or not, in which a child is really saved, is when he or she believes in the Lord Jesus Christ. Perhaps for years Lois and Eunice had been teaching the Old Testament to Timothy while they, themselves, did not know the Lord Jesus. And, if so, they were teaching him the type without the antitype—the riddles without the answers—but it was good teaching, for all that, since it was all the Truth of God which they then knew.

How much happier, however, is our task, since we are able to teach concerning the Lord Jesus so plainly, having the New Testament to explain the Old! May we not hope that even earlier in life than Timothy, our dear children may catch the thought that Christ Jesus is the Sum and Substance of Holy Scripture and, so, by faith in Him may receive power to become the sons of God? I mention this, simple as it is, because I want all teachers to feel that if their children do not as yet know all the doctrines of the Bible and if there are certain higher or deeper Truths of God which their minds have not yet grasped, still, children are saved as soon as they are wise unto salvation through faith which is in Christ Jesus! Faith in the Lord Jesus, as He is set forth in Scripture, will surely save. "If you believe with all your heart, you may," said Philip to the eunuch—and we say the same to every child—you may confess your faith if you have any true faith in Jesus to confess. If you believe that Jesus is the Christ and so put your trust in Him, you are as truly saved as though gray hairs adorned your brow.

Notice that by this faith in Christ Jesus, we continue and advance in salvation. The moment we believe in Christ we are saved, but we are not at once as wise as we may be and hope to be. We may be, as it were, saved unintelligently. I mean, of course, comparatively so, but it is desirable that we should be able to give a reason for the hope that is in us and so be wise unto salvation. By faith, children become little disciples and, by faith, they go on to become more proficient. How are we to go on to wisdom? Not by quitting the way of faith, but by keeping to that same faith in Christ Jesus by which we began to learn. In the school of Grace, faith is the great faculty by which we make advances in wisdom. If by faith you have been able to say A, B and C, it must be by faith that you shall go on to say D, E and F, until you shall come to the end of the alphabet and be an expert in the Book of Wisdom. If by faith you can read in the spelling book of simple faith, by the same faith in Christ Jesus you must go on to read in the classics of full assurance and become a scribe well instructed in the things of the Kingdom of God. Keep, therefore, close to the practice of faith from which so many are turning aside.

In these times men look to make progress by what they call thought, by which they mean vain imagination and speculation. We cannot advance a step by doubt—our only progress is by faith. There are no such things as "steppingstones of our dead selves." Unless, indeed, they are steppingstones down to death and destruction! The only steppingstones to life and Heaven are to be found in the Truths of God revealed to our faith. Believe God and you have made progress! So let us pray for our children, that they may constantly know and believe more and more, for the Scripture is able to make them wise unto salvation, but only through faith which is in Christ Jesus. Faith is the result to aim at. Faith in the appointed, anointed and exalted Savior. This is the anchor to which we would bring these little ships, for here they will abide in perfect safety!

Observe that the text gives us a plain intimation that by faith, knowledge is turned into wisdom. Exceedingly practical is the difference between knowledge and wisdom. See it in the text, "From a child you have known." But it is faith, faith alone, that turns that knowledge into wisdom—and thus the Holy Scriptures are "able to make wise unto salvation." "Knowledge is power," but wisdom is the application of that power to practical ends! Knowledge may be bullion, but wisdom is the minted gold, fit for circulation among men! You can give your children knowledge without their having faith, but they must have faith given them of the Holy Spirit before that knowledge can become wisdom! Scriptural knowledge is wisdom when it influences the heart, when it rules the mind, when it affects the daily life, when it sanctifies the spirit, when it renews the will. O Teachers, pray for your dear children that God would give them faith in Christ Jesus so that the knowledge which you have given them may turn to wisdom! Go as far as you can go with the teaching, but always cry mightily unto the Lord that His Holy Spirit may work regeneration, create faith, impart wisdom and give salvation.

Learn yet, again, that faith finds her wisdom in the use of knowledge conferred by the Scriptures. "From childhood you have known the Holy Scriptures, which are able to make you wise unto salvation through faith." Faith never finds her wisdom in the thoughts of men, nor in pretended revelations. She resorts to the Inspired Writings for her guidance. This is the well from which she drinks, the manna on which she feeds. Faith takes the Lord Jesus to be her wisdom. The knowledge of Christ is, to her, the most excellent of the sciences. She asks only—What is written? And when that question is answered, her difficulties are ended! I know it is not so with this unbelieving age and this it is which causes me to go mourning and lamenting. Alas for a Church which rejects the testimony of the Lord! As for us, we abide by the Word of the Lord and from it we will not stir an inch!

See then, my Hearers, what is needed for all of you who are unconverted. The Holy Scriptures must be made the means of your salvation through faith. Know the Bible, read the Bible, search the Bible—and yet the Bible, alone, will not save you! What did our Lord, Himself, say? "You search the Scriptures, for in them you think you have eternal life; and they are they which testify of Me; and you will not come unto Me that you might have life." If you come not to Jesus, you will miss eternal life! Searching the Scriptures is able to make you wise unto salvation "through faith which is in Christ Jesus"—but not without that faith! Pray, you Sunday school teachers, that you may see this faith worked in the children whom you teach! What a blessed groundwork for faith, your teaching of the Holy Scriptures will be! But never mistake it for the building, itself, which is of faith alone!

III. Time fails me. I cannot dwell as I would upon other points, but I beg you to notice, in the third place, that sound instruction in Holy Scripture, when quickened by a living faith, CREATES A SOUND CHARACTER. The man who, from childhood has known the Holy Scriptures, when he obtains faith in Christ, will be grounded and settled upon the abiding principles of the unchanging Word of God. I wish it were so with the bulk of those who profess and call themselves, "Christians." In these days we are surrounded by unsettled minds, "ever learning, but never coming to a knowledge of the Truth of God." These are carried about by every wind of doctrine. What numbers of professors I have known who go into one place of worship and hear one form of doctrine and apparently approve it because the preacher is "a clever man!" They hear an opposite teaching and they are equally at home, because, again, it is "a clever man!" They join with a Church and you ask them, "Do you agree with the views of that community?" They neither know nor care what those views may be—one doctrine is as good as another to them. Their spiritual appetite can enjoy soap as well as butter! They can digest bricks as well as bread!

These religious ostriches have a marvelous power of swallowing everything—but they have no spiritual discernment, no appreciation of the Truth of God. They follow any "clever" person and, in this, prove that they are not the sheep of our Lord's pasture, of whom it is written, "A stranger will they not follow, for they know not the voice of strangers." We desire to build up a Church with those who know what they know and can give a reason for what they believe. The true Believer's great reason for his faith is, "It is written." Christ our Master met the tempter in the wilderness with, "It is written." Though He was, Himself, Inspired, yet His teaching was full of the Old Testament—He was always quoting the Words of the Inspired Book and, therein, setting us an example.

If you and I would contend with Satan and with an evil world, so as to overcome in the conflict, we must take care to take our stand squarely and firmly upon the Scriptures! Let us treat our opponents to volleys of Scripture! Let us fire point-blank with sacred texts! These are arguments which wound and kill! Our own reasonings are mere paper pellets, but Scriptural proofs are bullets of steel! Our opponents will find it useless to try to lead us away from the old faith when they perceive that we will not budge an inch from Holy Scripture. We are bomb-proof when we shelter beneath the Word of the Lord. The cunning craftiness of deceivers is foiled by the clear simplicity of, "Thus says the Lord."

Those who know the Scriptures and so believe in Jesus, are pillared upon a personal acquaintance with the foundations of their faith. "From childhood you have known the Holy Scriptures"—they were not treated with an ignorant reverence, but with an intelligent homage. How much I desire that each one of you may be a personal student of the Holy Scriptures! We need to know them for ourselves! Personally grasping them as a Revelation of God to himself, the godly man loves them, studies them, feels them, lives upon them and so knows them! By this means he becomes as independent of other men. Paul is to die. Poor Timothy! Yes, it will be, "poor Timothy!" if he carries his faith in Paul's bosom and has none in his own heart! But Timothy's Bible is not going to die! Timothy's knowledge of Scripture is not going to be taken from him, nor is the Holy Spirit about to depart from him!

Look at some of our Churches—while a well-instructed Gospel minister leads the way, the Brethren abide in their steadfastness. The good man dies and where is the Church? No doubt, those who are instructed in the Scriptures remain in their places, but the more ignorant are scattered like chaff! There are numbers, now, in this part of London, wandering about, who were once zealous for the faith, but are now almost indifferent to it. I will not mention names, but I could do so readily enough—I mean the names of esteemed Brethren who gathered an earnest following about them, but they are gone—and with their going, numbers of their followers have gone, too! I fear there could not have been a sound knowledge of the Word of God, or these people would have survived the great loss of their teacher. Oh, to have a good personal building up upon the solid Word of God! Then you will know what you know and you will hold fast to it—and there will be no driving you away from the standards of the faith. I labor for this among you and I pray that I may not labor in vain.

The man that has been taught the Scripture from his youth is anchored by the Divine influences of that Scripture. It has so operated upon him that he knows for himself its Divine power. He knows the difference between the Truth of God and error by the effect produced on his heart and life. Without any boasting, he is able to discern between things that differ because about Scriptural Truth there is a strange, mysterious unction which does not attend the teachings of the most learned of men. I cannot explain to you what this unction is, but every child of God knows it. When I read a text of Scripture, even if I do not now it to be a text of Scripture by memory, I perceive its Divine origin at once by a mystic influence which it exerts over my heart. The most striking passages of any sermon are well-placed texts. A sentence from the mouth of God will have more permanent power over a Christian man than the best composed of human statements! God's Word is living, powerful and has a power to enter the heart beyond that of any other word! The Words of the Bible strike and stick—they enter and abide.

He that has been taught in Scripture, steeped in Scripture, saturated with Scripture—is conscious of its permeating influence and it gives him permanence of conviction. Like the crimson dye in cloth, the tint of Scripture is not to be gotten out of the soul when once fixed there! It is dyed ingrain—it enters into the very nature of the man! Bible Truths influence his thoughts, words and deeds—it is all-pervading—he begins to eat, drink and sleep Holy Scripture. The man's heart is fixed on God, fixed in the Truths of God and fixed in holy living. He will stand fast, however evil the days. Though all the rest should apostatize, this man cannot, for the Divine Word, through faith, has bound him to the Altar of the Lord and, in the Truth of God he must and will both live and die, come what may.

Besides, a man that has once been taught in the Scripture and to whose soul the Spirit has blessed that teaching, has come to yield himself to the supremacy of Scripture and this must operate to the shaping of his character. I confess that sometimes I come across a text which does not, at first blush, agree with other teachings of Scripture which I have already received—and this startles me for the moment. But one thing is settled in my heart, namely, that I will follow the Scripture wherever it leads me and that I will renounce the most cherished opinion rather than shape a text or alter a syllable of the Inspired Book. It is not mine to make God's Word consistent, but to believe that it is so! When a text stands in the middle of the road, I drive no further. The Romans had a god they called, "Terminus," who was the god of landmarks. Holy Scripture is my sacred landmark and I hear a voice which threatens me with a curse if I remove it! Sometimes I say to myself, "I did not think to find this Truth to be just so, but as it is so, I must bow. It is rather awkward for my theory, but I must alter my system, for the Scripture cannot be broken." "Let God be true, but every man a liar."

We want our children to have this deep reverence for Scripture, even as we have it ourselves. There it stands! The eternal pen has written it and we accept it! If God has said it, we have no desire to question it, lest the Scripture should say to us, "No but, O man, who are you that replies against God?" We must bow before the Infallibility of the Holy Spirit and say, "Lord, teach me what this means. What I know not, teach me." He who goes through the world with an intense reverence for Scripture will be a man, indeed. The Lord will make good in him that Word—"Them that honor Me I will honor." Angels and men, before long, reverence the man who reverences the Word of God. Feed your mind on the pulse of Scripture and, like Daniel and his comrades, your countenance shall appear fairer and fatter in flesh than all the children who eat the portion of the king's meat from the philosophic tables of the world.

While on this point, I would also say that this kind of instruction will hold a man fast against the differing seductions of the age. Here I go into one place of worship and I see a pretty little dolls' house at the far end and people are bowing down before some paper flowers and candlesticks! Around the building I see pictures of virgins and saints, but he who has read his Bible enters not into this modern idolatry! A priest once said to a poor Irishman, "There will be no good come of your reading the Bible." "Why," replied the man, "it is written, 'Search the Scriptures.' Please, your Reverence, I was just reading, 'you shall read it to your children' and the priests have no children—how can you account for that?" "Ah!" replied the priest, "the likes of you cannot understand the book." "Well," said the man, "if I cannot understand it, it will do me no harm, but if I can understand it, it will do me great good."

Just so! The Bible is a very dangerous book to superstition, but to nothing else! Spread it, then, to the winds of Heaven and read it, every one of you! To the Law and to the Testimony! If we speak not according to this Word, it is because there is no Light of God in us! He that holds to the Bible will be equally free from the dangers of rationalism which are now so abundant and he will keep himself clean from the ravings of anarchy which now sound like the cries of dragons from the dark places of the earth! People are beginning to forget the Commandment, "you shall not steal," and they are planning various methods of political thievery by which the foundations of society will be shaken. Love of Holy Scripture will be the sheet anchor of the State as well as of the Church! If men are thoroughly grounded in Holy Scripture, we shall undergo political changes with great advantage—but if not, there is mischief brewing. The Bible is the cornerstone of our future hope.

IV. Now, lastly. As this early teaching creates a fine solid character, so will it PRODUCE GREAT USEFULNESS. I will say nothing more than just this. Thus Timothy became above all others a choice companion for Paul, one upon whom Paul looked with love and remembered with joy. Companions for Apostles are only to be produced in the school of Holy Scripture. Those who have communed with Moses, David and the Prophets, are fit to associate with an Apostle. It is something to produce out of a child a comrade for a veteran servant of the living God! Let a man of God get side by side with a youth who knows the Scriptures and he feels, "This is fit company for me." Paul, worn with years of persecution, strokes his gray beard and his eyes light up with joy as he looks on that young Timothy! What is there about him more than about any other? Why, only that he knows the Scriptures and they have made him wise unto salvation!

There were, no doubt, fine young fellows to be found who gloried in preferring the advanced thought of philosophers to the stereotyped teachings of Holy Scripture. But had they begun to talk to the Apostle upon their new theories, Paul would have dismissed them with words of warning. He knew nothing of them or of their "other Gospel," except that they troubled him and the Churches. Without Scriptural training, a convert has no grit, no backbone and no soul in him. But when Paul looked on a gracious youth who knew the Scriptures and held fast to them, he thanked God and took courage.

This young man became a minister and an Evangelist. He was a preacher of such a sort that we should have been glad to have heard him. God send us many such! Perhaps we might have said,

> "The young man's opinions were rather crude and his expressions were somewhat rough, but we can put up with that from so young a man. On the other hand, what a richness of Scripture there was in him! What depth of thought! Did you not notice he had not got through a dozen sentences before he had quoted Scripture? And when he came to prove his point, he did not give half-a-dozen rationalistic arguments, but he brought out a single Word from the Lord and the point was settled."

You must agree with a man who is at home with his Bible. This is the kind of preacher that we need more of! Instruct your children well, beloved Teachers, that they, also, may become Scriptural teachers in due time.

Timothy became, also, a great champion for the faith. He came forward and in the midst of all those who were preaching false doctrine, he stood firm to the end—he was steadfast, unmovable, courageous— because as a child he had known the Scriptures! O Teachers, see what you may do! In your schools sit our future Evangelists. In that infant class sits an Apostle to some distant land! There may come under your training hand, my Sister, a future father in Israel! There shall come under your teaching, my Brother, those that are to bear the banners of the Lord in the thick of the fray! The ages look to you each time your class assembles!

Oh, that God may help you to do your part well! We pray with one heart and one soul that the Lord Jesus Christ may be with our Sunday schools from this day and till He comes. Amen and Amen!

19

A Last Look-Out

(Sermon No. 989)

"The time of my departure is at hand" (2 Timothy 4:6).

S O NEAR, SO VERY NEAR the change—his removal from this to another world; and so very conscious of it; yet Paul looked back with calm satisfaction; he looked forward with sweet assurance; and he looked round with deepest interest on the mission that had engaged his life. As you must have noticed while we were reading the chapter, in his case "the ruling passion was strong in death." Writing what he well knows is the last letter he shall ever write, its main topic is care for the church of God—anxiety for the promotion of the truth—zeal for the furtherance of the gospel. When he is dead, and gone from the post of service, the scene of suffering, the field of enterprise, on whom shall his mantle fall? He desires that in Timothy he may find a worthy successor, strong in the faith, sincere of heart, and having dauntless courage withal, one who will wield the sword and hold the banner when his hand is palsied in death. Men have usually shown us what lies at the bottom of their heart when they have come to die. Often their last expiring expressions have been indicative of their entire character. Certainly you have before you in the last sentences of Paul's pen a fair epitome of his entire life. He is trusting in the Savior; he is anxious to show his love for that Savior. The welfare of the Christian church and the advancement of the holy cause of the gospel are uppermost in his mind. May it be yours and mine to live wholly for Christ, and to die also for him. May this ever be foremost in our thoughts, "How can I advance the kingdom of our Lord and Savior? By what means can I bless his church and people?" It is very beautiful to observe the way in which Paul describes his death in this verse. According to our translation he speaks of it as an offering. "I am now ready," saith he, "to be offered." If we accept this version he may be

315

supposed to mean that he felt as one standing like a bullock or a lamb, ready to be laid on an altar. He foresaw he would die a martyr's death. He knew he could not be crucified as his brother Peter had been, for a Roman citizen was, as a rule, exempt from that ignominious death. He expected to die in some other manner. Probably he guessed it would be by the sword, and so he describes himself as waiting for the sacrificial knife to be used, that he might be presented as a sacrifice. So I say the words of our translation would lead us to think. But the original is far more instructive. He here likens himself, in the Greek, not to an offering, but to the drink-offering. Every Jew would know what that meant. When there was a burnt-sacrifice offered, the bullock or the victim then slain was the main part of the sacrifice. But sometimes there was a little, what if I say an unimportant, supplement added to that sacrifice—a little oil and a little wine were poured on to the altar or the bullock, and thus a drink-offering was said to be added to the burnt-offering. Now, Paul does not venture to call himself an offering,—Christ is his offering. Christ is, so to speak, the sacrifice on the altar. He likens himself only to that little wine and oil poured out as a supplement thereto, not necessary to its perfection, but tolerated in performing a vow, or allowed in connection with a free will offering, as you will find if you refer at leisure to the fifteenth chapter of Numbers, from the fourth to the eighth verses. The drink-offering was thus a kind of addendum, by which the person who gave it showed his thankfulness. So Paul is resolved to show his thankfulness to Christ, the great sacrifice, and he is willing that his blood should be poured as a drink-offering on the altar where his Lord and Master was the great burnt-offering. He rejoices when he can say, "I am ready to be presented as a drink-offering unto God."

We have mainly to do with the second description which he gives of his death. What does he say when the hour that this grim monster must be grappled with is at hand? I do not find him sad. Those who delight in gloomy poetry have often represented death in terrible language. "It is hard," says one—

"To feel the hand of death arrest one's steps,

Throw a chill blight on all one's budding hopes,
And hurl one's soul untimely to the shades."

And another exclaims—

"O God, it is a fearful thing,
To see the human soul take wing,
In any shape, in any mood!
I've seen it rushing forth in blood,
I've seen it on the breaking ocean,
Strive with a swollen convulsive motion."

Not so the apostle Paul. I do not even hear him speak of flying through the gate as our grand old poet has described death. He does not say, "The hour of my dissolution is at hand"—a very proper word if he had used it; but he is not looking so much at the process as at the result of his dying. He does not even say, "The hour of my death is at hand," but he adopts a beautiful expression, "The time of my departure"—words which are used sometimes to signify the departure of a vessel from the port; the pulling up of the anchor so that it looses its moorings, when about to put out to sea—so he feels himself like a ship lying at the harbor for awhile—but he says, "The time for pulling up the anchor, the time for letting loose the cable, and cutting from the mooring is at hand; I shall soon be launched upon my voyage." And he knew right well where that voyage would end, in the fair havens of the port of Peace in the better country, whither his Lord had gone before him.

Now we will proceed very briefly to say a word about *departure;* and then a shorter word still about the time of our departure; and then a little more about *the time* of our departure *being at hand*—trying here, especially, to bring forward some lessons which may be of practical usefulness to each one of us.

I. First, then, dear brethren, let us think a little about OUR DEPARTURE.

It is quite certain we shall not dwell here for ever: we shall not live here below as long as the first man did, or as those antediluvian fathers, who tarried some eight or nine hundred years. The length of human life then led to greatness of sin. Monstrosities of evil were ripened through the long continuance of physical strength, and the accumulating force of eager passions. All things considered, it is a mercy that life is abridged and not prolonged to a thousand years. Amidst the sharp competition of man with man, and class with class, there is a bound to every scheme of personal aggrandisement, a limit to all the spoils of individual despotism, a restraint upon the hoardings of any one's avarice. It is well, I say, that it should be so. The narrow span of life clips the wings of ambition, and baulks it of its prey. Death comes in to deprive the mighty of his power, to stay the rapacity of the invader, to scatter abroad the possessions of the rich. The most reprobate men must end their career after they have had their three score years and ten, or their four score years of wickedness. And as for the good and godly, though we mourn their exit, especially when we think that they have been prematurely taken from us, we remember how the triumphs of genius have been for the most part achieved in youth, and how much the world has been enriched by the heads and hearts of those who have but sown the seeds of faith and left others to reap the fruits. If into less than the allotted term they have crowded the service of their generation, we may save our tears, for our regrets are needless. The summons will reach each one of us ere long. We cannot stop here as long as the grey fathers of our race: we expect, and it is meet that we should prepare, to go. The world itself is to be consumed one day. "The elements shall melt with fervent heat." The land on which we stand we are wont to call *terra firma*, but beneath it is probably an ocean of fire, and it shall itself feel the force of the ocean. We must not marvel, the house being so frail, that the tenants are unsettled and migratory. Certainly, whether we doubt it or not, we shall have to go. There will be a departure for us. Beloved believer in Christ Jesus, to you the soft term, "Departure" is not more soft than the truth it represents. To die is to depart out of this world unto the Father. What say you about your departure? What say you of that from which you go, and what think you of that land to which you go? Well, of the land from which we go, my brethren, we might say many hard things if we would, but I think we had better not. We shall speak more correctly, if we say the hard things of ourselves. This land, my brethren, has been a land of mercy to us: there have been sorrows in it; but in bidding it farewell we will do it justice and speak the truth concerning it. Our sorrows have usually sprung up in our own bosoms, and those that have come from the soil itself would have been very light if it had not been for the plague of our hearts, which made us vex, and fret over them. Oh, the mercy you and I have enjoyed even in this life! It has been worth while to live for us who are believers. Even had we to die like a dog dieth, it has been worth while to live for the joy and blessedness which God has made to pass before us. I dare not call that an evil country in which I have met my Savior, and received the pardon of my sin. I dare not call that an ill life in which I have seen my Savior, though it be through a glass darkly. How shall I speak ill of that lamb where Zion is built, beautiful for situation, the joy of the whole earth, the place of our solemn assemblies, where we have worshipped God? No; cursed of old as the earth was to bring forth the thorn and the thistle, the existence of the church of God in that land seems to a great degree to have made reparation for the blight to such as know and love the Savior. Oh, have we not gone up to the house of God in company with songs of ecstatic joy, and have we not when we have gathered round the table of the Lord—though nothing was upon it but the type and emblem—have we not felt it a joyous thing to be found in the assembly of the saints, and in the courts of the Lord's house even here? When we loose our cable, and bid farewell to earth, it shall not be with bitterness in the retrospect. There is sin in it, and we are called to leave it; there has been trial in it, and we are called to be delivered from it; there has been sorrow in it, and we are glad that we shall go where we shall sorrow no more. There have been weakness, and pain, and suffering in it, and we are glad that we shall be raised in power; there has been death in it, and we are glad to bid farewell to shrouds and to knells; but for all that there has been such mercy in it, such loving-kindness of God in it, that the wilderness and the solitary place have been made glad, and the desert has rejoiced and blossomed as a rose. We will not bid farewell to the world, execrating it, or leaving behind us a cold shudder and a sad remembrance, but we will depart, bidding adieu to the scenes that remain, and to the people of God that tarry therein yet a little longer, blessing him whose goodness and mercy have followed us all the days of our life, and who is now bringing us to dwell in the house of the Lord for ever.

But, dear brethren, if I have had to speak in a somewhat apologetic manner of the land from which we depart, I shall need to use many apologies for my own poor talk about the land to which we are bound. Ah, whither goest thou, spirit loosened from thy clay—dost know? Whither goest thou? The answer must be, partly, that we know not. None of us have seen the streets of gold of which we sang just now; those harpings of the harpers, harping with their harps, have never fallen on these ears; eye hath not seen it, ear hath not heard it: it is all unrevealed to the senses; flesh and blood cannot inherit it, and, therefore, flesh and blood cannot imagine it. Yet it is not unknown, for God hath revealed it unto us by his Spirit. Spiritual men know what it is to feel the spirit, their own new-born spirit, living, glowing, burning, triumphing within them. They know, therefore, that if the body should drop off they would not die. They feel there is a life within them superior to blood and bone, and nerve and sinew. They feel the life of God within them, and none can gainsay it. Their own experience has proven to them that there is an inner life. Well, then, when that inner life is strong and vigorous, the spirit often reveals to it what the world of spirits will be. We know what holiness is, do we not, brethren? Are we not seeking it? That is heaven—perfect holiness is heaven. We know what peace means; Christ is our peace. Rest—he gives us rest: we find *that* when we take his yoke. Rest is heaven. And rest in Jesus tells us what heaven is. We know, even to-day, what communion with God is. If any one should say, "I do not know it," I should reply to him thus: Suppose I said to you, "You know not what it is to eat and drink:" the man would tell me that I belied him, for he knew, as he knew his own existence, what it was to eat and drink; and, as surely as I live, I have communion with God. I know it as certainly as you know that I have declared it to you. Well, friends, that is heaven. It has but to be developed from the germ to the produce, and there is heaven in its full development.

Communion with saints in like manner—know we not what that is? Have we not rejoiced in each other's joys, been made glad with the experience of our brethren? That, too, carried to perfection, will be heaven. Oh, to throw yourself into the bosom of the Savior and lie there taken up with his mind and his love, yielding all things to his supremacy, beholding your King in him! When you have been in that state you have had an antepast of heaven. Your view may have been but as one seeing a man's face in shadow yet you would know that man again even by the shadow; so know we what heaven is. We shall not be strangers in a strange land when we get there. Though, like the Queen of Sheba, we shall say, "The half has not been told me," yet we shall reflect on it thus:

"I did surmise there would be something of this sort. I did know from what I felt of its buddings in my soul below that the full-blown flower would be somewhat of this kind."

Whither away, then, spirit that art departing to soar through backs to thyself unknown? Thine answer is,

"I am away: away to the throne of him whose cross first gave me life, and light, and hope. I am away to the very bosom of my Savior, where I hope to rest and to have fellowship with the church of the firstborn, whose names are written in heaven."

This is your departure that you have in near prospect.

Suppose, dear friend, the thought of departing from this world to the glory-world should ever startle you, let me remind you that you are not the first that ever went that way. Your vessel is in the pool, as it were, or in the dock; she is going out on her voyage; oh, but you will not go alone, nor have to track your course through paths unnavigated or unknown before! When the Portuguese captain first went by the Cape of Storms it was a venturous voyage, and he called it the Cape of Good Hope when he had rounded it. When Columbus first went in search of the New World, his was a brave spirit that dared cross the unnavigated Atlantic.

But oh, there are tens of thousands that have gone whither you go. The Atlantic that severs us from Canaan is white with the sails of the vessels that are on voyage thither. Fear not, they have not been wrecked; we hear good news of their arrival there is good hope for you. There are no icebergs on the road, no mists, no counter currents, and no sunken vessels or quicksands; you have but to cut your moorings, and with Christ on board you shall be at your desired haven at once.

Remember, too, your Savior went that way. Have you to depart? So Christ departed too. Some of my brethren are always so pleased—pleased as some children are with a new toy—at the idea that they shall never die; that Christ will come, it may be before the time of their decease; for, "we shall not all sleep, but we shall all be changed." Well, let him come, ay, let him come; come quickly. But if I had my choice, were it permitted me to choose, I would prefer to pass through the portals of the grave. Those that are alive and remain unto the coming of the Lord will not prevent, go before, or steal a march on them which are asleep. But surely they will lack one point of conformity to their Lord, for he disdained not to sojourn awhile in the tomb, though it was impossible that he should be holden of death. Let the seal of death, then, be set upon this face of mine, that my fate in the matter may be like his. Enoch and Elias were exempt from this privilege—privilege, I call it—of conformity to his death. But it is safe to go by the beaten track, and desirable to travel by the ordinary route to the heavenly city. Jesus died. Through the valley of shadows, the vale of death-shades, there are the foot-prints of Immanuel all the way along: go down into it and fear not. Bethink you, too, dear brethren and sisters, that we may well look forward to our departure, and look forward to it comfortably too? Is it not expedient by reason of nature? Is it not desirable by reason of grace? Is it not necessary by reason of glory? I say, is not our departure needful by reason of nature? Men are not, when they come to hoary age, what they were in the prime of their days. The staff is needed for the foot, and the glass is wanted for the eye; and after a certain number of years, even those on whom Time hath gently laid his hand, find the taste is gone. They might proclaim, like old Barzillai, that they know not what they eat or drink. The hearing fails, the daughters of music are silent, the whole tenement gets very crazy. Oh, it were a melancholy thing if we had to continue to live! Perhaps there is no more hideous picture than that which the satirist drew of men who lived on to six or seven hundred years of age—that strange satirical man, Swift. Be thankful that we do not linger on in imbecility. Kind Nature says we may depart; she gives us notice, and makes it welcome by the decays that come upon us. Besides, grace desires it; for it were a poor experience of his kindness as our best and truest friend that did not make us long to see our Savior's face. It is no mere drivelling sentiment, I hope, when we join to sing—

"Father, I long, I faint to see,
The place of thine abode;
I'd leave thy earthly courts, and flee,
Up to thy seat, my God!"

I must confess there was one verse in the hymn we sung just now which I could not quite chime in with. I am not eagerly wishing to go to heaven this night. I have a great deal more to do here; therefore I do not want to take a hasty leave of all below. To full many of us, I suppose, there are times of quiet contemplation and times of rapt devotion, when our thoughts surmount these lower skies, and look within the veil and then, Oh, how we wish to be there! Yet there are other times; times of strenuous activity when we buckle on the armor and press to the front; and then we see such a battle to be waged, such a victory to be won, such a work to be wrought, that we say:

"Well to abide in the flesh, to continue with you all for the joy and furtherance of your faith, seems more loyal to Christ, more needful for you, and more in accord with our present feelings."

I think it is idle for us to be crying, to go home; it is too much like the lazy workman, that wants Saturday night to come when it is only Tuesday morning. Oh, no; if God spare us to do a long life's work, so much the better. At the same time, as a spark flies upward to the sun, the central source of flame, so does the newborn spirit aspire towards heaven, towards Jesus, by whom it was kindled. And, I add, that glory demands it, and makes our departure needful. Is not Christ in heaven praying that we may be with him where he is? Are there not the saints in heaven, of whom it is said, they without us cannot be perfect? The circle of the skies cannot be completed until all the redeemed be there. The grand orchestra of glory misses some notes as yet. What if the bass be full, there are wanting still some trebles and tenors! There are some sopranos that will be requisite to swell the enchanting melodies, and consummate the worship of the Eternal! What, therefore, nature prepares for, grace desires, and glory itself demands, we have no just cause to shudder at. Our departure need not make us afraid.

II. Having thus occupied so much time on this first point, I have little or no room to enlarge on the second.

THE TIME OF OUR DEPARTURE, though unknown to us, is fixed by God, unalterably fixed; so rightly, wisely, lovingly settled, and prepared for, that no chance or haphazard can break the spell of destiny. The wisdom of divine love shall be proven by the carefulness of its provision. Perhaps you will say: "It is not easy to discern this; the natural order of things is so often disturbed by casualties of one kind or another." Let me remind you, then, that it is through faith, only through faith, we can understand these things; for it is as true now of the providence of God as it was of old of the creation of God that *"things* which are seen were not made of things which do appear."* Because the *mode* of your departure is beyond your own ken, it does not follow that the *time* of your departure is not foreseen by God. "Ah! but," say you, "it seems so shocking for any one to die suddenly, unexpectedly, without warning, and so come to an untimely end!" I answer you thus. If you take counsel with death your flesh will find no comfort; but if you trust in God your faith will cease to parley with these feverish anxieties, and your spirit will enjoy a sweet calm. Dire calamities befell Job when he was bereaved of his children and his servants, his herds and his flocks. Yet he took little heed of the different ways in which his troubles were brought about; whether by an onslaught of the Sabeans or by a raid of the Chaldeans; whether the fire fell from heaven, or the wind came from the wilderness; it mattered little. Whatever strange facts broke on his ear, one thought penetrated his heart, and one expression broke from his lips. "The Lord gave, and the Lord hath taken away; blessed be the name of the Lord." So, too, beloved, when the time of your departure arrives—be it by disease or decay, be it by accident or assault, that your soul quits its present tenement—rest assured that "thy times are in his hand;" and know of a surety that "all his saints are in his hand" likewise. Besides this, dear friends, since the time of our departure must come, were the manner of it at our own disposal, I think we should most of us say, "What I shall choose, I wot not." Fevers and agues, the pangs and tortures of one malady and another, or the delirium incident to sickness, are not so much to be preferred to the shock of a disaster, or the terror of a wreck at sea, because one is the prolonging of pain, and the other the dispatch of fate, that we need to covet, and desire weeks or months spent in the vestibule of the grave. Rather should we say, Let the Lord do with me as seemeth him good. To live in constant communion with God is a sure relief from all these bitter frettings. Those who have walked with him have often been favored with such presentiments of their departure as no physician could give them. Survivors will tell you that though death seemed to come suddenly to the godly merchant, he had in the last acts of his life appeared to expect and prepare for it, and even to have taken an affecting farewell of his family while in the vigor of health, as though he were aware that he was setting out on his last journey, which a few hours afterwards it proved to be. So, too, the minister of Christ has sometimes fallen, expiring in his pulpit with a *nunc dimittis,* "Now lettest thou thy servant depart in peace" on his lips; secretly, but surely, made ready to depart and to be with his Lord. There is a time to depart; and God's time to call me is my time to go.

III. Now, to our third point—THE TIME AT HAND. "The time of my departure is at hand."

In a certain sense, every Christian here may say this; for whatever interval may interpose between us and death, how very short it is! Have you not all a sense that time flows faster than it did? In our childish days, we thought a year was quite a period of time, a very epoch in our career; now as for weeks—one can hardly reckon them! We seem to be travelling

325

by an express train, flying along at such a rate that we can hardly count the months. Why, the past year only seemed to come in at one door and go out at the other; it was over so soon. We shall soon be at the terminus of life, even if we live for several years; but in the case of some of us, God knows of whom, this year, perhaps this month, will be our last. I think to-morrow night we shall have to report at the church meeting the deaths of nine members of this church within the last eight or nine days. Since these have gone, some of us may expect to follow them. There are those who will evidently go; disease has set in upon them. Some of those disorders that in this land seem to be always fatal, tell these dear friends that the time of their departure is undoubtedly at hand. And then old age, which comes so gracefully and graciously to many of our matrons and our veterans, shows, past all dispute, "the time of your departure is at hand." The lease of your life is almost up. Not indeed that I would address myself to such special cases only. I speak to every brother and sister in Christ here. "The time of our departure is at hand." What then, dear friends?

Is not this a reason for surveying our condition again? If our vessel is just launching, let us see that she is seaworthy. It would be a sad thing for us to be near departing, and yet to be just as near discovering that we are lost. Remember, dear friends, it is possible for any one to maintain a decent Christ profession for fifty years, and be a hypocrite after all; possible to occupy an office in the church of God, and that of the very highest, and yet to be a Judas; and one may not only serve Christ, but suffer for him too, and yet, like Demas, may not persevere to the end; for all that looks like grace is not grace. Where true grace is, there it will always be; but where the semblance of it is, it will ofttimes suddenly disappear. Search thyself, good brother; set thine house in order, for thou must die and not live. Hast thou the faith of God's elect? Art thou built on Christ? Is thy heart renewed? Art thou verily an heir of heaven? I charge every man and woman within this place, since the time of his departure may be far nearer than he thinks, to take stock, and reckon up, and see whether he be Christ's or no.

But if the time of my departure be at hand, and I am satisfied that it is all right with me, is there not a call for me to do all I can for my household? Father, the time of your departure is at hand; is your wife unsaved? Will you pass another night without lovingly speaking to her of her soul? Are those dear boys unregenerate? Is that girl still thoughtless? The time of your departure is at hand. You can do little more for the lads and lasses; you can do little more for the wife and the brother. Oh! do what you can now. Sister, you are consumptive; you will soon be gone. You are the only Christ in the family. God sent you there to be a missionary. Do not have to say, when you are dying, "The last hope of my family is going out, for I have not cared for their souls." Masters, you that have servants about you, you must soon be taken away. Will you not do something for their souls? I know if there were a mother about to go to Australia, and she had to leave some of her children behind, she would fret if she thought, "I have not done all that needs to be done for those poor children. Who will care for them now their mother is gone?" Well, but to have neglected something necessary for their temporal comfort would be little in comparison with not having cared for their souls! Oh, let it not be so! Let it not be a thorn in your dying pillow that you did not fulfill the relations of life while you had the opportunity. "The time of my departure is at hand."

Then there is a third lesson. Let me try to finish all my work, not only as regards my duty to my family, but in respect to all the world so far as my influence or ability can reach. Rich men, be your own executors. Do what you can with your substance while it is your own. Men of talent, speak for Jesus before your tongue has ceased to articulate, and becomes a piece of clay. George Whitfield may supply us with a fine model of this uniform consistency. He was so orderly and precise in his habits, and so scrupulous and holy in his life, that he used to say he would not like to go to bed if there were a pair of gloves out of place in the house, much less were his will not made, or any part of his duty unfulfilled to the best of his knowledge. He wished to have all right, and to be fully prepared for whatever might happen, so that, if he never woke again from the slumbers of the night, nobody would have cause to reflect upon anything he had left undone, entailing needless trouble on his wife or his children. Such care bestowed on what some account to be trifles is a habit; worthy of our imitation. The main work of life may be sadly spoiled by negligence in little things. This is a striking test of character. "He that is faithful in that which is least is faithful also in much: and he that is unjust in the least is unjust also in much." Oh, then! time is fleeting, dispatch is urgent; gather up your thoughts, quicken your hands, speed your pace, for God commandeth thee to make haste. If you have ought to do, you must do it soon. The wheels of eternity are sounding behind you. Press on! If you are to run a race you must run it fast, for Death will soon overtake you. You may almost feel the hot breath of the white horse of Death upon your cheeks already. O God, help us to do something ere we go hence and be no more seen. It was grand of the apostle that in the same breath, when he said, "The time of my departure is at hand," he could also say, "I have fought a good fight, I have finished my course, I have kept the faith." So may we be able to say when the time of our departure has arrived.

If the time of our departure is at hand, let it cheer us amid our troubles. Sometimes, when our friends go to Liverpool to sail for Canada, or any other distant region, on the night before they sail they get into a very poor lodging. I think I hear one of them grumbling, "What a hard bed! What a small room! What a bad look-out" "Oh," says the other, "never mind, brother; we are not going to live here; we are off to-morrow." Bethink you in like manner, ye children of poverty, this is not your rest. Put up with it, you are away tomorrow. Ye sons of sorrow, ye daughters of weakness, ye children of sickness, let this cheer you:—

> "The road may be rough,
> But it cannot be long;
> And I'll smooth it with hope,
> And cheer it with song."

Oftentimes when I have been travelling on the Continent I have been obliged to put up at an hotel that was full, where the room was so inconvenient, that it scarcely furnished any accommodation at all. But we have said, "Oh, never mind: we are off in the morning! What matters it for one night?" So, as we are soon to be gone, and the time of our departure is at hand, let us not be ruffling our tempers about trifles, nor raise evil spirits around us by cavilling and finding fault. Take things as you find them, for we shall soon be up and away.

And if the time of my departure is at hand, I should like to be on good terms with all my friends on earth. Were you going to stop here always, when a man treated you badly, apart from a Christ spirit, you might as well have it out with him; but as we are going to stop such a little while, we may well put up with it. It is not desirable to be too ready at taking an offense. What if my neighbor has an ugly temper, the Lord has to put up with him, and so I may. There are some people with whom I would rather dwell in heaven for ever than abide with them half an hour on earth. Nevertheless, for the love of the brethren, and for the peace of the church, we may tolerate much during the short time we have to brook with peevish moods and perverse humors. Does Christ love them, and shall not we? He covers their offenses; why, then, should we disclose them or publish them abroad? If, any of you have any grievances with one another, if there is any bickering, or jealousy between you, I should like you to make it up to-night, because the time of your departure is at hand. Suppose there is some one you spoke harshly to, you would not like to hear to-morrow that he was dead. You would not have minded what you said to him if he had lived, but now that the seal is set upon all your communications one with another, you could wish that the last impress had been more friendly. There has been a little difference between two brothers—a little coldness between two sisters. Oh, since one or other of you will soon be gone, make it up! Live in love, as Christ loved you and gave himself for you. If one of you were going to Australia to-morrow, never to come back again, and you had had a little tiff with your brother, why I know before you started you would say, "Come, brother, let us part good friends." So now, since you are so soon to depart, end all strife, and dwell together in blessed harmony till the departure actually occurs.

If the time of my departure is at hand, then let me guard against being elated by any temporal prosperity. Possessions, estates, creature comforts dwindle into insignificance before this out-look. Yes, you may have procured a comfortable house and a delightful garden, but it is not your rest: your tenure is about to expire. Yes, you may say, "God did prosper me last year, the bank account did swell, the premises were enlarged, and the business thrived beyond all expectation." Ah! hold them loose. Do not think that they are to be your heaven. Be very jealous lest you should get your good things here, for if you do you will not have them hereafter. Be not lifted up too much when you grasp the pain, of which you must so soon quit your hold. As I said of the discomfort of the hotel, we did not think much of it, because we were going away. So, if it happens to be very luxurious, do not be enamoured of it, for you must go to-morrow. "These are the things," said one, when he looked at a rich man's treasures, "that make it hard to die." But it need not be so, if you hold them as gifts of God's kindness, and not as gods to be worshipped with self-indulgence, you may take leave of them with composure; "knowing in yourselves that ye have in heaven a better and an enduring substance."

Lastly, if the time of our departure is at hand, let us be prepared to bear our testimony. We are witnesses for Christ. Let us bear our testimony before we are taken up and mingle with the cloud of witnesses who have finished their course and rested from their labors. Dost thou say, "I hope to do that on my dying bed?" Brother, do it now: do it now, for you may never have opportunity to do it then. Mr. Whitfield was always desirous that he might bear a testimony for Christ in the hour of death; but he could not do so at that momentous crisis, for as you well know, he was suddenly taken ill after preaching, and very soon expired. Was this to be grievously deplored? Ah, no. Why, dear friends, he had borne so many testimonies for his Lord and Master while he was alive, there was no need to add anything in the last few moments before his death, or to supply the deficiencies of a life devoted to the proclamation of the gospel. Oh, let you and I bear our testimony now! Let us tell to others wherever we can what Christ hath done for us. Let us help Christ's cause with all our might while it is called to-day. Let us work for Jesus while we can work for him. As to thinking we can undo the effect of our idleness by the spasmodic effort of our dying breath, that were a vain hope indeed compared with living for Jesus Christ. Your dying testimony, if you are able to bear it, will have the greater force if it is not a sickly regret, but a healthy confirmation of your whole career.

I only wish these words about departure were applicable to all here. "Precious in the sight of the Lord is the death of his saints." But, "As I live, saith the Lord God, I have no pleasure in the death of the wicked, but that the wicked turn from his ways, and live." O unconverted man, the time for letting loose your cable draws nigh; it is even at the door. You must shortly, set sail for a far country. Alas! then yours is not the voyage of a passenger, with a sweeter clime, a happier home, a brighter prospect in view. Your departure is the banishment of a convict, with a penal settlement looming in the distance; fear all rife, and hope all blank, for the term of your banishment is interminable. I fear there are some of you who may depart ere long full of gloom with a fearful looking for of judgment and of fiery indignation. I seem to see the angel of death hovering over my audience. He may, perhaps, select for his victim an unconverted soul. If so, behind that death-angel attends there something far more grim. Hell follows death to souls that love not Christ. Oh, make haste, make haste! Seek Christ. Lay hold on eternal life; and may infinite mercy save you, for Jesus Christ's sake. Amen and Amen.

20
Paul—His Cloak and His Books

(Sermon No. 542)

"The cloak that I left at Troas with Carpus, when you come, bring with you, and the books, but especially the parchments" (2 Timothy 4:13).

FOOLISH PERSONS HAVE MADE remarks upon the trifles of Scripture. They have marveled why so little a matter as a cloak should be mentioned in an Inspired Book. But they ought to know that this is one of the many indications that the Book is by the same Author as the Book of Nature. Are there not things which our short-sightedness would call trifles in the volume of Creation around us? What is the peculiar value of the daisy upon the lawn, or the buttercup in the meadow? Compared with the rolling sea, or the eternal hills, how inconsiderable they seem!

Why has the humming bird a plumage so wondrously bejeweled and why is so much marvelous skill expended upon the wing of a butterfly? Why such curious machinery in the foot of a fly, or such a matchless optical arrangement in the eye of a spider? Because to most men these are trifles, are they to be left out of Nature's plans? No. Because greatness of Divine skill is as apparent in the minute as in the magnificent—even so in Holy Writ—the little things which are embalmed in the amber of Inspiration are far from inappropriate or unwise.

Besides, in Providence are there not trifles? It is not every day that a nation is rent by revolution, or a throne shaken by rebellion—far oftener a bird's nest is destroyed by a child, or an anthill overturned by a spade. It is not at every hour that a torrent inundates a province, but how frequently do the dewdrops moisten the green leaves? We do not often read of hurricanes, tornadoes and earthquakes, but the annals of Providence could reveal the history of many a grain of dust borne along in the summer's gale, many a sear leaf rent from the poplar and many a rush waving by the river's brim.

Learn to see in the little things of the Bible the God of Providence and Nature. Observe two pictures and you will, if thoroughly skilled in art, detect certain minute details which indicate the same authorship if they are by the same hand. The very little things often, to men of artistic eye, identify the painter more certainly than the more prominent strokes, which might far more easily be counterfeited. Experts detect a handwriting by a slight quivering in the upstrokes, the turn of the final mark, a dot, a cross, or even less matters.

Can we not see the legible handwriting of the God of Nature and Providence in the very fact that the sublimities of Revelation are interspersed with homely, everyday remarks? But they are not trifles. I venture to say that my text has much in it of spiritual instruction. I trust that this cloak may warm your hearts this morning, that these books may give you instruction, and that the Apostle himself may be to you an example of heroism, fitted to stir your minds to imitation.

I. First, let us LOOK AT THIS MEMORABLE CLOAK which Paul left with Carpus at Troas. Troas was a principal seaport town of Asia Minor. Very likely the Apostle Paul was seized at Troas on the second occasion of his being taken before the Roman emperor. The soldiers usually appropriated to themselves any extra garments in the possession of an arrested person, such things being considered as the perquisites of those who made the arrest. The Apostle may have been forewarned of his seizure, and therefore prudently committed his few books and his outer garment, which made up all his household stuff, to the care of a certain honest man named Carpus.

Although Troas was a full six hundred miles' journey from Rome, yet the Apostle Paul is too poor to purchase a garment, and so directs Timothy, as he is coming that way, to bring his cloak. He needs it much, for the sharp winter is coming on and the dungeon is very, very chilly. This is a brief detail of the circumstances. What kind of cloak it was, certain learned commentators have spent whole pages in trying to discover. But as we know nothing at all about it, ourselves, we will leave the question to them—believing that they know as much as we do, but no more.

1. But what does the cloak teach us? There are five or six lessons in it. The first is this—let us perceive here, with admiration, the complete self-sacrifice of the Apostle Paul for the Lord's sake. Remember, my dear Friends, what the Apostle once was. He was great, famous, and wealthy. He had been brought up at the feet of Gamaliel. He was so zealous among his brethren that he could not but have commanded their sincere respect. He was attended by a guard of soldiers when he went from Jerusalem to Damascus. I do not know whether the horse on which he rode was his own, but he must have been a man of importance to have been allotted so important a post in religious matters.

He was a man of good standing in society and doubtless everybody looking at young Saul of Tarsus would have said,

"He will make a great man. He has every chance in life. He has a liberal education, a zealous temperament, abundant gifts and the general esteem of the Jewish rulers. He will rise to eminence."

But when the Lord met him that day on the road to Damascus, how everything changed with him! Then he could truly say,

"But what things were gain to me, those I counted loss for Christ. Yes, doubtless and I count all things but loss for the excellency of the knowledge of Christ Jesus my Lord: for whom I have suffered the loss of all things and do count them but dung, that I may win Christ and be found in Him."

He begins to preach—away goes his character. Now nothing is too bad for Paul among his Jewish associates. "Away with such a fellow from the earth. It is not fit that he should live," was the exact expression of Jewish feeling towards him. He continues his labors and away has gone his wealth—he has either scattered it among the poor, or it has been sequestered by his former friends. He journeys from place to place at no small sacrifice of comfort. The wife to whom he was probably once united—for no unmarried man could vote in the Sanhedrim as Paul did against Stephen—had fallen sick and died and the Apostle now preferred a life of singleness, that he might give himself entirely to his work.

If only in this world he had hope, he would have been of all men the most miserable. He has at last grown gray, and now the very men who owed their conversion to him have forsaken him. When he first came into Rome they stood with him, but now they have all gone like winter's leaves, and the poor old man, "such an one as Paul the aged," sits with nothing in all the world to call property but an old cloak and a few books—and those are six hundred miles away. Ah, how he emptied himself, and to what extremity of destitution was he willing to bring himself for Christ's name sake!

Do not complain that he mentions his clothes—a greater than he did so and did so in an hour more solemn than that in which Paul wrote the Epistle. Remember who it was that said, "They parted My garments among them and upon My vesture did they cast lots." The Savior must die in absolute nakedness and the Apostle is made something like He as he sits shivering in the cold.

Brethren, was Paul right in all this? Were his sacrifices reasonable? Was the object which he contemplated worthy of all this suffering and self-denial? Was he carried away by an excessive heat of fanaticism to spend upon an inferior object what was not required of him? No Believer here thinks so. You all believe that if you could give up substance and talent and esteem, yes, and your own life, also, for Christ, it would be well spent. I say you think so, but how many of us have ever carried it out? Had I not better say, how few of us? There are some who seldom have an opportunity for sacrificing for Christ at all. What they give is spared from their superfluity—they never feel it.

It is a high luxury when a man has such a love for Jesus that he is able to give until he pinches himself. If Paul were reasonable, what are you and I? If Paul only gives as a Christian should do, how ashamed should we be of ourselves? If he will bring himself to poverty for Christ, what shall we say of those base-born professors who will not lose a trifle in their trade for honesty's sake? What shall we say of those who say "I know how to get money and I know how to keep it, too," and look with scorn upon those who are more generous than they? If you are content to condemn Paul and charge him with folly, do so. But if not, if this is but a reasonable service and such as the infinite Grace of God which Paul experienced required of him, then let us do something of the like sort. If you have experienced as much love, love the Lord as much and spend and be spent for the Lord Jesus!

2. Secondly, dear Friends, we learn how utterly forsaken the Apostle was by his friends. If he had not a cloak of his own, could not some of them lend him one? Ten years before, the Apostle was brought in chains along the Appian way to Rome. And fifty miles before he reached Rome, a little band of members of the Church came to meet him. And when he came within twenty miles of the city, at the "Three Taverns," there came a still larger group of the disciples to escort him, so that the chained prisoner, Paul, went into Rome attended by all the Believers in that city.

He was then a younger man. But now for some reason or other, ten years afterward, nobody comes to visit him. He is confined in prison and they do not even know where he is, so that Onesiphorus, when he comes to Rome, has to seek him out very diligently. He is as obscure as if he had never had a name and though he is still as great and glorious an Apostle as ever, men have so forgotten him, and the Church has so despised him that he is friendless! The Philippian Church, ten years before, had made a collection for him when he was in prison. And though he had learned in whatsoever state he was, to be content, yet he thanked them for their contribution as an offering of a sweet smelling savor unto God.

Now he is old and no Church remembers him. He is brought to trial and there are Eubulus and Pudens and Linus—will not some of them stand by his side when he is brought before the emperor? "At my first answer no man stood with me." Poor soul, he served his God and worked himself down to poverty for the Church's sake, yet the Church has forsaken him! Oh, how great must have been the anguish of the loving heart of Paul at such ingratitude! Why did not the few who were in Rome, if they had been ever so poor, make a contribution for him? Could not those who were of Caesar's household have found a cloak for the

Apostle? No. He is so utterly left, that although he is ready to die of fever in the dungeon, not a soul will lend or give him a cloak.

What patience does this teach to those similarly situated! Has it fallen to your lot, my Brother, to be forsaken of friends? Were there other times when your name was the symbol of popularity, when many lived in your favor like insects in your sunbeam? And has it come to this, now, that you are forgotten as a dead man out of mind? In your greatest trials do you find your fewest friends? Have those who once loved and respected you fallen asleep in Jesus? And have others turned out to be hypocritical and untrue? What are you to do now?

You are to remember this case of the Apostle. It is put here for your comfort. He had to pass through as deep waters as any that you are called to ford, and yet remember, he says, "Notwithstanding, the Lord stood with me and strengthened me." So now, when man deserts you, God will be your Friend. This God is our God forever and ever—not in sunshiny weather only, but forever and ever! This God is our God in dark nights as well as in bright days.

Go to Him, spread your complaint before Him. Murmur not. If Paul had to suffer desertion, you must not expect better usage. Let not your faith fail you as though some new thing had happened to you. This is common to the saints. David had his Ahithophel, Christ his Judas, Paul his Demas—and can you expect to fare better than they? As you look at that old cloak, as it speaks of human ingratitude, be of good courage and wait on the Lord, for He shall strengthen your heart. "Wait, I say, on the Lord."

3. There is a third lesson. Our text shows the Apostle's independence of mind. Why did not the Apostle borrow a cloak? Why did he not beg one? No, no, no! That is not to the Apostle's taste at all. He has a cloak and though it is six hundred miles away, he will wait until it comes. Though there may be some that may lend, he knows that they who go a borrowing go a sorrowing, and that they who beg are seldom welcome. I do not think a Christian man should blush to borrow or to beg if he is absolutely brought to it, but I never like that class of people who do either systematically.

I wish many of the poor would not damage the charity of others by being so ready to beg on every presence of necessity. A Christian man would do well to remember that it is never to his honor, though it is not always to his dishonor, to beg. "I cannot dig, to beg I am ashamed," said the unfaithful steward. And if he had been a faithful one he would have been more ashamed, still. I say again, when it comes to the pinch and a man must ask of his fellows, let him do it boldly. But let him never be too ready to do it, but, like the Apostle, as long as he can do without it, let him say, "I have labored with my own hand and eaten no man's bread for nothing."

He taught that the minister of God had a right to be supported by the people. "If you partake of their spirituals," says he, "it is right that you give of your temporals." He insists upon it that they are not to muzzle the mouth of the ox that treads out the corn. Yet though he holds this as a great general principle, he never takes anything himself. He follows his trade of tent making. He stitches away at the canvas and earns his own living so that he is chargeable unto no man. Noble example! How anxious all Christians ought to be to see that they do not come to want in their old age!

Yet Paul does come to poverty—his independent spirit is not broken at the last, for he will wait till his own cloak is brought six hundred miles rather than ask any man to give or lend. Let the Christian man be quite as independent, for though independence is not a Christian grace, yet it is a common grace which, when wreathed with Christianity, is very beautiful and befits the character of a son of God.

4. The fourth remark is—see here, how very little the Apostles thought about how they were dressed. Paul wants enough to keep him warm. He asks no more. There is no doubt whatever that the other parts of his garments were getting very dilapidated—that he was, indeed, in a state of rags. And so he needed the cloak to wrap about him. We read in olden times of many of the most eminent servants of God being dressed in the poorest manner. When good Bishop Hooper was led out to be burnt, he had been long in prison and his clothes were so gone from him that he borrowed an old scholar's gown, full of rags and holes, that he

might put it on and went limping with pains of sciatica and rheumatism to the stake.

We read of Jerome of Prague, that he lay in a damp, cold dungeon and was refused anything to cover him in his nakedness and cold. Some ministers are very careful lest they should not always be dressed in a canonical or gentlemanly manner. I like that remark of Whitfield's, when someone of a bad character wondered how he could preach without a cassock. "Ah," he said, "I can preach without a cassock, but I cannot preach without a character." What matters the outward garment, so long as the character is right?

This is a lesson to our private members, too. We sometimes hear them say, "I could not come out on the Sunday—I had not fit clothes to come in." Any clothes are fit to come to the House of God with, if they are paid for, no matter how coarse they may be. If they are the best God has given you, do not murmur. Inasmuch as the trial of raiment is a very sharp one to some of the poorest of God's people, I think this text was put into the Bible for their comfort. Your Master wore no soft and dainty raiment. His garment was the simple peasant's smock-frock—woven from the top throughout without seam—and yet He never blushed to wear it in the presence of kings and priests.

I shall always believe that the Christian ought to cultivate a noble indifference to these outward things. But when it comes to the pinch of absolute want of clothing, then he may comfort himself in this thought, "Now am I companion with the Master. Now do I walk in the same temptation as the Apostles. Now I suffer even as they also suffered." Every saint is an image of Christ. But a poor saint is His exact image, for Christ was poor. So, if you are brought to such a pinch with regard to poverty that you scarcely know how to provide things decent by way of raiment, do not be dispirited. But say, "My Master suffered the same, and so did the Apostle Paul." And so take heart and be of good cheer.

5. Paul's cloak at Troas shows me how mighty the Apostle was to resist temptation. "I do not see that," you say. The Apostle had the gift of miracles. Our Savior, though able to work miracles, never worked anything like a miracle on His own account. Nor did His Apostles.

Miraculous gifts were entrusted to them with Gospel ends and purposes—for the good of others and for the promotion of the Truth of God. But never for themselves. Our Savior was tempted of the devil, you will remember, when He was hungry, to turn stones into bread. That was a strong temptation—to apply miraculous powers which were intended for other ends—to His own comfort.

But He rebuked Satan and said, "Man shall not live by bread alone." Paul also had power to have created a cloak if he had liked. Why could he not? His very shadow healed the sick! If he had willed it, he could have prevented the cold and damp from having any effect upon himself. He who had once raised to life dead Eutychus, when he had fallen from a loft, and brought back the vital heat, could certainly have kept the heat in his own body if he had chosen. And I am bold to say the devil often came to him and said,

"If you are an Apostle of God, if you can work miracles, command this atmosphere to rise in temperature, or these rags to be joined together and form you a comfortable raiment."

You do not know—you cannot tell, for you were never put to it—what were the stern struggles the Apostle must have had in resisting the foul temptation to use his miraculous gifts for himself. O Brothers and Sisters, I am afraid you and I are much more ready to give way to self than was the Apostle. We preach the Gospel and if God helps us, oh, directly the devil will have us to take some of the praise. "You preached a good sermon this morning," said one to John Bunyan, as he came down the stairs. "You are too late," said Honest John, "the devil told me that when I was preaching." Yes, God works the miracles, but we take the honor to ourselves.

There is the temptation for any man who has gifts to use them to his own purposes. And if he does, he is an unfaithful steward to his Master. I do beseech you, whether in the Sunday school or the Church, never let the miracle-working power which God has given you be used for yourselves. You can do for Christ's sake mighty things through faith and prayer, but never let prayer and faith be prostituted to so base a purpose as to minister unto the flesh. I know carnal minds will not comprehend this, but spiritual minds, who know the temptations of the devil, will know how stern must be a life-long battle to keep ourselves back from doing that which might apparently make us happy, but which would at the same time make us unholy.

6. The sixth lesson from this cloak is we are taught in this passage how precisely similar one child of God is to another. I know we look upon Abraham and Isaac and Jacob as being very great and blessed beings—we think that they lived in a higher region than we do. We cannot think that if they had lived in these times, they would have been Abraham, Isaac, and Jacob. We suppose that these are very bad days and that any great height of Divine Grace, or self-denial is not very easily attainable.

Brethren, my own conviction is that if Abraham, Isaac and Jacob had lived now—instead of being less, they would have been greater saints—for they only lived in the dawn, and we live in the noon. We hear the Apostles often called "Saint" Peter and "Saint" Paul. And thus they are set up on high as on an elevated niche. If we had seen Peter and Paul we should have thought them a very ordinary sort of people— wonderfully like ourselves. And if we had gone into their daily life and trials, we should have said, "Well, you are wonderfully superior to what I am in Grace, but somehow or other, you are men of like passions with me. I have a quick temper, so have you, Peter.

"I have a thorn in the flesh, so have you, Paul. I have a sick house, Peter's wife's mother lies sick of a fever. I complain of the rheumatism, and the Apostle Paul, when aged, feels the cold and wants his cloak." Ah, we must not consider the Bible as a Book intended for transcendental super-elevated souls—it is an everyday Book and these good people were everyday people. They had more Divine Grace, but we can get more Grace as well as they could—the Fountain at which they drew is quite as full and as free to us as to them. We have only to believe after their fashion and trust to Jesus after their way—and although our trials are not the same as theirs, we shall overcome through the blood of the Lamb.

I like to see religion brought out in everyday life. Do not tell me about the godliness of the Tabernacle. Tell me about the godliness of your shop, your counter, and your kitchen. Let me see how Divine Grace enables you to be patient in the cold, or joyful in hunger, or industrious in labor. Though Grace is no common thing, yet it shines best in common things. To preach a sermon, or to sing a hymn is but a paltry thing compared with the power to suffer cold and hunger and nakedness for Christ's sake.

Courage then, courage then, fellow Pilgrim! The road was not smoothed for Paul any more than it is for us. There was no royal road to Heaven in those days any more than there is now. They had to go through sloughs and bogs and mire—just as we do—

"They wrestled hard as we do now,
With sins and doubts and fears,"

but they have gained the victory at last, and even so shall we! So much then, for the cloak which was left at Troas with Carpus.

II. We will LOOK AT HIS BOOKS. We do not know what the books were, and we can only form some guess as to what the parchments were. Paul had a few books which were left, perhaps wrapped up in the cloak, and Timothy was to be careful to bring them. Even an Apostle must read. Some of our very ultra-Calvinistic Brothers and Sisters think that a minister who reads books and studies his sermon must be a very deplorable specimen of a preacher. A man who comes up into the pulpit, professes to take his text on the spot and talks any quantity of nonsense is the idol of many.

If he will speak without premeditation, or pretend to do so, and never produce what they call a dish of dead men's brains—oh, that is the preacher! How rebuked are they by the Apostle! He is Inspired and yet he wants books! He has been preaching at least for thirty years, and yet he wants books! He had seen the Lord, and yet he wants books! He had had a wider experience than most men, and yet he wants books! He had been caught up into the third Heaven and had heard things which it was unlawful for a men to utter, yet he wants books! He had written the major part of the New Testament, and yet he wants books!

The Apostle says to Timothy, and so he says to every preacher, "Give yourself unto reading." The man who never reads will never be read. He who never quotes will never be quoted. He who will not use the thoughts of other men's brains proves that he has no brains of his own. Brothers and Sisters, what is true of ministers is true of all our people. You need to read. Renounce as much as you will all light literature, but study as much as possible sound theological works, especially the Puritan writers and expositions of the Bible. We are quite persuaded that the very best way for you to be spending your leisure is to be either reading or praying. You may get much instruction from books which afterward you may use as a true weapon in your Lord and Master's service. Paul cries, "Bring the books"—join in the cry.

Our second remark is that the Apostle is not ashamed to confess that he does read. He is writing to his young son, Timothy. Now some old preachers never like to say a thing which will let the young ones into their secrets. They suppose they must put on a very dignified air and make a mystery of their sermonizing. But all this is alien from the spirit of truthfulness. Paul wants books and is not ashamed to tell Timothy that he does. And Timothy may go and tell Tychicus and Titus if he likes—Paul does not care.

Paul herein is a picture of industry. He is in prison. He cannot preach—what will he do? As he cannot preach, he will read. As we read of the fishermen of old and their boats, the fishermen were out of them. What were they doing? Mending their nets. So if Providence has laid you upon a sick bed and you cannot teach your class—if you cannot be working for God in public, mend your nets by reading. If one occupation is taken from you, take another and let the books of the Apostle read you a lesson of industry.

He says, "Especially the parchments." I think the books were Latin and Greek works but the parchments were Oriental. And possibly they were the parchments of Holy Scripture. Or, as likely, they were his own parchments, on which were written the originals of his letters which stand in our Bible as the Epistles to the Ephesians, the Philippians, the Colossians, and so on. Now, it must be, "Especially the parchments" with all our reading. Let it be especially the Bible. Do you attach no weight to this advice? This advice is more needed in England now than almost at any other time, for the number of persons who read the Bible, I believe, is becoming smaller every day.

Persons read the views of their denominations as set forth in the periodicals. They read the views of their leader as set forth in his sermons or his works. But the Book, the good old Book, the Divine Fountainhead from which all Revelation wells up—this is too often left. You may go to human puddles until you forsake the clear crystal stream which flows from the Throne of God. Read the books, by all means, but especially the parchments. Search human literature, if you will, but especially stand fast by that Book which is Infallible, the Revelation of our Lord and Savior Jesus Christ.

III. We now want to have AN INTERVIEW WITH THE APOSTLE PAUL HIMSELF, for we may learn much from him. It is almost too dark to see him—we will find him in that frightful den! The horrid dungeon—the filth lies upon the floor till it looks like a road which is seldom scraped—the draft blows through the only little slit which they call a window. The poor old man, without his cloak, wraps his ragged garment about him. Sometimes you see him kneeling down to pray and then he dips his pen into the ink and writes to his dear son, Timothy. No companion, except Luke, who occasionally comes in for a short time. Now, how shall we find the old man? What sort of temper will he be in?

We find him full of confidence in the religion which has cost him so much. For in the first chapter, at the twelfth verse, we hear him say,

"For this reason I also suffer these things: nevertheless I am not ashamed: for I know whom I have believed and am persuaded that He is able to keep that which I have committed unto Him against that day."

No doubt, often the tempter said to him,

"Paul, why you have lost everything for your religion! It has brought you to beggary. See, you have preached it and what is the reward of it? The very men you have converted have forsaken

344

you. Give it up, give it up, it cannot be worth all this. Why, they will not even bring you a cloak to wrap round you. You are left here to shiver and very soon your head will be struck from your body. Take off your hand from the standard and retire."

"No," says the Apostle, "I know whom I have believed." Why, I have heard of professors who say, "Ever since I have been a Christian I have lost in my business and therefore I will give it up." But our beloved Apostle clings to it with a life grip. And oh, there is no heart in our piety if our afflictions make us doubt the Truth of our religion. For these trials, inasmuch as they work patience, and patience experience, and experience hope, render us such that we are not ashamed, but we do the more firmly hold on to Christ. Just think, you hear the Apostle say, "I know whom I believe." It is very easy for us to say it. We are very comfortable, sitting in our pews. We shall go home to our plentiful meal. We shall be clothed comfortably.

We have friends about us who will smile at us and it is not hard to say, "I know whom I have believed." But if you were vexed on the one hand by Hermogenes and Philetus, and on the other hand by Alexander the coppersmith, and De-mas, you would not find it quite so easy to say, "The Lord is faithful." Behold this noble champion who is just as much unmoved at the worst as he was at the best times. "I know how to be full," said he once. And now he can say, "I know how to suffer hunger— I know how to abound and how to suffer loss."

But he is not only confident. You will notice that this grand old man is having communion with Jesus Christ in his sufferings. Turn to the second chapter, at the tenth verse. Did ever sweeter language than this come from anyone?

"Therefore I endure all things for the elect's sakes, that they may also obtain the salvation which is in Christ Jesus with eternal glory. It is a faithful saying: For if we are dead with Him, we shall also live with Him: If we suffer, we shall also reign with Him. If we deny Him, He also will deny us: if we believe not, yet He abides faithful: He cannot deny Himself."

Ah, there are two in the dungeon—not only the man who is suffering trouble as an evildoer, even unto bonds—but there sits with him One like unto the Son of Man, sharing all his griefs and bearing all his despondencies and so lifting up his head. Well may the Apostle rejoice that he has fellowship with Christ in his sufferings, being made conformable unto his death.

Nor is this all. Not only is he confident for the past and in sweet communion for the present, but he is resigned for the future. Look at the fourth chapter and the sixth verse. "I am now ready to be offered, and the time of my departure is at hand." It is a beautiful emblem taken from the sacrificial bullock. There it is, tied to the horns of the altar, and ready to be offered. So the Apostle stands as a sacrifice ready to be offered upon the altar. I am afraid that we cannot all say we are ready to be offered. Paul was ready to be a burnt offering. If God willed it, he would be burnt to ashes at the stake. Or he would be a drink offering, as he did become, when a stream of blood flowed under the sharp sword.

He was ready to be a peace offering, if God willed it, to die in his bed. In any case, he was a freewill offering unto God, for he offered himself voluntarily. As he says, "I am now ready to be offered and the time of my departure is at hand." Glorious old man! Many a professed Christian has been clothed in scarlet, and fared sumptuously every day and yet never could say he was ready to be offered. Rather he looked upon the time of his departure with grief and sorrow. As you think, then, of poor, shivering, ragged Paul, think of the jewel which he carried in his breast. And O you sons of poverty, remember that the magnificence of a holy life and the grandeur and nobility of a consecrated heart can deliver you altogether from any shame which may cling to your rags and poverty! For as the sun at setting paints the clouds with all the colors of Heaven, so your very rags, poverty, and shame may make your life the more illustrious as the splendor of your piety lights them with heavenly radiance!

We have not quite concluded with the Apostle. We find him not only resigned, but triumphant. "I have fought a good fight, I have finished my course, I have kept the faith." See the Grecian warrior just returned from battle? He has many wounds and there is a gash across his brow. His breast is streaming here and there with cuts and flesh wounds. One arm is dislocated. He halts, like Jacob, on his thigh. He is covered with the smoke and dust of battle. He is besmeared with much blood. He is faint, and weary, and ready to die, but what does he say? As he lifts up his right arm, with his buckler tightly clasped upon it, he cries, "I have fought a good fight, I have kept my shield." That was the object of ambition with every Grecian warrior. If he kept his shield he came home glorious.

Now, faith is the Christian's shield. And here I see the Apostle, though he wears all the marks of the conflict, yet he triumphs in these marks of the Lord Jesus, saying, "I have fought a good fight. My very scars and wounds prove it. I have kept the faith." He looks to that golden buckler of the faith fastened to his arm and rejoices in it. The tyrant Nero, nor all the warriors of Rome never had such triumph as the Apostle Paul! None of them had such true glory as this solitary man who has trod the winepress alone. And of the people—there were none with him—who has stood against the lion, a solitary champion, with no eye to pity and no arm to save, still triumphant to the end? Brave spirit! Never mind the old cloak at Troas, so long as your faith is safe.

Once more. He not only triumphs in the present, but he is in expectation of a crown. When the Grecian wrestler had fought a good fight, a crown was presented to him. And so Paul, who writes about the old cloak, also writes—

"Henceforth there is laid up for me a crown of righteousness, which the Lord, the righteous Judge, shall give me at that day: and not to me only, but unto all them also that love His appearing."

When I was picturing Paul, and talking of the poverty of many Believers—"Ah," said the Sinner, "Who would be a Christian? Who would suffer so much for Christ? Who would lose everything as Paul did?" Worldly minds here are thinking—"What a fool, to be led away by such an excitement!" Ah, but see how the tables have turned! "Henceforth there is laid up for me a crown!" What if he had been robed in scarlet, had

347

rolled in wealth, and been great? And what if there had been no crown for him in Heaven? No joy hereafter—but a fearful looking for of judgment? See, he springs from his dungeon to his throne! Nero may cut off his head, but that head shall wear a starry crown. Courage, then, you that are downtrodden, afflicted, and despairing! Be of good cheer, for the end will make up for the way. And all the roughness of the pilgrimage will be well recompensed by the Glory which shall await all those who are resting upon Christ Jesus.

We close, having done with this old cloak, when we say, is it not beautiful as you read this Epistle, and, indeed, all the Apostle's letters, to see how everything which the Apostle thought of was connected with Christ? How he had concentrated every passion, every power, every thought, every act, every word—and set the whole upon Christ. I believe that there are many who love Christ after a sort, just as the sun shines today. But you know if you concentrate the rays of that sun with a magnifying glass and fix all the rays upon any object, then what heat there is, what burning, what flame, what fire!

So many men scatter their love and admiration on almost any and every creature, and Christ gets a little, as we all get some rays of the sun. But that is the man, who, like the Apostle Paul, brings all his thoughts and words to a focus. Then he burns his way through life. His heart is on fire. Like coals of juniper are his words. He is a man of force and energy. He may have no cloak, yet for all that, he is a great man and the Czar in his imperial mantle is but a driveling dwarf by the side of this giant in the army of God. O, I wish we could set our thoughts on Christ this morning. Are we trusting in Him this morning? Is He all our salvation and all our desire? If He is, then let us live to Him.

Those who are wholly Christ's are not many. O that we were espoused as chaste virgins unto Christ—that we might have no other lover and know no other object of delight! Blind are these eyes to all but Christ. And deaf these ears to any music but the voice of Christ. And lame these feet to any way but that of obedience to Him! Palsied these hands to anything but work for Him. And dead this heart to every joy if Jesus cannot move! Even as a straw floats upon the river and is carried to the ocean, so would I be bereft of all power, and will to do anything but that which my Lord would have me do—and be carried along by the stream of His Grace right onward, ready to be offered up, or ready to live, ready to suffer, or ready to reign just as He wills—only that He may be served in my living and dying!

It will little matter what cloak you wear, or if you have not any at all, if you have but such a concentration of all your bodily and mental powers and spiritual energies upon Christ Jesus and upon Him alone. May those of you who have never trusted Jesus be ready to rely upon Him now. He did not forsake Paul, even in extremity, and He will not forsake you—

"Trust Him, He will never deceive you, though you hardly of Him deem. He will never, never leave you, nor will let you quite leave Him." Therefore trust Him now and forever, for Jesus' sake. Amen.

21

The Sick Man Left Behind

(Sermon No. 1452A)

"But Trophimus have I left at Miletum sick" (2 Timothy 4:20).

THESE ARE AMONG the last words of Paul the Apostle, for we find them in the closing verses of the last of his Epistles. The chapter reminds us of a dying man's final adieu to his best friend, in the course of which he calls to mind the associates of his life. Among his memories of love we find Paul recollecting Trophimus who had frequently shared with him the perils of rivers and perils of robbers which so largely attended the Apostle's career. He had left the good man ill at Miletum and as Timothy at Ephesus was within an easy journey of him, there was no need to add a hint that he should visit him, for he would be sure to do it.

The love of Jesus works great tenderness and unity in the hearts of His disciples. The overflow of our Lord's great soul has saturated all His true followers with brotherly affection—because Jesus has loved Paul, Paul loves Timothy and Timothy must love Trophimus. From this love there arises communion of feeling so that in sympathy they share each other's joys and griefs. When one member rejoices, the body rejoices—and when one member suffers the whole body suffers with it. Trophimus is sick and Paul cannot forget him, though he, himself, expects in a few weeks to die a martyr's death! Neither would he have Timothy ignorant of the fact, though twice, within a few verses, he hurries him to come to Rome, saying, "Do your diligence to come shortly unto me."

If Timothy could not personally visit the sick friend, yet it was well that he should know of his affliction, for he would then remember him in his prayers. "Beloved, let us love one another, for love is of God." Let us remember those who are one with us in Christ and especially let us bear on our hearts all those who are afflicted in mind, body, or estate. If we have had to leave Trophimus at Miletum, or at Brighton, or at Ventnor, let us leave our heart's love with him. And if we hear that another Trophimus lies sick not far from our own home, let us accept the information as in itself a sufficient summons to minister to the afflicted friend.

May holy sympathy pervade all our souls, for however active and zealous we may be, we have not yet reached a perfect character unless we are full of compassion, tender-hearted and considerate of the sorrowful, for this is the mind of Christ. Simple as the statement of our text certainly is, it is found in an Inspired Book and it is, therefore, more than an ordinary note in a common letter. Like another verse of the same chapter, "The cloak that I left at Troas with Carpus, when you come, bring with you, and the books, but especially the parchments," has been judged to be beneath the dignity of Inspiration, we think not so. The God who counts the hairs of our heads in Providence may well mention His sick servant on the pages of Inspiration!

Instead of quibbling at the littleness of the recorded fact, let us admire "the love of the Spirit" who, while He lifts Ezekiel and Daniel above the spheres and raises the language of David and Isaiah to the utmost pitch of poetry and eloquence, yet deigns to breathe in such a line as this—"Trophimus have I left at Miletum sick." Can we learn anything more from this plain line of Apostolic penmanship? Let us see. If the same Divine Spirit who Inspired it, will shine upon it, we shall not read it in vain!

I. From the fact that Paul left Trophimus sick at Miletum we learn that IT IS THE WILL OF GOD THAT SOME GOOD MEN SHOULD BE IN ILL HEALTH. Whatever the malady may have been which affected Trophimus, Paul could certainly have healed him if the Divine Spirit had permitted the use of his miraculous powers to that end. He had raised up Eutychus from death and he had given back the use of his limbs to the cripple at Lystra. We feel, therefore, fully assured that had God allowed the Apostle so to use his healing energy, Trophimus would have left his bed and continued his journey to Rome.

Not so, however, had the Lord willed. The good fruit-bearing vine must be pruned and Trophimus must suffer—there were ends to be answered by his weakness which could not be compassed by his health. Instantaneous restoration could have been given, but it was withheld under Divine direction. This doctrine leads us away from the vain idea of chance. We are not wounded by arrows shot at a venture, but we smart by the determinate counsel of Heaven! An overruling hand is everywhere present, preventing or permitting ill and no one shaft of disease is ever let fly by stealth from the bow of death! If someone must be ill, it was a wise Providence which selected Trophimus, for it was better for him to be ill than Titus, or Tychicus, or Timothy.

It was well, too, that he happened to be ill at Miletum near to his own native city, Ephesus. We cannot always see the hand of God in Providence, but we may always be sure that it is there. If not a sparrow lights on the ground without our Father, surely not a child of the Divine family is laid low without His sacred will! Chance is a heathenish idea which cannot live in the Presence of an everywhere present, living and working God! Away with it from every Christian mind! It is dishonoring to the Lord and grievous to ourselves!

This also delivers us from regarding affliction as being always brought upon men by their personal sin. Many a sickness has been the direct result of intemperance, or some other form of wickedness—but here is a worthy, well-approved Brother laid aside and left on the road through a malady for which he is not blamed in any measure. It is too common, nowadays, for men to be of a hard and cruel spirit and ascribe the illnesses, even, of those who are true children of God to some fault in their habits of life. We wonder how they would like to be dealt with in this manner if they were suffering and could wash their hands in innocence in reference to their daily lives?

In our Lord's day they told Him, "Lord, he whom You love is sick." And Solomon, long before that time, wrote, "Whom the Lord loves He corrects; even as a father the son in whom he delights." This was a much better, more humane and more truthful speech than the frozen philosophy of modern times which traces each man's sickness to his own violation of natural law and, instead of pouring in the balm of consolation, pours out the sulfuric acid of slanderous insinuation! Let the afflicted examine himself to see if the rod is not sent to correct some secret evil and let him diligently consider where he may amend—but far be it from us to stand at his bedside like judges or lictors and look upon our friend as an offender as well as a sufferer!

Such brutality may be left to the philosophers, but it would ill become the sons of God! We may not think a shade the less of Trophimus because he is sick at Miletum. He is probably a far better man than any of us and perhaps for that very reason he is more tried. There is gold in him which pays for putting into the crucible—he bears such rich fruit that he is worth pruning—he is a diamond of so pure a water that he will repay the lapidary's toil. This may not be quite so true of any of us and, therefore, we escape his sharper trials. Let us, as James says, "count them happy that endure," and like David, say, "Blessed is the man whom You chasten, O Lord, and teach him out of Your Law."

What do the Scriptures say?—"For whom the Lord loves, He chastens and scourges every son whom He receives. If you endure chastening, God deals with you as with sons; for what son is he whom the father chastens not?" Lazarus of Bethany, Dorcas, Epaphroditus and Trophimus are a few of that great host of sick folk whom the Lord loves in their sicknesses, for whom the promise was written, "The Lord will strengthen him upon the bed of languishing: You will make all his bed in his sickness."

II. We have only strength and space for mere hints and so we notice, secondly, that GOOD MEN MAY BE LAID ASIDE WHEN THEY SEEM TO BE MOST NEEDED—as Trophimus was when the aged Apostle had but a scanty escort and required his aid. Paul needed him, badly enough, soon after he had been obliged to leave him at Miletum, for he writes sorrowfully, "Demas has forsaken me, having loved this present world, and is departed unto Thessalonica; Crescens to Galatia, Titus unto Dalmatia. Only Luke is with me." "And Tychicus have I sent to Ephesus." How glad he would have been with Trophimus, for we see how he begs

Timothy to come with all speed and to bring Mark, whose service he greatly needed with him.

Yet not even for Paul's sake can Trophimus be suddenly raised up! His Lord sees it to be necessary that he should feel the heat of the furnace and into the crucible he must go. We think that the Church cannot spare the earnest minister, the indefatigable missionary, the faithful deacon, the tender teacher—but God thinks not so! No one is indispensable in the household of God! He can do His own work not only without Trophimus, but even without Paul! Yes, we go further—it sometimes happens that the work of the Lord is quickened by the decease of one upon whom it seemed to depend! When a broad, far-spreading tree is cut down, many smaller trees which were dwarfed and stunted while it stood, suddenly shoot up into vigorous growth—even so, one good man may do much and yet, when he is removed, others may do more!

Temporary illnesses of great workers may call to the front those who would otherwise, from modesty, have remained in the rear—and the result may be a great gain. Poor Trophimus had, in his healthier days, been the innocent cause of bringing Paul into a world of trouble, for we read in Acts 21:27 that a tumult was made by the Jews because they imagined that Paul had brought Trophimus into the Temple and so had defiled it. Now, when he could have been of service, he is sick and, no doubt, it was a great grief to him that it should be so. Yet for him, as oftentimes for us, there was no alternative but to submit himself under the hand of God and feel that the Lord is always right.

Why do we not yield at once? Why do we chomp the bit and paw the ground, restless to be on the road? If our Lord bids us stand still, can we not be quiet? Active spirits are apt to become restive spirits when under the restraining hand—energy soon sours into rebellion and we quarrel with God because we are not allowed to glorify Him in our own way—a foolish form of contest which at bottom means that we have a will of our own and will only serve God upon condition of having it indulged!

Brothers and Sisters, he who writes these lines knows what he writes and this is the verdict of his experience—God's work needs us far less than we imagine and God would have us aware of this fact, for He will not give His Glory to human instruments any more than He will allow His praise to be bestowed on graven images!

III. Our text clearly shows us that GOOD MEN WOULD HAVE THE LORD'S WORK GO ON WHATEVER BECOMES OF THEM. Paul did not desert Trophimus, but left him, because a higher call summoned him to Rome. Trophimus, we may be sure, did not wish to delay the great Apostle, but was content to be left. No doubt they both felt the separation but, like true soldiers of Christ, they endured hardness and, for the sake of the cause, parted company for a while. It would be a great grief to a true-hearted worker if he knew that any fellow-laborer slackened his pace for his sake. The sick in an army of an earthly monarch are necessarily an impediment, but it need not be so in the army of the King of kings!

Spiritual sickness is a sore hindrance, but sickness of body should not delay the host. If we cannot preach we can pray. If one work is out of our reach, we can try another and if we can do nothing, our inability should serve as a call to the vigorous to be doing all the more! Trophimus is sick, then let Timothy be the more energetic! Trophimus cannot attend the Apostle, then let Timothy be the more diligent to come before winter! Thus, by acting as an incentive, the lack of one man's service may produce tenfold more in others who are awakened to extra exertions.

Brethren, it will be the sweetest alleviation to the pains of a sick pastor if he sees you each and all nerved to special diligence. His enforced rest will be the better enjoyed if he knows that the Church of God is not a sufferer because of it. And his whole mind and spirit will minister to the health of his body if he sees the fruit of the Spirit of God in all of you, keeping you faithful and zealous. Will you not see to this for Jesus' sake?

❧ ❧

Printed in Great Britain
by Amazon